THE RELUCTANT MODERNISM OF HANNAH ARENDT

MODERNITY AND POLITICAL THOUGHT

Series Editor: Morton Schoolman
State University of New York at Albany

This unique collection of original studies of the great figures in the history of political and social thought critically examines their contributions to our understanding of modernity, its constitution, and the promise and problems latent within it. These works are written by some of the finest theorists of our time for scholars and students of the social sciences and humanities.

The following titles are available as New Editions from
Rowman & Littlefield Publishers, Inc.

THE RELUCTANT MODERNISM OF HANNAH ARENDT

NEW EDITION

SEYLA BENHABIB

ROWMAN & LITTLEFIELD PUBLISHERS, INC.
Lanham • Boulder • New York • Toronto • Oxford

For Colombe Benhabib
with love and gratitude

ROWMAN & LITTLEFIELD PUBLISHERS, INC.

Published in the United States of America
by Rowman & Littlefield Publishers, Inc.
A wholly owned subsidary of The Rowman & Littlefield Publishing Group, Inc.
4501 Forbes Boulevard, Suite 200, Lanham, Maryland 20706
www.rowmanlittlefield.com

PO Box 317, Oxford, OX2 9RU, UK

British Library Cataloguing in Publication Information Available

The Library of Congress cataloged the previous edition of this book as:

Benhabib, Seyla.
    The reluctant modernism of Hannah Arendt / Seyla Benhabib.
        p.   cm. — (Modernity and political thought; vol. 10)
    Includes bibliographical references and index.
        1. Arendt, Hannah—Contributions in political science.
2. Heidegger, Martin, 1889–1976—Contributions in political science.
3. Political science—Philosophy.
I. Title. II. Series.
JC251.A74B45   1996
320.5'092—dc20   95-50247

ISBN 0-7425-2150-8 (cloth : alk. paper)—ISBN 0-7425-2151-6 (pbk. : alk. paper)

Printed in the United States of America

Contents

Preface to the New Edition

At the cusp of the twenty-first century, Hannah Arendt's reputation as one of the most important political thinkers of late modernity has been established worldwide. Such eminence was by no means always assured. Although a widely acclaimed political writer and public intellectual during her lifetime, her views were always contested. Arendt was also accused, and often, of meddling in areas like Jewish history, the Holocaust, and American desegregation debates—to name but a few—in which she was not a specialist. Actually, she objected to being called a "philosopher" and described herself to Karl Jaspers, her former teacher, as having become "something between a historian and a publicist." All this has changed. Certainly, controversy has not ceased to accompany her even after her death, particularly after the 1998 publication of her correspondence with Martin Heidegger whose student and lover she had been. Yet Hannah Arendt has become a "classical" political philosopher and has assumed her place alongside the male stars of the Western intellectual canon.

The Reluctant Modernism of Hannah Arendt was written as the contemporary Arendt renaissance was gathering momentum. My purpose in this work was, and remains, to offer a rereading of her political philosophy in the light of newly gained insights into the historical and cultural contexts of her thought. It is my thesis that German *Existenz* philosophy, and particularly the thought of Martin Heidegger, inspired some of Arendt's best known categories, such as world, action, and plurality. But what enabled Arendt to transform Heidegger's teachings into an original political philosophy were her experiences as a German Jewish woman in the age of totalitarianism.

Although the details of Arendt's life and her passionate involvement with twentieth-century, and especially Jewish, politics were well known since the publication of Elisabeth Young-Bruehl's 1982 biography, *For Love of the World,* there were few attempts to integrate the essayistic and journalistic writings with the more well-known philosophical and political works. What I called the "standard view" of Arendt dominated, and in fact, still governs much interpretation of her work. The standard view maintains that Arendt is a political philosopher of nostalgia, an anti-modernist for whom the Greek "polis" remained the quintessential political experience. It is easy then to conclude not only that Arendt's thought is irrelevant to contemporary concerns but that she is an elitist reactionary when it comes to assessing the prospects of liberal democracies. I believe that this view is wrong and one-sided, and that the major text upon which it is based, *The Human Condition,* needs to be read in a more subtle and nuanced way, as engaging in multiple complex dialogues with Aristotle as well as with Martin Heidegger and Karl Marx.

To clarify Arendt's philosophical intentions, I identify two orientations that run like a red thread through her work. On the one hand, she practices the method of fragmentary historiography for which Walter Benjamin was her prime example. After the break with tradition, one could no longer approach the past with the intention of transposing past insights into contemporary wisdom. Rather, one had to think of human history as sediments in layers of language and of concepts. Particularly during moments of rupture, displacement, and dislocation, the history of concepts themselves bore witness to the more profound tectonic shifts occurring beneath the visible course of events. Such a "fragmentary" approach to history would involve a remembering, in the sense of a creative act of rethinking and reappropriating the past, just as a collector or as an artist might do. Arendt practiced this method brilliantly in her masterpiece *The Origins of Totalitarianism,* but this way of reading is demonstrated in *On Revolution* as well as in her essays collected in *Between Past and Future*. On the other hand, Arendt's thoughts are also influenced by the phenomenological attempt to find an originary state of the phenomena as being the privileged one. As opposed to rupture, displacement, and dislocation, this view emphasizes the continuity between the origin and the present and seeks to uncover at the origin the lost and concealed essence of phenomena. Philosophical thinking becomes an exercise in mimetic recollection, of allowing beings "to represence" themselves, in Heideggerian terminology. Thus, Arendt searches for the "original meaning of politics," for the "lost" distinction between the public and the private.

Whereas the first approach emphasizes creative rupture through which configurations of new meanings can emerge, the second approach views thinking as an exercise in retrieval. Although I recognize the powerful influence of both the fragmentary and the originary strains in Arendt's thought, my sympathies are with the Benjaminian Arendt rather than with the Heideggerian. Through an extensive analysis of her concepts of the social and the political, the public and the private, in their institutional as well as phenomenological meanings, I attempt to show that we, as readers of Arendt, can "think with Arendt against Arendt" and cull from these distinctions fragments which can be rendered fruitful for a political philosophy of late modernity. (See especially chapter 5).

In that spirit, I open this book with a little-known text of Arendt's, *Rahel Varnhagen: The Life of a Jewish Woman*. Begun in 1929, shortly after Arendt completed her dissertation on St. Augustine's concept of love, this study was not finished until 1938, and it was first published in 1957. In Arendt's story of Varnhagen I read not only the traces of disappointment and sadness over her failed love affair with Martin Heidegger, but I also discover an "alternative genealogy of modernity." According to this alternative account of modernity, the transformation of the household from a productive unit within a subsistence economy into an "intimate" sphere of the bourgeois family is accompanied, in certain historical contexts, with the rise of "salons." These were spaces within the household—usually a festive living room—in which individuals from different ranks, groups, and classes, even faiths, could mix and mingle; literary and artistic works were read and discussed. They presented occasions for experimentation with self-fashioning and with less hierarchical, more fluid modes of interaction.

Salons such as Varnhagen's revealed the presence within modern society of an alternative form of public sphere, one that is more egalitarian, fluid, experimental, and in which lines between intimacy and sociability, the public and the private are renegotiated and resignified. Thus, at the very beginnings of Arendt's career as a thinker we see her presenting an alternative genealogy of modernity and a public sphere radically different from the inegalitarian, exclusive, male, and hierarchical spaces of the Greek polis. Arendt, I claim, never lost sight of this alternative account of modernity, but neither did she fully accept it.

II

It did not escape the attention of careful readers of my book that in locating this alternative account of modernity in Arendt's work and in stressing the modernist, egalitarian, politically experimental, and even revolutionary aspects of her teaching, I was inspired by Juergen Habermas's *The Structural Transformation of the Public Sphere.*[1] From the start, Habermas makes very clear that in focusing upon the category of the "public sphere" (*Oeffentlichkeit*), he is both following in the footsteps of and establishing his distance from Arendt's discussion of the "public space" (*der oeffentliche Raum*) in *The Human Condition* (See chapter 6). Thus to the charge that I may have been reading Arendt as if she were a Habermasian, my answer would simply be that for many years now, my concern has been rather the converse, namely to show the respects in which Habermas is an Arendtian. Not only the recovery of the public world under conditions of modernity, but the very understanding of political power as flowing "from the action in concert" of equals, united through their deliberative pursuit of the common good, testify to the Arendtian traces in Habermas's work.

Surely, though, it would be a mistake to overlook their profound differences as well. Habermas was able to show, contra Arendt and contra Adorno and Horkheimer in *The Dialectic of Enlightenment*, the presence of an emancipatory moment of reason within modernity. Calling this "communicative reason" in contradistinction to instrumental reason, Habermas's life work has been devoted to extending an understanding of communicative rationality into fields as diverse as the pragmatics of speech acts, sociological action theory, and democratic and legal philosophy. Although I follow the broad outlines of Habermas's program in ethics and politics, my goal has never been a vindication of Habermas against Arendt. Quite to the contrary, I have argued that the emphasis on the validity of speech acts misses the narrative and interpretive dimensions of human action, which Arendt so acutely highlights. Habermas's exclusive focus on the justifiability of principles in ethics also ignores the role of judgment in morals and politics, an issue to which Arendt devoted considerable attention. Lastly, Habermas's emphasis on the emancipatory potential of modern liberal democracies may run the risk of minimizing the decline of the public sphere in our societies and of ignoring the weakness of citizens' movements and deliberative organizations when compared to markets and professional lobbying. Just as we are getting too smug about the ideals of the Enlightenment, a dose of Arendtian pessimism may be necessary to keep us honest as thinkers. Far from vindicating one against the other, this book is situated in the force field created by these interpretive tensions which run deep in my own work.

III

While completing *The Reluctant Modernism of Hannah Arendt* I did not have access to the Arendt–Heidegger correspondence. Since the letters in Arendt's possession were also closed to scholars, I had to rely upon excerpts from the correspondence as reported in Elzbieta Ettinger's *Hannah Arendt-Martin Heidegger*.[2] Since then these letters have been published in German as *Hannah Arendt/Martin Heidegger Briefe 1925 bis 1975*.[3] In the new appendix to this edition of my work, I offer a reevaluation of the fraught Arendt and Heidegger saga and at several points I indicate my deep disagreement with Ettinger's interpretation of this personal as well as intellectual relationship.

Taking my cue from Arendt's 1954 lecture titled "Concern with Politics in Recent European Political Thought" (see pp. 52 ff.), I place the concept of the "world" not only at the center of my reconstruction of certain leitmotifs in Arendt's work, but I use it as the key to access the complex philosophical relationship of Arendt and Heidegger, as well. Arendt thought that with the fundamental analysis of being human in terms of "being-in-the-world," Heidegger had created an unprecedented possibility for the philosopher to think about the specifics of human action and the realm of politics. At the same time, Arendt claimed, Heidegger denigrated the public realm as one of "distantiality, averageness, and leveling down."[4] Yet it remained Heidegger's fundamental insight that "By reason of this with-like Being-in-the-world, the world is always the one that I share with Others."[5]

Hannah Arendt's central philosophical categories, such as action, plurality, and natality, through which she defined "the human condition," are indebted to Heidegger and yet subvert Heideggerian ontology. Whereas for Heidegger the most authentic form of being is the being-unto-death of the self, for Arendt, natality, that every child born is also potentially the initiator of freedom, of new and unprecedented deeds and words, is crucial. Whereas for Heidegger "being-with" remains a problematic and often inauthentic form of existence, for Arendt human beings live most authentically in a world they share with others like themselves and with whom they are in constant communication and to whom they appear through speech and action. Whereas Heidegger develops in great detail forms of activity through which objects are made disposable for human purposes as well as forms of aesthetic activity, moral and political interaction do not receive any special ontological treatment in his system. By contrast, Hannah Arendt is the philosopher of human plurality, action, and natality. Her focus is on words and deeds through which the "web of human affairs" comes into existence and is sustained. The depth and originality of these philosophical contributions that proceed at the level of ontology (the mode of being qua human) and phenomenology (experiential access to appearances) have not been adequately appreciated. Together with Jacques Taminieux and Dana Villa, I see this subversive reappropriation of Heidegger to be Arendt's genuine philosophical, in contradistinction to her political, contribution.[6]

Dana Villa's *Arendt and Heidegger: The Fate of the Political* is the most comprehensive treatment of this philosophical relationship.[7] Despite our crucial agreement on certain fundamentals, Villa presents a reading of Arendt the main aim of which is to emphasize the "performative" rather than the deliberative and communicative aspects of Arendt's understanding of political action (Villa, pp. 53-54). Since Villa's work appeared shortly after *The Reluctant Modernism of Hannah Arendt,* I would like to explore these differences briefly. Villa and I agree that Arendt did not merely appropriate Heideggerian categories—an assumption repeated by Richard Wolin most recently[8]—but that she transformed them. We also agree that the categories of action and plurality are crucial to this transformation, and that Heidegger's reading of Aristotle in the years 1924–1925 in Marburg left indelible marks upon Arendt. It is through a revival of the Aristotelian distinction between *praxis* (the doing of fine and noble deeds) and *poiesis* (making) that Arendt arrives at her own concept of action.

Finally, I agree with Villa that "Throughout her work, Arendt focuses on deliberative speech. . . . Political speech, then, is nothing other than the process of debate and deliberation, the 'talk and argument,' the 'persuasion, negotiation and compromise' that precedes the deed. . . . Political debate is end-constitutive: its goal does not stand apart from the process, dominating it at every point, but is rather formed in the course of 'performance' itself" (Villa, p.12).

Nevertheless, Villa is concerned to show that the deliberative and universalist reading does Arendt an injustice. "The problem is that Benhabib's redemption of the deliberative dimension of Arendt's political theory comes at the expense of the initiatory or performative dimension" (Villa, p. 70). Villa reaches this conclusion from a strikingly original, but unconvincing reading of Arendt's concept of political action. According to Villa, Arendt did not simply follow the Aristotelian distinction between *praxis* and *poiesis,* between doing and making; she radicalized this distinction along one dimension. This is the sense in which activities can be said to be "self-sufficient" or "self-contained." "In some cases," says Aristotle, "the activity is the end, in others, the end is in some product beyond the activity. In cases where the end lies beyond the action the product is naturally superior to the activity."(As quoted in Villa, p. 21.) For Aristotle "praxis," the doing of fine and noble deeds, are ends-in-themselves and not undertaken for the sake of a product or a consequence which follows from the deed. *Praxis* for Aristotle flows from the right moral character and, for the good man, the praxis of virtue is an end-in-itself. But political activity is for the sake of the good life: deliberating, judging, and acting in the polis present "proximate goals"; they are aimed at the good life, which is the ultimate goal.

Villa claims that, unlike Aristotle, for Arendt political action is self-sufficient and *atelic*; "freedom," for Arendt, "resides in the self-contained-ness of action" (Villa, p. 25). This means that political action must be judged by standards intrinsic to it. Neither morality nor economics, neither aesthetics nor justice are the goal of politics. Politics, in the Arendtian sense, has no goal that is extrinsic to itself. Villa admits that a "self-contained politics" entails a certain kind of talk: "The structure of political action is one in which debate and disagreement reflect an overarching commitment to a particular public world and the mode of being together that it makes possible" (Villa, p. 39). However, such debate and disagreement is not engaged in for the sake of reaching consensus; such processes through which the inevitable plurality and perspectivality of the human world shines forth, are ends-in-themselves. Villa concludes that for Arendt the performative dimension has priority over the deliberative and the dialog-ical.[9]

Villa's provocative reading is based not only on a misreading of Aristotle but upon a distortion of the meaning of reaching communicative agreement as well. When Aristotle distinguishes between praxis and poiesis, he does so on the basis of his theory of the virtues. For the man of practical wisdom, whom Aristotle identifies with the "good man," *tout court*, the "doing of fine and noble deeds" is an end-in-itself because it flows from a firm disposition of heart and habit. Its origin is moral character. Actions can only exhibit virtue when they are undertaken not for the sake of pleasure, utility, or influence, but for the sake of doing the right thing. Aristotle is not unlike Kant in this respect. Virtue is its own goal because it has to be undertaken for its own sake alone. For Aristotle only activities which flow from a firm moral disposition and which have a clear moral good as their purpose are ends-in-themselves. If, however, one rejects Aristotle's teaching of the virtues, there is very little sense left to the notion of praxis being "an end-in-itself."

I see little evidence in Arendt's work that she is concerned with the concept of an end-in-itself or, for that matter, with Aristotle's teaching of the virtues. It is not the self-containedness of action—a category foreign to Arendt but crucial to Villa's reading of her—but rather the unique and irreducible way in which words and deeds reveal "who" the person is that is at the center of Arendt's reflections. Repeatedly Arendt tells us that humans "appear" to others through their words and deeds, and that human life unfolds within the "web" of human relationships (See p. 110 ff.). Villa ignores the narrative constitution of self and action in Arendt's work and cannot establish the case for the priority of the performative for several reasons.

First, the performative interpretation of action simply cannot explain how the "web" of narratives is constituted through ordinary speech and deliberation. Performativity, a vague but very fashionable category, leaves unclear how the performer and the spectator come to share and exchange standards of understanding and evaluation. Performance also communicates through narrative, deliberation, and mutual reasoning. The meaning of a play is no clearer to us than the meaning of a contested piece of legislation. It is in the medium of ordinary everyday discursive exchange and deliberation that the *what* as well as the *how* of the performance is identified and appropriated.[10] This is why Arendt had to appeal to Kant's theory of reflective judgment to mediate the standpoint of the actor and the spectator.

Furthermore, Villa sees a sharp contrast between communication aimed at consensus and reaching agreement, and properly political speech and deliberation. He even suggests that the ethos of agreement "*instrumentalizes* action and judgment" (Villa, 70. Emphasis in the text.). This is based upon a misunderstanding of the status of the communicative validity claims in Habermas's work and of my deployment of them. In assuming that the other with whom one is engaged in conversation is capable of judging the validity of one's claims—their truth, rightfulness, sincerity, or appropriateness—one is in fact treating the other human being as an end-in-him or -herself, as a person capable of assessing the claims of others through reason. This form of interaction is referred to as "communicative up-take" in conversation, deliberation, and debate. The emphasis here is on individuals' capacities to be communicative agents and to judge for themselves.

In communicating with you on the basis of reason, I am respecting your ability to be a reasoning being. There is no instrumentalization here. Quite to the contrary, it is when I try to achieve certain effects upon you without giving you reasons or by giving you false ones—as in propaganda, advertising, seducing, and various forms of scare tactics—that I fail to treat you as an end-in-itself and attempt to influence your person or behavior without sharing my reasons for aiming at those effects. If performativity is made primary, then politics is not "action in concert among equals" but indeed a "politics of heroic display" and "an immoralist celebration of greatness as its own morality" (Villa, 55). But Arendt was no admirer of Zarathustra, and Achilles was not one of her idols but, in her eyes, a foible of male vanity and of the search for vainglory.

Teasing out categorial distinctions from her theoretical texts, Villa leaves aside Arendt's historical–political writings. But it is in the latter that one should have searched for evidence for the kind of self-contained political action that Arendt ostensibly glorified. Do her references to the lost treasures of revolutions, revived through the deliberative councils of ordinary sailors in the Kornstadt rebellion, of ordinary citizens in the Hungarian uprising of 1956, or during the anti-Vietnam war movement of the 1960s, vindicate a performative politics of greatness over a deliberative one? Hardly. The truth rather is that while there were moments of great deeds performed by ordinary individuals in these events, there were also processes of "action in concert" and deliberative politics. Arendt's historical reflections do not permit such clear dichotomies. The "priority of the performative" reflects Villa's own philosophical choices and is not a hermeneutic approach which can integrate the political with the philosophical, the ontological with the historical dimensions of Arendt's work. It offers a truncated reading of Arendt, through which she is placed more firmly in the company of Nietzsche and Heidegger than of Aristotle and Kant. But the cost of this repositioning is, as I will attempt to show in the following chapters, a neglect of Arendt's reflections on concrete historical and political phenomena of the twentieth century.

V

The Reluctant Modernism of Hannah Arendt was translated into German in 1998 as *Hannah Arendt: Die Melancholische Denkerin der Moderne* (Hannah Arendt: The Melancholy Thinker of Modernity).[11] The choice of the term "melancholy" was misunderstood by several critics.[12] Many assumed that I intended to describe an emotional or psychological state of mind. However, what I intended to convey through this term was an attitude of meditative reflection on the *necessity* as well as *impossibility* of attaining certain results in human affairs. The passage which inspired me to use this term reads as follows: "These facts and reflections offer what seems an ironical, bitter, and belated confirmation of the famous arguments with which Edmund Burke opposed the French Revolution's Declaration of the Rights of Man."[13] Arendt is discussing the condition of statelessness and the loss on the part of millions of human beings of "the right to have rights." She is reflecting on the irony that just as men and women of the twentieth century have emancipated themselves from the ontology of nature as well as from the metaphysics of history, and just as the sheer fact of being human should serve as a guarantee for entitlement to rights and for the protection of one's "right to have rights," human beings become disposable bodies in space and time. Shoved across national borders, hunted down by the police, criminalized because they lack adequate papers, and deprived, in many cases, of the protection of the national states into which they were born, human beings seem to lose all rights at the point when they have nothing to lose but their "their abstract nakedness."

I read these concluding reflections of the second section of *The Origins of Totalitarianism* as "melancholy" because they outline wonderfully the necessity of guaranteeing universal human rights to all human beings in virtue of their "naked humanity," while at the same time expressing deep skepticism that this can be done without the protection of nation-states. Yet, as Arendt herself admits, these observations are "ironical and bitter."[14] For it is the regime of territorial sovereignty of a supposedly homogenous nation-state that leads in the first place to practices of denaturalization, discrimination against minority rights, and disenfranchisement of unwanted ethnic, linguistic, and religious groups.

These reflections, like so much else in Arendt's work, have proved extremely prescient. It is not only her insights about the significance of a vibrant and free public sphere in democratic civil societies, East and West, which has earned her the title of the "theorist of the post-totalitarian moment." It is also Arendt, the theorist of minority rights and statelessness, of refugees and deported peoples, whose words strike the deepest chord in a world still shaken by civil wars and ethnic massacres, cultural self-determination movements and assertive nation-states. The dilemmas of "the right to have rights" and the predicament of stateless peoples, refugees, asylum-seekers, illegal migrants, and undocumented workers will prove as central to a state-centric world in deep crisis as totalitarianism did in the previous century. In reflecting on these matters as well, "thinking with Arendt against Arendt" can illuminate new possibilities as well as pitfalls.[15]

Except for minor stylistic and bibliographic corrections and the new appendix, this book reproduces the 1996 Sage publication edition of *The Reluctant Modernism of Hannah Arendt.* Complete references to Arendt's texts can be found in the bibliography at the end.

Notes

1. See Maria Pia Lara and Joan V. Landes, Review of *The Reluctant Modernism of Hannah Arendt, Hypatia,* 14 (3)[1999], pp. 162-169; Rahel Jaeggi, "Authentizitaet und Alltag. Die Hannah Arendt Rezeption zwischen Kritischer Theorie und Postmoderne," *Deutsche Zeitschrift fuer Philosophie,* 45 (1) [1997], pp. 147-165; Dana Villa, *Arendt and Heidegger. The Fate of the Political* (Princeton, N.J.: Princeton University Press, 1996).

2. Ettinger, Elzbieta. *Hannah Arendt-Martin Heidegger* (New Haven, Conn.: Yale University Press, 1995).

3. *Hannah Arendt/Martin Heidegger Briefe 1925 bis 1975,* ed. Ursula Ludz (Frankfurt: Vittorio Klostermann, 1998).

4. Martin Heidegger, [1927] *Being and Time,* trans. by John Macquarrie and Edward Robinson (New York: Harper and Row, 1962), p. 165.

5. Ibid., p. 155.

6. Jacques Taminieux, *La Fille de Thrace,* translated into English as *The Thracian Maid and the Professional Thinker. Arendt and Heidegger.* Trans and ed. Michael Gendre (Albany: State University of New York Press, 1997).

7. Dana Villa, *Arendt and Heidegger. The Fate of the Political* (Princeton, N.J.: Princeton University Press, 1996).

8. See *Heidegger's Children. Hannah Arendt, Karl Loewith, Hans Jonas, and Herbert Marcuse* (Princeton, N.J.: Princeton University Press, 2001), pp. 30-70. Richard Wolin, who has attacked Arendt's person and work in his previous reviews, continues his one-sided presentation in this book as well, by subsuming both the person and the work under the shadow of Heidegger. In addition to the hardly concealed sexism of his comments on the Arendt-Heidegger affair, it is interesting to note that his views most clearly represent what I have named the "standard interpretation" of Arendt. Thus one of the chapters on Arendt is revealingly titled, *"Kultur,* 'Thoughtlessness', and *Polis En*vy." (31) For Wolin's earlier attacks on Arendt, see "Hannah and the Magician," *The New Republic,* vol. 213 (October 9, 1995), pp. 27-37; "Within Four Walls," *The New Republic,* vol. 223, No. 22 (November 2000), pp. 27-35. See also my review of Richard Wolin's *Heidegger's Chidren,* "Taking Ideas Seriously," *Boston Review,* vol. 27, No. 6 (December 2002), pp. 40-44.

9. There are certain passages in Arendt's text in which the criterion of "greatness" with reference to judging action is emphasized (Arendt, *The Human Condition,* 8th edition [Chicago: University of Chicago Press, 1973 {1958}], p. 205). Greatness seems to me related to Arendt's understanding of freedom and natality, to our capacity to initiate the new and the unprecedented. Such actions require a reevaluation of our old values, a reconsideration of the

common yardsticks by which we pass judgments. Indeed, greatness can entail both good and evil for Arendt, whereas ordinarily we are inclined to think of it with reference to the morally good alone. But if we emphasize what is unprecedented in human affairs and the need "to think without banisters," then we see that totalitarian crimes require criteria of evaluation which are just as novel as truly great or heroic actions. Arendt's emphasis upon greatness as a quality of certain actions does not render moral evaluations suspect, but rather highlights the need to rethink them. For example, if a regime is based upon organized crime, such as mass murder of the Jews was under the Nazis, how does one use criteria of personal responsibility to judge anonymous bureaucrats? Arendt believed that this was possible but not without some prior transvaluation of values. Villa, in my judgment, thinks that greatness displaces or renders superfluous additional moral and political criteria. I do not think that it does. To the contrary, greatness forces a reevaluation of traditional categories but not their elimination.

10. The status of performativity has always been a bone of contention for theorists influenced by postmodernism and discourse ethics. I have dealt with the narrative/performative distinction in several other contexts as well. See Benhabib, "Sexual Difference and Collective Identities: The New Global Constellation," *Signs: Journal of Women in Culture and Society*, 24 (2) [1999], pp. 335-361.

11. Seyla Benhabib, *Hannah Arendt. Die Melancholische Denkerin der Moderne*. Mit einem Nachwort von Otto Kallscheuer, trans. by Karin Wordemann (Rotbuch Verlag: Hamburg, 1998)

12. Ronald Schindler, "Melancholische Denkerin der Moderne? Zur deutschen Ausgabe von Seyla Benhabibs Studie ueber Arendts Politische Theorie," *Hannah Arendt Newsletter*, No. 3 (July 2000), pp. 32-37.

13. Arendt, Hannah. *The Origins of Totalitarianism* (New York: Harcourt Brace Jovanovitch, 1979 [1951]), p. 299.

14. Ibid., p. 299.

15. I have started developing these issues in several recent writings. See Seyla Benhabib, *Transformations of Citizenship. Dilemmas of the Nation-State in the Era of Globalization. The Spinoza Lectures* (Amsterdam: Van Gorcum 2000); *The Claims of Culture. Equality and Diversity in the Global Era* (Princeton, N.J.: Princeton University Press, 2002); and "Political Geographies in a New World: Arendtian Reflections," *Social Research*, vol. 69, No. 2 (Summer 2002): pp. 539-566.

Series Editor's Introduction

S eyla Benhabib's *The Reluctant Modernism of Hannah Arendt* is the tenth volume in the Rowman & Littlefield series **Modernity and Political Thought** to be published in a second edition. It follows publication of the new editions of William E. Connolly's *The Augustinian Imperative: A Reflection on the Politics of Morality*, Richard E. Flathman's *Thomas Hobbes: Skepticism, Individuality and Chastened Politics*, Michael Shapiro's *Reading "Adam Smith": Desire, History and Value*, Tracy B. Strong's *Jean-Jacques Rousseau: The Politics of the Ordinary*, George Kateb's *Emerson and Self-Reliance*, Jane Bennett's *Thoreau's Nature: Ethics, Politics, and the Wild*, Thomas Dumm's *Michel Foucault and the Politics of Freedom*, Stephen White's *Edmund Burke: Modernity, Politics, and Aesthetics*, and Fred Dallmayr's *G.W.F. Hegel: Modernity and Politics.*[1] In addition, new works for **Modernity and Political Thought** are under way, and, among others, will focus on such diverse thinkers as Plato, Aristotle, Thomas Aquinas, Thomas More, Niccolo Machiavelli, John Locke, Karl Marx, Friedrich Nietzsche, John Stuart Mill, William James, and Sigmund Freud, as well as on a selection of contemporary political theorists. As those who are familiar with the previous works of series authors will expect, taken together their studies adopt a variety of approaches and pose importantly different questions. As contributors to **Modernity and Political Thought,** however, their efforts also are commonly devoted to effecting critical examinations of major political theorists who have shaped our understanding of modernity—its constitution, problems, promises, and the dangers that are latent within it.

Among the distinctions earned by Seyla Benhabib's work, perhaps the most important, though certainly the one especially significant for its current impact on political thought, is her contribution to the reconstitution of critical social theory. While Jurgen Habermas has been acknowledged as the architect of the restructuring of critical theory since the publication in 1968 of his *Knowledge and Human Interests,* during the latter years of the following decade there were signs that the evolution of critical theory had reached a new plateau. Further theoretical progress appeared to wait upon Habermas's response to attacks on the rationalist tradition from largely counter-Enlightenment schools of thought that posed serious challenges to presuppositions that formed the basis of his model of communicative interaction. Habermas's response came with the 1981 publication of *The Theory of Communicative Action* and the 1986 appearance of his *Philosophical Discourse of Modernity.* Yet, his attempts to meet the critical challenges of feminism, poststructuralism, and postmodernism, in particular, have received important assistance from other theorists, notably among them Seyla Benhabib. Her work in this area in several ways may prove decisive, as her support of Habermas's project promises to push the theory of communicative action to a new level. And of particular importance for our immediate purposes, it also opens with a sweeping reassessment and revaluation of the thought of Hannah Arendt.

In *Critique, Norm, and Utopia,* widely acknowledged as a landmark study of the historical evolution and philosophical foundations of critical social theory, Benhabib lays the groundwork for her contribution to its theoretical development.[2] At the outset of any discussion of Benhabib's work, what first should be stressed is her passionate devotion to the idea that every human being is worthy of the same moral respect. By so recognizing her allegiance to universalism, the danger is swiftly averted that her equally powerful allegiance to commitments articulated by feminist, postmodernist, and poststructuralist thinkers could be read as an unqualified opposition to the liberal tradition. Sharing this normative principle with liberalism, she is likewise committed to equality; democratic processes; civil, legal, and political rights; and institutionalized forms of justice, such as constitutionalism, through which universal rights and entitlements are protected.

Benhabib's devotion to universalism establishes her ties to Habermas, who more than any other contemporary political theorist has come nearest to formulating a universalist position on rationality and ethics that grounds universal norms. As does Habermas, Benhabib locates the resources to realize the values underwritten by universal rationality within modernity. Modernity embodies the as yet unexploited potential of the Enlightenment for achieving human emancipation through a sphere of public discourse and action within which every norm governing collective life can be contested and validated. Modernity is an unfinished human project. However, it is an endangered human project, as well. Modernity has been imperfectly realized in established liberal democratic practices, which are the heir to nearly three hundred years of bourgeois revolutions culminating in the one-sided institutionalization of a rationality that threatens to entirely erode moral values and moral capacities not related instrumentally to systemic goals and interests.

Benhabib and Habermas are clearly deeply rooted in the tradition of critical thinking that grew out of the Enlightenment thought, which they hold in common and that serves as the foundation of their work. Their shared roots are evident in several commitments intrinsic to Benhabib's thought. Through her commitment to public discourse, at an explicit level of analysis Benhabib endorses an inextricable connection between the claim of a communicatively grounded reason and individual freedom and justice for the whole, while at an implicit level she denies any division between ethics and politics. Through her commitment to the normative legitimacy of the public sphere, she embraces a normative standpoint in relation to existing social structures, beliefs, and practices. Through her commitment to a normative standpoint that can be institutionally represented through public discourse and action, she subscribes to the view that individuals fall victim to ideologies that can be exposed through forms of communicative interaction designed to contest and validate their interpretations of needs and examine the consequences of their satisfaction. And, finally, through her commitment to the critique of ideology, Benhabib shares critical theory's notion of praxis, according to which the relationship of theory to the individuals and groups whom it addresses is always problematic with regard to how, under what conditions, and to what end or ends theory can play a part in their political struggles. To begin to appreciate the originality of her contribution to critical theory, Benhabib's understanding of the notion of praxis becomes uniquely important. For our present purposes, what is striking is her grasp of the analytical discipline this idea imposes on the theorist. It instructs the intelligence that circulates throughout her examination of the Enlightenment tradition from Hobbes to Kant and the critical tradition from Hegel to Habermas. And it enables Benhabib's discovery that the theory of communicative action must accommodate the insights generated by feminism, postmodernism, and poststructuralism and of the ways and extent to which such a theoretical accommodation can occur.

Because the relationship of critical theory to its addressee is problematized by the notion of praxis, the relationship of the theorist to critical theory becomes problematic, as well, particularly with respect to how critique's relationship to its addressee must be guided conceptually. By thematizing such a special reflective relationship of the theorist to critical theory, the idea of praxis informs Benhabib's design of a conceptual framework that permits her to highlight conflicts, tensions, and ambiguities characterizing the project of critical theory in a variety of ways since its Hegelian inception. "Norm" and "utopia," the twin poles of Benhabib's framework corresponding to two visions of politics, illuminates these conflicts as they have appeared throughout the history of critical thought. "Norm," she explains, envisions a community of rights and entitlements, and corresponds to a "politics of fulfillment" where society in the future more adequately attains what present society promises but has not achieved. "Utopia" envisions a community of needs and solidarity, and corresponds to a "politics of transfiguration" emphasizing the emergence of qualitatively new needs and modes of association that burst open the utopian possibilities of the existing society. Norm and utopia are concerned, respectively, with justice at the one extreme, and at the other with forms of life that can be fulfilling. Conflicts, tensions, and ambiguities within critical theory have arisen when theory gravitated toward one of the two poles at the expense of the other, limiting the power of its sociological and philosophical assumptions and arguments. Theory can avoid its past foundering on the rocks of either Scylla or Charybdis by unfolding between these two poles. "A critical social theory is only rich enough to address us in the present," Benhabib proposes, "insofar as it can do justice to both moments."[3]

Benhabib's analysis of Habermas's theory of communicative action brilliantly illustrates how the framework of "norm and utopia" exposes conflicts internal to critical social theory that compromise its normative and explanatory efficacy. Though Benhabib's study is far too comprehensive of Habermas's work to be examined in its entirety, in the context of a discussion of the insights generated by "norm and utopia" one dimension of her discussion can be taken up. Benhabib recalls Habermas's concern that the theory of communicative action, preoccupied with the emancipatory potential of moral–political discourse, might focus on normative validity, justice, and freedom to the neglect of the integrity of cultural values, images of the good life, and those qualities of individual life histories and collective life forms that make them fulfilling or unfulfilling. Put in terms of Benhabib's conceptual framework, a theory confined to holding societies accountable for realizing promises rooted in Enlightenment universalism is wanting. Restricting critique to the reformism of keeping promises relinquishes the utopian ideals whose achievement presupposes the "transfiguration" of social orders. Incorporating—or rather, reincorporating—transfiguration into critique would return it to the utopian tradition that, beginning with Marx, included both fulfillment and transfiguration in the project of emancipation. With this in mind, Benhabib remarks,

> Let me ask, therefore, if the goal of realizing bourgeois universalism, of making good the unfulfilled promise of justice and freedom, must exhaust itself in a "joyless reformism," or whether, speaking with Benjamin, one cannot see a *Jetztzeit,* a moment of transfiguration, in this very process? I want to suggest that the seventh stage of moral development postulated by Habermas as a corrective and extension of the Kohlbergian [six stage] scheme, that is, the stage of "universalizable need interpretations," has an unmistakable utopian content to it, and that it points to a transfigurative vision of bourgeois universalism.[4]

Benhabib's interest lies in Habermas's argument that an appropriate moral language can serve individuals as a cognitive vehicle for interpreting both their particular needs as well as needs they hold in common with others and about which they can reach consensus. To capture the force of

Habermas's contention, Benhabib points out that what it requires of moral discourse far exceeds the limits of conventional, Kantian universalistic ethical theories. Since the perspective of conventional universalistic ethical theories, conceptualized in terms of stage six of Kohlberg's moral theory, operate at a level of public discourse concerned with rights and entitlements, they are able to contest neither the needs on behalf of which rights are exercised nor the "concept of entitlement which the ethos of a right-bearing and invariably adult male implies."[5] From this Benhabib concludes that Habermas's demand that "universalistic need interpretation"—the requirement that needs and the cultural tradition through which they are interpreted—become the subject of discursive argumentation, is not simply the *evolution* of the perspective of conventional moral theories. On the contrary, Benhabib argues, by insinuating needs into the heart of moral argumentation Habermas's correction of the Kohlbergian scheme constitutes a "utopian break" with the perspective of conventional universalistic moral theories, a break that Benhabib describes as a "transfiguration." In this new light Benhabib casts on Habermas's theory of communicative ethics, it becomes clear that in communicative interaction questions of justice would be inseparable from questions of the good life, and questions of the universal validity of norms governing the life of all would appear to be inseparable from the value to individuals of the cultural norms through which by themselves or together they live their lives.

Yet, although communicative ethics appears in this light to inhabit the terrain lying between the poles of norm and utopia, Benhabib is not satisfied with the manner in which Habermas conceptualizes the "community of needs and solidarity." While Habermas's idea of "universalizable need interpretation" acknowledges that needs and their interpretations are thematized in moral discourse and enter into moral theory, he also conceptualizes needs in aesthetic–expressive terms and limits debate about need interpretation to aesthetic–expressive discourse concerned with issues that are semipublic, nonuniversalizable, and culturally specific. At best, then, the problematic distinction between normative and aesthetic–expressive discourse on which this move is based establishes an ambiguous position for the place of need interpretation in the model of communicative ethics. At worst, configuring need interpretation in aesthetic–expressive rather than normative terms purifies moral discourse of any genuine theoretical contact with needs and their interpretations. Such a purification unfortunately undermines the utopian pole and transfigurative moment of critical theory. It does so by perpetuating in communicative ethics the alignment with what, in universalistic ethical theory, is construed as a "moral point of view" with the standpoint of the "generalized other." For the standpoint of the "generalized other," as Benhabib argues,

> requires us to view each and every individual as a rational being entitled to the same rights and duties we would want to ascribe to ourselves. In assuming this perspective, we abstract from the individuality and concrete identity of the other. We assume that the other, like ourselves, is a being who has concrete needs, desires, and affects, but that what constitutes his or her moral dignity is not what differentiates us from each other, but rather what we, as speaking and acting rational agents, have in common . . . [The] moral categories that accompany [the interactions of generalized others] are those of right, obligation, and entitlement; the corresponding moral feelings are those of respect, duty, worthiness and dignity, and the vision of community is one of rights and entitlements.[6]

To the standpoint of the generalized other Benhabib opposed that of the "concrete other," which requires that individuals be thought of emphatically in terms of their identities, particular life histories, beliefs and understandings, needs, desires, feelings, and emotions. Concrete otherness, in other words, recovers for the moral point of view the utopian dimension that norm, rights, entitlements, and the generalized other leave out. It entails the recognition of the distinctiveness in addition to the commonality of the other, the demonstration of sincere interest in and effort to comprehend the other affectively, and the confirmation of the other's talents and capacities. In one of the most eloquent passages of *Critique, Norm, and Utopia,* Benhabib, reflecting on the moral ideals of a communicative ethic that valorizes difference in its breadth and depth, explicates the norms of interaction among individuals whose ethical orientations are informed by a respect for concrete otherness.

> The norms of our interaction are usually private, noninstitutional ones. They are the norms of solidarity, friendship, love, and care. Such relations require in various ways that I do, and that you expect me to do in the face of your needs, more than would be required of me as a right bearing person. In treating you in accordance with the norms of solidarity, friendship, love, and care, I confirm not only your *humanity* but your *individuality.* The moral categories that accompany such interactions are those of responsibility,

bonding, and sharing. The corresponding moral feelings are those of love, care, sympathy, and solidarity, and the vision of community is one of needs and solidarity.[7]

By building the notion of the concrete other into communicative ethics, Benhabib turns it unambiguously in the direction of a radical participatory, pluralist conception of politics. With this reformulation and recovery of its utopian moment, communicative ethics now provides for discursive practices in a public sphere within which an individual's worldviews, along with the cultural traditions, life histories, and self-conceptions from which every individual's view of the world is born, can emerge in the context of dialogue oriented toward the creation of shared beliefs and understandings. An authentic commonality of perspectives—what Benhabib calls a "unity-in-difference"—is created because communicative discourse is able to reflect the actual existing plurality of differences. And an authentic plurality of differences is reflected in communicative discourse because discursive practices are informed by an ethic that expresses the "concreteness" of differences that prevail among the multiplicity and diversity of forms of life.

But the new sensibility that Benhabib introduces into communicative interaction with the concept of concreteness is also remarkable for the process of individual self-transformation that it installs into the creation of every unity-in-difference. Through the experience of developing commonality, individuals learn to see the world from the perspectives of others. In effect, this reciprocity of perspectives enables participants in discourse to become an other and by so doing to *provisionally* adopt a standpoint that may compel a revision of their own worldview. Adopting perspectives belonging to others encourages respect for the dignity of the generalized other, who is our equal, and an awareness of the generalized other's difference. Moreover, at the same time that participants in discourse are taught to see the world from perspectives not originally their own, they make self-discoveries about their own distinctiveness, their own uniqueness, and their identity. Taken as a whole the process of self-transformation that accompanies the development of shared beliefs and understandings seems to include the essence of what it means to exercise moral judgment.

Critique, Norm, and Utopia's examination of the evolution of critical theory is significant for purposes beyond those for which it was expressly written. By setting out to learn which of critical theory's arguments and assumptions should either be discarded or appropriated and revised to mount a theoretical renewal of the project of modernity, and by discovering those philosophical and sociological shortcomings that crippled past insights in order to avoid reproducing flawed patterns of argumentation, Benhabib's approach laid the foundations for the renewal launched in *Situating the Self*, a study steadily making an important impact on contemporary social and political thought.[8] Here Benhabib concentrates on a defense of universalism, the bulwark of modernity's rationality, against recent assaults by communitarianism, feminism, and postmodernism, which have taken modernity to task for its perpetuation of war, environmental destruction, economic exploitation, victimization of minorities, and promotion of forms of life that satisfy human needs at the cost of human dignity and destroy the bases of human solidarity. Her defense, however, is not unqualified, nor does it entail a rejection of communitarianism, feminism, and postmodernism. Rather, by staging an engagement with its critics, her intention first and foremost is to reconstruct moral and political universalism in order to restore the validity and authority of the ideals universalism sustains. Specifically, such a reconstruction will allow us to imagine the trajectory along which modernity might be reformed and partly reconstituted to provide new political and institutional supports for the ideals of universal respect for every person by virtue of simply being human; the moral autonomy of the individual; economic and social justice and equality; democratic participation; the most extensive civil and political liberties compatible with principles of justice; and the establishment of solidaristic human associations. Benhabib's reconstruction also has the additional importance of drawing out elements of communitarianism, feminism, and postmodernism that possess value beyond the terms of their own frameworks.

Situating the Self isolates three themes around which Benhabib believes the reconstruction of Enlightenment universalism ought to proceed. Communitarians, feminists, and postmodernists, Benhabib recalls, have

(1) voiced skepticism toward the claims of a 'legislating' reason to be able to articulate the necessary conditions of a 'moral point of view,' an 'original position,' or an 'ideal speech situation;' (2) they have questioned the abstract and disembodied, distorting and nostalgic ideal of the autonomous male ego which the universalist tradition privileges; (3) they have unmasked the inability of such universalist, legislative reason to deal with the indeterminacy

and multiplicity of contexts and life-situations with which practical reason is always confronted.[9]

Benhabib agrees that there is much truth to these critiques from which contemporary universalist theorists can learn. If, in their light, universalism is reconceptualized to be "interactive" rather than legislative, to recognize gender differences rather than being gender blind, and to be appreciative of, rather than indifferent to, the diversity specific to cultural contexts, a "post-Enlightenment" defense of universalism, as Benhabib refers to it, is yet viable. Indeed, communitarianism, feminism, and postmodernism can find an ally in universalism, and the alliances forged can speak together to the complexities of the cultural and political situation of late modernity far more powerfully than any of these schools of thought or the tradition of universalism can alone.

A post-Enlightenment defense of universalism, Benhabib explains, must distance itself from the metaphysical assumptions of its Enlightenment predecessor. To be precise, a post-Enlightenment universalism is also a post-metaphysical universalism, having dispensed with the metaphysical "illusions" peculiar to universalistic moral theories since Kant. Among those metaphysical assumptions belonging to the Enlightenment tradition, Benhabib reformulates universalism without regard to three essential assumptions—that reason is both able to provide grounds for and is transparent to itself; that reason is "disembodied," or undetermined by anything other than itself; and that reason can discover an objective standpoint external to history and culture. With the rejection of these assumptions, for all intents and purposes Benhabib discards the Enlightenment concept of reason.

Alternatively, Benhabib shifts to Habermas's model of communicative rationality, a move that was implicit in her critical examination of his theory of communicative ethics in *Critique, Norm, and Utopia.* Free of the metaphysical baggage that makes Enlightenment reason vulnerable to contemporary critiques of the universalist tradition, the communicative model of rationality works with radically different presuppositions. Rather than legislated by a solitary individual who, endowed with a self-sufficient reason, can arrive autonomously at a moral point of view, reason—cognitive capacities, linguistic competences, and needs—develops through the contextualized social interactions of human community. Processes of individual socialization, which are thematized by such an interactive model of rational development, can then be conceptualized in "narrative" terms, whereby the identity of an individual has a narrative unity such that who a person comes to be and what a person comes to believe presumes an "I" that incorporates the expectations of others. A narratively constituted identity, in other words, is based upon a social relation that is inherently normative. This, again, foretells of morality as the achievement of an interactive form of rationality, as opposed to a timeless moral standpoint dictated by Reason.

As her earlier study anticipated, however, Benhabib does not adopt Habermas's model of communicative rationality without revisions. In particular, she emphasizes those features of discursive ethics that are universalistic without being rationalistic and that foreground understanding among individuals while recognizing that a consensus of all is an illusion. Of greatest importance to Benhabib, then, are those aspects of communicative rationality that are sensitive to "difference"—differences of identity, in modes of reasoning, in needs—without finally obscuring or denying difference in favor of some concept of "uniform rational autonomy." Benhabib's revised orientation toward communicative ethics entails loosening its relationship to the rationalist tradition. To accomplish this, Benhabib develops arguments first outlined in *Critique, Norm, and Utopia* pertaining to the reciprocity of perspectives, the formation of a moral point of view, the relationship of moral claims to gender differences without relativizing moral principles, and the demonstration of how a universalist and context sensitive morality complement each other's versions of moral judgment. As Benhabib puts it succinctly, the overarching objective of these arguments is "to situate reason and the moral self more decisively in the contexts of gender and community, while insisting upon the discursive power of individuals to challenge such situatedness in the name of universalistic principles, future identities, and as yet undiscovered communities."[10]

There can be no doubt that in light of the challenges a variety of schools of thought today pose not only to critical theory, but to political philosophy generally, communicative ethics can go forward only along the guidelines proposed by Benhabib, for two reasons. Drawing universality into the same orbit with the historical and cultural specificities of identities and differences, and the particularities of beliefs and understandings, hopes, fears, needs and aspirations, her reformulation of communicative rationality pushes decisively in the direction of a radical participatory and procedural-

ist model of democratic life. But it is the ethical impulse underlying Benhabib's project—to articulate a universalistic theory that as it is elaborated
becomes increasingly rather than less sensitive to diversity—that is most
palpable. By arriving at a concept of universalism truly inclusive of particularity, Benhabib is forcing Habermas's theory to live up to the normative
commitments that it, in turn, demanded be kept by modern social orders
born of the Enlightenment.

As controversial as Benhabib's project may prove to be, it promises now
to become even more so with this highly controversial reading of Hannah
Arendt. Arendt, who has seemed to so many interpreters to be an idiosyncratic thinker who failed to address central questions in political philosophy with consistency and coherence, through Benhabib's reading speaks
directly and powerfully to issues she explored in the works I have discussed
here. Already in these earlier studies, in fact, Benhabib either had drawn
Arendt's thought into a dialogue with critical theory directly or had established the terms for such a dialogue. Thus, *Critique, Norm, and Utopia*
prefaces this engagement by thematizing interrelated categories commonly
important to critical theory and to an analytical understanding of Arendt—
the "public sphere," the "interpretive indeterminacy of action," "enlarged
thinking," "plurality," the "web of narratives," and others. Through these
categories and against the backdrop of reconstructing critical social theory,
in *Situating the Self* Benhabib then begins to frame the argument that will
form the basis of her subsequent work on Arendt's political philosophy.[11]
Two examples from this work illustrating how it suggests a framework
for *The Reluctant Modernism of Hannah Arendt* will serve to indicate the
direction of the new study.

In *Situating the Self* Arendt's concept of public space is problematized
from the standpoint of whether the divide she creates between the public
and the private spheres entails a blindness to the moral and political significance of gender. Does not her conceptualization of the public sphere,
Benhabib proposes, which plays a decisive role in Arendt's thinking, dis-
pose her theory to a neglect of the ordinary, everyday moral interactions
of the private sphere, such as in the family where women's activity traditionally has been concentrated, and thus reproduces the deficiencies of conventional universalistic theories? Yet, at the same time, has not their relative
confinement to this private sphere, where the human dimensions of social
relations are fostered and cared for, provided women with privileged access

to the "art of the particular," in Benhabib's words, to the particularities nurtured within that "web of stories" Arendt believes narratively constitutes the who and what of the world we all share? It is precisely this truncated movement in Arendt's work between the extreme of universality and the extreme of particularity, recalling the Scylla of "norm" and the Charybdis of "utopia" of *Critique, Norm, and Utopia*, that Benhabib brings to the surface but also finds promising as a polarity that compels us to reflect on the need for a dialectical relationship between universals and particulars. When, to cite a second and similar example, Benhabib finds that Arendt limited the scope of the public sphere and its agenda, and further undermined both with a narrow concept of morality, she also looks to discover in Arendt's theory ways to introduce *inside* this rarefied and foreshortened universality opportunities for participants to redraw the lines of public space to make it far less exclusive. Here Arendt's notion of "enlarged thinking" or "enlarged mentality," with which Benhabib develops a concept of political judgment, embraces the full perspectival quality of the political world for the public sphere—the perspectives of concrete others, the particularities of identities and their differences, of the excluded and neglected. Thinking with Arendt against Arendt in this way, Benhabib closes the theoretical and practical distance between the universal and concrete contexts of beliefs, understandings, and actions. She softens the tendencies in Arendt's thought toward modeling political and ethical life on an uncompromising universalism, while continually pressing in her own thought toward a concept of the public sphere that makes the quality of enlarged thinking available to each of its participants.

Accordingly, Arendt can figure prominently in Benhabib's efforts to democratize the idea of political judgment and to conceptualize an interactive universalism that elaborates the import of Arendt's philosophy for a post-Enlightenment morality, politics, and critical theory. *The Reluctant Modernism of Hannah Arendt* will alter our understanding of Hannah Arendt as it contributes to the development of critical social theory.

I am especially grateful to Mary Carpenter, our new series editor at Rowman & Littlefield, for continuing the work of shepherding **Modernity and Political Thought** through the transitional stages to our new publisher and home, and for her thoughtfulness and professionalism that make it possible for editors and authors alike to produce their best work. And while each of the authors of series volumes will earn rewards and punishments commensurate with his or her contribution, as the hidden architects of the series each must also share credit with me for developing **Modernity and Political Thought.**

—Morton Schoolman
State University of New York at Albany

Notes

1. William E. Connolly, *The Augustinian Imperative: A Reflection on the Politics of Morality*; Richard E. Flathman, *Thomas Hobbes: Skepticism, Individuality and Chastened Politics*; Michael Shapiro, *Reading "Adam Smith": Desire, History and Value*; Tracy B. Strong, *Jean-Jacques Rousseau: The Politics of the Ordinary*; George Kateb, *Emerson and Self-Reliance*; Jane Bennett, *Thoreau's Nature: Ethics, Politics, and the 'Wild'*; Thomas Dumm, *Michel Foucault and the Politics of Freedom*; Stephen White, *Edmund Burke: Modernity, Politics, and Aesthetics*; Fred Dallmayr, *G.W.F. Hegel: Modernity and Politics* (Lanham, Md.: Rowman & Littlefield, 2002).

Modernity and Political Thought was first published by Sage Publications, Newbury Park, California. Volume 1, William E. Connolly, *The Augustinian Imperative: A Reflection on the Politics of Morality* (1993); Volume 2, Richard E. Flathman, *Thomas Hobbes: Skepticism, Individuality, and Chastened Politics* (1993); Volume 3, Fred Dallmayr, *G.W.F. Hegel: Modernity and Politics* (1993); Volume 4, Michael Shapiro, *Reading 'Adam Smith': The Politics of Desire* (1993); Volume 5, Stephen K. White, *Edmund Burke: Modernity, Politics, and Aesthetics* (1994); Volume 6, Tracy Strong, *Jean-Jacques Rousseau: The Politics of the Ordinary* (1994); Volume 7, Jane Bennett, *Thoreau's Nature: Ethics, Politics, and the 'Wild'* (1994); Volume 8, George Kateb, *Emerson and Self-Reliance* (1994); Volume 9, Thomas Dumm, *Michel Foucault and the Politics of Freedom* (1996); Volume 10, Seyla Benhabib, *Hannah Arendt's Reluctant Modernism* (1996).

2. Seyla Benhabib, *Critique, Norm, and Utopia. A Study of the Foundations of Critical Theory* (New York: Columbia University Press, 1986).

3. Ibid., p. 13.

4. Ibid., pp. 329-330.

5. Ibid., p. 336.

6. Ibid., pp. 340-341.

7. Ibid., p. 341.

8. Seyla Benhabib, *Situating the Self: Gender, Community and Postmodernism in Contemporary Ethics* (New York: Routledge, 1992).

9. Ibid., p.3.

10. Ibid., p. 8.

11. Ibid.; see especially pp. 89-144.

Introduction:
Why Hannah Arendt?

Hannah Arendt is widely recognized as a brilliant and controversial political thinker of the twentieth century. The first theorist of totalitarianism who appreciated this phenomenon as a wholly novel form of political power in human history, the publicist of the bitterly contested phrase *the banality of evil,* and the creator of such controversial distinctions as those between "work" and "labor," "force," "power," and "violence," Hannah Arendt remains a fiercely independent mind whose work defies classification in terms of established schools of political thought.

More than two decades after her death on December 4, 1975, the interest in Arendt's work shows no signs of abating. One can even note a contemporary Arendt renaissance: every year brings new publications and analyses of her work; an increasing number of papers about her thought are delivered at philosophical and political associations; a new generation of scholars is busy examining various aspects of her theories, ranging from her views on Zionism to her affinities with Albert Camus, from postmodernist and Nietzschean themes in her views of action to her relevance for contemporary politics of identity.[1]

With the publication of the monumental Hannah Arendt-Karl Jaspers correspondence (1926–1969) in English,[2] with the posthumous edition of some of her papers collected in the Library of Congress,[3] and with the recent documentation of Hannah Arendt's friendship and exchanges with Mary McCarthy,[4] the historical and intellectual context of Arendt's work is assuming new and sharper contours.

The purpose of this book is to offer a rereading of Hannah Arendt's political philosophy in the light of newly gained insights into the historical and cultural contexts of her work. It is my thesis that German "Existenz philosophy" of the 1920s, and in particular the thought of Martin Heidegger, were the inspiration for some of Arendt's best known philosophical categories such as those of world, action, and plurality.[5] Heidegger's reading of Aristotle in his lectures at Marburg during the years 1924 and 1925 left indelible marks upon Arendt's thinking. What enabled Arendt, however, to radically transform these categories into an original political philosophy were her experiences as a German Jewish woman in the age of totalitarianism. Hannah Arendt first confronted the politics of the twentieth century as a persecuted Jew, as a stateless émigré in Paris, as a new immigrant and eventually an American citizen in the United States. Her reflections on the dilemmas and paradoxes of Jewish identity in the modern age, the search for a political homeland for the Jewish people, and her always problematic relationship with nationalist Zionism are at the origin of some of her most provocative political theses: namely, the distinction between the pariah and the parvenu; the critique of nationalism; her reflections on the paradoxes of the rights of man; and her faith in the capacity of human beings to begin anew and to create a common space of political power. German Existenz philosophy and her identity as a German Jewish woman are the wells out of which Hannah Arendt's political thought springs, and to which we must return to understand her more fully. The great tensions in Arendt's systematic reflections on politics and society, and the unresolved contradictions in some of her formulations, can be traced back to this twofold spiritual-intellectual legacy. Expressed in somewhat stylized form: although Hannah Arendt, the stateless and persecuted Jew, is the philosophical and political modernist, Arendt, the student of Martin Heidegger, is the antimodernist Grecophile theorist of the *polis* and of its lost glory.

There is by now a standard and widespread reading of Hannah Arendt's work. Placing *The Human Condition* as the definitive expression of Arendt's political philosophy at the center, this view argues that Hannah Arendt is a political philosopher of nostalgia, an antimodernist lover of the Greek polis.[6] It is said that she views modernity simply as initiating a decline of the "public sphere" of politics. Very few of her categories, indeed if any at all, are relevant for understanding the contemporary world, it is argued. Perhaps her concepts of action, judgment, and the public sphere contain a few insights for democratic politics, these critics contend, but beyond this, not much can be gained from Hannah Arendt.

This view was first challenged by Elisabeth Young-Bruehl's 1982 biography of Hannah Arendt, *For Love of the World*. Young-Bruehl documented the intensity with which Arendt reflected about the political and cultural issues of the twentieth century as well as her passionate involvement with Jewish politics all her life. With the appearance of Arendt's essays from various Jewish German immigrant newspapers and their publication under the title *The Jew as Pariah* in 1978,[7] we have also learned of her daily interventions in Jewish politics and cultural life in the 1940s. Yet the philosophical implications of this discovery of Arendt's "Jewish identity" for her political thought at large were not addressed by Young-Bruehl,[8] and the standard reading of Arendt's work was not revised. As Hanna Pitkin has recently written, "Only when the remote, abstract, Grecophile concepts of *The Human Condition* are traced back to their roots in Arendt's life does their true political power and contemporary public relevance emerge."[9]

It is a principal goal of this book to decenter the place of *The Human Condition* in our reading of Hannah Arendt. Although I do not question the forceful brilliance of the work, it is my thesis that only when we read *The Human Condition* in the light of the historical development of Arendt's thought as a whole can we interpret its import. *The Human Condition* is the result of Arendt's dialogue with two thinkers: Martin Heidegger, whose philosophy she appropriates and subverts, and Karl Marx, whom she criticizes but does not dismiss.

Despite its richness and complexity, there is on the surface a simple plot that dominates *The Human Condition*. This is the presentation of the modern age and of the transformations undergone by Western societies, and increasingly by societies in other parts of the globe, in terms of a history of the decline of the public sphere of politics and the rise of a social sphere of economic activity and bureaucratic domination. If we read Hannah Arendt from her beginnings, though, we see that this picture of modern society, with its contradictions and tensions, is a caricature contradicted by her own far more nuanced analysis of modernity, already contained in her early book on Rahel Varnhagen and then developed in *The Origins of Totalitarianism*. The author of *Rahel Varnhagen*, which was subtitled *The Life of a Jewish Woman*, discovered the dialectic of modernity to reside in the tension between political equality and sociocultural, ethnic, religious, linguistic (and more problematically gender) forms of difference. The author of *The Origins of Totalitarianism* analyzed how the anti-Semitism of European society, the racist confrontation with Africa on the part of the colonial powers of Europe, and the paradoxes in the declaration of the rights of man were some of the trends in modern society through which this tension between the principle of universal political equality and sociocultural, linguistic, racial, and ethnic difference was reenacted. Modernity, for Hannah Arendt, was not a seamless historical development but a process rich in contradictions. The universalist promises of the Enlightenment, of the various bourgeois revolutions, of the declaration of the rights of man and citizen were repeatedly in tension with forms of particularist identity. Reflecting on the paradoxes of Jewish assimilation into modern society, Arendt borrowed the terms *pariah* and *parvenu* from the French journalist Bernard Lazare: while the pariah is the one who is cast aside, marginalized, and treated with contempt by society because of his or her otherness, the parvenu denies her otherness so as to become accepted by the dominant society. As the twentieth century progressed, the sociocultural paradoxes of maintaining particularistic identities gave way to a politics of the annihilation of otherness through the racial policies of extermination in the hands of National Socialism.

The Origins of Totalitarianism is the work in which the two spiritual legacies of Arendt's thinking meet and form a powerful synthesis. On the one hand, in this work Arendt delves deeper into the paradoxes of equality/difference under conditions of modernity through her analysis of anti-Semitism, racism, and imperialism; on the other hand, the central explanatory categories of this work, such as the existential phenomenology of totalitarianism developed through her accounts of loneliness and isolation, are deeply indebted to Martin Heidegger's *Being and Time* and are unintelligible without a knowledge of Heidegger's critique of the conditions of modern *Dasein*, of "being-there."

* * *

The first three chapters of this work deal with Hannah Arendt's biography of Rahel Varnhagen; her confrontation in the late 1920s with German Existenz philosophy and Zionist politics, and her theory of totalitarianism. I begin with an examination of a much neglected early text by Hannah Arendt, *Rahel Varnhagen: The Life of a Jewish Woman.* Completed during her exile in France in 1938 and not published in English until 1957, this work is the only text of Hannah Arendt's in which the "mirroring effect" between the narrator and the narrated object is intense, complicated, and multileveled. Arendt's biography of Rahel Varnhagen von Ense, a German Jewish woman known for her Berlin salon and for her lively correspondence with famous figures of the German romantic movement and the Prussian aristocracy, sets the tone for a number of Arendt's subsequent preoccupations. The quality of life as an "outsider," of one who is culturally, religiously, and perhaps psychologically "other" within the confines of a conformist bourgeois society; the proper "place" in which to express this otherness; the manner in which the world of politics can intrude upon and destroy the supposed sanctuaries of private life—these themes are suggested by Arendt's biography of Varnhagen and prefigure some of the central issues of her later work. The eventual fate of Rahel Varnhagen's salon and of her circle of friends, who gathered together between 1795 and 1806, is like the dystopia of the ideal community of friendship, equality, self-disclosure, and mutual appreciation that still guides Arendt's mature political thought.

Having identified an alternative account of the genealogy of modernity in Arendt's treatment of Rahel Varnhagen's story, in Chapter 2 I examine her struggles to find a viable form of Jewish politics in the face of National Socialism and the Holocaust. Arendt sharply distinguished between the ideals of the "Jewish homeland," a political and social space in which those members of the Jewish people who agreed with certain principles could gather to form a community, and that of the "nation-state." Despite her sympathies for the Zionist movement and settlements in Palestine, the nation-state was not the only desirable or even viable model of realizing this aspiration for a Jewish homeland. After discussing her breathtaking 1945 essay "Zionism Reconsidered," I look at another essay from 1946 called "What Is Existenz Philosophy?" Written for *Partisan Review* to introduce some of the tenets of European philosophical currents to an American audience, this essay contains Arendt's first public attempt to come to grips with Martin Heidegger's involvement with the Nazis.

Chapter 3 is dedicated to *The Origins of Totalitarianism*. It is my belief that, despite all its flaws, this work is the crowning achievement of Arendt's political, as opposed to more strictly philosophical, reflections. The profound irony in Arendt's analysis of the phenomenon of totalitarianism is that the thought of one tempted by National Socialism, Martin Heidegger, now provides some of the central categories for an analysis of totalitarianism and the rise of mass movements. The key in solving this hermeneutic puzzle is Heidegger's category of the "world." In a lecture first given in 1954, Arendt wrote that "it is almost impossible to render a clear account of Heidegger's political thoughts which may be of political relevance without an elaborate report on his concept and analysis of 'world.' "[10] Through his analysis of the fundamental human condition as being-in-the-world, Arendt thought that Heidegger had created an unprecedented possibility for the philosopher to think productively about the political realm. Arendt herself did so. From her early emphasis on the worldlessness that characterized the circle of friends gathered in Rahel Varnhagen's salons to her poignant diagnosis of the double loss of world and home by millions of refugees, stateless peoples, and persecuted minorities, this category remained a leitmotif in Arendt's work.

Why, however, was Heidegger himself unable to illuminate the political? Why was it that he not only expressed "the old prejudices of the philosopher against politics" but also committed such a fatal error as supporting the National Socialist movement, even if briefly? In her answer to this last question, Arendt vacillated: her 1946 essay titled "What Is Existenz Philosophy?" established an internal link between some of Heidegger's philosophical commitments and his politics while in her

1969 article, "Martin Heidegger at Eighty," Arendt explained Heidegger's mistake in "characterological" terms, as expressing personal and professional blindness and lack of judgment.

Read against this background, *The Human Condition*, which is at the center of Chapter 4, documents the theoretical saga of Hannah Arendt and Martin Heidegger. In this work, Hannah Arendt for the first time not merely applied but radically transformed the categories of Heideggerian philosophy. The crucial step of this transformation is the passage from being-in-the-world as a form of being-with-others to human plurality as the basic human condition. Although Heidegger always acknowledged that being-in-the-world was a form of being-with-others, he viewed this latter condition with great ambivalence. More often than not, being-with-others represented inauthentic and problematic forms of togetherness. For Hannah Arendt, however, being-with-others in the world who are like one and yet different than one is the human condition par excellence.

Appropriating the phenomenological category of the world, developed by Husserl and Heidegger, Arendt discovers the worldliness of the human condition to be its characteristic of plurality, which is unthinkable without action and speech, without what Aristotle called "praxis." Praxis, speech and action, is the actuality, that is, the most accomplished ontological reality of beings such as humans are. Beasts have no praxis because they have no words; gods need no praxis because they have no need for company, for togetherness. Only bodily, dependent, and finite beings exist through words and deeds. Their mode of being is in the space of appearance created by the web of narratives and unfolding through the reality of words and deeds. This condition is revealed most characteristically through speech and action; and most human action for Hannah Arendt takes place in the form of speech. Linguistically mediated human action is Dasein's form of being-in-the-world.

Having established this phenomenological account, Arendt analyzes how action and speech are the central activities through which the political is constituted. Labor, work, and action are fundamental constituents of the human condition, but it is the capacity for speech and action that creates and sustains the political. With this thesis, Arendt was finally able to unite her phenomenological philosophy with her political reflections. Martin Heidegger's fundamental ontology was left behind, and the mature categories of Arendt's political philosophy emerged. I suggest in this context that "public space" is the socio-political, and historical correlate of a much more fundamental human condition, which is that of "only being actual within a space of appearance."

Because Arendt often considered political philosophy in the twentieth century to reside in the art of making distinctions, the final two chapters of this work deal with this Arendtian art. Chapter 5 examines the Arendtian distinctions between labor, work, and action; and the social and the political as they unfold through various phases of her writing. I reject Arendt's "phenomenological essentialism," her contention that each human activity has a proper place in the world, in which it must be carried out and within which it unfolds. I maintain that this thesis is neither defensible on its own right nor consistently deployed by Arendt herself.

The task of Chapter 6 is systematic. It asks what we can retain from the Arendtian art of making distinctions today for thinking further upon our political condition. After a discussion of *Eichmann in Jerusalem,* I consider Arendt's theory of judgment, and I conclude by appropriating Arendtian insights for the restructuring of the public and private spheres in contemporary societies.

* * *

How can we account for the contemporary Arendt renaissance, and what does this suggest for the legacy of Hannah Arendt's political thought? The current Arendt renaissance is motivated by three complex and interrelated sets of sensibilities and concerns. After the demise of authoritarian communism and the worldwide retreat of Marxist theory, Hannah Arendt's thought has emerged as the critical political theory of the post-totalitarian moment. In addition, the rise of identity politics, from the politics of gender to the politics of nationalism and ethnicity, sends us back to Hannah Arendt. Finally, there is Hannah Arendt and the "woman question."

Rejected by the Left because of its problematic analogies between Stalinism and National Socialism, denounced by the Right for its irreverence toward the polarizing thinking of cold war camps, and derided by empirical political scientists for its overly journalistic, literary, and philosophical generalizations, *The Origins of Totalitarianism* became one of the notorious texts of twentieth-century political theory. Indeed, Margaret Canovan, one of Arendt's most penetrating interpreters, shares this unease about Arendt's theory of totalitarianism and concludes her recent book, *Hannah Arendt: A Reinterpretation of Her Political Thought,*[11] with the observation that

> if we trace her thought trains to their source, it must be admitted that the first thing we find when we do go back to her thinking about Nazism and Stalinism may be something of an embarrassment: a brilliant, ambitious and highly questionable interpretation of totalitarianism and modernity.

I see more merit to Arendt's theory of totalitarianism than does Canovan. Arendt's theory of totalitarianism presents us today not with an "embarrassment" but with something of a paradox. And it is this paradox that makes her the thinker of the post-totalitarian moment. The contemporary experience of post-totalitarian societies in eastern and central Europe has proven the *normative centrality and desirability* of reconstructing civil society and associational life for the success of democracy, very much along the lines suggested by Hannah Arendt's concepts of the public space and of democratic politics. By defining totalitarianism as an "iron band" that squeezed people together until they became one, thus eliminating the "public spaces" between them, Arendt was on to something central about the political experience of totalitarianism. It is as if the revolutions of 1989 in the heart of Europe have placed her analyses of revolutions, but unfortunately also her diagnosis of the darker sides of totalitarianism, once more on the world historical agenda. When in the joyous last days of 1989 the communist regimes of central and eastern Europe started to topple like a house of cards, and in country after country citizens' initiatives and forums, with varying degrees of success, began to "do politics," the categories of Arendt's analyses of revolutions came alive again.[12]

Yet, despite its power to illuminate the political experiences and normative aspirations of peoples of eastern and central Europe after 1989, the *analytical and explanatory* power of Arendt's theory of totalitarianism is limited, and this is also the source of Canovan's misgivings about it. Her reinterpretation of Arendt would have been considerably stronger if she had stated more directly what exactly was objectionable in Arendt's "interconnected accounts of totalitarianism, modernity and 'society.' "[13] For Hannah Arendt did not subscribe to the slippery slope view that totalitarianism was an inevitable growth of Western modernity; in many ways, she regarded it as a total perversion of much that was essential to the Western tradition.[14] Like many social theorists of her generation, though, she did see a link between the growth of mass society, the creation inside and outside the borders of European nation-states of a mass of "superfluous human beings," and totalitarianism. For Arendt, the breakdown of civil and associational life, the experiences of uprootedness, statelessness, and homelessness, were phenomena that preceded and enabled the rise of totalitarianism. Clearly under the influence of Martin Heidegger's analysis of *das Man*, she described the fundamental ontological experience of the individual who would fall prey to totalitarianism as that of "loneliness."

Recent historical research has shown the degree to which previously existing local organizations and associations were not destroyed by the Nazis but to the contrary could often be successfully integrated into their power hierarchy.[15] This seriously challenges the explanatory centrality of categories such as "loneliness" and "mass society" in explaining the rise of totalitarianism. Furthermore, there are serious problems with the parallel discussion of National Socialism and Stalinism undertaken by Arendt. In the case of Stalinism, the formation of mass society and the creation of "superfluous human beings" did not precede but succeeded Stalinism. This phenomenon was a consequence of Stalinism, rather than being among its causes. Despite these empirical shortcomings, Hannah Arendt's political sociology of totalitarianism paved the way for a wholly original manner of thinking about this experience. It is east European dissidents such as Václav Havel and Georg Konrad who today are the true heirs to the Arendtian theory of totalitarianism. In the post-totalitarian moment, Arendt will remain a central interlocutor.[16]

Arendt identified the central dialectic of Enlightenment and modernity as the clash between the universalistic principles of the "Rights of Man and Citizen" embodied in the various bourgeois constitutions, and the yearnings toward otherness, difference, and particularistic identities that also accompanied modernity. A political modernist, who melancholically reflected upon the fragility of human rights, Hannah Arendt repeatedly focused on the dialectic of equality and difference. In this sense, her political thought anticipates some of the major preoccupations of today's identity politics. Arendt's observations on the paradoxes of the nation-state and her touching reflections on the condition of statelessness and homelessness in a world of inflamed ethnic passions and weak states are more pertinent than ever. Although she herself could ultimately offer no philosophical justification either for her belief in universal human rights or for the category of crimes against humanity, her articulations of the issues involved can still guide us. The category of "crimes against humanity" is now an internationally recognized legal norm such that individuals can be charged with committing this crime and can be brought before a tribunal of the World Court for doing so. It is clear that Arendt would have wanted a similar international practice and institution permanently to protect members of minorities from becoming refugees and stateless peoples. The feeble institution of the United Nations High Commissioner for Refugees is a pale incorporation of this Arendtian political sensibility.

The contemporary Arendt renaissance is rooted not only in the post-totalitarian moment and the problems of equality/difference encountered by identity politics but in the tremendous surge of the Women's Movement and feminist thought and practice in the last three decades. Arendt remains a formidable and enigmatic example, one of our "early mothers." Although the sheer facts of her life and the brilliance of her intellectual achievement make us want to reappropriate her for feminist thought, her theoretical framework as well as her overt dislike of certain ways of posing the woman's problem make this a formidable task. Arendt remains the mother who eludes us. Although from her early book on Rahel Varnhagen to her sensitive portraits of Rosa Luxemburg and Isak Dinesen (Karen Blixen),[17] female figures and masterful reflections on their lives are present in Arendt's historical and journalistic writings, women and their activities are invisible in her theory of politics. Hannah Arendt's political thought, like the Western tradition in general, remained "gender blind." Even worse, some of Arendt's characteristic distinctions as between the "public realm of politics" and the "private realm of the house-hold" appear to condemn women in the most traditional ways to the private sphere of care for the necessities of daily life. It is my thesis that, despite this apparent antagonism between feminist goals and Hannah Arendt's political thought, engaging in a "dialectical conversation" with Hannah Arendt about the concepts of the public and private is indispensable for contemporary feminist theory.

Understanding Arendt adequately on questions of women is of one cloth with understanding her properly on the Jewish question. These seemingly theoretically marginal but existentially crucial categories of identity—a woman and a Jew—or, more correctly, Arendt's identity as a German Jewess in the twentieth century, are the sources out of which Arendt's thought flows and to which we, her readers, must attend to understand her properly.

A word about method and interpretation in political philosophy: in general, to understand another's thought and to evaluate its cogency, it is necessary to know the questions and puzzles a thinker seeks to answer. To understand these questions and puzzles, in turn, it is necessary to reconstruct those social, historical, personal, and conceptual contexts that form the horizon of inquiry for a thinker. As Hans-Georg Gadamer has shown, the reconstruction of past arguments and theories always involves a "fusion of horizons."[18] Understanding always means understanding within a framework that makes sense for us, from where we stand today. In this sense, learning the questions of the past involves posing questions to the past in the light of our present preoccupations. The reconstruction and interpretation of another's thought is a dialogue in which one asks a question, seeks to comprehend whether this question is meaningful for the other, listens and reformulates the answer of the other, and, in light of this answer, rearticulates one's original position. Every interpretation is a conversation, with all the joys and dangers that conversations usually involve: misunderstandings as well as ellipses, innuendos as well as surfeits of meaning.

Hannah Arendt's voice has guided me in my philosophical conversations and questionings since I discovered her reflections on anti-Semitism thirty years ago when I first entered Yale Graduate School as a student of philosophy in 1972. My deep admiration and affinity for her thought is no doubt rooted in my profound identification with her as a Jewish woman from a European tradition, in my case not the German Jewish but the Spanish Sephardic one. And like her, for better or for worse, it is the legacy of classical German philosophy from Immanuel Kant to Jürgen Habermas that has provided me with the philosophical framework within which I have—not always explicitly—reflected on these issues. In this sense, this is a very personal book.

Over the years, I have had many conversations with many individuals about Hannah Arendt. Elisabeth Young-Bruehl first aroused my curiosity about Arendt and Heidegger by recounting their love story one evening over dinner in New Haven in 1974. In 1987, Professor Dan Diner asked me to contribute an article to a volume titled *Zivilisationsbruch: Denken nach Auschwitz* (Civilizational Rupture: Thinking After Auschwitz).[19] This invitation led me to reflect seriously about Hannah Arendt and the Jewish question in the twentieth century. This book grew out of my contribution to that volume. I thank Dan Diner for his original suggestion and for many subsequent conversations on Hannah Arendt.

I owe to Jürgen Habermas, Richard J. Bernstein, Albrecht Wellmer, and Jerome Kohn, all Arendt friends, many fortuitous exchanges on her thought. To Morris Kaplan, whose passionate admiration of Hannah Arendt I share, a special word of thanks for nearly twenty years of discussions on these issues. From 1981 to 1984, I had the pleasure of working on Hannah Arendt with Maurizio Passerin d'Entrèves. His fine dissertation and book on her thought have taught me a great deal and have pushed my own thinking further. More recently, Dana Villa and Bonnie Honig have provoked me through conversations as well as publications. Although we disagree more often than we agree, I acknowledge the kinship in their deep involvement with the thought of Hannah Arendt.

I would like to thank my research assistants Lynne Eckenberg, Michaele Ferguson, April Flakne, and Patchen Markell for first-rate comments on earlier drafts of various chapters. Michaele Ferguson has provided the bibliography for this volume; Patchen Markell has been a meticulous commentator and copy editor.

The research for this book was supported in its initial stages by an American fellowship from the Leona J. Beckmann and Susan B. Anthony Endowment of the American Association of University Women (January to December 1992). I would also like to thank the Radcliffe College Junior Partnership Program for allocating funds to enable Lynne Eckenberg to act as my research assistant during the spring and summer of 1994, and the Lewis Clarke research fund of Harvard University for supporting the completion of this manuscript through a grant in the summer of 1995.

I dedicate this book, with love, to my deceased mother, Colombe Benhabib.

Notes

1. Margaret Canovan's first book on Hannah Arendt appeared in 1974 (*The Political Thought of Hannah Arendt* [London: J. M. Dent]); in 1979, several former students of Arendt collaborated to produce a collection of essays titled *Hannah Arendt: The Recovery of the Public World*, ed. Melvyn A. Hill (New York: St. Martin's, 1979). In the early 1980s, there were also a number of Arendt publications: Bikhu Parekh, *Hannah Arendt and the Search for a New Political Philosophy* (London: Macmillan, 1981); Elisabeth Young-Bruehl, *Hannah Arendt: For Love of the World* (New Haven, Conn.: Yale University Press, 1982); George Kateb, *Hannah Arendt: Politics, Conscience, Evil* (Totowa, N.J.: Rowman and Allanheld, 1984). In this period, the edition of Hannah Arendt's *Lectures on Kant's Political Philosophy* (ed. R. Beiner) also played a major role (Chicago: University of Chicago Press, 1982). A selective list of monographs since 1989 devoted to her work would include Leah Bradshaw, *Acting and Thinking: The Political Thought of Hannah Arendt* (Toronto: University of Toronto Press, 1989); Shiraz Dossa, *The Public Realm and the Public Self: The Political Theory of Hannah Arendt* (Waterloo, Ontario: W. Laurier University Press, 1989); Dagmar Barnouw, *Visible Spaces: Hannah Arendt and the German-Jewish Experience* (Baltimore: Johns Hopkins University Press, 1990); Michael S. Gottsegen, *The Political Thought of Hannah Arendt* (Albany: SUNY University Press, 1993); Maurizio Passerin d'Entrèves, *The Political Philosophy of Hannah Arendt* (London: Routledge, 1994); and the recent collection by Lewis P. Hinchman and Sandra K. Hinchman, *Hannah Arendt: Critical Essays* (Albany: SUNY Press, 1993). *Feminist Interpretations of Hannah Arendt*, ed. Bonnie Honig (University Park: Pennsylvania State University Press, 1995) gives a very good sampling of the debates raging around Arendt's work among contemporary feminist theorists.

2. See *Hannah Arendt-Karl Jaspers Correspondence 1926–1969*, ed. Lotte Köhler and Hans Saner, translated from the German by Robert and Rita Kimber (New York: Harcourt Brace Jovanovich, 1992).

3. See *Arendt: Essays in Understanding: 1930–1954*, ed. Jerome Kohn (New York: Harcourt Brace Jovanovich, 1994).

4. *Between Friends: The Correspondence of Hannah Arendt and Mary McCarthy, 1949–1975*, ed., with an introduction by, Carol Brightman (New York: Harcourt Brace Jovanovich, 1995).

5. With the publication of excerpts from the Hannah Arendt-Martin Heidegger correspondence, which was hitherto inaccessible to the scholarly public, in Elzbieta Ettinger's *Hannah Arendt-Martin Heidegger* (New Haven, Conn.: Yale University Press, 1995), the contours of the personal relationship between Arendt and Heidegger have become clearer. Unfortunately, Ms. Ettinger's interpretation of this material is psychological, partial, and, from the standpoint of philosophical scholarship, naïve. Nonetheless, the publication of this work has rapidly evoked a controversy because a number of scholars have proceeded to use the personal

relationship of Arendt and Heidegger to dismiss Arendt herself as a political thinker and, worse still, to denounce her as a Jew. See Richard Wolin, "An Affair to Remember: Hannah and the Magician," *New Republic,* October 9, 1995, pp. 27-37. For further discussion, see p. 221.

6. For a polemical dismissal of Hannah Arendt's thought along these lines, see Isaiah Berlin's statements: "I do not greatly respect the lady's ideas, I admit. Many distinguished persons used to admire her work. I cannot . . . she produces no arguments, no evidence of serious philosophical or historical thought. It is all a stream of metaphysical associations." The interviewer asks: "Have you read any of her books?" "Yes, I have read several of her books since some of my friends praised her to me. . . . Then I read *The Human Condition,* it seems based on two ideas, both historically false. The first is that the Greeks did not respect work, but that Jews did." Commenting on the influence that German thinkers had on Arendt's thought, Berlin quips: "But I have not yet discovered something of hers which I find arresting, which stimulates thought, or illuminates one" in *Conversations With Isaiah Berlin,* by Ramin Johanbegloo (London: Peter Halban, 1992), pp. 82-83. Sir Isaiah Berlin is, of course, entitled to his views and opinions; to any careful reader of Hannah Arendt, his criticism of her work in this interview and his rather off-the-cuff remarks about Greek and Jewish attitudes toward work in *The Human Condition* exhibit neither a deep understanding of nor an engagement with Arendt's thought. What is offensive about this passage, though, is the disrespectful, almost petulant, dismissal of the ideas of a major, even if controversial, thinker of this century. The comment about the "lady's ideas," and the claim that she never produces arguments but writes in streams of consciousness, sound like gender stereotyping; women's thought is nonsystematic, associative rather than argumentative, and so on. To read Isaiah Berlin's dismissal of Hannah Arendt is to be reminded once more of some of the bitter conflicts, divisions, and personal animosities that characterized their generation of European Jewish émigrés in the 1930s and 1940s.

7. Hannah Arendt, *The Jew as Pariah: Jewish Identity and Politics in the Modern Age,* ed., with an introduction by Ron H. Feldman (New York: Grove, 1978).

8. Dagmar Barnouw in *Visible Spaces* gives the most comprehensive account to date of Arendt's involvement with Jewish culture and politics but does not raise philosophical questions concerning her political thought that this historical evidence suggests. See also Richard J. Bernstein, *Hannah Arendt and the Jewish Question* (Oxford: Polity Press, 1996).

9. Hanna Pitkin, "Conformism, Housekeeping and the Attack of the Blob: The Origins of Hannah Arendt's Concept of the Social," in *Feminist Interpretations,* ed. Honig, p. 65. Cf. Hanna Pitkin, *The Attack of the Blob: Hannah Arendt's Concept of the Social* (Chicago: University of Chicago Press, 1998).

10. See Hannah Arendt, "Concern With Politics in Recent European Philosophical Thought," in *Hannah Arendt: Essays in Understanding,* p. 446.

11. Cambridge, UK: Cambridge University Press, 1992, p. 279.

12. See Timothy Garton Ash's wonderful account of these revolutions in *The Magic Lantern* (New York: Random House, 1990).

13. Margaret Canovan, *Hannah Arendt: A Reinterpretation of Her Political Thought* (London: Cambridge University Press, 1992), p. 280.

14. I think Canovan's claim that "the seeds of totalitarianism were deeply planted in modernity itself" (p. 202) is not an adequate characterization of Arendt's position. Arendt never ceased to emphasize the "contingency" of totalitarianism, stressing that it could have been otherwise. One should only recall the somewhat ingenious claim that after the death of Lenin the Soviet system could have headed in a different direction. "At the moment of Lenin's

death the roads were still open. The formation of workers, peasants, and middle classes need not necessarily have led to the class struggle which had been characteristic of European capitalism. Agriculture could still be developed on a collective, co-operative, or private basis, and the national economy was still free to follow a socialist, state-capitalist, or a free-enterprise pattern. None of these alternatives would have automatically destroyed the new structure of the country." Arendt, *The Origins of Totalitarianism* (New York: Harcourt Brace Jovanovich, 1979, reprint of 1951 edition), p. 319. The title is abbreviated as *OT*.

15. See the massive project undertaken by Martin Broszat and his coworkers that documents the involvement with, as well as resistance to, the Nazi power machine by provincial associations: *Bayern in der NS-Zeit: Soziale Lage und politisches Verhalten der Bevölkerung im Spiegel vertraulicher Berichte*, ed. Martin Broszat, Elke Fröhlich, and Falk Wiesemann (Munich: R. Oldenburg Verlag, 1977). I would like to thank Danny Goldhagen for conversations around this issue.

16. See Tony Judt's insightful article, "At Home in This Century," in the *New York Review of Books* 42 (April 6, 1995): 9-15.

17. Isak Dinesen (pseudonym for Karen Blixen, née Karen Christentze Dinesen, 1885-1963) was a Danish author most renowned for her somewhat autobiographical novel *Out of Africa* (1937).

18. Hans-Georg Gadamer, *Truth and Method*, trans. Garrett Barden and John Cumming (New York: Seabury, 1975).

19. See Seyla Benhabib, "Hannah Arendt und die erlösende Kraft des Erzählens," in *Zivilisationsbruch: Denken nach Auschwitz*, ed. Dan Diner (Frankfurt: Fischer, 1988), pp. 150-175; this article has appeared in altered form as S. Benhabib, "Hannah Arendt and the Redemptive Power of Narrative." *Social Research* 57, no. 1 (1990): 167-196. Copyright 1990, *Social Research: An International Quarterly of the Social Sciences*. Used with permission.

1

The Pariah and Her Shadow: Hannah Arendt's Biography of Rahel Varnhagen

A Methodological Preamble

Hannah Arendt's self-consciousness of herself as a Jew, and her belief that in the twentieth century to be Jewish had become a "political" and unavoidable fact, stand in sharp contrast to her almost total silence on the women's question.[1] Although the fate of the Jewish people is at the center of her public-political thought, her identity as a woman and the social-political, cultural dimensions of being female in the modern world do not

AUTHOR'S NOTE: A shorter version of this chapter has previously appeared as "The Pariah and Her Shadow," *Political Theory* 23, no. 1 (1995), pp. 5-24, and in *Feminist Interpretations of Hannah Arendt*, ed. Bonnie Honig (University Park: Pennsylvania State University Press, 1995), pp. 83-105. Copyright © *Political Theory*, 1995. Research on earlier versions of this chapter was supported by an American fellowship from the Leona J. Beckmann and Susan B. Anthony Endowment of the American Association of University Women (January 1992 to December 1992).

find explicit recognition in her work. We know from her biographer Elisabeth Young-Bruehl that Arendt "was suspicious of women 'who gave orders,' skeptical about whether women should be political leaders, and steadfastly opposed to the social dimensions of Women's Liberation."[2]

This perplexing constellation becomes clearer, if also more troubling, when one turns to the opening pages of *The Human Condition*. Here a first reading easily gives one the impression that Arendt not only ignored the women's question but was almost a reactionary on the issue in that she accepted the age-old confinement of women to the private realm of the household and their exclusion from the public sphere. In *The Human Condition* she writes,

> The fact that the modern age emancipated the working classes and women at nearly the same historical moment must certainly be counted among the characteristics of an age which no longer believes that bodily functions and material concerns should be hidden. It is all the more symptomatic of the nature of these phenomena that the few remnants of strict privacy even in our own civilization relate to the "necessities" in the original sense of being necessitated by having a body.[3]

It is hard to avoid the impression that in these early passages of *The Human Condition*, Arendt ontologized the division of labor between the sexes and endorsed the presumption that aspects of female anatomy forced women to be confined to the household sphere alone. This was certainly the conclusion drawn by Adrienne Rich in her powerful comments on *The Human Condition*:

> In thinking about the issues of women and work . . . I turned to Hannah Arendt's *The Human Condition* to see how a major political philosopher of our time, a woman greatly respected in the intellectual establishment, had spoken to the theme. I found her essay illuminating, not so much for what it says, but for what it is. . . . The withholding of women from participation in the *vita activa,* the "common world," and the connection of this with reproductivity, is something from which she does not so much turn her eyes as stare straight through unseeing. . . . To read such a book, by a woman of large spirit and great erudition, can be painful, because it embodies the tragedy of a female mind nourished on male ideologies. In fact, the loss is ours, because Arendt's desire to grasp deep moral issues is the kind of concern we need to build a common world which will amount to more than "life-styles."[4]

Adrienne Rich's verdict on Hannah Arendt is based upon certain heuristic assumptions that led her to the conclusion that one should read Arendt's work "not so much for what it says, but for what it is." Reading Hannah Arendt's work from the standpoint of a question that she herself did not place at the center of her thought, namely, the women's question, and examining her political philosophy in this light requires certain innovative hermeneutical and interpretive principles that go beyond those traditionally deployed, and shared by Rich as well. One very commonly shared principle in the interpretation of texts can be characterized as *disinterested historicism,* which requires that we understand a text, a theory, a thinker's views in the context of their genesis. This obvious and unproblematic beginning point of any interpretive effort is inadequate when it is accompanied by the further assumption that to understand can only mean to understand in context and that to pose contemporary questions to historical texts is to fall into anachronism. Since Hans-Georg Gadamer's work on hermeneutics, we know that all understanding involves interpretation. We can be said to understand an "x" only if it makes sense to us, appears meaningful to us, within the context of a framework "y," which we always already presuppose. In this sense, understanding involves a "fusion of horizons," a dialogue across time, a meeting of generations and perspectives.[5] In interpreting "x" in light of "y," we bring two meaning contexts to bear upon one other; we simulate a dialogue between them. In this process, we, as contemporary readers, cannot help but pose certain questions to the texts and thinkers of the past, for we come to the reading of these texts with certain presuppositions that constitute a meaning horizon for us. It is in light of these presuppositions, which can be more or less explicit, that the process of making sense of a text proceeds. For this reason, there can never be mere "disinterested historicism" in the reading of the past; we can never divest ourselves of all our interpretive presuppositions, for every act of reading is always a conversation of understanding as well as misunderstanding that extends across interpretive horizons.

The second commonly shared postulate of interpretation, and the one most prominently displayed by Adrienne Rich, can be named *the self-righteous dogmatism of the latecomers.* In posing questions to the past, this attitude assumes that our already attained answers are the right ones. This kind of reading of past texts is particularly prevalent among activists

of social movements who, very often, simply juxtapose the misunderstandings of the past to the truths of the present. For the collective
self-understanding of social movements, this kind of simplistic heuristic
may be part of an inevitable process of political identity formation that
requires a breaking away from the past and an assertion of one's identity
as distinct from the legacy of the past. For the art of reading and appropriating the past, however, such an attitude is inadequate. If we approach
tradition and thinkers of the past only to "debunk" them, then there really
is no point in seeking to understand them at all. Such dogmatism kills the
spirit and dries up the soul, and it is certainly not conducive to the task of
building "a common world," in Adrienne Rich's words, "which will
amount to more than 'life-styles.' "[6]

In approaching Hannah Arendt's thought from where we stand today
and in probing it from the standpoint of her identity as a German Jewish
woman, neither principle is adequate: disinterested historicism is inadequate because it kills the interests of contemporary readers in past texts
by blocking the asking of any questions that transcend the immediate
historical context in which these texts were written. Applied to Hannah
Arendt's work, this would mean that all questioning of her work, particularly on the women's issue, would be considered anachronistic and insensitive to her own historical concerns. Yet, as I hope to show in the rest of
this chapter, such questioning is neither anachronistic nor insensitive to
Arendt's own preoccupations but, on the contrary, can allow us to pursue
certain lines of interpretation that shed unusual light on the initial concerns that motivated her work.

The self-righteousness of latecomers is also misleading as a hermeneutic approach, in that it would lead us to assume that we can no longer learn
from Arendt, that her work has ceased to engage us, that we can treat her
as a sociological and psychological curiosity exemplifying the "male-
identified female mind." In view of the enormity of Arendt's contribution
to political thought in this century, this conclusion is clearly wrong.

How then should we proceed? Asking the women's question, as always,
signifies a movement from margin to center in the hermeneutic task.[7] We
begin by searching in the footnotes, in the marginalia, in the less recognized works of a thinker for those "traces" *(Spurren)* that are left behind
by women's presence and more often than not by their absence. For
Hannah Arendt's work, this method means that one begins not with *The
Human Condition* but with a text that certainly does not occupy a central

place in any systematic interpretation of her political philosophy, namely, *Rahel Varnhagen,* subtitled *The Life of a Jewish Woman.*

Rahel Levin Varnhagen's Quest for the "World"

Hannah Arendt's intellectual biography of Rahel Varnhagen, born Rahel Levin in Berlin in 1771, was begun in 1929, shortly after she completed her dissertation on Augustine's concept of love under Karl Jaspers's directorship in Heidelberg. This study appears to have been intended as her *Habilitationsschrift,* which was to win her the right to teach in a German university.[8] It was completed in 1933 except for the last two chapters, which were finished during her exile in France in 1938. The book appeared almost twenty years later in 1957 in English translation; the first German edition came out in 1959.[9] *Rahel Varnhagen,* which Arendt subtitled in German *Lebensgeschichte einer deutschen Juedin aus der Romantik* (The Life History of a German Jewess From the Romantic Period), is a difficult text. An early reviewer found it to be

> a relentlessly abstract book—slow, cluttered, static, curiously oppressive; reading it feels like sitting in a hothouse with no watch. One is made to feel the subject, the waiting distraught woman; one is made aware, almost physically, of her intense femininity, her frustration. (Sybille Bedford)[10]

"The relentless abstractness" of the book is in part due to Arendt's methodological angle, which she herself admits is "unusual." "It was never my intention," explains Arendt,

> to write a book *about* Rahel; about her personality, which might lend itself to various interpretations according to the psychological standards and categories that the author introduces from outside; nor about her position in Romanticism and the effect of the Goethe cult in Berlin, of which she was actually the originator; nor about the significance of her salon for the social history of the period; nor about her ideas and her "Weltanschauung," insofar as these can be reconstructed from her letters. *What interested me solely was to narrate the story of Rahel's life as she herself might have told it.* . . . My portrait therefore follows as closely as possible Rahel's own reflections upon herself, although it is naturally couched in different

language and does not consist solely of variations upon quotations. (pp. xv-xvi, emphasis added)

This claim to "narrate the story of Rahel's life as she herself *might have told it*" is astonishing. Arendt's confidence in her judgments about Rahel Varnhagen is so deep that she does not fear correcting Rahel's husband's presentation of her. In fact, at one level the book reclaims Rahel's life and memory from the clutches of her husband—the generous and giving, but upright and boring, Prussian civil servant Karl August Varnhagen von Ense, who, Arendt maintains, presented Rahel's life so as to make her "associations and circle of friends appear less Jewish and more aristocratic, and to show Rahel herself in a more conventional light, one more in keeping with the taste of the times" (p. xv). One might wish to ask what gives Arendt this confidence that she in fact could know or could claim to know this woman better than her husband? How can she, Arendt, separated from Rahel's death in March 7, 1833, by almost 100 years at the time of composing her book on Rahel, claim to narrate Rahel's story as she herself "might have told it"? What hermeneutical mysteries does this little subjunctive phrase *might have told it* contain?

The facts of Rahel Varnhagen's life story are well known: Rahel was born in Berlin on May 19, 1771, the eldest child of the well-to-do merchant Markus Levin. She had three younger brothers and a younger sister. Her parental household was still Orthodox Jewish and uneducated in German culture. Rahel's early letters are written in Yiddish, that is, with Hebrew characters.[11] After the death of her father in 1790, her brother Marcus assumed the family business and provided Rahel and her mother with a regular income. Between 1790 and 1806, Rahel held a salon in her attic room on Jaegerstrasse. Among her guests were the Humboldt brothers (Alexander and Wilhelm), Friedrich Schlegel, Friedrich Gentz, Schleiermacher, Prince Louis Ferdinand of Prussia and his mistress Pauline Wiesel, the classical philologist Friedrich August Wolf, Jean Paul, Brentano, and the Tieck brothers. From 1790 to 1804, Rahel had a series of friendships and love affairs with aristocrats of various European origins, ranging from the Swedish ambassador, Karl Gustav von Brinckmann, to Count Karl von Finckenstein, and to Friedrich von Gentz (a career diplomat who was to play a significant role in the Vienna Congress of 1815).[12] In the winter of 1795–1796, Rahel was engaged to Finckenstein; their affair ended in 1800, and he retreated from this unusual Jewish woman to the clutches of his aristocratic family. In 1801–1802, Rahel fell into one of the stormiest love affairs of her life with the secretary of the Spanish Legation, Don Raphael d'Urquijo, and was engaged to him until 1804.

With the entry of Napoleon into Berlin on October 27, 1806, Rahel's salon and circle of friends were scattered. A wave of nationalism and anti-Semitism began to sweep the intellectual and aristocratic circles that had formerly befriended Varnhagen. This period heralded the end of one of the first cycles of "German-Jewish symbiosis." Family and financial difficulties followed suit in Rahel's life. Her mother moved out of the home on Jaegerstrasse and died shortly thereafter in 1809. Rahel, who had met Karl August von Varnhagen in 1808, now moved from Berlin to Teplitz. After several short separations, she was baptized on September 27, 1814, and married Varnhagen. Von Varnhagen, who was a career civil servant, moved between several cities, such as Frankfurt and Karlsruhe. In 1819, they resettled in Berlin, and from 1821 to 1832, the Berlin salon of the Varnhagens ran. Among the guests were Bettina von Arnim, Heinrich Heine, Prince Pueckler-Muskau, G. W. F. Hegel, T. Ranke, and Eduard Gans. Rahel died on March 7, 1833.

Arendt's reconstruction of Rahel's story is based primarily upon the unprinted letters and diaries from the Varnhagen collection of the Manuscript Division of the Prussian State Library. In her 1956 preface, she indicates that this manuscript was stored in the eastern provinces of Germany during the war and "what happened to it remains a mystery, so far as I know."[13] We know now that the entire collection turned up at the library in Krakow, Poland.[14] Arendt herself had to rest content with quoting from old excerpts, photostats, and copies of documents.

There are manifold layers of reading and interpretation that must be disentangled from one another in approaching Arendt's attempt to tell Rahel's story as she herself "might have told it." In the early 1930s, Arendt's own understanding of Judaism in general and her relationship to her own Jewish identity were undergoing profound transformations. These transformations were taking her increasingly away from the egalitarian, humanistic Enlightenment ideals of Kant, Lessing, and Goethe toward a recognition of the ineliminable fact of Jewish difference within German culture. The Rahel book documents the paradoxes of Jewish emancipation between the breakdown of the Ghetto and the emergence of the nineteenth-century bourgeois-Christian modern nation-state. It is in this small intermezzo between 1790 and 1806, at which point Napoleon enters Berlin, that Rahel Levin's salon in her "Berliner Dachstube" flourishes. With categories such as the *"parvenu"* and the *"pariah,"* which she borrows from the French journalist Bernard Lazare, Arendt penetrates an extremely interesting episode of German Jewish social history—that of the Jewish salonnières and the world of one among them.[15] Ironically, it is her perspective 100 years later, and her "awareness of the doom of German Judaism" (p. xvii), that allows her to tell Rahel's story in a way in which Rahel could not but might have told it.

In telling Rahel Varnhagen's story, Arendt was engaging in a process of self-understanding and self-redefinition as a German Jew. Her correspondence with Karl Jaspers, who follows the development of Arendt's work on this book with amazement bordering on irritation and bewilderment, is quite revealing in this respect.

On March 30, 1930, Karl Jaspers writes to Hannah Arendt concerning a lecture of hers on Rahel Varnhagen. Unfortunately, this lecture is no longer available. The exchange of letters between Jaspers and Arendt gives the distinct impression that Arendt here is breaking new ground and taking the *Existenzphilosophie* of her teacher Jaspers in new directions. Jaspers indicates that he wants to "get a clearer idea in the give and take of our conversation of what you mean."[16] He continues,

> You objectify "Jewish Existence" existentially—and in doing so perhaps cut existential thinking off at the roots. The concept of being-thrown-back-on-oneself can no longer be taken altogether seriously since it is *grounded* in terms of the fate of the Jews instead of being rooted in itself. . . . The passage from the letters, which you have chosen so well, suggests something quite different to me: "Jewishness" is a *façon de parler* or a manifestation of a selfhood originally negative in its outlook and not comprehensible from the historical situation. It is a fate that did not experience liberation from the enchanted castle. (emphasis in the original)[17]

Jaspers is clearly puzzled by the status of the category of "Jewish existence," and by whether or not Arendt is attributing a more fundamental status to this fact than is allowable by the categories of existential philosophy. Jaspers himself sees "Jewish existence" as a wholly contingent or accidental matter—or, as he puts it, *"a façon de parler,"* a manner of speaking, or "the manifestation of a selfhood originally negative in its outlook." Neither individually nor collectively, however, can he see in the matter of "being Jewish" more than a contingency of culture and history or an accident of birth.

Arendt's answer is cautious: she indicates that she has not tried

to "ground" Rahel's existence in terms of Jewishness—or at least I was not conscious of doing so. This lecture is only a *preliminary* work meant to show that on the foundation of being Jewish a certain possibility of existence *can* arise that I have tentatively and for the time being called fatefulness. This fatefulness arises from the very fact of "foundationlessness" and can occur *only* in a separation from Judaism. (emphasis in the original)[18]

It is noteworthy that for Arendt "Jewishness" permits a certain kind of existential condition, one that she designates as "fatefulness." In other words, being Jewish is a form of fate—it is more than an accident, because fate, although accidental, determines one's life more fundamentally and more continuously than does an accident. So Arendt is attributing a more fundamental role to the "fact" of being Jewish than Jaspers is ready to do at this point. Yet, Arendt also agrees with Jaspers that an authentic existential attitude, aware of its own "fatefulness," is only possible when one has already distanced oneself from traditional Judaism—as she phrases it—"in a separation from Judaism." The authentic existential attitude cannot emerge for a self who is still submerged in given categories of cultural and social existence; it is the confrontation with life itself, without reliance upon the social and cultural givens of one's background, which would guide one here. Yet, is Arendt really satisfied with the abstract individualism of *Existenzphilosophie?* Does not her analysis of Rahel Varnhagen betray, *malgré elle,* the multiple, complex, and fragmentary crisscrossing of collective cultural identities in determining the fate of an individual?

Given the perspective of hindsight and what it would signify to be Jewish in Germany by the end of the 1930s, this exchange is almost astonishing in its abstractness and aloofness. Neither Jaspers nor Arendt could have anticipated a situation when the fact of being Jewish would indeed be fateful for millions and millions. Yet it is interesting that Arendt is full of premonition, that she seems to be sensing a certain "uncanniness" *(das unheimliche)* in Rahel's own attempt to live life as her "fate." With reference to Rahel, Arendt writes:

> What this all really adds up to—fate, being exposed, what life means—I can't really say in the abstract (and I realize that in trying to write about it here.) Perhaps all I can try to do is illustrate it with examples.[19]

Eventually, Arendt comes to describe Rahel's own attitude toward her Judaism as a move away from the psychology of the parvenu to that of the pariah. Whereas the parvenu denies "fatefulness" by becoming like the others of the dominant culture, by erasing difference and assimilating to dominant trends, the pariah is the outsider and the outcast who either cannot or chooses not to erase the fate of difference. The latter is the self-conscious pariah, who transforms difference from being a source of weakness and marginality into one of strength and defiance. This is ultimately what Arendt admires in Rahel: commenting on Rahel's reflections on her life as "Friederiké Varnhagen," the respectable wife of a Prussian civil servant, she writes,

> She had at last rid herself of Rahel Levin, but she did not want to become Friederiké Varnhagen, née Robert. The former was not socially acceptable; the latter could not summon the resolution to make a fraudulent self-identification. For "all my life I considered myself Rahel and nothing else."[20]

Rahel's Jewish identity and Arendt's own changing understanding of what this means in the 1930s in Germany are the central hermeneutic motifs in the Varnhagen story.[21] In telling Rahel's story, Hannah Arendt was bearing testimony to a political and spiritual transformation that she herself was undergoing. There is thus a mirror effect in the narrative. The one narrated about becomes the mirror in which the narrator seeks to understand and interpret herself. Retelling and reconstructing Rahel Varnhagen's life story was clearly a medium for Hannah Arendt to reflect upon aspects of her own identity as a German Jew. The collapse of Rahel's salon and along with it of the ideals of the German Enlightenment, which assimilated German Jews, including Arendt's own mother, had deeply believed in; Rahel's eventual recognition of her status as a pariah and a Jew, although occurring nearly one hundred years prior to the time in which Arendt was composing the book, provide a parallel narrative, almost a parable, for the experiences and transformations of Arendt's own lifetime.[22]

There is an additional dimension to this narration, and it is one that leads more directly to future themes in Arendt's political philosophy. In telling Rahel's story, Arendt is concerned to document a certain form of romantic *Innerlichkeit* (inwardness). Arendt cites Rahel's nearly tautological phrase, "Everyone has a Destiny who knows what kind of Destiny he has" (p. xvi). This concept of Destiny, Arendt maintains, reduces Rahel to a certain passivity, to a certain refusal to choose and to act. In choosing and acting, one would not live but would "make life happen." To live life "as if it were a work of art," writes Arendt, "to believe that by 'cultivation' (Bildung) one can make a work of art of one's life was the great error that Rahel shared with her contemporaries" (p. xvi). The "claustrophobic" feeling about the book that was noted above, the sensation, namely, that "one is in a hothouse without a watch" (Sybille Bedford), derives from Arendt's literary success in conveying this sense of endless expectation, of an endless yearning without fulfillment, of inaction coupled with the wish to live and experience most intensely—"What am I doing?" asks Rahel. "Nothing. I am letting life rain upon me" (quoted on p. xvi). It is this "worldless" sensibility that Arendt finds most objectionable about Rahel. In the opening chapters of the Varnhagen biography, which deal with romantic introspection, Arendt indicates what she sees as the greatest weakness and ultimately as the "apolitical" quality of romantic inwardness:

> Introspection accomplishes two feats: it annihilates the actual existing situation by dissolving it in mood, and at the same time it lends everything subjective an aura of objectivity, publicity, extreme interest. In mood, the boundaries between what is intimate and what is public become blurred; intimacies are made public, and public matters can be experienced and expressed only in the realm of the intimate—ultimately, in gossip.[23]

Romantic introspection leads one to lose a sense of reality by losing the boundaries between the private and the public, the intimate and the shared. Romantic introspection compounds the "worldlessness" from which Rahel Varnhagen suffers to the very end. The category of the "world" is the missing link between the "worldless" reality of Rahel Levin Varnhagen and her contemporaries, and Hannah Arendt's own search for a recovery of the "public world" through authentic political action in her political philosophy. Romantic inwardness displays qualities of mind and feeling that are the exact opposite of those required of political actors and that Arendt highly valued. Whereas romantic introspection blurs the boundaries between the personal and the political, the political qualities of distinguishing sharply and precisely between the public good and the personal sphere are extremely important for Arendt. Whereas the ability to judge the world as it appears to others and from many different points of view is the quintessential epistemic virtue in politics, romantic inwardness tends to eliminate the distinction between one's own perspective and those of others through mood. Finally, an interest in the world and a commitment to sustain it are fundamental for politics, whereas romantic inwardness cultivates the soul rather than sustaining the world.[24]

Varnhagen's search for a place in the "world" was defined by her identity not only as a Jew and as a Romantic but also as a woman. Although Arendt does not place this theme at the center, her story of Rahel begins to reveal an unthematized gender subtext. In Arendt's account, Varnhagen attempts to gain a place in the world for herself by using typically female strategies. In the concluding paragraphs of her 1956 preface to *Rahel Varnhagen,* Arendt remarks,

> The modern reader will scarcely fail to observe that Rahel was neither beautiful nor attractive; that all the men with whom she had any kind of love relationship were younger than she herself; that she possessed no talents with which to employ her extraordinary intelligence and passionate originality; and finally, that she was a typically "romantic" personality, and that the Woman problem, that is the discrepancy between what men expected of women "in general" and what women could give or wanted in their turn, was already established by the conditions of the era and represented a gap that virtually could not be closed. (p. xviii)

Rahel's strategies for dealing with the fate of her Jewishness were typically female ones: assimilation and recognition through love affairs, courtships, and eventually marriage with Gentile males. It may also not be unimportant that according to Jewish law the Jewish male who married a Gentile woman and had children by her could not consider his children Jewish, whereas to this day Jewish law recognizes that a child born of a

Jewish woman is Jewish. This matrilineal aspect of the Jewish tradition may have made it easier for upper-class Jewish women to retain their identity while marrying Gentile men to become successful in the world. The female strategy of assimilation through marriage is, of course, made possible by a gender-asymmetrical world in which it is the husband's public status that defines the woman, rather than the other way around. Rahel Levin Varnhagen's life was full of stories of failed love affairs, broken promises, and unsuccessful engagements. By giving herself to the right man, Rahel hoped to attain the "world" that was denied her as a Jew and as a female.

But "where" is the world, and "who" is it composed of? Interestingly, Arendt's most explicit definition of this category comes much later, in a 1960 essay on Lessing that focuses on *Nathan der Weise.* "But the world and the people who inhabit it," writes Arendt,

> are not the same. The world lies between people, and this in-between . . . is today the object of the greatest concern and the most obvious upheaval in almost all the countries of the globe. Even where the world is still halfway in order, or is kept halfway in order, the public realm has lost the power of illumination which was originally part of its very nature . . . [The] withdrawal from the world need not harm an individual; . . . but with each such retreat an almost demonstrable loss to the world takes place; what is lost is the specific and usually irreplaceable in-between which should have formed between this individual and his fellow men.[25]

Arendt made this speech in 1959, upon receiving the Lessing Peace Prize from the city of Hamburg. Her melancholy reflections on the loss of the "world" as that fragile "space of appearances" that "holds men together" stand in interesting contrast with the theme of "worldlessness" that dominates the *Varnhagen* book. Rahel and her contemporaries failed to create a world except in that brief intermezzo between 1790 and 1806 when a few exceptional Prussian Jews could emerge into the world of genteel society, only to be pushed back into obscurity with the onslaught of anti-Semitism in Prussia after the victory of Napoleon. The fragility and almost illusory character of the world of the "salons" that Jewesses such as Rahel Varnhagen and Henriette Herz created for a brief moment stands in sharp contrast to the fate of the "stateless" and "worldless" people that the Jews would become in the twentieth century. By the time she gives the Lessing speech, however, Arendt is preoccupied by yet another phenomenon: this time it is not the loss of a common world through the onslaught of murderous regimes and totalitarian politics that concerns her but the disappearance of a common world of "speech and action" through the privatistic value systems of capitalist consumer societies and the increasingly fabricated world of political truth created by the mass media that are her concern. The "recovery of the public world" of politics under conditions of modernity is a guiding theme of Hannah Arendt's political philosophy. The personal story of Rahel Varnhagen, of her circle of friends, of the failure of her salon, and of the political naïveté of her generation of Jews is like a *negative utopia* of Arendt's concept of political community in her subsequent works. Nonetheless, this cluttered and at times awkward youthful text retains themes, issues, and preoccupations that are much closer to the nerve of Arendt's existential concerns than some of her subsequent formulations. As Dagmar Barnouw has written,

> Arguably, however, much of her peculiarly sharp and consistent concreteness in perceiving, analyzing, and presenting the destructive mechanisms underlying the Jewish experience of assimilation and anti-Semitism was informed by the fact that she analyzed it first in the life story of a woman to whom she, as a woman, was particularly close and of whom she, as a woman, was particularly critical. Rahel's subtext was immediately accessible to her. Bringing it to the surface was not an act of indiscretion, imposition, or hindsight falsification; rather, it was, in peculiarly personal, unmediated terms, a historical reclamation of deleted parts of a life story by one articulate woman relating, through judgment, to another in expressing kinship *and* difference. In this sense, Arendt's collating of the Jewish situation and the "Woman Question" in its emphasis on the pariah's self-critical perspective contributes significantly to an understanding of the cultural-historical meaning of both issues.[26]

The Salons as Female "Public Sphere"

Rahel Varnhagen's life and her moment of "glory" coincided with that brief intermezzo in German cultural history when the Enlightenment, the ideals of the French Revolution, the spirit of Prussian reforms and German

Romanticism came together to make possible that ephemeral but still fascinating public sphere—"the Jewish salonnières of Berlin." Rahel Varnhagen's salon was by no means the only one in an illustrious group, which included Dorothea (Mendelssohn) Veit Schlegel, Henriette Hertz, Rebecca Friedlander, and Amalie Beer. Nonetheless, this crucial period of German intellectual and cultural history (1780–1806) would come to be known as *die Rahelzeit*. Commenting on this period in her most comprehensive and illuminating study, *Jewish High Society in Old Regime Berlin*, Deborah Hertz writes,

> During the quarter century between 1780 and 1806 the city's Jewish salons caused a stir at home and abroad. Visitors from across Europe hailed the swift assimilation accomplished by the Jewish salonnières, whose social prominence was achieved at a time when the majority of central and eastern European Jews were still poor peddlers and traders, living in small villages, speaking Yiddish and following a traditional way of life. Surely here, in the drawing rooms of Berlin's rich and sophisticated Jewish women, was to be found the realization of the dream of emancipation that was just then being proposed by avant-garde intellectuals. . . . When the French salonnière Madame de Stäel visited Berlin in 1804, she found it easier to gracefully entertain princes alongside humble writers than elsewhere in Germany.[27]

The Jewish salonnières of Berlin were the daughters and wives of well-to-do Jewish merchants and intellectuals who ran large and complex households and whose fathers and husbands were frequently absent from the house in the world of commerce and community affairs. These women accomplished a triple feat through their social activities: first, they emancipated themselves from traditional patriarchal families. Often they refused to marry their designated Jewish future spouses to be; some converted to Christianity and lost all ties to the religion of their forebears. Their emancipation as "women" was often coupled with their rejection of traditional Judaism. Second, they helped create high culture in a crucial era at the end of the Enlightenment and the outbreak of Romanticism. They did so by creating a "social space" in which Berlin's intelligentsia, writers, artists, as well as civil servants and aristocrats, could gather together, exchange ideas, views, and texts, mix and mingle with each other, be seen, heard, and noticed by others. In this respect, they acted as the patrons of the intelligentsia in a city that at the time lacked a university, a parliament, and a generous court. Finally, the salons forged bonds across classes, religious groups, and the two sexes, creating the four walls within which new forms of *sociability* and *intimacy* could develop among members of an emergent civil society.

The French salons, which were also dominated by women and predated the Berlin ones by half a century, also accomplished a parallel feat. The salons were *spaces* in which individuals from different and traditionally segregated groups, ranks, and classes could mix and mingle; primarily members of the bourgeoisie and the intelligentsia mixed with the nobility. They were *social events* in which literary and artistic works were read, discussed, contracted, and exchanged; they were *social processes* through which individuals of a hierarchical ancien régime with its formalized manners of speech, intercourse, and even affection learned new and non-hierarchical, more fluid forms of self- and other presentation. The salons were social experiments of a period of transition from the old to the new in prerevolutionary Europe.[28] Such experimentation included not only the crossing of social boundaries, but very often an experimentation with gender roles and sexual expectations as well. The salons, both in the French and in the German context, allowed the creation of new, experimental, and transgressive modes of self- and other presentation.

Gatherings with the characteristics of salons have been located as early as classical Greece and twelfth-century French courts, but it is only beginning with the Renaissance that they became more regularized and less episodic phenomena.[29] Although historically not unprecedented, the salons become a recurring feature of sociability only with the emergence of modern civil society. Urban life, peace, prosperity, a certain refinement of tastes in dress, manners, consumption as well as in art and literature are preconditions of salons. As Hertz explains,

> The word *salon* came into use to describe a public room that began to appear in wealthy European homes between the sixteenth and eighteenth centuries as the "great hall," which had been the center of medieval family life, gradually lost its private character and four-poster beds were moved into separate rooms. The great hall, now called the salon, was a lavishly decorated public space where the piano was played, feasts served and guests received.[30]

The salons of early modernity are topographically confined and structured spaces, but the forms of sociability and social intercourse that they exemplify and help to foster and develop are not themselves topographically confined. As modern civil society spreads, the forms of sociability and intimacy prefigured by the salons become in part social reality; in part they remain ideals defining the utopian self-understanding of early bourgeois society.

What then are the forms of sociability appropriate to the salons? Here again a distinction must be made between the French and the German versions of this occurrence. In the French salons, which developed in the shadow cast by the courtly reign of *le Roi Soleil,* more stylized, ceremonial, and hierarchically defined manners are the norm. In the German salons, developing against the background of a weak aristocracy and a nonexistent courtly public sphere, more spontaneous and less stylized ceremonial manners are the norm. In both cases, the salons bring to life the Enlightenment idea of *l'homme, der Mensch,* the human being as such. This is the vision that underneath it all, when divested of all our social, cultural, religious accoutrements, ranks, and distinction, we are all humans like each other. There is no greater proof of our common humanity than the fact that we can communicate with and understand each other. The salons are social gatherings in which the "joy of conversation," the joy of communication and understanding as well as misunderstandings and lack of communication, is discovered. This is indeed Rahel Varnhagen's strength to which her admirers testify: the magic of her language, her capacity to express herself, her witticisms, her judgments; Rahel opens a world for those with whom she is communicating through her speech. The joy of speech culminates in friendship, in that meeting of hearts, minds, and tastes between two individuals. Particularly in the case of the German salons, the search for a *Seelensfreund,* a friend of one's soul, one who understands oneself perhaps better than oneself, is predominant. For Rahel, Pauline Wiesel, the mistress of King Ludwig of Prussia, who in her old age would also try to seduce Rahel's husband, August von Varnhagen, was such a "friend." With friends one shares one's soul; however, to share the soul—an entity that itself comes to be discovered in this new process of individuation—one has to project a certain depth of the self, one has to view the self as a being whose public presence does not reveal all. The

public reveals and conceals at the same time; it is only in the withdrawal
from the public into the sheltered space of a two- or three-person relationship that one can also move inward, toward who one really is. In this
respect as well, the salon is a fascinating space: unlike an assembly hall,
a town square, a conference room, or even simply the family dinner table,
the salon, with its large, luxurious, and rambling space, allows for moments of intimacy; in a salon, people are with each other but must not
always be next to each other. Salons are amorphous structures with no
established rules of entry and exit for those who have formed intimacy;
in fact, it may be a sign of good manners to foster and to allow the
formation of intimacy among members of the salon. What is important
here is the fluidity of the lines between the gathering as one and the
gathering as many units of intimacy, and how the salons can be both public
and private, both shared and intimate.

A new ideal of humanity, the joy of conversation, the search for
friendship, and the cultivation of intimacy—these are the ideals and
aspirations of the salon phenomena in the age of modernity. Of course,
the cleavage between ideals and reality accompanies the salons no less
than other social phenomena: despite their egalitarian humanist rhetoric,
class, rank, and religious differences continue to play a role. The salons
are not spaces for the whole people, including the laborers, the gardener,
the milk maid, and the coach driver. They are largely upper-middle-class
phenomena. The working and laboring classes of Europe in this period
share a different mode of sociability of their own. As Rahel Varnhagen's
own experience shows, many of her lovers of noble descent (most notably
Count von Finckenstein) are unable to overcome class biases; and with
the defeat of the German armies at the hands of Napoleon and the rise of
German nationalism, anti-Semitic feelings immediately come to the fore.
Neither are the salons protected spaces of friendship and intimacy alone;
intrigues, petty fighting, and even treachery have their place there, as do
erotic and sexual jealousy, infidelity, and betrayal.

Finally, the discovery of the "joy of conversation" should not lead one
to overlook the fact that the salons were fascinating gatherings in which
the written and the spoken word often flowed into each other; even
private, confidential letters were often written to be read out loud in
public. Written texts were often first presented, improvised, and altered
in the process. Even the literary creations of the amateurs, and most often

of the women, were circulated in this space.[31] And this is precisely what Rahel Varnhagen has left of her work to posterity: not a literary or philosophical or political text, but her letters, her copious correspondence with her many friends.

Letter writing in the late eighteenth century, the art in which Rahel excelled, is closely related to the emergence of a new form of individuality and self-understanding in European culture. Letters often have the writer, her moods, thoughts, reflections, as their subject: they are frequently confessional as well as informational. They create a special bond between the writer, the addressee, and the larger public that these writers of the eighteenth century never quite lose sight of. Because of their quasi-public, quasi-private quality, because they lend themselves so readily to expressions of intimacy, letters become almost the preferred "feminine" pattern of prose. Women here discover a medium through which they can communicate from the intimate toward the public, so to speak. Beginning with what is closest to one and the mundane realities of the everyday, the letter allows women to venture toward, as well as appropriating for themselves, a "public" world from which they were effectively excluded. The use of the first person pronoun in writing letters also permits women to craft for themselves a language of literature and expression that otherwise excludes them. Women, through their letters, appear to re-create themselves as texts, thus overcoming their own silencing in the major texts of the tradition, which as educated upper- and middle-class females, they would have had to read. The letter form, like the salon, is a transgressive mode: it is a mode in which boundaries are crossed, erased, renegotiated, and re-created.

The phenomenon of the salons, the predominance of the women among them, the kinds of public spaces they are, and the forms of interaction, speech, and writing most closely associated with them pose fascinating problems for Hannah Arendt's political philosophy. Almost in ᵉvery respect, the salons, as modes of the public sphere, contradict the *agonal* model of the public sphere of the polis that predominates in *The Human Condition*. Whereas the Greek polis and the public sphere characteristic of it exclude women (and other members of the household like children and servants generally), the salons are spaces dominated by female presence. Whereas speech in the public spaces of the polis is "serious," guided by the concern for the "good of all," speech in the salons is playful, amorphous, and freely mixes the good of all with the advantage of each. Whereas the public sphere of the polis attempts to exclude and to suppress eros, the salons cultivate the erotic. Of course, the erotic is never silenced in the Greek public sphere either: more often than not, it assumes a homosexual rather than heterosexual form. Whereas the spaces of the polis are governed by the ideals of "visibility" and "transparency," eighteenth-century salons are governed by "visibility" but not by "transparency": self-revelation and self-concealment, even pretending to be quite other than one is, are the norms.

Yet the salons and the polis also have features in common: they are based on assumptions of equality among the participants. In the case of the polis, this is the *isonomia* of political rank as citizen and of economic independence as *oikos despotes*. For the salon participants, equality is an ideal based upon their shared humanity and their specific talents, abilities, and capabilities as individuals sharing certain tastes and sensibilities. Such equality prevails against otherwise existing social, economic, and even political inequality among salon members. Both the public spheres of the polis and the salons aid in the creation of bonds among their members. According to Aristotle, "friendship" among citizens of the polis is the virtue that good lawgivers try most to cultivate; for, without friendship, there cannot be justice, whereas with justice alone, friendship may be lacking.[32] The salons are also spaces in which friendships are formed: these friendships are more personal than political, but here again the lines are not clear; the salons are spaces in which personal friendships may result in political bondings (what we nowadays ubiquitously refer to as "networking"). In effect, both the polis and the salons contribute to the formation of "civic friendship," either among a group of citizens or among a group of private, like-minded individuals who can gather for a common political purpose.[33]

If we proceed to decenter Arendt's political thought, if we read her work from the margins toward the center, then we can displace her fascination with the polis to make room for her more modernist and women-friendly reflections on the salons. The salons must be viewed as transitory but fascinating precursors of a certain transgression of boundaries between the public and the private. Arendt developed her political philosophy to ward off such transgressions, but as a radical democrat she could not but welcome

such transgressions if they resulted in authentic political activity, in a community of "speech and action." The following observations by Deborah
Hertz make clear that the salons were typically female forms of the public
sphere, and that for a brief moment indeed they may have allowed Rahel
Varnhagen to recover a piece of the "public world."

> That the home could be a public as well as private place was obviously one
> reason why salons were organized by women. The synthesis of the private
> and the public in salons was evident in the curious, bygone way that guests
> arrived at the door. . . . That social institutions like salons should ever have
> appeared in preindustrial Europe, even intermittently, came to seem quite
> odd. It was odd that private drawing rooms should have been public places,
> odd that in an age when women were excluded from educational and civic
> institutions, even wives of rich and powerful men should lead intellectual
> discussions among the most learned men of their cities. It was odd that men
> and women should have had important intellectual exchanges during cen-
> turies when the two sexes generally had little to say to each other and few
> public places in which to say it.[34]

Arendt's own relentless pessimism about the significance of the salons
certainly cannot be separated from the tragic ending of the utopian and
optimistic hopes they had initially kindled in the souls of many German
Jews. As she notes in the preface to *Rahel Varnhagen*:

> The present biography was written with an awareness of the doom of
> German Judaism (although, naturally without any premonition of how far
> the physical annihilation of the Jewish people in Europe would be carried);
> but at that time, shortly before Hitler's coming to power, I did not have the
> perspective from which to view the phenomenon as a whole. . . . On the
> other hand, it must not be forgotten that the subject matter is altogether
> historical, and that nowadays not only the history of the German Jews, but
> also their specific complex of problems, are a matter of the past (p. xvii)

Written in 1956, these melancholy reflections distance Hannah Arendt
herself from this biography by "historicizing" Rahel and the fate of the
German Jews to whom she belonged. Yet, for us, as Arendt's readers, the
questions posed by her biography of Rahel Varnhagen cannot be restricted
to this tragic-historical context alone. For early works are also beginnings,
and beginnings are frequently closer to the nerve of a thinker's oeuvre,

precisely because time, experience, sophistication, and the apparatus of scholarship have not cluttered the existential questions and preoccupations that are at the origins of thought. When read in the light of this hermeneutic principle, Arendt's early treatment of Rahel Varnhagen suggests a set of issues that go well beyond the fate of German Jewry and of the salonnières among them, and that point us to the heart of her political theory. I will assemble these issues under a question mark: "An Alternative Genealogy of Modernity?" I want to suggest that at the beginnings of Arendt's work, we discover a different genealogy of modernity than the one so characteristic of her later writings. The "rise of the social," in this alternative genealogy of modernity, would not refer to the rise of commodity exchange relations in a burgeoning capitalist economy but would designate the emergence of new forms of sociability, association, intimacy, friendship, speaking and writing habits, tastes in food, manners and arts, as well as hobbies, pastimes, and leisure activities. Furthermore, in the midst of this alternative genealogy of the social is a curious space that is in the home yet public, that is dominated by women yet visited and frequented by men, that is highly mannered yet egalitarian, and that is hierarchical toward "outsiders" and egalitarian toward its members. What leads Arendt to lose sight of this "other modernity" with which she began, and to replace it with a relentless pessimism? Of course, at one level the answer to this question is the Holocaust and the fate of European Jewry, which nullified all the ideals of the Enlightenment and modernity in which Rahel's generation still believed. At another level, though, the answer may be that perhaps Arendt never did lose sight of this other modernity and that her purported "Grecocentrism" is as much a fiction created by us, her readers, as it is based upon her own texts. Let us reread the meaning of the concept of the "social" in Arendt's work in light of what I am suggesting is an alternative genealogy of modernity.

The Rise of the Social

Consider the standard reading of Arendt's political philosophy. For many, Arendt is a nostalgic and antimodernist thinker, who sees in modernity the decline of the public sphere of politics and the emergence of an amorphous, anonymous, uniformizing reality that she calls "the social." In this account, the social, by which is meant a form of glorified national housekeeping in economic and pecuniary matters, displaces the concern with the political, with the *res publica,* from the hearts and minds of men. The social is the perfect medium in which bureaucracy, the "rule by nobody," emerges and unfolds.

As an account of modernity, this view is jarring in so many ways that it requires a great deal of hermeneutic uncharity to attribute it to a thinker who was as historically grounded and sophisticated as Hannah Arendt. First, this model of the rise and decline of the public sphere operates with a gross historical oversimplification: if the Greek polis and, to a lesser extent, the early phases of the Roman republic are the model of the "public sphere" that Arendt praises, what happens to the Middle Ages, the Renaissance, and early modernity? What was the configuration of the *oikos* and the *polis* during these times? Are these terms even relevant to describe these sociohistorical formations? Do we simply skip over them? Do we treat them as if they were "blank pages" of history (Hegel)? Second, if the "social" arises, it must rise out of something. Arendt suggests that it rises out of "the shadowy interior of the household" into the public light. But what was it that was formerly confined to the household and eventually emerged into the light of the public?

There are three dominant meanings of the term *social* in Arendt's work. At one level, the *social* refers to the growth of a capitalist commodity exchange economy. At the second level, it refers to aspects of mass society. In the third and least investigated sense, the *social* refers to sociability, to the quality of life in civil society and civic associations.

To document the first meaning of the social, it will be helpful to place Arendt's views on the emergence of a modern exchange economy alongside those of Karl Marx and Karl Polanyi. In a trenchant definition, Arendt writes, "Society is the form in which the fact of mutual dependence for the sake of life and nothing else assumes public significance and where the activities concerned with sheer survival are permitted to appear in public" (*HC,* p. 46). The emergence of such a sphere of universal economic exchange and production, in which everything, including labor power, could be bought and sold as a commodity in the marketplace, has been seen by many thinkers before Hannah Arendt as marking an epochal turning point in human history. A century ago, G. W. F. Hegel had named this sphere "the system of needs," namely, the sphere in which economic exchange activities for the sole satisfaction of the needs and interests of the exchangers would become the norm of human interaction.[35]

For Karl Marx, the spread of free exchange relations and the transformation of all objects, all products of human activity, and of human activities themselves into commodities, revealed an almost ontological truth about human society. In the prophetic words of *The Communist Manifesto*,

> The bourgeoisie, wherever it has got the upper hand, has put an end to all feudal, patriarchal, idyllic relations. It has pitilessly torn asunder the motley feudal ties that bound man to his "natural superiors," and has left no other nexus between man and man than naked self-interest, than callous "cash payment." . . . All fixed, fast frozen relations, with their train of ancient and venerable prejudices and opinions, are swept away, all new-formed ones become antiquated before they can ossify. All that is solid melts into air, all that is holy is profaned, *and man is at last compelled to face with sober senses his real conditions of life and his relations with his kind.* (emphasis added)[36]

From a Marxian standpoint, the exchange market indeed means the rise of the "social" because bourgeois society is the first one in history in which the legitimation of social and political relations of power and inequality are grounded not upon "nature" but upon principles and criteria that are immanent to human relations themselves.[37] Marx has in mind here the principles of the social contract, as advocated by political theorists from Thomas Hobbes to J. G. Fichte; he reads the norms of civic, political, and legal equality and liberty, advocated by contract theorists, in light of a narrowly economic focus as norms that are required, as well as made possible by, the new form of commodity exchange relations.[38]

Even more illuminating for understanding this particular sense of the "rise of the social" in Arendt's work than Karl Marx's anatomy of the exchange market is Karl Polanyi's concept of the "disembedded economy." Polanyi, like Marx, focuses on the "demystifying" aspects of the commodity exchange market.[39] The "demystification" occurs in the way in which economic relations, which in all previously known forms of human societies were regulated by religious, magical, mythical, and other normative criteria, are now freed from the sanctions of these. With the eventual collapse of previously existing political, religious, and cultural barriers prohibiting and limiting private appropriation of the land; with the transformation of all objects and potentially of all aspects of physical reality into an object of "property"; and with the uprooting of human beings themselves from their embedded identities in communities, a process of social disembedding and cultural leveling occurs.[40] The economy is no longer "embedded" in the Greek *oikos,* in the feudal manor, or *das ganze Haus* of the Middle Ages; exchange relations, production for the sake of selling and buying, now become the norm.

This disembedded economy contributes to the rise of the social insofar as exchange relations emerge as an open and unrestricted medium of social interaction for all persons who happen to be commodity owners. The logic of capitalist exchange relations is to level all distinctions of status and hierarchy except those based on the appropriation of means of wealth. The anonymous, infinite, multiple crisscrossings of production, exchange, and distribution create, in the words of the young Hegel, "an elemental animal-like movement,"[41] whose logic is governed by an "invisible hand." In this elemental movement that catches all in its web, Arendt notes, "society [becomes] the form in which the fact of mutual dependence for the sake of life and nothing else assumes public significance and where the activities concerned with sheer survival are permitted to appear in public" (*HC,* p. 46). When read against the background of the emergence of a commodity exchange economy, Arendt's diagnosis of the rise of the social loses some of its oddities; the rise of the social is better named the rise of a commodity exchange market.

There is a second sense of the *social* for Hannah Arendt. The term now shifts its meaning from the spread of a market of commodity exchange to "mass society" as such. When focusing upon this aspect of the rise of the social, Arendt introduces such contrasts as between "behavior" and "action." Whereas "behavior" is the ideal typical activity of individuals insofar as they are the bearers of social roles, that is, the bureaucrat, the businessman, the executive, and so on, "action" is individuating and individualizing behavior; it reveals the self rather than concealing him or her behind the social mask. "It is decisive that society," writes Arendt, on all its levels, excludes the possibility of action, which formerly was excluded from the household. Instead, society expects from each of its members a certain kind of behavior, imposing innumerable and various rules, all of which tend to "normalize" its members, to make them behave, to exclude spontaneous action or outstanding achievement. (*HC,* p. 40)

There is no analysis, in Arendt's considerations on these matters in *The Human Condition,* of the mechanisms of social control and integration through which such homogenization, leveling, and "normalization" are achieved. We do not find in Arendt's work, as we do later in Max Weber's, an analysis of the logic of formal and instrumental rationality as an organizational principle that demands that behavior be rendered predictable and uniform, that tasks be broken down into compatible and interchangeable units, that efficiency and obedience to formal criteria of performance dominate.[42] Neither do we find in Arendt's diagnosis of the "social," as it becomes transformed into "mass society," an analysis of what Michel Foucault has called "disciplinary institutions," such as the hospital, the school, the army, and the prison system.[43] Arendt presupposed that such normalizations occur without explicating the social mechanisms of the exercise of power, or the microphysics of power, which make such normalization possible. As a contribution to *social theory,* her reflections on the leveling and homogenizing effects of the rise of the social are thin and at times reductionist. It is only when we read these passages against the background of much other work in nineteenth- and twentieth-century social theory, and place Arendt in the company of Marx, Weber, Polanyi, and Foucault by supplementing her insights and aphorisms with their more comprehensive treatments of the dynamics of modern societies, that her diagnosis of the "rise of the social" loses some of its initial implausibilities.

To begin to explore the third and last meaning of the term *social* for Arendt, namely, the "social" as sociability and as the quality of civic-associational life,[44] consider the following passage:

But society equalizes under all circumstances, and the victory of equality in the modern world is only the political and legal recognition of the fact that society has conquered the public realm, and *that distinction and difference have become private matters of the individual.* (*HC,* p. 41, emphasis added)

By "equality" in this passage, Arendt not only means political and legal equality but also the equalization of tastes, behavior, manners, and life-styles, which is executed by mass society. Under such conditions, "distinction and difference have become private matters of the individual." But have they really? Arendt's historical and political writings on the Jewish question, beginning with her biography of Rahel Varnhagen, reveal quite a different picture. They show that the constant struggle and tension between "equality" and "difference," in both the social and the political domains, is characteristic of modernity. In one of her most illuminating remarks on this dialectic of equality and difference, Arendt notes,

> Equality of condition, though it is certainly a basic requirement for justice, is nevertheless among the greatest and most uncertain ventures of modern mankind. The more equal conditions are, the less explanation there is for the differences that actually exist between people; and thus all the more unequal do individuals and groups become. . . . Whenever equality becomes a mundane fact in itself, without any gauge by which it may be measured or explained, then there is one chance in a hundred that it will be recognized simply as a working principle of a political organization *in which otherwise unequal people have equal rights*; there are ninety-nine chances that it will be mistaken for an innate quality of every individual, who is "normal" if he is like everybody else and "abnormal" if he happens to be different. *This perversion of equality from a political into a social concept is all the more dangerous when a society leaves but little space for special groups and individuals, for then their differences become all the more conspicuous. (OT,* p. 54, emphasis added)[45]

For Arendt, this tension between political equality and social difference is at the root of modern secular anti-Semitism as opposed to religiously based anti-Semitism. When social contacts between Jews and Gentiles increase in modern societies, when commercial relations multiply, when Jewish children attend the same schools as their countryfolk, when Jewish women shop and dine in the same shops and restaurants as the non-Jewish members of the dominant religious groups in society, whether Christian or not, the increase in these social exchanges makes the fact of Jewish difference less comprehensible and more problematic in the eyes of others (*OT,* pp. 52 ff.). It is against the background of growing social and political equality that difference can first be noted; in inegalitarian societies, difference signifies otherness. In the ancient, hierarchical order of pre-bourgeois societies, the otherness of the other does not present the same problems of discrimination and prejudice, precisely because this otherness is thought to reflect and to be grounded upon an order of society that ultimately mirrors an extrasocietal normative order. It is only with the rise of the ideals of political and legal equality and the universalistic claim of the Enlightenment that "we are all humans" that the fact of Jewish difference becomes a social fact for which all modern anti-Semitic movements seek an explanation. Arendt's work as a historian of anti-Semitism brilliantly documents this dialectic of equality and difference as well as showing how much more complicated and multilayered the dynamics of the social are. This complex picture is hard to reconcile with the more undifferentiated and reductive claims concerning the social in *The Human Condition*. As noted above, in *The Human Condition* "distinction" and "difference" are said to become private matters of the individual. Arendt's reflections and analyses as a social and cultural historian show, however, that such matters of "distinction" and "difference" are never merely individual but always concern the identities and social positions of collectivities.

Several issues are worthy of attention here. Note that in the context of these latter considerations, the *social* does not mean the "housekeeping" activities of the market on a national scale, nor does the *social* mean a "mass society" of like-behaving consumers. Rather, the *social* in this context means "sociability": patterns of human interaction; modalities of taste in dress, eating, leisure, and lifestyles generally; differences in aesthetic, religious, and civic manners and outlooks; patterns of socializing and forming marriages, friendships, acquaintanceships, and commercial exchanges. In short, the *social* signifies *civil and associational society,* that sphere of human relations that is not economic, or political, or military, or bureaucratic-administrative. This meaning of the term *social* is closely related to the 18th-century understanding of a refined society of tastes and manners of *la bonne société,* in French, or *die gute Gesellschaft* in German. It is also what Norbert Elias has described as "the civilizing process."[46] It is within this sphere that the homogenization of tastes, attitudes, manners, and lifestyles begins to spread in modernity; this is the sphere in which the "parvenu" dominates, the one who craves social recognition through social equality and acceptance.

By contrast, the "pariah" does not fare well in "society." The pariah is an outsider in matters of taste, manners, habits, and friendships. She breaks social conventions and flouts social norms; she goes against established traditions and plays with social expectations. The self-conscious pariah insists upon the fact of difference and distinction, but does so in a manner that is not wholly individualistic. The complete pariah would be the total outsider, the marginal bordering on suicide, insanity, or criminality. The self-conscious pariah is one who lives with difference and distinctness in such a way as to establish her difference in the "eyes" of society. The self-conscious pariah requires visibility, requires to be seen as "other" and as "different," even if only by a very small group, by a community of like-minded friends.

This is precisely what Rahel Varnhagen's salon was: a space of sociability in which the individual desire for difference and distinctness could assume an intersubjective reality. This space of sociability, of which the salons are only one instance, points to a dimension in Arendt's genealogical account of the rise of the social that is wholly missing in *The Human Condition*. Having begun with "her eyes" on this phenomenon in the Rahel Varnhagen biography, why does Arendt lose sight of this social space in her later work? And what does its disappearance in the later work mean for her political philosophy as a whole? Furthermore, where if anywhere is there room to express difference and distinctness in "modern societies"? Are "difference" and "distinctness" political, social, or cultural categories? In which "sphere," to speak with Arendt, can they be best expressed?

The alternative genealogy of modernity suggested by Arendt's Rahel Varnhagen biography leaves its traces throughout her work and suggests a major rereading of her understanding of modernity and of the place of politics under conditions of modernity. According to this alternative genealogy, modernity cannot simply be identified with the spread of commodity exchange relations and the growth of a capitalist economy; nor can modernity be reduced to the spread of mass society alone. Modernity also brings with it new forms of social interaction, patterns of association, habits, and mores. For Arendt, this other dimension of modernity is significant on several counts. First, as a historian of anti-Semitism and totalitarianism, Arendt focuses on transformations occurring in these spheres of modern societies as they eventually lead to the formation of a mass society. Both the dialectics of identity/difference that lie at the root of modern anti-Semitism and the political power of totalitarianism are located by Arendt, the social and cultural historian, in this domain of modern society. This treatment requires further analysis. Second, this aspect of the social is important not only for Arendt the historian but for Arendt the political theorist as well. The kind of revitalization of public life that Arendt envisaged in her later work had at least two salient characteristics: on the one hand, Arendt was a political universalist, upholding egalitarian civil and political rights for all citizens while supporting nonconformism and the expression of pariahdom in social and cultural life; on the other hand, Arendt's call for a recovery of the public world is antistatist—indeed, we can complain that Arendt's philosophy as a whole suffers from a certain "state blindness." However, if such revitalization of public life does not mean the strengthening of the state but the growth of a political sphere independent of the state, where must this sphere be located, if not in civic and associational society?

My task in the next chapters will be to document the complexity of Arendt's account of modernity as this emerges from her historical writings and to explore the implications of this picture for her political philosophy as a whole.

Notes

1. One of Arendt's earliest publications is a book review of *Das Frauenproblem der Gegenwart* by Alice Ruehle-Gerstel, which appeared in the journal *Die Gesellschaft*, affiliated with the Weimar socialists (vol. 10, 1932, pp. 177-179); this review has recently been published in English under the title, "On the Emancipation of Women," in *Arendt: Essays in Understanding: 1930–1954*, ed. Jerome Kohn (New York: Harcourt Brace Jovanovich, 1994), pp. 66-68. In this review, Arendt matter-of-factly reports on the book's findings about continuing discrimination against women in the economic and political realms.

2. Elisabeth Young-Bruehl, *Hannah Arendt: For Love of the World* (New Haven, Conn.: Yale University Press, 1982), p. 238.

3. Hannah Arendt, *The Human Condition*, 8th ed. (Chicago: University of Chicago Press, 1973), p. 73. All future references in the text are to this edition and the title is abbreviated as *HC*.

4. A. Rich, "Conditions for Work: The Common World of Women," in *On Lies, Secrets, and Silence* (New York: Norton, 1979), p. 212.

5. See Hans-Georg Gadamer, *Truth and Method*, trans. Garrett Barden and John Cumming (New York: Seabury, 1975).

6. See Rich, "Conditions for Work," p. 212.

7. See bell hooks, *Feminist Theory From Margin to Center* (Boston: South End Press, 1984).

8. See Dagmar Barnouw, *Visible Spaces: Hannah Arendt and the German-Jewish Experience* (Baltimore: Johns Hopkins University Press, 1990), pp. 30-31.

9. I am using the 1974 edition of the English translation by Richard and Clara Winston, *Rahel Varnhagen: The Life of a Jewish Woman*, rev. ed. (New York: Harcourt Brace Jovanovich, 1974). All page references in the text are to this edition.

10. Sybille Bedford, "Emancipation and Destiny," in "Book Notes" in the *Reconstructionist*, December 12, 1958, as quoted in Barnouw, *Visible Spaces*, p. 48.

11. For the cultural and social background of Rahel Varnhagen and the Jewish salonnières in general, I have benefited greatly from Deborah Hertz's study, *Jewish High Society in Old Regime Berlin* (New Haven, Conn.: Yale University Press, 1988), p. 2.

12. For further discussion of the unusual character of Gentz, his anti-Semitism, and the subversive gender speculations of his letters, see Hannah Arendt, *Rahel Varnhagen*, pp. 80-81, and Marlis Gerhardt, "Einleitung: Rahel Levin, Friederike Robert, Madame Varnhagen," in *Rahel Varnhagen: Jeder Wunsch und Frivolität genannt: Briefe und Tagebücher* (Darmstadt: Luchterhand, 1983), pp. 22 ff. In 1803, Gentz writes to Rahel: "Do you know, my Dear, why our relationship has become so great and perfect? I will tell you why. You are an infinitely producing and I, an infinitely, receptive being. You are a great man; I am the first among all females who have ever lived. I know it: had I been a female physically, I had brought the whole world to kneel at my feet." As quoted by Gerhardt, "Einleitung," p. 23.

13. Preface, *Rahel Varnhagen*, p. xiii.

14. See Sybille Wirsing, "Urworte, nich orphisch, sondern weiblich," review of the *Gesammelte Werke* of Rahel Varnhagen in ten volumes, ed. Konrad Feilchenfeldt, Uwe Schweikert, and Rahel E. Steiner (Munich: Matthes and Seitz Verlag, 1983). The review appeared in *Frankfurter Allgemeine Zeitung*, no. 18 (January 21, 1984). This edition of Rahel's collected works is based on the early edition from the nineteenth century, originally edited by Rahel's husband, Karl August Varnhagen von Ense.

15. The themes of feeling alien, different, and other, the consciousness of oneself as a "pariah," as an outcast who does not fit in, as they are present in Varnhagen's as well as Hannah Arendt's own life, are explored by Ingeborg Nordmann in "Fremdsein ist gut: Hannah Arendt über Rahel Varnhagen," in *Rahel Levin Varnhagen: Die Weiderentdeckung einer Schriftstellerin*, ed. Barbara Hahn and Ursula Isselstein (Göttingen: Vandenhoeck & Ruprecht, 1987), pp. 196-207.

16. *Hannah Arendt-Karl Jaspers Briefwechsel*, ed. Lotte Köhler and Hans Saner (Munich: Piper Verlag, 1985), p. 46; English translation, *Hannah Arendt-Karl Jaspers Correspondence 1926–1969*, ed. Lotte Köhler and Hans Saner, trans. Robert and Rita Kimber (New York: Harcourt Brace Jovanovich, 1992), p. 10. On the whole, I have used the quite excellent English edition of the correspondence. All future references to the *Arendt-Jaspers Correspondence* are to this edition.

17. *Arendt-Jaspers Correspondence*, p. 10.

18. *Arendt-Jaspers Correspondence*, p. 11.

19. Arendt, *Rahel Varnhagen*, p. 48.

20. Arendt, *Rahel Varnhagen*, p. 212.

21. The continuing fascination with Rahel Varnhagen's life and letters, particularly given that interpretations of her work were developed in the light of different authors' perceptions of anti-Semitism and Jewish identity, has been analyzed by Konrad Feilchenfeldt, "Rahel Philologie im Zeichen der antisemitischen Gefahr (Margarete Sussman, Hannah Arendt, Käte Hamburger)," in *Rahel Levin Varnhagen,* ed. Hahn and Isselstein, pp. 187-195.

22. Hannah Arendt's story of Rahel Varnhagen has been interpreted as a sublimation of her love affair with Martin Heidegger; see Young-Bruehl, *For Love of the World,* pp. 58 ff. Although I do not deny that the pain caused by the end of her love affair with Martin Heidegger may have influenced Arendt's reconstruction of Rahel's innumerable heartbreaks, the Arendt-Jaspers correspondence, on which I draw in this chapter, suggests to me that a different set of existential concerns, namely, those about her Jewish identity, were at the center of this biography. Some of the details of this biographical background will be taken up in Chapter 2.

23. Arendt, *Rahel Varnhagen,* p. 21.

24. In her doctoral dissertation, "Der Liebesbegriff bei Augustin: Versuch einer philoso-phischen Interpretation" (Berlin: Julius Springer Verlag, 1929), Hannah Arendt focused on the tension between the otherworldly demands of Christian love and the this-worldliness of social life. Arendt quotes Augustine: "This world is for the faithful what the desert was for the people of Israel," and replies: "Would it not then be better to love the world in cupidity and be at home? Why should we make a desert out of this world?" (An English translation, titled *Love and St. Augustine: An Essay in Philosophical Interpretation,* was completed by E. B. Ashton—though never published—and can be found in the Hannah Arendt Papers in the Library of Congress, in containers 66 and 67. The citation here is to p. 033143. A new English translation is *Love and Saint Augustine,* ed., with an interpretive essay by Joanna V. Scott and Judith C. Stark, Chicago: University of Chicago Press, 1996.) In a forthcoming article, "Love and Worldliness: Hannah Arendt's Reading of St. Augustine," Ronald Beiner relies on this early work to argue that the fundamental structures of Arendt's political thought date back to an earlier phase of her thought, and that Arendt did not arrive at her preoccupa-tions as a political philosopher under the pressure of the traumatizing events of the 1930s and 1940s alone (in *Hannah Arendt: Twenty Years Later,* ed. Jerome Kohn and Larry May, forthcoming from MIT Press). Although I agree with Beiner that the concern with the themes of "world," "worldliness," "finding a home in the world" are at the origins of Arendtian philosophical thought, it is also clear that it was Martin Heidegger's philosophical influence that opened Arendt's eyes to the significance of these concepts. As I will document in the next two chapters, Arendt had already studied with Heidegger in Marburg from 1924 to 1926 before leaving for Heidelberg to complete her dissertation under the supervision of Karl Jaspers. What is unique in Arendt's achievement is the transformation of abstract epistemo-logical and ontological categories into conceptual grids through which the political phenom-ena of this century can be comprehended. See Chapter 2, and in particular the third section, "The Concept of the 'World' in Martin Heidegger's *Being and Time.*"

25. Hannah Arendt, "On Humanity in Dark Times: Thoughts About Lessing," in *Men in Dark Times* (New York: Harcourt Brace Jovanovich, 1968), p. 4.

26. Barnouw, *Visible Spaces,* p. 51.

27. Hertz, *Jewish High Society,* p. 3.

28. A very fine historical analysis of the transition from the reign of absolutism to the formation of Enlightenment modes of sociability, and the emergence of "society" as a sphere separate from the state and the church, has been recently provided by Daniel Gordon, *Citizens*

Without Sovereignty: Equality and Sociability in French Thought, 1670–1789 (Princeton, N.J.: Princeton University Press, 1994), pp. 9-43.

29. Hertz, *Jewish High Society*, pp. 14-15.

30. Hertz, *Jewish High Society*, p. 14.

31. See Peter Seibert, "Der Salon als Formation im Literaturbetrieb zur Zeit Rahel Levin Varnhagens," and Konrad Feilchenfeldt, "Die Berliner Salons der Romantik," both in *Rahel Levin Varnhagen*, ed. Hahn and Isselstein, pp. 164-172 and 152-163, respectively. The relation of the letter-writing form to "female" expressions of subjectivity is also explored by Petra Mitrovic, "Zum Problem der Konstitution von Ich-Identität in den Briefen der Rahel Varnhagen" (master's thesis, University of Frankfurt, Institut für Deutsche Sprache und Literatur, 1982).

32. Aristotle, *Nicomachean Ethics*, in *The Basic Works of Aristotle*, ed., with an introduction by Richard McKeon, 20th printing (New York: Random House, 1966), Bk. VIII, chap. 8, pp. 1068 ff.

33. The political dimensions of the salons in the age of the Enlightenment and the French Revolution have been discussed by Jürgen Habermas, *The Structural Transformation of the Public Sphere*, trans. T. Burger and F. Lawrence (Cambridge: MIT Press, 1989), and more recently from a perspective that takes gender differentials into account by Joan B. Landes, *Women and the Public Sphere in the Age of the French Revolution* (Ithaca, N.Y.: Cornell University Press, 1988).

34. Hertz, *Jewish High Society*, p. 18.

35. G. W. F. Hegel, "The System of Needs," in *Hegel's Philosophy of Right*, trans., with notes by T. M. Knox (Oxford: Oxford University Press, 1973), pp. 126 ff.

36. Karl Marx, "Manifesto of the Communist Party" (1848), in *The Portable Karl Marx*, ed. Eugene Kamenka (New York: Penguin, 1983), pp. 206-207.

37. See Jürgen Habermas, "Technology and Science as 'Ideology'," in *Toward a Rational Society*, trans. Jeremy J. Shapiro (Boston: Beacon, 1970), pp. 113 ff.

38. See Karl Marx, *Grundrisse: An Introduction to the Critique of Political Economy*, trans. Martin Nicolaus (Middlesex: Penguin, 1973), pp. 238-250; Marx, "On the Jewish Question," in *The Marx-Engels Reader*, ed. Robert C. Tucker (New York: Norton, 1972), pp. 26-53.

39. See Karl Polanyi, "Aristotle Discovers the Economy," in *Trade and Market in the Early Empires: Economics in History and Theory*, ed. Karl Polanyi, C. M. Arensberg, and Harry W. Peasner (Chicago: Regnerry, 1971).

40. See Maurice Godelier, *Perspectives in Marxist Anthropology*, trans. Robert Brain (London: Cambridge University Press, 1977), Pts. III and IV.

41. G. W. F. Hegel, *Natural Law*, trans. T. M. Knox; introduction by H. B. Acton (Philadelphia: University of Pennsylvania Press, 1975). The original German, *Ueber die wissenschaftliche Behandlungsarten des Naturrechts*, is dated from 1802–1803.

42. Max Weber, *The Theory of Social and Economic Organization*, ed., with an introduction by Talcott Parsons (New York: Free Press, 1964), pp. 115-118, 181-309, 324-341.

43. Michel Foucault, *Discipline and Punish: The Birth of the Prison*, trans. Alan Sheridan (New York: Pantheon, 1977).

44. See Daniel Gordon's statement: "Before the late seventeenth century, the word *société* did not refer to a durable and large-scale community. Instead, it referred to small associations and to the convivial life that took place within them. . . . Here *societe* appears to be more of

an activity than a space; a pastime among friends rather than a network of permanent relationships among a large mass of people." *Citizens Without Sovereignty,* p. 51.

45. For Arendt, this sharp distinction between the "social" and the "political" is crucial; it is at the heart of her complete universalism in the sphere of human rights and political institutions, and of her attempt to restrict the expression of "difference" to society alone. See below, Chapter 5, especially pp. 138-166.

46. Norbert Elias, *The Civilizing Process,* trans. E. Jephcott (Oxford, UK: Basil Blackwell, 1994).

2

Jewish Politics and German "Existenz Philosophy": The Sources of Hannah Arendt's Thought

Constructing a Homeland for a Worldless People

Hannah Arendt left Germany in the spring of 1933, after a brief encounter with the German police,[1] to settle in Paris. At this time, all but the last two chapters of the Varnhagen biography were complete. Having been intended possibly as her *Habilitationsschrift,* which was to embark her upon an academic career at a German university, this work, and the symbiosis of German-Jewish culture that Rahel and her circle represented, were rendered irrelevant by history. On January 1, 1933, Hitler and the National Socialist Party came to power. Politics, which Hannah Arendt had not been particularly interested in during her years as a student of philosophy, now became the overwhelming and inescapable fact of her life. Reflecting upon this reorientation of her existential interests, Hannah Arendt wrote much later to Karl Jaspers that in the intervening years since they had last corresponded, she had become something "between a historian and a political publicist."[2]

In discussing this period of her life, Elisabeth Young-Bruehl also comments that neither Hannah Arendt's temperament nor her inclination made her fit for political action and public life. Yet Arendt had encountered a form of politics and political action before the course of history had thrust her into it. During her student years, she became acquainted with and came under the considerable influence of Kurt Blumenfeld, a German Zionist leader.[3] Arendt's reflections on "the Jewish Question" preceded her entry into world politics.[4]

Already the last chapters of the Rahel Varnhagen biography, which were completed in exile in Paris, reveal this new orientation in her life. Chapter 12 of the Varnhagen biography introduces the categories of the "pariah" and the "parvenu," while the last chapter is titled significantly, "One Does Not Escape Jewishness."[5] Arendt observes,

> Rahel had remained a Jew and pariah. Only because she clung to both conditions did she find a place in the history of European humanity . . . [Heinrich] Heine's affirmation of Jewishness, the first and last resolute affirmation which was to be heard from an assimilated Jew for a long time, derived from the same reasons and the same feeling for truth as Rahel's negation. Both had never been able to accept their destiny serenely; both had never attempted to hide it behind big words or boastful phrases; both had always demanded an accounting.[6]

For Hannah Arendt and her generation, the "Jewish Question" meant something quite different than it had for the generation of Enlightenment Jews, of whom Rahel Varnhagen was a member. Arendt used Lessing's play *Nathan the Wise* to express this point. In her Lessing prize acceptance speech, with reference to the answer of Nathan the Wise, she writes: "As for the statement with which Nathan the Wise . . . countered the command: "Step closer, Jew"—the statement: I am a man—I would have considered nothing but a *grotesque and dangerous evasion of reality*."[7] The Enlightenment appeal to our common humanity; the faith that beneath the cloaks that culture, civilization, and society had imposed upon us, we all possessed fundamentally the same human nature and the same capacity for human reason; the search amidst a world of deception *(Verkehrung)* and displacement *(Entstellung)* for those few "kindred and like souls" with whom one could continue the "conversation of mankind"—this appeal, this faith, and this search appeared to Arendt, writing in 1959, to be a grotesque and dangerous evasion of reality.

For the generation of German Jewish intellectuals immediately preceding hers, and among whom she counted Franz Kafka, Karl Kraus, as well as Walter Benjamin, the "Jewish Question" had meant something different yet again: for this group of individuals, the "Jewish Question" referred primarily to the burden of the intellectuals who, although radically alienated from the spiritual content of Judaism, continued to experience their Jewishness as a "social fact."[8] On the one hand, there was the attitude of assimilated Jews, whose representatives wanted to remain Jews without wanting to acknowledge their Jewishness; on the other hand, there was the dilemma of the Jewish intellectuals who, in the words of Moritz Goldstein, "had to administer the intellectual property of a people which denies us the rights and the ability to do so."[9] This version of the Jewish question was thinkable only after political emancipation and the attainment of equal civil and political rights had allowed the Jews of Europe to participate in bourgeois society without, however, granting them full social recognition as legitimate members. This dilemma gave rise to two attitudes that Arendt, following the French journalist Bernard Lazare, had identified as those of the "pariah" and the "parvenu."[10] The pariah accepted the position of the outsider, and retained the otherness that bourgeois society continued to impose upon him or her, whereas the parvenu sought to overcome his or her outsider status and otherness either by denying difference altogether or by exaggerated identification with the values and behavior of that "genteel Christian society" whose recognition he or she sought. Under these circumstances, the "Jewish Question" was an issue of *social recognition*: how to be a full member of bourgeois society, from its commercial to its literary circles, without at the same time denying who one was.

For Hannah Arendt and her generation of German Jews, the "Jewish Question" was no longer one of social recognition as it had been in the late nineteenth and early twentieth centuries; and it had long ceased to be the search of the Enlightenment for mutual respect on the basis of one's shared humanity. In answering Nathan the Wise's question, "Who are you?" with the statement "A Jew," Arendt writes, "I was only acknowledging a political fact through which my being a member of this group outweighed all other questions of personal identity or rather had decided them in favor of anonymity, of namelessness."[11] This answer was not to be understood in an ontological sense, as if to be a Jew meant to be a special kind of human being (a form of thinking that Arendt attributed rather to the Nazis), nor did one thereby privilege a specific form of historical identity. For Arendt, this answer was primarily a *political* one: in the political realm, one "can resist only in terms of the identity that is under attack."[12]

To translate an "identity under attack" into a viable collective political project, and in particular to reconstruct Jewish collective identity in a form that would not repeat the bygone repertoire of political alternatives, such as Enlightenment cosmopolitanism, nineteenth-century assimilationism, or nineteenth-century nationalism, was Hannah Arendt's unrealized wish. When she left Germany in 1933, she was employed first by the Baronesse de Rothschild as a secretary. Later, she became the leading organizer of the Paris branch of the Jugend-Aliyah group, a Zionist organization that helped young emigrants prepare for life in Palestine.

After arriving in the United States in 1941, Arendt attempted to influence Jewish politics through articles and newspaper columns. In the period from 1941 to 1942, she advocated the formation of a Jewish army that would fight against the Nazis in cooperation with Allied forces.[13] Arendt's call for a Jewish army to enable the Jews to join the fight against Hitler "as a European people" expressed two concerns: she wanted the Jews to defend themselves politically, by fighting for themselves; she also hoped that such action would rid the Jewish people of long-established habits of dependence upon kings, courtiers, philanthropists, or pro-Semitic statesmen. Dependence upon the goodwill of non-Jewish others had characterized life in the Diaspora. To fight for one's rights as a people would allow the Jews to enter the public space of politics as independent and equal members; furthermore, Arendt was also hoping that after the defeat of Nazi Germany, there would be room in Europe for a Jewish homeland, as part of a Federation of European Peoples. This position brought Arendt into open conflict with two main streams in the Jewish politics of that period: on the one hand, she ran into conflict with those circles who saw in the efforts of the Allied forces alone the future hopes of the Jewish people; on the other hand, she became unpopular among Zionists, because she did not share their exclusive focus upon Palestine and their ideology of an "organic unity of the people" *(organischer Volkseinheit)*.[14]

As the extent of the crimes committed against the Jews, and the Holocaust perpetrated upon them, became clear, Arendt's hopes for a European solution of the Jewish question were destroyed. "The comity of European peoples went to pieces, when, and because, it allowed its weakest member to be excluded and persecuted."[15] With the foundation of the state of Israel in 1948, Arendt joined Judah Magnes's campaign for the establishment in Palestine of a federated state based on a common government but grounded in Jewish-Arab community councils. After the death of Judah Magnes that year, Arendt addressed a Jewish public in Massachusetts concerning his efforts.[16] She was booed and brought to silence. This event deeply discouraged her. Almost 15 years before the controversy over the Eichmann book, this event showed that there was no room in the Jewish politics of the times for Hannah Arendt's political views. She would become a self-conscious pariah in the Jewish community.

In the autumn of 1945, Arendt published a major essay in the Jewish journal *Menorah* titled "Zionism Reconsidered."[17] This essay is breathtaking not only for its political perspicacity—Arendt anticipates the dilemmas that were to plague Israeli-Arab relations for the next half century—but also for the synthesis of Jewish politics with the emergent categories of Arendt's mature political thought that it displays. Arendt begins the essay by commenting on the resolution of the American Zionist Congress, adopted in Atlantic City in October 1944, demanding that a "free and democratic Jewish commonwealth . . . shall embrace the whole of Palestine, undivided and undiminished."[18] Arendt notes in dismay that the fact that the Arab residents of Palestine were not mentioned suggests that they were forced to choose between voluntary emigration or second-class citizenship. With this resolution, she concludes, the more mainstream and moderate wing of the Zionist movement under the leadership of Chaim Weizmann and Ben-Gurion has given in to the demands of the extremists led by Jabotinsky.[19] "The Zionists," Arendt writes, "have now indeed done their best to create that insoluble 'tragic conflict' which can only be ended through cutting the Gordian knot" ("ZR," p. 132). Under the historical circumstances of the period, cutting the Gordian knot meant the partition of Palestine and the establishment of an independent Jewish state.

Arendt had political as well as theoretical reasons for doubting that a Jewish state in Palestine was viable. Politically, even as late as 1950, after the 1948 United Nations Resolution recognizing the partition of Palestine and the establishment of the state of Israel, she thought that such a state could only remain in existence by oppressing the Arab population within its borders and by perpetual belligerency against its neighbors. Continuing war with the Arab countries and increasing repression at home was the price she predicted the newly established state of Israel would have to pay. Furthermore, she saw it as inevitable that the Jewish minority in Palestine would ask for protection from outside powers against their neighbors ("ZR," p. 133). The belief that a Jewish state could only be established by brokering with the powers that be reflected, according to Arendt, a deep-seated tendency in European Zionism, as Theodor Herzl considered it, to act as a "broker" of Great Power interests, and to try to use the vacuum and the cracks that emerged in this process to further Jewish goals ("ZR," p. 153). Noting also the growing significance of American Jewry in the World Zionist Movement, and addressing the possible conflict of interests that may develop for this community between their "vital interests in Palestine as the homeland of the Jewish people" and their commitments as American citizens, Arendt anticipated a scenario that would begin to govern American foreign policy toward Israel after 1968. It is well known that the Soviet Union was the only major power in 1948 to support unequivocally the establishment of an independent Jewish state in Palestine;[20] during the Suez crisis of 1956, it was Britain and France, but not the United States, who acted as major powers in the region.[21] Anticipating the post-1968 development of U.S. foreign policy, Arendt writes,

> If Palestine Jewry could be charged with a share in the care-taking of American interests in that part of the world, the famous dictum of Justice Brandeis would indeed come true: you would have to be a Zionist in order to be a perfect American patriot. And why should this good fortune not come to pass? ("ZR," p. 159)

Unless and until the Jewish-Arab conflict in Palestine was settled, Arendt considered it inevitable that a Jewish state would have to rely on foreign superpowers to protect it, and would never become integrated into the "Mediterranean basin" ("ZR," p. 133).

Much of this is now history. In 1948, the state of Israel was established; indeed, continuing war with Israel's Arab neighbors, and the repression of the Palestinian Arab population within Israel and the occupied territories, ensued. The Soviet Union and the United States changed positions as key players in the conflict. The Soviet influence over the Arab regimes, particularly the military Ba'ath parties of Syria and Iraq, increased, while the American-Israeli friendship solidified and became one of the unquestioned cornerstones of U.S. foreign policy after 1968. Arendt anticipated with amazing clarity some of the key faults along which the major players in the area would move; but she was wrong in her judgment concerning the ability of the state of Israel to survive, with all its problems, as a more or less democratic entity, and in her evaluation of the tremendous historical and ethical importance of Israel for Jews all over the world.

In view of the historical realities of 1945, namely, the tremendous tragedy suffered by European Jewry and the near destruction of their collective identity, memory, and culture, it can be thought that Arendt should have been more sympathetic as well as realistic in her assessment of efforts to establish a Jewish home in Palestine. After all, the United States still did not allow mass Jewish immigration; the remaining Jewish population of Europe, the survivors and displaced persons from concentration camps, needed safety, security, a home, and a new world. In fact, Arendt draws a distinction between the idea of a *Jewish homeland* and the idea of a *Jewish nation-state*. Arendt's views on this issue are part and parcel of her theoretical and normative rejection of nationalism and the idea of a nation-state. This distinction, coupled with her critique of nationalism, makes her position more understandable.

In May 1948, Arendt wrote an essay called "To Save the Jewish Homeland: There Is Still Time."[22] The essay concludes with a set of programmatic goals that clearly articulate the distinction between the homeland and the nation-state. "The real goal of the Jews in Palestine," writes Arendt, "is the building up of a Jewish homeland. *This goal must never be sacrificed to the pseudo-sovereignty of a Jewish state*" ("JH," p. 192, emphasis added). Yet limited immigration in numbers and time is the only "irreducible minimum" in Jewish politics.[23] The independence of Palestine, according to Arendt, can be achieved only on a solid basis of Jewish-Arab cooperation. "Local self-government and mixed Jewish-Arab municipal and rural councils, on a small scale and as numerous as possible, are the only realistic political measures that can eventually lead to the political emancipation of Palestine" ("JH," p. 192). Extensive local democracy, in which Arabs and Jews participated commonly, and a federative state structure, integrated into a larger community of nations in the

Mediterranean,[24] were the only viable political structures that Arendt saw for a just and flourishing Jewish homeland in Palestine.

These proposals, although historically moot, are remarkable for a number of reasons. First, as we shall see in Chapter 5, Arendt advocated council democracy as the most defensible form of political participation on a number of different occasions. From her praise of the Jeffersonian ward model, to her support of the revolutionary councils of Paris in 1871 and the Kronstadt Sailors' Rebellion, Arendt had a deep and lasting philosophical support and political admiration for this form of government.[25] It is interesting to see that perhaps the earliest articulation in her thought of local council democracy emerges in the context of her reflections on Jewish-Arab politics in Palestine. Second, and equally noteworthy, is Arendt's skepticism toward the nation-state as a viable entity, and her reference to the "pseudosovereignty" of a Jewish state. The critique of nationalism, and skepticism toward the viability of the political sovereignty of nation-states, are at the heart of the deepest political conclusions Arendt drew from the European catastrophe.

From the beginning, Arendt criticized the Zionism of Theodor Herzl for its blind acceptance of the crudest form of European nationalist thinking, for its presumption that only the establishment of a Jewish state could end anti-Semitism, and for its Eurocentric arrogance in searching "for a country without a people for a people without a country" (Israel Zangwill).[26] Herzl's kind of Zionism belonged to those nineteenth-century political movements "that carried ideologies, *Weltanschauungen,* keys to history, in their portmanteaus" ("JH," p. 140). A key element in this ideology was the thesis that "the nation was an eternal organic body, the product of inevitable natural growth of inherent qualities; and it explains peoples, not in terms of political organizations, but in terms of biological superhuman personalities" ("JH," p. 156). For Arendt, this kind of thinking was prepolitical in its roots, because it applied metaphors from the domain of prepolitical "life," such as organic bodies, family unities, and blood communities, to the sphere of politics. Politics, for Hannah Arendt, is the realm of plurality, difference, perspectivity; political actors are not single entities but pluralities. Any ideology that denies this plurality can only do so via repression and injustice. All nationalisms, Zionism not excluded, are potentially repressive because they introduce into the political sphere categories of unity and homogeneity that can only lead to repression of difference and otherness.

Arendt distinguishes the grand French idea of the "sovereignty of the people" from "the nationalist claims of autarchical existence" ("JH," p. 156). The sovereignty of the people refers to the democratic self-organization and political will of a group of people, who may or may not be members of the same nationality, to constitute themselves as a self-governing and self-legislating body politic. Through such acts of sovereignty a nation is constituted—but as a self-legislating and self-governing collectivity, as a nation of citizens, as opposed to a nation of ethnic affiliation. Arendt is struggling with a distinction between *ethnos* and *demos*. The *demos* signifies the nation as a self-governing democratic body of citizens who may or may not be ethnically homogeneous, while the *ethnos* means the nation as an entity that is ethnically, linguistically, or religiously homogeneous. The conflict between the ethnos and the demos had been playing itself out in European political history since the French Revolution, and to the detriment of the idea of the demos, of the sovereign people.[27] Arendt was unwilling to support a movement among the Jewish people that would recapitulate these past errors of European nationalisms.

Arendt also criticizes nationalism for its political obsolescence. She makes the paradoxical observation that

> as for nationalism, it was never more evil or more fiercely defended than since it became apparent that this once great and revolutionary principle of the national organization of peoples could no longer either guarantee true sovereignty of the people within or establish a just relationship among different peoples beyond the national borders. ("JH," p. 141)

The end of the Austro-Hungarian and Ottoman empires after World War I had demonstrated to Arendt the tragedies as well as ineffectualities of the "nationalities system." The "successor states" established in the wake of these multinational empires created only more and more "stateless peoples" who were denaturalized by nationalist majorities in their home countries. Political absurdities, like the concept of a "state people," as opposed to national minorities, were also not uncommon in the mayhem that followed the collapse of the European order. The political and moral absurdities of trying to create ethnically homogeneous nation-states out of multinational societies is the theme of one of Arendt's most brilliant discussions in *The Origins of Totalitarianism*.[28] Her observation that nationalism becomes virulent when it becomes unviable must be understood in this context. Reflecting on the weaknesses of the nation-system in central and eastern Europe, Arendt saw in Herzlian Zionism a recipe for repeating these follies in Palestine. Add to this the Eurocentric hubris of considering Palestine a "country without a people," as if the Arabs of Palestine did not exist, and Arendt saw in Herzlian Zionism a recipe for disaster.

Arendt's critique of Herzlian Zionism was also linked to her critique of the antiprogressive and antidemocratic politics of top-down management implied in Herzl's vision.[29] Commenting on the different strands that went to constitute Zionism, Arendt writes,

> In sharp contrast to their eastern comrades, these western Zionists were no revolutionaries at all; they neither criticized nor rebelled against the social and political conditions of their time; on the contrary, they wanted only to establish the same set of conditions for their own people.[30]

Arendt admires the social-revolutionary zeal of the "Eastern comrades" among the Zionists, primarily the Jews of Poland and Russia, who were inspired by the German *Jugendbewegung* as well as by the ideas of Zionist revolutionary thinkers such as Ber Borochov.[31] These revolutionary Zionists sought a spiritual and moral regeneration of the Jewish people in the *Yishuv* (the Jewish settlements in Palestine). Their goal was to create a new Jewish community, freed from the distortions, neuroses, character perversions, and social ugliness caused by living as an oppressed and dispersed people in the Diaspora. In her 1945 essay, Arendt is clearly skeptical toward this movement, even if more admiring of it than of Herzlian Zionism. Her admiration for this movement is expressed in her judgment that

> they did succeed in creating a new type of Jew, even a new kind of aristocracy with their newly established values; their genuine contempt for material wealth, exploitation and bourgeois life; their unique combination of culture and labor; their rigorous realization of social justice within their

small circle; and their loving pride in the fertile soil, the work of their hands, together with an utter and surprising lack of any wish for personal possession. ("ZR," p. 138)

Her skepticism toward this movement is based on the pioneers' lack of interest in *Realpolitik,* their inability to think of new and fresh solutions to the Arab-Jewish conflict, and their insistence on not employing Arab labor. Originally intended to prevent the exploitation of the local population and to teach the "people of the Book" to become farmers and laborers, this decision not to employ Arab labor in the settlements exacerbated economic differences between the two communities as well as preventing the sharing of higher standards of agriculture and technological know-how between the Jewish settlers and the Arab farmers. Arendt concludes with regard to this group that "in a sense, indeed, they were too decent for politics" ("JH," p. 138).[32]

In her reflections on the pioneers of the Kibbutz movement, we find echoes of Arendt's commentary on Rahel Varnhagen and her circle: lack of realistic political judgment about the world, romantic inwardness that concentrates more on saving the soul and one's small circle of friends than the larger world. This lack of realism, coupled with a tendency toward Messianic outbursts, gave Jewish history, until the catastrophe of the Holocaust, its peculiarly "unworldly" character.[33] Commenting on the Messianic movement of Sabbatai Zvi in the sixteenth century, and its ignoble end—Zvi converted to Islam when confronted with the *force majeur* of the Ottoman sultan—Arendt sees the collapse of this movement in catastrophic terms. "From now on, the Jewish body politic was dead and the people retired from the public scene of history."[34] However, it was not only the great wars of Europe and the Holocaust that would return Jewish people to "the public scene of history." By a curious dialectical twist, Arendt sees in Jewish mysticism the sources of popular action expressed through the hopes for world redemption and the return to Zion. Nonetheless, tempering revolutionary Messianism with a worldly politics, which would be based upon the principles of equal respect and democratic self-governance among Jews and Arabs, remained the unrealized task of Jewish politics in the 1940s.

When Hannah Arendt reflected upon Jewish politics in the 1940s, her thinking was decidedly modernist and universalist. She searched for political structures that would create a homeland for a part of the Jewish people in Palestine, structures that would not recapitulate the blindness of European nationalism and the worldlessness of Diaspora Judaism. It was important for her to find a political form for a Jewish homeland that would transcend the European conflict between the "nation" and the "modern state." As she would elaborate subsequently in *The Origins of Totalitarianism,* although the modern states established after the American and French Revolutions made the recognition of the individual as a rights-bearing person the basis of their legitimacy, nationalist developments in Europe in particular revealed that one's right to be a person was only safeguarded insofar as one was a member of a specific nation.

> From the beginning, the paradox involved in the declaration of the inalienable human rights was that it reckoned with an "abstract" human being who seemed to exist nowhere. . . . The whole question of human rights, therefore, was quickly and inextricably blended with the question of national emancipation; only the emancipated sovereignty of the people, of one's own people, seemed to be able to insure them. (*OT,* p. 291)

Arendt remained a political modernist insofar as she pleaded for the fulfillment of this basic principle of political modernity, that is, one's recognition of *the right to have rights* simply because one was a member of the human species. The political movement of the Jewish people to establish a homeland should not abrogate this principle of political modernity.

Analyzing Arendt's writings on Jewish politics, we see how deeply she was involved in these events and how passionately she thought about twentieth-century political issues as they affected not only Jews but other peoples as well. Her prescient insistence on the need to find a political solution to the Israeli-Palestinian conflict, her critique of nationalism, her plea for local democracies protected by federated structures, her observation that it does not suffice to save one's soul if the world around one is going up in flames and ashes, and her search for a worldly and just public political space for the Jews are all themes that resonate deeply with her mature political thought. The themes of the perspectivality and essential plurality of the political, the cultivation of "worldliness" as a quality of political judgment and action, and faith in the political capacity of the common people to determine their fate are cornerstones of Arendt's search for a recovery of the public world in the twentieth century. I have emphasized Arendt's little known essays on Zionism and Jewish politics to reveal the depth of her commitment to political modernism and universalism, and to indicate some of the little known sources of the concepts of world, worldliness, and the public sphere in her thought.

When Hannah Arendt left Germany to go to Paris in 1933, she had been a student of classical German philosophy as well as a young Jewess caught in the throes of history. Any presentation of her thought that does not emphasize the formative experience of German philosophy as well as of Jewish politics would be grossly inadequate, because German "Existenz philosophy" of the 1920s, and in particular the thought of Martin Heidegger, as well as her political experiences as a German Jewish intellectual, are the dual sources of her philosophy. And it is the tension between these traditions of thought and value, and the continuing attempt to renegotiate their legacy, that make Hannah Arendt's political theory so vibrant.

What Is "Existenz Philosophy"?

In 1946, Arendt published an essay in *Partisan Review* with the title, "What Is Existenz Philosophy?"[35] This essay is one among others in which she attempts to explain the main tenets and legacy of European, and particularly classical German, philosophy to American audiences.[36] She was shy about trying her hand at philosophy again after having written on politics, culture, and history for several years. In a letter to Karl Jaspers, she explains that she was also nervous about sending this essay to her old teacher.[37] A wide-ranging and largely expository essay, this piece analyzes the historical and cultural roots of *Existenz philosophy.* By this term, Arendt understands those currents in German philosophy, originating with Immanuel Kant, that principally deny the identity of thought and being. In Kant's theory of knowledge, the concepts of our understanding, for example, cause and substance, are radically distinguished from the sensory impressions that originate in our sense organs and that Kant names the "material of our intuitions." Although I can identify this bottle of wine, let us say, to be a Bordeaux 1989 only via the use of concepts such as those of substance, which allow me to designate a distinct object as this bottle of wine in space and time, the use of such concepts as "Bordeaux 1989" can never be a substitute for the taste of this wine on my palate. The "that" of our conceptual apparatus can never explain the "what" of our sense perceptions. Despite Hegel's efforts to restore the ancient unity of thought and being, much modern philosophy in the post-Hegelian period proceeds from the failure to synthesize and to reestablish the unity of thought and being.

> The unity of Being and thought presupposed the preestablished coincidence of essence and existence, that, namely, everything thinkable also exists and every existent, because it is knowable, must also be rational. This unity was destroyed by Kant, the true, if also clandestine, founder of the new philosophy: who has likewise remained till the present time its secret king.[38]

Arendt views Kant as the "clandestine founder of the new philosophy" not only because Kant established the irreducible opposition of thought and being, concept and intuition, but also because, in doing so, Kant subjugated man himself to a set of dualisms and antagonisms. Because humans are creatures of thought and matter, in epistemological terms, they possess both concepts and sensory impressions, which Kant calls *"Anschauungen,"* intuitions. As bodies in space and time, they, like all matter, are subjected to the laws of motion of the natural sciences: they are determined, in ways that are obscure and unintelligible to them, by forces in nature. But they are also creatures of reason, who can determine their own actions on the basis of principles that they alone formulate. Humans are creatures of freedom insofar as they determine their actions in accordance with general principles that they themselves have articulated; however, as material bodies and as creatures in space and time, they are subject to the laws of nature.

> Man, free in himself, is hopelessly surrendered to the course of nature alien to him, a fate contrary to him, destructive of his freedom. . . . While Kant made Man the master and measure of Man, at the same time he lowered him to a slave of Being. Every new philosopher since Schelling has protested against this devaluation.[39]

Returning in "What Is Existenz Philosophy?" to a theme that dominated her Varnhagen biography as well as her reflections on Jewish politics,

Arendt now uncovers the sources of the "modern feeling of homelessness in the world" (p. 35) as these become manifest in modern philosophy. Rendered insecure after Kant concerning the capacity of reason to go beyond its limits, caught between the world of causality and natural laws on the one hand, and the world of freedom and rationality on the other, modern man no longer has "a home in this world" (p. 35). Arendt continues,

> However one may interpret this homelessness sociologically or psychologically, its philosophical basis lies in the fact that though the functional context of the world, in which also I myself am involved, can always justify and explain that there are, for example, tables and chairs generally, nevertheless it can never make me grasp conceptually that *this* table *is*. And it is the existence of *this* table, independent of tables in general, which evokes the philosophical shock.[40]

Arendt, in one of the nicest turns of phrase in the history of twentieth-century philosophy, interprets Husserlian phenomenology as an attempt to "evoke magically a home again out of the world which has become alien" (p. 36).

The concept of the "world," and its opposite "worldlessness," are the leitmotifs of Arendt's early political as well as philosophical thought. What will dominate Arendt's later thinking are neither the epistemological problems created by the Kantian dualisms nor the failed Hegelian synthesis of Being and Thought. Furthermore, Arendt was not really interested in the Husserlian attempt to reestablish magic in the world by gaining access to the "phenomena themselves" through the analysis of the intentional structures of consciousness. Nor was she taken by neo-Kantian developments in the logic and philosophy of science, such as those initiated by Heinrich Rickert[41] and Max Weber,[42] and in which her own teacher of philosophy, Karl Jaspers, was schooled. Rather, it was the moral, political, and cultural dimensions of "homelessness in the modern world" that fascinated her. After Kant, philosophy defied the dualisms and dichotomies of human existence by choosing one horn of the dilemma: either it accepted fate and the forces of history as determinants of human action, as was the case with Hegel's philosophy of history and Marx's transformation of it, or philosophy dwelled on the inscrutability, ultimate absurdity, and contingency of human existence. If human reason is limited, if man can never escape being subject to the forces of nature, if freedom is a "fact of reason" (Kant) for which no further rational proof can be given, then the individual cannot help but be drawn to those "limit" situations and conditions *(Grenzsituationen)* in which the antinomies of human existence reveal themselves most forcefully. Arendt explains,

> *Death* is the guarantee of the *principium individuationis,* since death, as the most common of occurrences, nevertheless strikes me unavoidably alone. *Contingency* as guarantee of reality as only given, which overwhelms and persuades me precisely through its incalculability and irreducibility to thought. *Guilt* as the category of all human activity which is wrecked not upon the world but upon itself, insofar as I always take responsibilities upon myself which I cannot overlook, and am compelled through my decisions themselves to neglect other activity. Guilt is thus the mode and the manner in which I myself become real, plunge into reality.[43]

The themes of death, contingency, and guilt dominate Existenz philosophy after Kant and Hegel; they are at the heart of Søren Kierkegaard's, Friedrich Nietzsche's, Karl Jaspers's, Jean-Paul Sartre's, and Martin Heidegger's philosophies. In the subsequent development of existentialism out of Existenz philosophy, what is lost is not only the confidence of human reason to be at home with the things of this world but, more significantly, the shared human world, the world of human affairs, actions, and stories. The individual of Existenz philosophy is the Self. Arendt notes: "The 'Self' has entered in place of Man" (p. 48).

A central thesis of my interpretation of Hannah Arendt is that the recovery of the public world of politics in her thought was not only a political project but a philosophical one as well. Arendt herself, as well as her commentators, have failed to note *the philosophical significance* of her search for a recovery of the public world. Although not an epistemologist and not interested in issues of epistemology, in her eventual rejection of Existenz philosophy and in her transformation of the Heideggerian concept of the "world," Arendt restored "being-in-the-world-with," or the condition of human plurality, to the center of our experience of worldliness. The discovery of human plurality as a fundamental existential condition is Arendt's real answer to the Existenz philosophy in which she was schooled, and to its most forceful representative, namely, Martin Heidegger. The discovery of human plurality will allow

Arendt to undertake fundamental revisions in the concepts of human action and identity and finally in the category of the "world" itself.

The Concept of the "World" in
Martin Heidegger's *Being and Time*

Hannah Arendt had arrived in Marburg to study philosophy in 1924. She studied with Martin Heidegger as well as Nicolai Hartmann and Rudolf Bultmann during this time.[44] During the winter semester of 1923–1924, Heidegger was developing themes and lectures that subsequently were to constitute the core of *Being and Time*. Arendt attended these seminars and lectures on Aristotle's notion of *aletheia* (truth) and Plato's *Sophist*. In 1925, she had been not only Heidegger's student but his lover as well. She left Marburg in the fall of 1925 to study with Husserl, and did not return; instead, she proceeded to Heidelberg to study with Karl Jaspers.

In my reconstruction of Hannah Arendt's indebtedness to Heidegger, I take my cue from a 1954 lecture titled "Concern With Politics in Recent European Philosophical Thought."[45] In a note appended to the first version of the text, Arendt writes, "It is almost impossible to render a clear account of Heidegger's political thoughts that may be of political relevance without an elaborate report on his concept and analysis of 'world.'"[46] Arendt thought that with the fundamental analysis of being human in terms of "being-in-the-world," Heidegger had created an unprecedented possibility for the philosopher to think about the political realm; and at the same time, through his own phenomenological account of what constitutes being-in-the-world, so Arendt claimed, Heidegger expressed "the old prejudices of the philosopher against politics as such."[47] How are we to understand the claim that Heidegger's concept of the world opens up and yet also closes down philosophical access to the phenomena of the political?

As is well-known, Heidegger maintained that human beings are the only kind of beings in nature for whom the question of being has constitutive significance. The most primordial condition, in the phenomenological sense of being the most basic and all-pervasive, and not in the empirical sense of being the first in time, is that of being-there, *Dasein*, at a certain locality in space and time. But how is this thereness of Dasein to be characterized? Heidegger's answer here is that the individual is always already in-the-world, in an environment, in an *Umwelt*, constituted by everyday concerned involvement with things. "Because Being-in-the-world belongs essentially to *Dasein*, its being towards the world is essentially concern" ["Weil zu Dasein wesenhaft das In-der-Welt-sein gehört, ist sein Sein zur Welt wesenhaft Besorgen"].[48] The world is the totality of those contexts of involvement with the things and affairs around one; it is the *Um-welt* (literally, "the world around one") in which one orients oneself by signs that are taken for granted, by references that are treated as recognized, by trust in the way in which the things of the world, and particularly equipment and gadgets, function. These are the first constituents of the analytic of Dasein's being-in-the-world as laid out in the opening sections of *Being and Time*.

It is hard to see why these abstract categories of concerned being-in-the-world should have any relation to the political realm and in particular why they should allow philosophical access to the political. The object of critique of these early analyses in *Being and Time* is the entire epistemological tradition from Descartes to Kant.[49] In the epistemological tradition, the mode of being of the I is reduced to that of the knower (the epistemological subject), whereas the mode of being of the world is treated in terms of the categories of "objecthood." A *res cogitans* faces a *res extensa*. It is assumed that the primordial mode of being-in-the-world is the act of cognition through which two substances of different kinds interact with one another.[50] In displacing this cognitive model through the model of concerned being-in-the-world, Heidegger opens up new avenues for much of twentieth-century philosophy.[51]

As abstract as Heidegger's categories are, the analytic of Dasein explicated in terms of concerned being-in-the-world allows Heidegger access to the "phenomena." He can allow the appearances to appear, to shine forth in their everydayness. Not only Hannah Arendt but thinkers as diverse as Herbert Marcuse and Günther Anders all experienced at this time the sheer phenomenological and descriptive power of the seemingly abstract and empty categories that initiated *Being and Time*.[52]

Arendt retained a lifelong admiration and respect for this aspect of Heidegger's thought, namely, its capacity to let the phenomena shine through. Yet, precisely in his analysis of the further determinations of the analytic of the category of the "world," she thought that Heidegger failed to live up to his own best insights. This is also the path to the political that is opened up and closed off. The crucial thesis here is simple:

> By reason of this with-like Being-in-the-world, the world is always the one that I share with Others. The world of *Dasein* is a with-world. Being-in is Being-with-Others. Their Being-in-themselves within-the-world is *Dasein*-with. [Auf dem Grunde dieses *mithaften* In-der-Welt-seins ist die Welt je schon immer die, die ich mit den Anderen teile. Die Welt des Daseins ist *Mitwelt*. Das In-Sein ist *Mitsein* mit Anderen. Das innerweltliche Ansichsein dieser ist *Mitdasein*].[53]

For Arendt, this was Heidegger's fundamental insight. Heidegger makes being-with-others a constitutive dimension of the thereness of Dasein in the world: *"die Welt ist nie nur eine Umwelt, es ist immer auch ein Mitwelt* [the world is never just the world around one, it is always also the world we share with others]." In Arendt's later terminology, the world is always a world shared with others because "plurality" is the fundamental human condition, that is, because humans inhabit a space with others to whom they are both equal and from whom they are distinct. Plurality, for Hannah Arendt, is expressed through in speech: "Speech corresponds to the fact of distinctness and is the actualization of the human condition of plurality, that is, of living as a distinct and unique being among equals."[54] But this is precisely the step that Heidegger does not take: although the world is always a world shared with others, although *Mitsein* is a fundamental condition of Dasein, the most authentic form for Dasein (i.e., that condition through which the meaning of being human is revealed) is not Mitsein but being-unto-death, the awareness of Dasein's temporality and finitude. Forms of Mitsein are inauthentic; they represent the fallenness of Dasein into the chatter *(die Gerede)* of the everyday world and its disappearance in the experience of the anonymous *das Man*. In Heidegger's well-known words:

> Distantiality, averageness, and leveling down, as ways of Being for the "they," constitute what we know as "publicness" *[die Öffentlichkeit]*.

Publicness proximally controls every way in which the world and *Dasein* get interpreted, and it is always right—not because there is some distinctive and primary relationship-of-Being in which it is related to "Things," or because it avails itself of some transparency on the part of *Dasein* which it has explicitly appropriated, but because it is insensitive to every difference of level and of genuineness and thus never gets to the "heart of the matter." By publicness everything gets obscured [das Licht der Öffentlichkeit verdunkelt alles], and what has thus been covered up gets passed off as something familiar and accessible to everyone.[55]

In her long struggle with Heidegger's thought and politics,[56] Arendt offered two different readings of these passages: in her early article, "What Is Existenz Philosophy?" of 1946, she interpreted such passages and others like them in which Heidegger reduced every form of human plurality to a form of inauthentic existence, as being the intrinsic sources of his sympathy for National Socialism. Arendt writes of Dasein:

The essential character of the Self is its absolute Self-ness, its radical separation from all its fellows. . . . The self in the form of conscience (*Gewissen*) has taken the place of humanity, and being-a-Self has taken the place of being human. . . . Later, and after the fact, Heidegger has drawn on mythologizing and muddled concepts like "folk" and "earth" in an effort to supply his isolated Selves with a shared, common ground to stand on. But it is obvious that concepts of this kind can only lead us out of philosophy and into some kind of nature-oriented superstition. If it does not belong to the concept of man that he inhabits the earth together with others of his kind, then all that remains for him is a mechanical reconciliation by which the atomized Selves are provided with a common ground that is essentially alien to their nature. All that can result from that is the organization of these Selves intent only on themselves into an Over-self in order somehow to effect a transition from resolutely accepted guilt to action.[57]

Nearly a decade and a half later, in 1969, a different interpretation of the relation between Heidegger's philosophy and politics emerges. Announced already in the lecture "Concern With Politics in Recent European Philosophical Thought,"[58] this reading holds that the presentation of Mitsein in terms of the experience of lonely individuals in a mass society reflects the contempt toward politics ingrained in the Western philosophical tradition. In a footnote that is no doubt flattering to Heidegger, even

when it appears to be damning, Arendt likens Heidegger's sympathies
for National Socialism, his joining the party and acting as rector in
Freiburg University, to Plato's sympathies for the tyrants of Sicily. Rising
to the ceremonial occasion for which this piece was written, a *Festschrift*
for Heidegger's eightieth birthday, Arendt concludes,

> We who wish to honor the thinkers, even if our own residence lies in the
> midst of the world, can hardly help finding it striking and perhaps exasper-
> ating that Plato and Heidegger, when they entered into human affairs,
> turned to tyrants and Führers. This should be imputed not just to the
> circumstances of the times and even less to preformed character, but rather
> to what the French call a *déformation proféssionelle.* . . . For the wind that
> blows through Heidegger's thinking—like that which still sweeps toward
> us after thousands of years from the work of Plato—does not spring from
> the century he happens to live in.[59]

Arendt forgave Heidegger his mistake; we may say that she even
rationalized it by presenting it in such lofty terms. Yet the 1946 critique
that establishes an internal, and not merely a contingent, relation between
the categories of Heidegger's fundamental ontology and the experience
of political authoritarianism cuts deeper. Here Arendt formulates an insight that is also crucial in her analysis of totalitarianism: namely, that
societal atomization; the breakdown of civic, political, cultural associations and the loneliness of atomized masses, prepares them for the recep-
tion of authoritarian and totalitarian movements. These conditions are
necessary even if not sufficient for the emergence of totalitarian regimes.
Heidegger's Dasein can give himself over to a *Führer,* or for that matter
to the Central Committee of the party, because atomized existence in a
mass society, the disappearance of social networks and associations into
which the individual is inserted, deprive such selves of fundamental
attributes of worldliness.

The worldlessness of this experience derives from several features: the
world is constituted by our common and shared experiences of it; we can
be in the world to the degree to which we implicitly trust that the
orientations we follow are more or less also followed by others. This
commonness of the world is the background against which the plurality
of perspectives that constitute the political can emerge. Politics requires
a background commonality and the recognition of the plurality and

perspectivality of the judgment of those who share this background commonality. It is over and against such a background that political action can unfold. Political action, action in concert, presupposes civic and political equality as well as the expression of the new and the unprecedented, the expression of that moment that distinguishes the doer from all others. Such an experience of the world signifies that individuals share in common a "public realm," a space of appearances in the world, constituted by the interplay of commonality and perspectivality, equality and distinction.

Although Heidegger, through his analysis of Dasein's worldliness as a form of Mitsein, made the experience of human plurality constitutive of the human condition, the fundamental categories of his existential analytic, rather than illuminating human plurality, testified to the progressing atomization, loneliness, and increasing worldlessness of the individual in the Weimar period in the 1920s. At least in one of her interpretive tracks toward Heidegger's ontology, Arendt shared the judgment of other students of Heidegger's such as Herbert Marcuse, who saw in *Being and Time* not the fundamental and history-transcending categories but an implicit cultural sociology of Weimar, and the premonition of a world in disarray.[60]

Notes

1. Hannah Arendt was arrested and detained by the police for eight days because she was collecting materials in the Prussian State Library on the extent of anti-Semitic actions in nongovernmental organizations, business associations, and professional circles. She was doing this work at the request of her friend Kurt Blumenfeld, who in turn was preparing this material to present it at the 18th Zionist Congress. See Elisabeth Young-Bruehl, *For Love of the World* (New Haven, Conn.: Yale University Press, 1982), for further details on the circumstances pertaining to Arendt's arrest, pp. 105 ff. See note 3 below on Kurt Blumenfeld.

2. Arendt's letter of November 18, 1945, to Karl Jaspers in *Arendt-Jaspers Correspondence*, Letter 31, p. 23.

3. See Young-Bruehl's discussion of Kurt Blumenfeld, and Hannah Arendt's first encounter with him during his visit in 1926 to the Zionist student club at the University of Heidelberg, in *For Love of the World*, pp. 70 ff. Before 1933, notes Young-Bruehl, Arendt was struck by Blumenfeld's analysis of the difficulties of Jewish responses to anti-Semitism, but emigration to Palestine or an exclusive focus on the rebirth of the Jewish nation in the *Yishuv* were never a part of her life plans (p. 73). Cf. *Hannah Arendt–Kurt Blumenfeld, Die Korrespondenz*, edited by Ingeborg Nordmann and Iris Philling (Nördlingen: Rotbuch, 1995).

4. In her letter of September 7, 1952, to Karl Jaspers, reflecting upon this period of her life and the Rahel Varnhagen biography, Arendt writes, "It was written from the perspective of a Zionist critique of assimilation, which I had adopted as my own and which I still consider basically justified today. . . . By virtue of my background I was simply naive. I found the so-called Jewish question boring. The person who opened my eyes in this area was Kurt Blumenfeld, who then became a close friend and still is." *Arendt-Jaspers Correspondence,* Letter 135, p. 197.

5. Arendt, *Rahel Varnhagen,* pp. 199-228.

6. Ibid., p. 227.

7. Arendt, "On Humanity in Dark Times: Thoughts About Lessing," in *Men in Dark Times* (New York: Harcourt Brace Jovanovich, 1968), pp. 17-18.

8. Arendt, "Walter Benjamin," in *Men in Dark Times,* pp. 183-184.

9. Moritz Goldstein, "Deutsch-Jüdischer Parnass," as quoted in *Men in Dark Times,* pp. 183-184.

10. See Arendt, *The Jew as Pariah: Jewish Identity and Politics in the Modern Age,* ed., an introduction by, Ron Feldman (New York: Grove, 1978). For Bernard Lazare, see *Job's Dungheap: Essays on Jewish Nationalism and Social Revolution,* with a "Portrait of Bernard Lazare" by Charles Peguy; trans. Harry Lorin Binsse; and preface by Hannah Arendt (New York: Schocken, 1948), pp. 65, 84-86. Lazare writes in a tone of messianic and emotional nationalism, which is actually quite alien to Arendt's more cerebral prose: "If the Jew did not exist as an outlet for the wrath of those who are despoiled, and thus as savior of the strongboxes anointed with the waters of baptism, certainly he would be invented. He is a pariah; emancipated or not, he will always be useful as a scapegoat for the Christian nations. So it is as an outcast that he must defend himself, through duty to his own being, for every human creature must know how to resist oppression and preserve his right to total development, his freedom to be and *to be himself*" (p. 85, emphasis in original).

11. Arendt, "On Humanity in Dark Times," in *Men in Dark Times,* p. 18.

12. Ibid., p. 18.

13. Arendt expressed this view in several articles written for the German-language daily *Aufbau* from 1941 to 1942; see "Die jüdische Armee: Der Beginn einer jüdischen Politik" ("The Jewish Army: The Beginning of a Jewish Politics"), in *Aufbau,* November 14, 1941, pp. 1-2; "Die 'sogenannte Jüdische Armee,' " in *Aufbau,* May 2, 1942, p. 20; "Von der Armee zur Brigade," in *Aufbau,* October 6, 1944, pp. 15-16. As Young-Bruehl documents, this call for a Jewish army temporarily landed Arendt in odd company. At the time, there was also a Committee for a Jewish Army, based in New York, and created by three Palestinian Jews of the extremist Revisionist Party and their leader Vladimir Ze'ev Jabotinsky. When Arendt and Joseph Maier, her colleague from the *Aufbau,* realized that the Committee for a Jewish Army was a Revisionist front, they formed a group of their own called Die jungjüdische Gruppe. The group met from March until June 1942 in New York. In a March 6, 1942, article, Arendt called the Revisionists, of whom Menachem Begin and Yitzhack Shamir were members, "Jewish fascists." See *For Love of the World,* pp. 173-180; see also Jeffrey Isaac's interesting discussion in *Arendt, Camus, and Modern Rebellion* (New Haven, Conn.: Yale University Press, 1992), pp. 206-216.

14. Martin Buber's essay "Nationalism" is an interesting case here. Buber attempts to distinguish between legitimate and illicit forms of nationalism, and between chauvinistic and justifiable concepts of a "people," but many of his formulations still bear the marks of a certain Romantic organicism. See his statements, for example: "peoples, that is, a new organic order growing out of the natural forms of the life of the people"; or a people "develops

as a living substance." Martin Buber, "Nationalism" (September 1921), in *A Land of Two Peoples: Martin Buber on Jews and Arabs,* ed., with commentary by Paul R. Mendes-Flohr (New York: Oxford University Press, 1983), pp. 48, 50-51, respectively.

15. Arendt, "Wir Flüchtlinge," in *Hannah Arendt Zur Zeit: Politische Essays* (Berlin: Rotbuch Verlag, 1986), p. 21 (originally published in 1943 as "We Refugees" in the *Menorah Journal*; reprinted in *The Jew as Pariah,* pp. 55-67); here p. 66.

16. See Young-Bruehl, *For Love of the World,* pp. 233 ff., for details.

17. There is a discrepancy in the scholarly literature about the precise date of publication of this essay. Young-Bruehl lists it as August 1945; see *For Love of the World,* p. 539; in *The Jew as Pariah,* ed. Feldman, it is listed as October 1944, p. 131. The correct date of publication of "Zionism Reconsidered" is *Menorah Journal* 32, no. 2 (October-December 1945), pp. 162-196 (abbreviated as "ZR" in the text).

18. Reprinted in *The Jew as Pariah,* p. 131.

19. Vladimir (Ze'ev) Jabotinsky (1880–1940) formulated the tenets of his revisionism after leaving the executive board of the Zionist council in 1923. In his view, it was not Zionism that needed to be revised but its current policies. "Jabotinsky and his followers were maximalists, claiming not only Palestine for the Jews but 'the gradual transformation of Palestine (including Transjordan) into a self-governing commonwealth under the auspices of an established Jewish majority.' " See Walter Laqueur, *A History of Zionism* (New York: Holt, Rinehart & Winston, 1972), p. 347. Laqueur also recounts that among Jabotinsky's followers, voices sympathetic to German and Italian fascism (without their anti-Semitism, of course) became increasingly loud after 1932, and titles this particular discussion, "Jewish Fascism?" pp. 361 ff.

20. See Laqueur, *A History of Zionism.* Laqueur observes that whereas American support for the Zionist cause was often ambiguous, "much to the surprise of the Zionists, the Soviet attitude was much more positive" (p. 578). Great Britain, the Arab countries (as expected), most Asian nations, and the State Department were all opposed to the 1947 partition plan (p. 581). Ultimately, "a hesitating President Truman gave his assent to the partition scheme on October 9, 1947" (p. 582).

21. "There was general agreement that any operation [against Nasser–SB] should be undertaken by the end of October. . . . To invade toward the end of the American election campaign. The participants assumed that Eisenhower would not oppose Israel and risk the Jewish vote so near to election day. Representatives of Israel, France, and Great Britain met secretly in France." Charles Smith, *Palestine and the Arab-Israeli Conflict* (New York: St. Martin's, 1988), p. 173.

22. In *The Jew as Pariah,* pp. 178-192. This essay originally appeared in *Commentary* 5 (May 1948), pp. 398-406. In subsequent references, the title is abbreviated as "JH."

23. Ibid., p. 193 (inverted commas in the original text).

24. The idea of a confederation of "Mediterranean peoples" is articulated by Arendt several times in the "Zionism Reconsidered" essay. See pp. 163 ff.

25. In *On Revolution,* Arendt writes, "Both Jefferson's plan and the French *sociétés révolutionnaires* anticipated with an almost weird precision those councils, *soviets* and *Räte,* which were to make their appearance in every genuine revolution throughout the nineteenth and twentieth centuries. Each time they appeared, they sprung up as the spontaneous organs of the people, not only outside of all revolutionary parties, but entirely unexpected by them and their leaders" (New York: Viking, 1963), p. 252 (hereafter abbreviated as *OR*). Arendt

was no doubt more than a little optimistic in overlooking the quasi-feudal structures of authority that prevailed among the Arab population of Palestine, and in seeing germs of democracy in the prevailing local councils.

26. This phrase is attributed to Israel Zangwill as "the land without people—for the people without land" in Amos Elon, *The Israelis: Founders and Sons* (New York: Holt, Rinehart & Winston, 1971), p. 149. The actual Israel Zangwill quote reads, "Palestine is a ruined country, and the Jews are a broken people. But neither is beyond recuperation. Palestine needs a people; Israel needs a country" in Israel Zangwill, "Zion, Whence Cometh My Help?" (July 1903) in *Speeches, Articles, and Letters of Israel Zangwill*, ed. Maurice Simon, with a foreword by Edith Aryton Zangwill (London: Soncino, 1937), p. 80; Arendt paraphrases this as "a people without a country would have to escape to a country without a people," in "The Jewish State: Fifty Years After: Where Have Herzl's Politics Led?" (May 1946) in Arendt, *The Jew as Pariah*, p. 171.

27. This is the theme of Hannah Arendt's discussion in the chapter titled "The Decline of the Nation-State and the End of the Rights of Man," in *The Origins of Totalitarianism*, pp. 267 ff. See the third section, "Imperialism and the End of the 'Rights of Man,'" in Chapter 3 of this book.

28. See Arendt, *The Origins of Totalitarianism*, pp. 249-290.

29. See her essay "Herzl and Lazare" (July 1942), reprinted in *The Jew as Pariah*, pp. 125-131.

30. Arendt, "Zionism Reconsidered," p. 146.

31. Ber Borochov (1881–1917) was born in the Ukraine. After working actively in the Social Democratic Party, he was expelled as a "Zionist deviationist." From then on, he devoted his life to developing Marxist-Zionist thought. He developed a theory of the social structure of the Jewish people that saw it as an inverted pyramid, with capitalists and financiers taking precedence over the proletariat. Among the spiritual tasks of regeneration that the Jewish state would achieve would be the creation of a Jewish proletariat and the setting right of the pyramid. He traveled throughout Europe after 1907 as party functionary for Poale Zion (Workers of Zion), including a trip to the United States after the outbreak of World War I. He returned to Russia after the Kerensky Revolution and died in Kiev. See Arthur Herzberg, ed., *The Zionist Reader: A Historical Analysis and Reader* (New York: Athanaeum, 1959), p. 353.

32. Again, historical realities have changed this condition. Although the Kibbutzim in general have been moderate politically with regard to the Palestinian-Israeli conflict and have pleaded for its peaceful resolution, they served in the Israeli army after the establishment of the state, and in this capacity often constituted an elite military group. Some of the leading politicians of postwar Israel, such as Moshe Dayan, came out of the Kibbutz movement. Dayan was born in Israel's first Kibbutz, Degania.

33. See Arendt's essay "Jewish History, Revised" (March 1948), reprinted in the *Jew as Pariah*, pp. 96-105, which is actually a review of Gershom Scholem's *Major Trends in Jewish Mysticism* (New York: Schocken, 1946).

34. Arendt, "Jewish History, Revised," p. 105.

35. Arendt, "What Is Existenz Philosophy?" *Partisan Review* 18, no. 1 (1946), pp. 35-56. This essay was published in German as "Was ist Existenz-Philosophie?" in *Hannah Arendt: Sechs Essays* (Heidelberg: Schneider, 1948). It has been reprinted in *Arendt: Essays in Understanding: 1930-1954*, ed. Jerome Kohn (New York: Harcourt Brace Jovanovich,

1994), as "What Is Existential Philosophy?" pp. 163-187. This English version was translated from the German by Robert and Rita Kimber, whereas the *Partisan Review* version was written in English by Arendt herself. All citations in the text are to the *Partisan Review* version in Arendt's own English. I will not follow the rendition of the title of this essay into English as "What Is Existential Philosophy?" because the term *Existenzphilosophie* in German connotes a much wider philosophical movement than the terms *existentialism* or *existential philosophy* do in English. Whereas Wilhelm Dilthey and his philosophy of life would be considered part of "Existenz philosophy," I am familiar with no characterization of Dilthey's thought as "existentialist." The terms *philosophies of life* or *philosophies of existence* capture Arendt's meaning more precisely than the terms *existentialism* or *existential philosophy*. I will follow Arendt's original usage in referring to this movement as "Existenz philosophy."

36. See also the essays "French Existentialism" and "Concern With Politics in Recent European Philosophical Thought," both reprinted in *Arendt: Essays in Understanding*, pp. 188-194 and 428-447, respectively.

37. Arendt refers to her "schoolgirl fear" in sending Jaspers this article; Letter 36 in *Arendt-Jaspers Correspondence*, p. 37, and in a subsequent letter writes, "Because, even today, and after all these years, our students' fear of being a 'pupil' is still so much in my bones or, more accurately, in my memory"; Letter 41, p. 47.

38. Arendt, "What Is Existenz Philosophy?" p. 38.

39. Ibid., p. 41.

40. Ibid., p. 35.

41. Heinrich Rickert (1863–1936) lectured from 1891 until 1916 at the University of Freiburg, and moved to the University of Heidelberg in 1916 to succeed Wilhelm Windelband. He belonged to the southwestern school of Neo-Kantianism. He studied the logical and epistemological foundations of the natural sciences and of the historical disciplines in the hope of arriving at a "unity of reality and values." He rejected the separation of the natural from the historical disciplines, which had been proposed by his predecessor Wilhelm Windelband, proposing instead that all reality was historical.

42. Max Weber (1864–1920) was the most prominent sociologist at the beginning of the twentieth century in Germany. He was a professor of economics from 1894 to 1897, first at Freiburg, then in Heidelberg. Although a severe nervous breakdown forced him into early academic retirement, he resided in Heidelberg as a private scholar, and he and his wife entertained one of the best known intellectual circles of their times, referred to as the "Max Weber Kreis." Karl Jaspers was very close to Max Weber, and several personal friends of Hannah Arendt's, such as Benno Georg Leopold von Wiese, frequented the Max Weber circle. See Young-Bruehl, *For Love of the World*, pp. 64-69. Karl Jaspers, in particular, had been influenced greatly by Weber's theory of constructing "ideal types" in explaining social action.

43. Arendt, "What Is Existenz Philosophy?" p. 45.

44. See Young-Bruehl, *For Love of the World*, pp. 48 ff.

45. See Arendt, "Concern With Politics in Recent European Philosophical Thought," in *Essays in Understanding*, pp. 428 ff.

46. Ibid., p. 446.

47. Ibid.

48. Martin Heidegger, *Being and Time*, trans. John Macquarrie and Edward Robinson (New York: Harper & Row, 1962), first published in 1927, p. 84; *Sein und Zeit*, 10th ed. (Tübingen: Max Niemeyer Verlag, 1963), p. 57.

49. See Heidegger, *Being and Time*, pp. 123 ff.; German ed., pp. 89 ff.

50. See Heidegger, *Being and Time*, pp. 125 ff.; German ed., pp. 90 ff.

51. The pragmatist tradition of John Dewey, proceeding from an insight parallel to Heidegger's, displaces the priority of cognition and reveals how every "knowing-that" is grounded in a "knowing-how." Pragmatism and existentialism, like the analytic of Dasein, have the rejection of the Cartesian-Kantian paradigm at their origin.

52. For Herbert Marcuse, see Herbert Marcuse and Frederick Olafson, "Heidegger's Politics: An Interview," *Graduate Faculty Philosophy Journal* 6, no. 1 (1977): 28 ff.; Günther (Stern) Anders, "Wenn ich verzweifelt bin, was geht's mich an?" in *Die Zerstörung einer Zukunft: Gespräche mit emigrierten Sozialwissenschaftlern,* ed. Mathias Greffrath (Hamburg: Rowohlt, 1979), pp. 22 ff.

53. Heidegger, *Being and Time,* German ed. p. 118; emphasis in the German original; English ed., p. 155.

54. Arendt, *The Human Condition,* p. 178.

55. *Being and Time,* German ed., p. 127; English ed., p. 165. The full German passage reads, "Abständigkeit, Durchschnittlichkeit, Einebnung konstituieren als Seinsweisen des Man das, was wir als 'die Öffentlichkeit' kennen. Sie regelt zunächst alle Welt- und Daseinsauslegung und behält in allem Recht. Und das nicht auf Grund eines ausgezeichneten und primären Seins-verhältnisses zu den 'Dingen', nicht weil sie über eine ausdrücklich zugeignete Durchsichtigkeit des Daseins verfügt, sondern auf Grund des Nichteingehens 'auf die Sachen,' weil sie unempfindlich ist gegen alle Unterschiede des Niveaus und der Echtheit. Die Öffentlichkeit verdunkelt alles und gibt das so verdeckte als das Bekannte und jedem Zugängliche aus."

56. I disagree with Richard Wolin's observation that "Arendt never made a concerted effort to come to grips with the dilemma of Heidegger's political engagement. She was more disposed to read Heidegger's Nazism in the manner of a character flaw than pertaining to his philosophy per se" in "Karl Löwith and Martin Heidegger—Contexts and Controversies: An Introduction," in Karl Löwith, *Martin Heidegger and European Nihilism,* trans. Gary Steiner (New York: Columbia University Press, 1995), p. 9.

57. Arendt, "What Is Existenz Philosophy?" in *Arendt: Essays in Understanding,* pp. 181-182.

58. Hannah Arendt, "Concern With Politics in Recent European Philosophical Thought," in *Arendt: Essays Understanding,* pp. 428 ff.

59. Arendt, "Heidegger at Eighty," p. 303, originally published, in German, in *Merkur* 10 (1969): 893-902; trans. Albert Hofstadter for the *New York Review of Books* 17, no. 6 (1971): 50-54; reprinted in Michael Murray, ed., *Heidegger and Modern Philosophy* (New Haven, Conn.: Yale University Press, 1978), pp. 293-303. All page references in the text are to the *Heidegger and Modern Philosophy* publication.

60. Marcuse and Olafson, "Heidegger's Politics: An Interview," pp. 32-33.

3

The Destruction of the Public Sphere
and the Emergence of Totalitarianism

T he work in which the legacy of German Existenz philosophy and the political catastrophes of the twentieth century are brought into a fateful synthesis is *The Origins of Totalitarianism*. It is also in this work that Martin Heidegger's continuing influence upon Arendt is most visible. Ironically, the thought of one who was tempted by National Socialism becomes an implicit framework for analyzing "the burden of our times," which was the title of this work when it first appeared in England.[1] Through her reflections upon the moral and political catastrophes that afflicted humanity in the first half of the twentieth century, through her diagnosis of "totalitarianism" as a new form of political rule in human history, Hannah Arendt reached an unprecedented synthesis of philosophy and political analysis in this work. The events of this century caused the conditions of "homelessness" and "worldlessness" that she had previously placed at the center of her presentation of Existenz philosophy

---

AUTHOR'S NOTE: A shortened version of this chapter has appeared as "Hannah Arendt and the Redemptive Power of Narrative," in *Social Research 57*, No. 1 (1990), pp. 167-196.

to become the real life situation of millions upon millions of human beings. Existenz philosophy was both a harbinger of things to come and, in the person of Martin Heidegger, implicated in the catastrophe of humanity. The full drama of Martin Heidegger's influence upon Hannah Arendt can be appreciated only after the elements of her theory of totalitarianism come to the fore.

Despite its many flaws, *The Origins of Totalitarianism* is no doubt a work of continuing brilliance and relevance. From the standpoint of established disciplinary methodologies, Arendt's work defies categorization while violating a lot of rules. It is too systematically ambitious and overinterpreted to be a strictly historical account; it is too anecdotal, narrative, and ideographic to be considered social science, and although it has the vivacity and the stylistic flair of a work of political journalism, it is too philosophical to be accessible to a broad public. Furthermore, the unity between the first part on anti-Semitism, the second part on imperialism, and the last part on totalitarianism is hard to discern at first glance. Thus, one of the first reviewers of this work, political philosopher Eric Voegelin, maintained that the arrangement of the book was "roughly chronological," and that it was "an attempt to make contemporary phenomena intelligible by tracing their origin back to the eighteenth century, thus establishing a time unit in which the essence of totalitarianism unfolded to its fullness."[2] Voegelin's interpretation of Arendt's thesis as one of *Geschichtsphilosophie* no doubt was more indebted to the curious distortions caused by his own hermeneutic lens; nonetheless, his question about the unity of the work, which prompted one of Arendt's infrequent attempts at methodological self-clarification, is a justified one.

Methodological and Historiographic Puzzles of Arendt's *Origins of Totalitarianism*

Hannah Arendt did not engage in methodological reflections, and on those few occasions when she characterized her own work, she appeared to confuse matters further, as in the case of her various prefaces to *The Origins of Totalitarianism,* where she distinguished between "comprehension" and "deducing the unprecedented from precedents,"[3] and between "totalitarianism" and "its elements and origins."[4] The "origins" of totalitarianism is actually a misnomer for this work, which Arendt originally intended to call *The Burden of Our Times*. More importantly, Arendt is not concerned to establish some inevitable continuity between the past and the present that would compel us to view what happens as what had to happen. She objects to this trap of historical understanding and maintains that the future is radically underdetermined,[5] and that, more significantly, to place the present in inevitable continuity with the past will result in a failure to recognize the novelty of what has taken place. The key terms that she uses to describe her method in *The Origins of Totalitarianism* are *configuration* and the *crystallization of elements*. Arendt is searching for the "elements" of totalitarianism; for those currents of thought, political events and outlooks, incidents and institutions, that once the "imagination of history"[6] gathered them together in the present, reveal an altogether different meaning than what they stood for in the original context. All historical writing is implicitly a history of the present. And it is the particular constellation and crystallization of elements into a whole at the present time that are the methodological guides to their past meaning. In language that resonates with Walter Benjamin's introduction to *The Origin of German Tragic Drama*,[7] Arendt explains,

> The book, therefore, does not really deal with the "origins" of totalitarianism—as its title unfortunately claims—but gives a historical account of the "elements" which "crystallized" into totalitarianism. This account is followed by an analysis of the "elementary structure" of totalitarian movements and domination itself. The elementary structure of totalitarianism is the hidden structure of the book while its more apparent unity is provided by some fundamental concepts which run like red threads through the whole.[8]

If one interprets the unity of the work as Arendt herself intended it to be read, one must begin not with the Enlightenment attitudes toward human nature and the social condition of the *Hofjuden* (court Jews), but with the chapter titled "Total Domination" on the extermination and concentration camps, and which in the 1951 edition was the final chapter preceding the inconclusive "Concluding Remarks" (in the 1966 edition Arendt expanded these remarks into a chapter, "Ideology and Terror"). The chapter "Total Domination" is significant not because it brings fresh empirical data into the discussion—it does not—but because of Arendt's interpretive thesis that the camps are the "guiding social ideal of total domination in general" or that "these camps are the true central institution of totalitarian organizational power."[9] The camps reveal elementary truths about the totalitarian exercise of power, about the structure of totalitarian ideology, as well as bringing to light those moral, political, and psychological presuppositions of the tradition that would be forever destroyed once the camps were established, and became part of human history.

Arendt is concerned to stress that the camps served no "utilitarian" purpose in totalitarian regimes and hence could not be explained in functionalist terms:[10] they were needed neither to intimidate and subdue the opposition nor to provide for "cheap and disposable" labor.[11] The camps are the living laboratories revealing that "everything is possible," that humans can create and inhabit a world where the distinctions between life and death, truth and falsehood, appearance and reality, body and soul, and even victim and murderer are constantly blurred. This totally fabricated universe reflects the ideological impetus of totalitarian regimes to create a universe of meaning that is wholly self-consistent but also curiously devoid of reality and immune to proof by it.

As the crystalline structure through whose blinding foci the totalitarian form of domination is revealed, the camps show, first, that the juridical person in humans had to be killed; second, that the moral person had to be destroyed; and, finally, that the individuality of the self had to be crushed. Arendt's analysis in the preceding sections of *The Origins of Totalitarianism* is designed to show how certain "elements" were present in the political and moral culture of European humanity in the preceding two centuries that, in retrospect, and in retrospect alone, could be viewed as harbingers of a new form of political power in human history.

The death of the juridical subject, of the person qua subject of rights, is the story Arendt tells in the section "Imperialism," when she traces the paradoxes of the nation-state and the fragility of the universal belief in the rights of man on the part of imperialist nations. She recounts the collapse of Western moral standards through the confrontation with Africa, both in the case of the Boer colonization of South Africa and in the case of the later "scramble for Africa." These experiences prove that mere humanity is no guarantee of one's juridical status as a subject of rights. The death of the juridical subject is signed and made historical testament when the Minority Treaties at the end of World War I create millions of homeless, nationless, and displaced persons. The juridical subject becomes a "superfluous" human being.

The murder of the moral person in humanity, the death of the moral self, accompanies the death of the juridical subject. The specifically modern form of anti-Semitic prejudice plays a special role in this process. Such anti-Semitism ascribes moral guilt and blame in a way that defies traditional moral categories. The traditional anti-Judaism of Christian doctrine and practice had blamed the Jews for a crime they committed against the Son of God. For one's crimes, one can atone by conversion, by penance, by denunciation of one's brethren. But modern anti-Semitism, which erupts when Jews begin to enter "society" en masse without fully becoming its members, is morally more perverse. Enlightened opinion distances itself from traditional conceptions of the murder of the Son of God; however, Jewishness now becomes an undefinable "essence," a condition that is at once other and undeniable; Jewishness becomes a "vice." Whereas a crime is an act, a vice is a condition, a spiritual disposition, a trait of character; its transformation is much harder because it is less easily identifiable. The figure of the Jew increasingly becomes associated with forces and powers that bear little or no relation to the empirical individual, and thus it ceases to be a morally accountable self and becomes instead a "specimen" of the species Jew.[12]

The third element in the crystalline structure of totalitarianism, as revealed via a retrospective analysis of the death camps, is the disappearance of the autonomous individual. This begins with the emergence of the mob and the universalization of the condition of worldlessness as a result of war, political upheavals, and mass unemployment. For Arendt, the mob is a new historical actor on the political scene, replacing *le peuple*. The mob is the precursor of the lonely masses of totalitarianism. It is composed of the "refuse" of bourgeois society, of those individuals who fall out of the cracks of the social system, who belong to no social class in particular, who can be identified with no specific trade or work, who have been made "superfluous" by the economic and social changes brought about by industrialization, urbanization, and commercialization. They are "worldless" in the sense that they have lost a stable space of reference, identity, and expectation that they share with others. Not having a particular social perspective from which to view the world, they are especially open to ideological manipulation: they can believe anything and everything, for they lack the definite perspective that is tied to having a certain place in the world. Their condition is one of loneliness. The destruction of the individual in concentration camps by methods of torture, terror, and behavior manipulation only shows that a humanity that has become worldless, homeless, and superfluous is also wholly eliminable. Arendt sums up:

> Loneliness, the common ground for terror, the essence of totalitarian government, . . . is closely connected with uprootedness and superfluousness which have been the curse of modern masses since the beginning of the industrial revolution and have become acute with the rise of imperialism at the end of the last century and the break-down of political institutions and social traditions in our own time. To be uprooted means to have no place in the world, recognized and guaranteed by others; to be superfluous means not to belong to the world at all.[13]

Even if it is possible to interpret the unity of Arendt's work in light of the principles of a "crystalline structure" or the "elements of a configuration," questions remain: Why did Arendt resort to such an indirect manner of exposition and to an even more obscure method of explanation in her account of totalitarianism? Is this yet another example of the idiosyncratic and at times bewildering nature of her political thought? Until now, concern with Arendt's intentions and methodology in *The Origins of Totalitarianism* has primarily focused on the following: the concept of totalitarianism,[14] the usefulness or obsolescence of this concept for "comparative studies of fascism" and for understanding the inner workings of totalitarian political movements,[15] the questionableness of treating Nazism and Stalinism as totalitarian regimes of the same kind, and the unevenness of her explanations in the case of the two regimes.[16] This last point is worth considering in more detail. Particularly in the wake of the cold war, research into totalitarianism itself underwent a change and became "operationalized" through the work of Carl Friedrich and Zbigniew Brzezinski to fit positivist understandings of social science. As a result of this work, the concept of totalitarianism came to be almost synonymous with Soviet-type societies.[17] Whatever the merits of this concept to help us understand the latter type of societies,[18] there is little doubt that Arendt's historical account did not illuminate Stalinism and Nazism to the same extent and in the same way.

Whereas it could be argued that there is some unity between the experiences of imperialism, anti-Semitism, and the subsequent triumph of National Socialism, these two phenomena, namely, imperialism and modern anti-Semitism, do not play the same formative-hermeneutic role in the emergence of Stalinism. Arendt treats nineteenth-century Pan-Slavism and Pan-Germanism as species of "continental imperialism," but this discussion is far too cursory, and the consequences of the latter movement for future developments in the Soviet Union remain unexplained. Arendt cannot really prove that the dislocations caused by World War I and the Russian Revolution amount to the creation of "mass" society, in the same way that the war experience, coupled with inflation and depression, did in Germany in particular. Ironically, mass society and the abolition of traditional classes, rather than preceding Stalinist rule, were consequences of it. It is Stalin's war against the peasantry that finally dissolves the fabric of traditional society on the land.[19] Finally, the absence of a racially based anti-Semitism as the centerpiece of Stalinist ideology (of course, anti-Semitism was used by Stalin, as the trial of the Jewish doctors reveals, but one cannot claim that it was the center of the Stalinist *Weltanschauung*) casts even greater doubt as to whether the developments outlined by Arendt in the first two sections of *The Origins of Totalitarianism* can be "crystalline elements" of National Socialism and Stalinism alike.[20]

An analogy may enable us to understand Arendt's intentions better: in *Democracy in America*, Alexis de Tocqueville emphasized that "a new political science is needed for a world itself quite new;"[21] otherwise, the "mind of men" would be left "to wander aimlessly," unable to extract meaning from the present. Tocqueville wrote *Democracy in America* because he saw tendencies in the life of North American society, such as the rise of social equality, the tyranny of the majority, and the spread of individualism, that he thought were exemplary of the developmental trends of modern societies at large. Nevertheless, the political institutions and trends of nineteenth-century America were not only exemplary but also unique or, better still, one could capture what was most exemplary about them—the tendency of modern societies toward "equality of conditions" and social leveling—by focusing on their uniqueness, namely, democracy not just as a political form of government but as a social condition of equality. Like Tocqueville's *Democracy in America*, Arendt's treatise is motivated by the desire to comprehend the new and to face the unprecedented.[22] Alexis de Tocqueville's analysis of the condition of democracy in America was more than just a methodological example for Hannah Arendt. Arendt appropriated precisely those aspects of Tocqueville's analysis that deal with "associations" under conditions of a mass society that for her own formulation of the concept of totalitarianism. It is this Tocquevillian strand in *The Origins of Totalitarianism* rather than Heidegger's phenomenological ontology of isolation that makes Arendt's work fruitful for an analysis of contemporary conditions.

Empirical-Analytical
Aspects of Arendt's Theory of Totalitarianism

Arendt's phenomenology of totalitarianism, articulated in light of the concepts of "loneliness" and "worldlessness," is indebted to the categorical structure as well as to specific phenomenological descriptions in Heidegger's *Being and Time*. Yet what constitutes the greatness of Arendt's account of totalitarianism is precisely her departure from such foundationalist thinking and her capacity to focus on the phenomena of history, sociology, and culture instead of taking flight into metaphysical abstractions. Arendt remained a phenomenologist of sorts all her life, but a phenomenologist who took seriously the world of appearances as they unfolded in the humble everydayness of human history. I want to suggest that what remains viable of Arendt's theory of totalitarianism today is not the *existential psychology or phenomenology of loneliness but the political sociology of the public sphere and of intermediate associations*.

In developing this point, I would first like to call to mind some aspects of Alexis de Tocqueville's analysis of associations in *Democracy in America*. Tocqueville attributes several functions to nonpolitical, civic associations in American democratic life. First and foremost, such associations serve as bulwarks against the tyranny of the majority by allowing like-minded individuals to come together in society to protect their interests, further their goals, and articulate their viewpoints. At this level, associational life allows diversity and acts to check the spreading forces of conformism, leveling, and homogeneity. "No countries need associations more—to prevent either despotism of parties or the arbitrary rule of a prince—than those with a democratic social state. In aristocratic nations secondary bodies form national associations which hold abuses of power in check," writes Tocqueville, and he continues,

> In countries where such associations do not exist, if private people did not artificially and temporarily create something like them, I see no other dike to hold back tyranny of whatever sort, and a great nation might with impunity be oppressed by some tiny faction or by a single man.[23]

In aristocratic and feudal societies, the division of society into hierarchically organized social classes, ranks, and orders situates individuals in certain ascribed contexts and hinders the exercise of totalizing political control. The despotism of the "ancien régime" is not totalitarianism precisely because despotism attempts to subordinate the exercise of power to a single source without, however, destroying the very identity of alternative social centers of power. Totalitarianism, by contrast, is like an "iron band" in that it seeks to compress society into one by eliminating all independent sources of power and spaces of association (*OT*, p. 466). Totalitarianism seeks to stamp out not only associations themselves but the very ability to form political associations. Hannah Arendt, in formulating this observation, was indebted to Tocqueville's reflections in the second volume of *Democracy in America*.

In Volume 2 of *Democracy in America*, composed thirteen years after the first, Tocqueville's theory of associations undergoes a notable change. Whereas in the first volume, civic, religious, and cultural associations are significant as bulwarks against "tyranny of whatever sort," in the second volume Tocqueville notes a development that he characterizes as a more insidious form of tyranny than the tyranny of the majority. This is individualism, a "calm and considered feeling which disposes each citizen to isolate himself from the mass of his fellows and withdraw into the circle of family and friends."[24] As social equality spreads, forms of life become increasingly homogenized, and the forces of the capitalist market dominate, individualism also increases. Tocqueville observes, "Each man is forever thrown back on himself alone, and there is danger that he may be shut up in the solitude of his own heart."[25] The freedom to associate, to come together with one's fellow human beings to form organizations of common purpose, counteracts such isolation and "the solitude of heart" that excessive individualism creates.

> As soon as common affairs are treated in common, each man notices that he is not as independent of his fellows as he used to suppose and that to get their help he must often offer his aid to them. . . . When the public governs, all men feel the value of public good will and all try to win it by gaining the esteem and affection of those among whom they must live. . . . Those frigid passions that keep hearts asunder must then retreat and hide at the back of consciousness. Pride must be disguised; contempt must not be seen. Egoism is afraid of itself.[26]

Freedom of association and the habit of associating force individuals out of their self-centeredness toward a concern for the good shared with others, and in Tocqueville's poetic words, melt "those frigid passions that keep hearts asunder." Arendt learned from Tocqueville that there could be no political freedom and democratic life if individuals could not exercise their right to associate and come together "in the manner of speech and action." Although under conditions of democratic individualism, associational life can atrophy and lose relevance, it can never quite disappear as long as some modicum of political freedom is guaranteed. Totalitarianism, however, seeks to eliminate not individualism but individuality as such; totalitarianism seeks not only to destroy associations, but it also imprisons all in the "frigid passions of the heart." In her reflections on the loneliness of the masses under totalitarian regimes, Arendt applied these Tocquevillian insights. In doing so, she departed from the existential phenomenology of solitude that she had learned from Heidegger and moved toward a more empirically grounded political sociology of associations.

Hannah Arendt decidedly did not subscribe to the slippery slope argument that totalitarian domination was either an inevitable or even an inescapable result of Western culture, reason, or modernity. She continued to emphasize the radical contingency of the historical moment that led to the constellation of elements resulting in the disasters of humanity in the twentieth century. Perhaps in ways that appear naive to us today, she insisted that "there existed an obvious alternative to Stalin's seizure of power and transformation of the one-party dictatorship into total domination, and this was the pursuance of the NEP policy as it had been initiated by Lenin."[27] Arendt did not implicate the European revolutionary tradition in the emergence of totalitarianism. In fact, her insistence upon the radical contingency of history and her stress that "it could have been otherwise" derive from the moral obligation that the political theorist, as narrator of past deeds, feels toward the political actor, who is always caught in the uncertain moment between past and future, namely, in the present. The "it could have been otherwise" is the hypothetical imperative guiding the action of those who want that this otherwise come to be in the future.

Even if historically contingent, totalitarian domination is possible only under conditions of mass industrialization and modern technology. The methods of social control, propaganda, surveillance, and extermination practiced by totalitarian regimes require the technical possibilities of modernity. This aspect of totalitarianism, and in particular the technological routinization of mass murder, has been amply researched and documented in recent years by historians of National Socialism.[28] What distinguishes Arendt's understanding of totalitarianism from more technological accounts is its decidedly institutional, and, I would like to suggest, "associationalist," methodology. She writes,

> No matter what the specifically national tradition or the particular spiritual source of its ideology, totalitarian government always transformed classes into masses, supplanted the party system, not by one-party dictatorships, but by a mass movement, shifted the center of power from the army to the police, and established a foreign policy openly directed toward world domination. (*OT,* p. 460)

The methods of domination whereby these goals are attained are the indiscriminate use of terror and the development of a totalizing ideology.

It is helpful in this context to distinguish analytically between totalitarian forms of government, totalitarian movements, and the totalization of society through the totalitarian state. Totalitarian movements are the social forces through which totalitarian governments destroy classes, create masses, and establish lawlessness and terror as a fundamental condition. The drive of the totalitarian state is to achieve the total domination of society. Resorting to spatial metaphors, Arendt likens constitutional government to a space where law is like hedges erected between buildings and one orients oneself on known territory; tyranny is like a desert. Under conditions of tyranny, one moves in an unknown, vast, and open space, where the will of the tyrant occasionally befalls one like the sandstorm overtaking the desert traveler. Totalitarianism has no spatial topology: it is like an iron band, compressing people increasingly together until they are formed into one (*OT*, p. 466). The purpose of totalitarian government is to convert society into such an iron band.

In my opinion, it is in the course of examining the processes of social, political, military, economic, and technological domination exercised by totalitarian governments so as to achieve the totalization of society that the political sociology of Hannah Arendt, based upon the centrality of the public sphere, becomes significant. Arendt's political sociology of the public sphere of associations has less relevance for explaining the *dynamics* of totalitarian movements in the process of their formation, but it is crucial for understanding the *routinization* of totalitarian political rule. For with the destruction of the old order, the social forces of totalitarianism must themselves be brought under control if the regime is to consolidate its power. Often the tension between the functional requirements of social mobilization to destroy the old and the establishment of order to achieve the new manifests itself under totalitarianism as a clash between the Party and the Movement. Historical cases of the Party turning against the Movement that once made it possible are well documented.[29] But once the Party has consolidated power, it must deal with the demands of the routinization of politics. It is under conditions of such routinized rule that society, or whatever remains of it, begins to assert itself against the Party. Total control, the goal of all totalitarian movements, is more readily attainable under conditions of war and continuous mobilization. Under conditions of routinized power, and in the absence of war or warlike social mobilization, the forces of society begin to assert themselves against the state. The self-organization of society is thus a threat to every totalitarian regime as well as a powerful indicator of the degree of detotalitarization at work.[30]

In a provocative piece titled "An Imaginary Preface to the 1984 Edition of Hannah Arendt's 'The Origins of Totalitarianism,'" Agnes Heller comments on the following observation in Arendt's 1966 preface to Part III of *The Origins of Totalitarianism*: "The clearest signs that the Soviet Union can no longer be called totalitarian in the strict sense of the term is, of course, the amazingly swift and rich recovery of the arts during the last decade."[31] Heller claims that Arendt was wrong, and concludes that "almost two decades have again elapsed since this paper was committed to paper, and totalitarianism has remained vigorous, indeed, it has even gained more ground."[32] After the spectacular collapse of communism in Eastern Europe and the Soviet Union at the end of the 1980s, we have to conclude that Heller was wrong, and that Hannah Arendt was right in predicting as early as in 1966 a process of "detotalitarization" in the Soviet Union.[33]

Certainly, it would be more than foolish to attribute the collapse of Soviet-style societies to the "flourishing of the arts." What Arendt was calling attention to with this observation was the development of shared spaces—alternative or subaltern publics[34]—in the interstices of these societies as evidence of the loosening of totalitarian rule and the reassertion of the self-organizing power of civil society. She also cites the public trial of the dissidents Sinyavsky and Daniel as evidence of the slow but palpable transformation of totalitarian rule.[35] We know now that the formation of oppositional or alternative public spaces in the interstices of totalitarian societies was far less advanced in the Soviet Union than in other eastern European countries such as Poland, the former Czechoslovakia, and Hungary.[36] Nor should one underestimate the impact, on the Soviet Union in particular, of the Afghan war (which seems to have been their Vietnam) in undermining army discipline and causing elite demoralization and a nascent antiwar movement. No doubt, to the elements of the transformation of Soviet totalitarianism will also have to be added the intensified nuclear arms race of the 1980s and the impact of the global markets on the loosening of Soviet control over the satellite economies of east central Europe and other Third World clients of the Soviet Empire, such as Syria in the Middle East. I am not suggesting that the political sociology of alternative public spaces can constitute more than one element in a larger explanatory framework about detotalitarization that would have to combine internal as well as external factors. Yet the political sociology of alternative public spheres and associations to be derived from Hannah Arendt's theory of totalitarianism does have empirical-analytical power in enabling us to rethink the conditions of transformation of totalitarian societies. A hypothesis can result from these considerations: totalitarian rule cannot allow and will prevent the formation of independent and alternative public spheres in its midst. A totalitarian society begins to transform its nature when the number, frequency, outreach, and intensity of modes of social relations constituting an alternative "public" begin to increase in number.

At this juncture, Arendt's diagnostic concepts of loneliness and worldlessness, which she saw as the hallmarks of totalitarianism in her time, lose their mooring in Martin Heidegger's fundamental ontology. Interpreted in the light of a political sociology of associations, these concepts serve to refocus our attention on the model of alternative or subaltern public spaces as crucial indicators of detotalitarization processes. Read in this light, Arendt's theory of totalitarianism can be said to have anticipated the currently growing and rigorous literature on the formation of civil societies in systems undergoing transitions from authoritarian and totalitarian rule to democracy,[37] for a multiplicity of public spaces are the sine qua non of an independent and vigorous civil society as a component of democratic cultures everywhere.

Imperialism and the End of the "Rights of Man"

Although both methodological and historical questions remain about Hannah Arendt's account of totalitarianism, and her use of this concept to describe National Socialism as well as Stalinist Russia, these perplexities are minor compared with the utter puzzlement that the contemporary reader is likely to face in view of Part II of *The Origins of Totalitarianism,* the section called "Imperialism." Long neglected by Arendt scholars,[38] this brief discussion contains one of the most insightful analyses of the phenomenon of European imperialism from the end of the nineteenth century to the end of World War I. Arendt's distinction between overseas and continental imperialism, her discussion of the British rule in India, the French conquest of Algeria, the Boer War in South Africa, the different cultural strands and national traditions that contribute to the formation of "racism," and her moving last chapter on the end of the "rights of man" are examples of brilliant synthesis of historically grounded empirical insights with philosophical depth. But what exactly is the place of these discussions in an analysis of totalitarianism? Whereas there is a clear historical relationship between the elements of European anti-Semitism analyzed in the first part and the third section on totalitarianism, it is very hard to discern any causal and/or historical links between the phenomena discussed under the heading of imperialism and the political problems of totalitarianism.

Consider that British imperialism, which serves Arendt as exemplary in setting up some of her key concepts for analyzing imperialism in general,[39] did not issue in totalitarianism. In fact, France and Great Britain, whose conquests of Egypt, Algeria, and India Arendt considers as paradigmatic imperialist ventures, were and remained democratic nations, except for France's capitulation to Nazi domination during the Vichy period. The Pan-Germanism and Pan-Slavism developing among the German-speaking and Slavic peoples certainly were movements that left traces upon the totalitarian regimes of National Socialism and Stalinism. But in fact, National Socialist theories of racial superiority owed as much, if not more, to the pseudoscientism of British social Darwinist thinking than they did to the metaphysical theories of tribal nationalism, widespread among the Pan-Germanists, with their emphasis on the "divine origin" of a people.[40] These are just a few of the ways in which the discussion of imperialism, brilliant though it may be, makes little theoretical sense when understood as offering a causal hypothesis about the genesis or causes of totalitarianism. How then should we interpret this discussion?

I propose two theses: (a) at the center of Arendt's reflections are the dilemmas of the modern nation-states and their historically proven incapacity to defend the "universal rights of man"; totalitarian movements absorbed lessons from this failure;[41] (b) at the margins of this analysis is the intuition, not fully proven, that the encounter with "non-European others" through imperialist conquests created moral and psychic patterns of racism in the pre- and unconscious of European settlers, which eventually were carried from overseas into the home country. As Arendt was to remark nearly twenty years later in her comments on the Vietnam war and the Watergate scandal, sooner or later the chickens come "home to roost."[42] Imperialism in other lands leaves indelible marks at home, upon the psyche of the nation as well. The other is not outside us in faraway lands; through the experiences of imperial domination and racism, we become prone to create the other within, in our midst.

Imperialism and the Dilemmas of the
Modern Nation-State

Using a pithy formula, the historical significance of which would not have been lost on anyone familiar with discussions of imperialism within the socialist workers' movements at the turn of the century, Arendt writes, "Imperialism must be considered the first stage in political rule of the bourgeoisie rather than the last stage of capitalism" (*OT*, p. 138). Arendt here is clearly referring to Lenin's text, *Imperialism: The Highest Stage of Capitalism*.[43] Polemicizing against Lenin, she distinguishes between capitalism as an economic system, the bourgeoisie as a social class, and the nation-state as a political formation. The force of her distinctions can be understood only against the background of debates concerning imperialism with which she was no doubt quite familiar.[44] It was largely accepted both by Marxist and non-Marxist political economists of the 1920s that capitalism essentially depended upon the existence of a "noncapitalistic world" to continue its process of growth, expansion, and capital accumulation. This dependence could be explained through various economic factors such as oversaving and maldistribution, which would then impel the capitalist nations to seek new ventures of investment and capital lending; or one could see the need for imperialist expansion, as did Lenin, to be the result of overproduction, which would then impel a capitalist economy to expand into new markets; or one could explain imperialist expansion through the search for new sources of material. Arendt is ready to accept all of these as factors that drive a capitalist economy to expand. However, she sides with Rosa Luxemburg against Lenin concerning the structural dynamics of this expansion. Rosa Luxemburg had maintained that capitalism, as an economic system, depended upon a noncapitalist and essentially a precapitalist environment, and not just at its final stage but at its inception. "Capitalism," wrote Rosa Luxemburg,

arises and develops historically amidst a non-capitalist society. In Western Europe it is found at first in a feudal environment from which it in fact sprang—the system of bondage in rural areas and the guild system in the towns—and later, after having swallowed up the feudal system, it exists mainly in an environment of peasants and artisans, that is to say a system of simple commodity production both in agriculture and trade. European

> capitalism is further surrounded by vast territories of non-European civilization ranging over all levels of development. . . . This is the setting for the accumulation of capital. . . . The existence and development of capitalism requires an environment of non-capitalist forms of production. . . . Capitalism needs non-capitalist social strata as a market for its surplus value, as a source of supply for its means of production and as a reservoir of labour power for its wage system.[45]

Arendt is in fundamental agreement with this thesis, which she calls "Rosa Luxemburg's brilliant insight into the political structure of imperialism" (*OT,* p. 148). She further concurs with Luxemburg that the capitalist mode of production "from the beginning had been calculated for the whole earth" (*OT,* p. 148). At a political and cultural level, the world-expansionist economic dynamic of modern capitalism requires that the confrontation of the "West with its others" be seen as a structural aspect of the development of modern capitalism in the West, and not just as an extraneous necessity imposed upon the system at a later stage by contingent factors such as overproduction, search for raw materials, and investment. In her subsequent essay on Rosa Luxemburg, Arendt comments,

> In other words, Marx's "original accumulation of capital" was not, like original sin, a single event, a unique deed of expropriation by the nascent bourgeoisie, setting off a process of accumulation that would then follow "with iron necessity" its own inherent law to the final collapse. On the contrary, expropriation had to be repeated time and again to keep the system in motion.[46]

Her fundamental agreement with Rosa Luxemburg, or, formulated more precisely, the profound influence Rosa Luxemburg exercised on Hannah Arendt,[47] no doubt led Arendt to see the most momentous developments of the modern world such as the rise of capitalism, imperialism, and totalitarianism in the West in a global context. Unfortunately, some recent commentators have judged Hannah Arendt through the experiences of black-white racial relations in the United States alone, and have thoroughly missed the import of Arendt's discussions of all forms of European imperialism, including the British, the French, the German, the Dutch, and the Russian, as being essential to the formation of European racism.[48]

Arendt's analysis of imperialism, though, differs from Luxemburg's in one fundamental respect: Arendt's threefold distinction between capitalism as a socioeconomic formation, the bourgeoisie as a social class, and the nation-state as a modern polity makes her avoid the reductionism of much Marxist theory that sees the state as an instrument for administering the interests of the capitalist class alone. Quite to the contrary: for Arendt, the political significance of imperialism derives "from the nation's losing battle against it" (*OT*, p. 132). The modern nation-state, established in the wake of the British (1648 and 1688), American (1776), and French Revolutions (1789), was based from the beginning on three potentially contradictory principles: the universal rights of man and citizen, the consent of the governed, and the sovereignty of the nation. The drive for ever-expanding lands, markets, and goods, the search for the domination of ever more remote peoples and parts of the earth, contradict, according to Arendt, the political principle of consent. For consent is dependent on the more or less stable formation of a public sphere of speech and action in common among human beings. But the principles of growth for growth's sake or accumulation for the aggrandizement of capital are forever forcing the limits of consent by following their own logic. "The limitless process of capital accumulation needs the political structure of so 'unlimited a power' that it can protect growing property by constantly growing more powerful" (*OT*, p. 143). The bourgeoisie hankers after a form of power that transforms the state into an instrument for the protection of its interests in ever-expanding growth. Imperialism is the temptation, very often realized at the expense of the population of the lands that one dominates, to escape the constraints of consent and to render power unaccountable. Imperialism teaches that power and consent can be dissociated, and that this is a permanent possibility within the modern state. Arendt agrees with Edmund Burke that "the breakers of law," in India, most notably Lord Hastings, cannot be trusted with obedience to the law at home.[49]

Unfolding the complex relations among the principle of "the rights of man" and the paradoxes of the nation-state is also the task of Arendt's penultimate chapter in the section on imperialism. This chapter explores the conceptual contradictions between the principles of universal rights of men and national sovereignty with much more clarity than her earlier reflections on capitalist growth and democratic consent. It also illustrates

Arendt's search for certain "crystalline structures" (see the first section in this chapter) in the culture and politics of the twentieth century that could be considered anticipatory elements of that complex configuration of events, trends, and developments characterized as totalitarianism. For the topic of this chapter is not the lawlessness of colonial administrations in the provinces of their empires and their attempt to free the exercise of power from the limits of consent. This chapter deals with the destruction of the European nation-state system at the end of World War I.

> Modern power conditions which make national sovereignty a mockery except for giant states, the rise of imperialism, and the pan-movements undermined the stability of Europe's nation-state system from the outside. None of these factors, however, has sprung directly from the tradition and the institutions of national-states themselves. Their internal disintegration came only after the first World War, with the appearance of minorities created by the Peace Treaties and of a constantly growing refugee movement, the consequence of revolutions. (*OT*, p. 270)

With the disintegration of the German Reich and the Austro-Hungarian and, at a more remote level, the Ottoman Empires, the peace treaties created many peoples in a single state calling them the "state people," such as the Czechs in what would be then Czechoslovakia and the Serbs in Yugoslavia, assuming thereby that Slovaks in the first case, and Croats and Slovenes in the second, were simply secondary groupings or nationalities. Furthermore, a third group of nationalities, such as the Jews in all the newly created east central European nation-states, or the Greeks in modern Turkey, became official minorities. The peace treaties concluded at the end of World War I brought the clash between the principles of respect for universal human rights and of national sovereignty to a head. Everybody was convinced, observes Arendt, that

> true freedom, true emancipation, and true popular sovereignty could be attained only with full national emancipation, that people without their own national government were deprived of human rights. In this conviction, which could base itself on the fact that the French Revolution had combined the Declaration of the Rights of Man with national sovereignty, they were supported by the Minority Treaties themselves, which did not entrust the governments with the protection of different nationalities but charged the League of Nations with safeguarding the rights of those who, for reasons

of territorial settlement, had been left without national states of their own. (*OT,* p. 272)

Minorities had existed before, but the recognition that millions of people would live outside normal legal boundaries and would need protection from an international body for the guarantee of their elementary human rights implied that only nationals could be citizens. The modern state was thereby transformed from being an instrument of the rule of law and the protection of the human rights of all its citizens to being an instrument furthering national interest alone. The ensuing creation of stateless peoples, of groups of people who were rejected by their respective nation-states, the massive denaturalizations of other groups of individuals who were deemed "alien" by their host countries, were simply juridical steps that increasingly transformed the nation-state into an instrument serving the needs and interests of one group of people alone. "In other words," writes Arendt,

> man had hardly appeared as a completely emancipated, completely isolated being who carried his dignity within himself without reference to some larger encompassing order, when he disappeared again into a member of a people. From the beginning the paradox involved in the declaration of inalienable human rights was that it reckoned with an "abstract" human being who seemed to exist nowhere, for even savages lived in some kind of a social order. . . . The whole question of human rights, therefore, was quickly and inextricably blended with the question of national emancipation; only the emancipated sovereignty of the people, of one's own people, seemed to be able to insure them. . . . The full implication of this identification of the rights of man with the rights of peoples in the European nation-state system came to light only when a growing number of people and peoples suddenly appeared whose elementary rights were as little safeguarded by the ordinary functioning of nation-states in the middle of Europe as they would have been in the heart of Africa. (*OT,* p. 291)

Arendt's words have proved prophetic: the nearly half century that has elapsed after the composition of these words has made the refugee problem a worldwide question; not only in east central Europe but in Africa, Asia, and the Middle East, ever-new groups of human beings—the Hutus and the Tutsis, the Cambodians, the Vietnamese, and the Kurds—are drawn into the vicious cycle of statelessness, minority status, and often elimination and extermination. Yet Arendt's reflections, as she herself observes, are "ironical," "bitter," and almost confirm Edmund Burke's critique of the French Revolution's Declaration of the Rights of Man (*OT,* p. 299). Leaving aside for a moment the daunting political question of how global human rights can be protected, we can ask Arendt what she offers in effect as a philosophical, conceptual reply to Edmund Burke. Is the whole category of "human rights," the "existence of a right to have rights," in her perspicacious phrase (*OT,* p. 296), a defensible one? Do human beings "have" rights in the same way in which they can be said to have body parts? If we insist that we must treat all humans as beings entitled to the right to have rights, on the basis of which philosophical assumptions do we defend this insistence? Do we ground such respect for universal human rights in nature, in history, or in human rationality? One searches in vain for answers to these questions in Arendt's text. But, by withholding a philosophical engagement with the justification of human rights, by leaving ungrounded her own ingenious formulation of the "right to have rights," Arendt also leaves us with a disquiet about the normative foundations of her own political philosophy. In the concluding chapters of this work, I will return to these issues and explore the limits of Arendt's political thought.

"We are not born equal; we become equal as members of a group on the strength of our decision to guarantee ourselves mutually equal rights," observes Arendt. "Our political life rests on the assumption that we can produce equality through organization, because man can act in and change and build a common world, together with his equals and only with his equals" (*OT,* p. 301). Political equality is always created against the background of difference, what Arendt names "the dark background of mere givenness" (Ibid.). So far we have examined this dialectic of equality and difference as it is manifested in the emergence of modern civil society, and in particular with respect to Jewish identity in the modern world; but on a global scale, what forever transformed European consciousness and confronted Europe with the most unsettling experience of racial difference was the "scramble for Africa." The European colonization of Africa created a hiatus between the white peoples of Europe and black peoples. This hiatus testifies to the permanent fragility of the polity within the walls of which alone equality can be guaranteed.

The Scramble for Africa
and the Curse of Racism

Arendt notes that race thinking in Europe originated in different intellectual and political currents, and was by no means restricted to the white-black divide. She singles out three major currents: the aristocratic racism of Count Arthur de Gobineau, who published in 1853 his *Essai sur l'inégalité des Races Humaines* (Essay on the Inequality of the Human Races) (*OT,* pp. 161 ff.), and the critique of the "rights of men" as opposed to the "rights of Englishmen," in British political thought, which is initiated by Edmund Burke (*OT,* pp. 175 ff.) but gives way in the late nineteenth century to pseudoscientific theories of social Darwinism (Ibid.). Arendt also explores how German nationalism, developing after the defeat of the old Prussian army by Napoleon in 1807, while first emerging as a patriotic movement against the French, eventually developed into Pan-Germanism and the belief in the unique destiny of the German nation. These forms of race thinking are largely reaction formations to the ideals of universal equality, human rights, and the brotherhood of men propagated by the French Revolution. Both Count de Gobineau and Edmund Burke sought to restore the ancien régime of Europe by destroying the egalitarian arguments of the French Revolution. They were searching more for "a race of aristocrats" than "a nation of citizens" (*OT,* pp. 161 ff.). What radically transformed these inter-European forms of race thinking into a confrontation between human groups whose differences were presumably "biologically" rather than "culturally" grounded was the "scramble for Africa." In the struggle for the domination of Africa, European man confronted a limit experience, namely, the limits of his own civility and civilization.

Hannah Arendt uses Joseph Conrad's well-known short story, *Heart of Darkness,* to frame and explore this experience.[50] In this story, Conrad examines the psychic regression of a German engineer, entrusted by his company with the supervision of an engineering project, in some unidentified Central African nation. Kurtz, confronted by the strangeness and alienness of tribal African life, increasingly develops a trancelike condition. He is unable to escape "the lure of the primitive," eventually loses all boundaries between himself and the natives, sleeps with native women, and lets himself be declared their king. Conrad's story serves Arendt as a device to explore the threat to the limits of European identity and civilization posed by this encounter with the "other" in the heart of Africa. Note that Conrad's title is ambiguous: the "heart of darkness" can refer to the heart of the Dark Continent of Africa, the innermost, secret being of Africa; but the "heart of darkness" can also refer to the darkness within Kurtz that he discovers as he travels from Europe to Africa, and as he regresses into ever deeper recesses of his psyche, into the night of memory. Arendt comments and quotes Conrad:

> The world of native savages was a perfect setting for men who had escaped the reality of civilization. Under a merciless sun, surrounded by an entirely hostile nature, they were confronted with human beings who, living without the future of a purpose and the past of an accomplishment, were as incomprehensible as the inmates of a madhouse. "The pre-historic man was cursing us, praying to us, welcoming us—who could tell? We were cut off from the comprehension of our surroundings; we glided past like phantoms, wondering and secretly appalled, as sane men would be, before an enthusiastic outbreak in a madhouse. *We could not understand because we were too far and could not remember, because we were traveling in the night of first ages that are gone leaving hardly a sign—and no memories.* The earth seemed unearthly, . . . and the men . . . No, they were not inhuman. Well, you know, that was the worst of it—this suspicion of their not being inhuman. It would come slowly to one. They howled and leaped, and spun, and made horrid faces; *but what thrilled you was just the thought of their humanity—like yours—the thought of your remote kinship with this wild and passionate uproar"* (*OT,* p. 190, quoting from Conrad, *Heart of Darkness,* emphasis added)

What interests Arendt, and what proves to be such a powerful guide for the exploration of Conrad, is this mixture of attraction and repulsion, kinship and antagonism that the European soldiers of fortune who dug into Africa in search of gold and riches, as well as the Boer settlers, felt for the natives. By referring to his travels in Africa as travels "in the night of the first ages," Conrad has the character of Kurtz affirm the shared humanity of the natives with the Europeans. The natives' way of life then becomes a permanent temptation, the temptation of regression to a condition in which everything is possible, and a dull engineer from Europe can deify himself as a god in the eyes of the believing natives.

Arendt's purpose in using Conrad and his character Kurtz to delve into these issues has been misunderstood. Anne Norton, for example, argues that

> it is in her own voice that Arendt says of the Africans "they had not created a human world." It is in her own voice that Arendt denies history and politics to the Africans. Yet if Arendt had written these words in another voice, marking them as foreign to her own sentiments, one would still have reason to question her views of racial difference and their significance for her political theory. Arendt put herself in the mind and circumstances of the Boer. She did not attempt to enter the minds and circumstances of the African. Arendt gave voice to the Boer. She left the African silent.[51]

Norton's dismissive reading is belied by the very historical and social distinctions that Arendt makes: first, "Africa," as such, as a whole unit, is a historically misleading category; it is the product either of the racist discourse of whites who assimilate all of Africa into one, or of the political rhetoric of Pan-Africanists. Arendt's refusal to speak of Africa "en bloc" is not an attempt to erase Africa, as Norton maintains; rather, it is the result of a political theory that takes political distinctions more seriously than culturally unexamined placatives of demonstrative political gestures. Recent debates among African American scholars concerning "essentialism" and "constructivism" in racial discourse show very well that the creation of fictive entities like "Africa" must always be challenged in the name of historical and cultural specificity and the differential experiences of racism to which different peoples, in different social classes and pertaining to different genders, religions, and ethnicities, are differentially subject. Arendt had a sense of these differences.[52] Second, precisely because she shares the discourse neither of white supremacism nor of Pan-Africanism, Arendt distinguishes the Arab countries such as Egypt, Tunis, Algeria, and Morocco in the north of Africa from the Cape of Good Hope and South Africa, and both from Central Africa (*OT,* pp. 187 ff.). Norton completely misses these distinctions and takes Arendt's characterization of the innermost peoples and tribes of Central Africa, as experienced by European settlers, fortune seekers, and crooks, to be descriptions in Arendt's own voice. Third, why indeed did Arendt try to analyze the mind of the Boer and leave "the African silent"? The answer simply is that Arendt analyzed the "scramble for Africa" from the standpoint of its influence upon the perversion of European morals, manners, and customs; she was concerned to explore how the experience of lawlessness, of civilizational regression, the threat to identity posed by otherness, all return back home from the "Dark Continent" to create the heart of darkness within Europe itself. Given that her topic is European racism, and the exploration of the alliance between capitalism and elements of the displaced and uprooted European mobs who sought to penetrate into Africa to seek their fortune, it is perfectly understandable that her methodological emphasis would lie on the one rather than the other perspective. Norton misses the moral, as well as political, significance of even exploring the links between the emergence of totalitarianism in Europe and the scramble for Africa. Arendt's brilliant insight was that experiences in the Dark Continent and the heart of darkness in Europe were profoundly related. But the weakness of her discussion has been identified at the beginning: she did not translate this insight into a causal or genetic account of the rise of European totalitarianism. We have to remain satisfied with her method of exploring "crystalline structures" rather than discovering a causal nexus. At this stage, a more in-depth exploration of Arendt's methodological considerations in writing *The Origins of Totalitarianism* can shed light on some of these perplexities.

The Politics of Memory and the
Morality of Historiography

Whereas for Alexis de Tocqueville a new reality required a new science to comprehend it and extract meaning from it, for Hannah Arendt totalitarianism required not so much a new science as a new "narrative." Totalitarianism could not really be the object of a "science of politics," even if Arendt believed that there could ever be such a thing as a "science" of politics, for totalitarianism signified the *end* of politics and the universalization of domination. Instead, one required a narrative that would once again reorient the mind in its aimless wanderings, for only such a reorientation could reclaim the past such as to build the future. The theorist of totalitarianism, as the narrator of totalitarianism, was engaged in a moral and political task. Put more sharply: some of the conceptual perplexities of Arendt's treatment of totalitarianism derive from her profound sense that because what had happened in Western civilization with the existence of Auschwitz was so radically new and unthinkable, telling its story required that one first reflect upon the moral and political dimensions of the historiography of totalitarianism. Although the *politicization of memory* was part of the destruction of tradition in the twentieth century that Arendt lamented, the *politics of memory* and *the morality of historiography* are at the center of her analysis of totalitarianism no less than of her subsequent reflections on Eichmann in Jerusalem.

My thesis is that the historiography of totalitarianism presented Arendt with extremely difficult methodological dilemmas with normative dimensions,[53] and that in reflecting upon these dilemmas, Arendt developed a conception of political theory as "storytelling." The task of this kind of political theory is to engage in "exercises" of thought by digging under the rubble of history so as to recover those "pearls" of past experience, with their sedimented and hidden layers of meaning, to cull from them a story that can orient the mind in the future.

For Hannah Arendt, writing about totalitarianism, but in particular about the extermination and concentration camps, which she saw as the most unprecedented form of human domination, presented profound historiographical dilemmas. These can be summed up around four issues: first, historicization and salvation; second, the exercise of empathy, imagination, and historical judgment; third, the pitfalls of analogical thinking; and fourth, the moral resonance of narrative language.

Historicization and salvation. All "historiography is necessarily salvation and frequently justification."[54] Historiography originates with the human desire to overcome oblivion and nothingness; it is the attempt to save, in the face of the fragility of human affairs and the inescapability of death, something "which is even more than remembrance." Proceeding from this Greek and even Homeric conception of history, for Arendt the first dilemma posed by the historiography of totalitarianism was the impulse to destroy rather than to preserve. "Thus my first problem was how to write historically about something—totalitarianism—which I did not want to conserve but on the contrary felt engaged to destroy."[55]

The very structure of traditional historical narration, couched as it is in chronological sequence and the logic of precedence and succession, serves to "preserve" what has happened by making it seem inevitable, necessary, plausible, understandable, and, in short, justifiable. Nothing seemed more abhorrent to Arendt than the dictum that *"Die Welt-geschichte ist das Weltgericht"* (world history is the judge of the world). Her response to this dilemma was the same as Walter Benjamin's: to break the chain of narrative continuity, to shatter chronology as the natural structure of narrative, to stress fragmentariness, historical dead ends, failures, and ruptures. Not only does this method of fragmentary historiography do justice to the memory of the dead by telling the story of history in terms of their failed hopes and efforts, it is also a way of "preserving the past" without being enslaved by it, in particular without having one's moral and political imagination stifled by arguments of "historical necessity." Arendt stumbled upon this historiographical dilemma when reflecting upon totalitarianism, but there is little question that this method of writing history in defiance of the traditional canons of historical narrative is also what guided her controversial account of the action of the *Judenräte* in the Eichmann book as well as her account of the French and American Revolutions in *On Revolution.*

Empathy, imagination, and historical judgment. Arendt maintained that there was a special relationship between historical *Verstehen* (understanding) and what Kant had called *Einbildungskraft.*[56] Both were exercises in reproductive imagination; in each case, one had to re-create from the evidence available to one a new concept, a new narrative, a new perspective. For historical understanding could never be the mere *reproduction* of the standpoint of past historical actors; to pretend that historical understanding amounted to complete empathy was an act of bad faith that served to disguise the standpoint of the narrator or the historian. Arendt painstakingly distinguished "judgment" from "empathy."[57] The historical narrator no less than the moral actor had to engage in acts of judgment, for *Verstehen* is a form of judging—certainly not in the juridical or moralistic sense of the delivery of a value perspective but in the sense of re-creating a shared reality from the standpoint of all involved and concerned. Historical judgment revealed the perspectival nature of the shared social world by representing its plurality in narrative form. At stake in such representational narrative was the ability "to take the standpoint of the other," which did not mean empathizing or even sympathizing with the other but re-creating the world as it appears through the eyes of others.

In re-creating this plural and perspectival quality of the shared world, the historian could accomplish his or her task only so far as his or her faculty of imagination was not limited to one of these viewpoints. Arendt here was drawing a fine line between the practice of judgment by the historian on the one hand and the moral dilemmas of objectivism and relativism on the other. The commitment to represent in narrative form every perspective may appear as the equivalent of the God's eye view of the universe. It may feed the illusion of total objectivity. Equally, the more pluralized and fragmentary social and historical reality appears, the more can one gain the conviction that there is no shared right or wrong at all but that all our moral concepts are smoke screens for our perspectives and preferences—a consequence that Nietzsche, whose perspectivalist epistemology certainly inspired Arendt, did not hesitate to draw.[58]

As in morality so in historiography, Arendt refused to deal with these problems via foundationalist positions and insisted that this is what the cultivation of historical and moral judgment amounted to: the ability to draw fine distinctions and to represent the *plural* nature of the *shared* human world by re-creating the standpoint of others.[59] According to some commentators, Arendt herself excelled in this art of representation to such an extent that she was more successful in capturing the mind of the anti-Semite than of the Jew, of the white Boer settlers than of African natives.[60]

The pitfalls of analogical thinking. One of Arendt's chief quarrels with the social sciences of her day was that the dominant positivist paradigm led to ahistorical modes of thinking and to hasty enthusiasm for analogies and generalizations. Because the method of science was considered to be an inductive one of assembling ever more instances of the same law, in social science as well, one searched for the generalizable and cross-culturally "similar," more often than not ending in banal generalizations.[61] For Arendt, the problem with this approach was not just methodological but also moral and political. This method dulled one's appreciation for what was new and unprecedented, thus failing to confront one with the task of thinking morally in the face of the unprecedented. Politically, this method also stultified one's capacity for resistance by making it seem that everything was possible and permissible.[62]

In the first edition of *The Origins of Totalitarianism*, Arendt employed the category of "radical evil" to describe what had happened in the death camps. Subsequently, and largely as a result of her analysis of Eichmann, she withdrew from this position to the term the *banality of evil*. Her biographer, Elisabeth Young-Bruehl, recounts that this change was a *"cura posterior"* for Arendt.[63] This cure meant, however, neither forgiveness nor forgetting (Arendt always insisted that Eichmann had to be condemned for his deeds—the question was on what principles and according to which justification).[64] By this much maligned and much misunderstood phrase Arendt simply raised a question that has remained unanswered till today: namely, how could "ordinary," dull, everyday human beings, who are neither particularly evil nor corrupt or depraved, be implicated in and acquiesce to the commitment of unprecedented atrocities?[65] A better phrase than the *banality of evil* might have been the *routinization of evil* or its *Alltäglichung*. Analogical thinking governs the logic of the everyday, where we orient ourselves by expected and established patterns and rules. For this reason, analogical thinking routinizes, normalizes, and renders familiar the unfamiliar. In doing so, it reinforces the "normal," the "everyday" quality of the unacceptable, the unprecedented, and the outrageous.

The moral resonance of narrative language. Arendt's first critics had praised her work as passionate and denounced it as sentimental.[66] Arendt's response to this was that she had parted quite consciously "with the tradition of *sine ira et studio*" (without passion and study) in her analysis of totalitarianism, for not to express moral indignation or not to seek to arouse it in the reader when writing about totalitarianism would have been equivalent to moral complicity. "To describe the concentration camps *sine ira* is not to be 'objective,' but to condone them; and such condoning cannot be changed by a condemnation which the author may feel duty bound to add but which remains unrelated to the description itself."[67] The moral resonance of one's language does not only, or even primarily, reside in the explicit value judgments that an author may pass on the subject matter; rather, such resonance must be an aspect of the descriptive narrative itself. The language of narration must match the moral quality of the narrated object. Of course, such ability to narrate makes the theorist into a storyteller, and it is not the mark of every theorist to find the language of the true storyteller.

The Theorist as Storyteller

It may seem less perplexing now that in reflecting about what she was doing, "storytelling" is one of the most frequent answers Arendt gives.[68] The vocation of the theorist as "storyteller" is also the unifying thread of Arendt's political and philosophical analyses from the *Origins of Totalitarianism* to her reflections on the French and the American Revolutions to her theory of the public space and to her final words in the first volume of *The Life of the Mind* on "thinking."

> I have clearly joined the ranks of those who for some time now have been attempting to dismantle metaphysics, and philosophy with all its categories, as we have known them from their beginning in Greece until today. Such dismantling is possible only on the assumption that the thread of tradition is broken and we shall not be able to renew it. Historically speaking, what actually has broken down is the Roman trinity that for thousands of years united religion, authority, and tradition. The loss of this trinity does not destroy the past. . . . What has been lost is the continuity of the past. . . . What you then are left with is still the past, but a *fragmented* past, which has lost its certainty of evaluation.[69]

The past that claims authority over us because it is the way things were done is "tradition." Arendt distinguishes between the nineteenth-century "revolt" against the authority of tradition and the twentieth-century "break" with tradition.[70] This nineteenth-century revolt is intelligible only if one assumes that the past that one is attempting to rid oneself of is sufficiently present such that the attempt to rid oneself of it makes genuine sense. The events of the twentieth century, however, have created a "gap" between past and future of such a magnitude that the past, while still present, is fragmented and can no longer be told as a unified narrative.

Under these conditions, we must rethink the gap between past and future anew for each generation; we must develop our own heuristic principles; we "must discover and ploddingly pave anew the path of thought."[71]

This recovery of the past must proceed and cannot but proceed outside the framework of established tradition, for tradition no longer reveals the meaning of the past. But to be without a sense of the past is to lose one's self, one's identity, for who we are is revealed in the narratives we tell of ourselves and of our world shared with others. Narrativity is constitutive of identity. Human actions are always identified in terms of "such and such has done so and so." Actions, unlike things and natural objects, live only in the narrative of those who perform them and the narrative of those who understand, interpret, and recall them. This narrative structure of action also determines the identity of the self. The human self, as opposed to things and objects, cannot be identified in terms of what it is, but only by who one is. The self is the protagonist of a story we tell, but not necessarily its author or producer (*HC*, pp. 184 ff.). The narrative structure of action and of human identity means that the continued retelling of the past, its continued reintegration into the story of the present, its continuous reevaluation, reassessment, and reconfiguration, are ontological conditions of the kinds of beings we are. If *Dasein* is in time, narrative is the modality through which time is experienced. Even when the thread of tradition is broken, even when the past is no longer authoritative simply because it has been, it lives within us and we cannot avoid placing ourselves in relation to it. Who we are at any point is defined by the narrative uniting past and present.

Narrative, then, or, to use Arendt's term, *storytelling,* is a fundamental human activity. Thus, there is a continuum between the attempt of the theorist to understand the past and the need of the acting person to interpret the past as part of a coherent and continuing life story. But what guides the activity of the "storyteller" when tradition has ceased to orient? What structures narrative when collective forms of memory have broken down, have been obliterated or manipulated beyond recognition? To elucidate the activity of the storyteller, Arendt resorts to "a few lines" that, according to her, say "better and more densely than I could" what one does in the attempt to cull meaning from a fragmented past. She quotes Shakespeare:

> Full fathom five thy father lies,
> Of his bones are coral made,
> Those are pearls that were his eyes.
> Nothing of him that doth fade
> But doth suffer a sea-change
> Into something rich and strange. (*The Tempest,* Act 1, Scene 2)[72]

After the storm, the theorist as storyteller is like the pearl diver who converts the memory of the dead into something "rich and strange." Arendt first cites this passage from Shakespeare in her 1968 essay on Walter Benjamin.

> Walter Benjamin knew that the break in tradition and the loss of authority which occurred in his lifetime were irreparable, and he concluded that he had to discover new ways of dealing with the past. In this he became a master when he discovered that the transmissibility of the past had been replaced by its citability and that in place of its authority there had arisen a strange power to settle down, piecemeal, in the present and to deprive it of "peace of mind," the mindless peace of complacency.[73]

In using the same lines from Shakespeare to characterize Benjamin's efforts and her own exercises in remembrance, Arendt revealed the significant influence that Benjamin's "Theses on the Philosophy of History" had on her views of historical narrative.[74] Of course, Arendt herself did not replace the transmissibility of the past by its citability, but quotations for her as well became interesting fragments, archaeological curiosities whose meaning lay "full fathom deep." To "find those pearls that were his eyes," one had to dive deep into the original meaning of the phenomena that lay covered under the sedimented layers of historical interpretation. Once one brought these pearls to the surface, one could unsettle the present and deprive it of its "peace of mind."

In Arendt's Benjamin essay, the figure of the pearl diver is accompanied by that of the collector:

> The figure of the collector, as old-fashioned as that of the *flâneur,* could assume such eminently modern features in Benjamin because history itself—that is the break in tradition which took place at the beginning of

this century—had already relieved him of this task of destruction and he only needed to bend down, as it were, to select his precious fragments from the pile of debris.[75]

Arendt was well aware that by arguing that the activity of the storyteller was like that of the pearl diver and of the collector, she was consciously leaving out poetry. Although she praises Benjamin for being a poet, there is ultimately no kinship between the poet who sings to eternalize the city and to save from oblivion those deeds of human greatness, and the modern storyteller who has no identifiable human city. The loss of the *Vaterstadt,* as Brecht knew, was not the loss of a place or an environment;[76] the city exemplifies home, tradition, and generationally transmitted remembrance. If the loss of the city seemed to dry up the sources of poetry, the storyteller, like the pearl diver and the collector, was still free to dig under the rubble for pearls to bring to the surface.

Arendt's account of the "rise of the social" and the decline of the public space of politics under conditions of modernity must be reread in light of this methodology of "fragmentary historiography" or "storytelling." Here we return to a theme already identified at the end of the Rahel Varnhagen discussion in Chapter 1: the presence of an alternative archaeology of modernity in Arendt's work. This alternative archaeology of modernity has both substantive and methodological dimensions. I began to explore some of the substantive issues involved in Arendt's analysis, such as the meaning of the *social,* in Chapter 1. This chapter has introduced the methodological aspects of fragmentary historiography, which is not an exercise in a nostalgic *Verfallsgeschichte,* a history of decline, but an attempt to think through the human history sedimented in layers of language and concepts. We must learn to identify those moments of rupture, displacement, and dislocation in history. At such moments, language is witness to the more profound transformations taking place in human life. Such a *Begriffsgeschichte* is a remembering, in the sense of a creative act of rethinking that sets free the lost potentials of the past.

The history of revolutions . . . could be told in a parable form as the tale of an age-old treasure which, under the most varied circumstances, appears abruptly, unexpectedly, and disappears again, under different mysterious conditions, as though it were a fata morgana.[77]

Arendt's thought, however, is not always free from aspects of an *Ursprungsphilosophie* that posits an originary state, in the phenomenological sense of the word, as being the privileged one. As opposed to rupture, displacement, and dislocation, this view emphasizes the continuity between origin and the present and seeks to uncover at the origin the lost and concealed essence of the phenomena. There are thus two strains in Arendt's thought, one corresponding to the method of fragmentary historiography, and inspired by Walter Benjamin; the other, inspired by the phenomenology of Husserl and Heidegger, and according to which memory is the mimetic recollection of the lost origins of phenomena as contained in some fundamental human experience. Along these lines, reminders abound in *The Human Condition* of "the original meaning of politics" or of the "lost" distinction between the "private" and the "public" (*HC*, pp. 22 ff., 68 ff.). The text in which the philosophical struggle between these two methodologies is played out, and in which Hannah Arendt once more returns to the thought of Martin Heidegger, is *The Human Condition*.

Notes

1. See Hannah Arendt, *The Burden of Our Times* (London: Secker and Warburg, 1951).

2. See Eric Voegelin, review of *The Origins of Totalitarianism* in *Review of Politics* 15 (January 1953): 69.

3. Arendt, 1950 preface to the first edition of *The Origins of Totalitarianism*, p. viii.

4. Arendt, 1967 preface to Pt. I of the *The Origins of Totalitarianism*, p. xv.

5. Arendt's claim that the future is radically underdetermined, and can never be foretold on the basis of the past, is rooted in her ontological analysis of human "spontaneity." This is the capacity to initiate the new and the unexpected. It corresponds to the human fact of birth. Just as every birth signifies a new life story, one that can never be foretold at birth, so the human capacity for action can always initiate the new and the unexpected (see *HC*, pp. 243 ff.). This capacity for spontaneity is essential for political life, for the building of the city is due to such an act of spontaneity, just as the continuity of the city is dependent upon the coordination of human activities. Totalitarianism aims at destroying this capacity for a new beginning, thus making political life impossible.

Arendt does not explore how this thesis of the spontaneity of human action is related to the perspective of the social sciences, which, by focusing on the enabling and antecedent conditions of action, enhances our understanding of the course of action while diminishing our sense of its spontaneity. Arendt would appear to be claiming that social science is possible only insofar as humans do not "act" but "behave," that is, insofar as they repeat socially established patterns. A more interesting account of the impossibility of a social science of a nomological and predictive nature, which bases this thesis on the narrative character of action rather than upon its spontaneity, is offered by Alasdair MacIntyre, *After Virtue* (Indiana: Notre Dame University Press, 1981).

6. This is the phrase used by Merleau-Ponty in describing Max Weber's analysis of the Protestant ethic and the spirit of capitalism; see Maurice Merleau-Ponty, *Les Aventures de la Dialectique* (Paris: Gallimard, 1955), p. 29.

7. See Walter Benjamin, *The Origin of German Tragic Drama,* trans. John Osbourne (London: New Left Review, 1977). See also Susan Buck Morss's exploration of the terms *configuration* and *crystallization of elements* as methodological categories of Benjamin's work in *The Origin of Negative Dialectics: Theodor W. Adorno, Walter Benjamin and the Frankfurt Institute* (New York: Free Press, 1977), pp. 96-111.

8. Hannah Arendt, "A Reply," exchange with Eric Voegelin about the latter's review of *The Origins of Totalitarianism,* in the *Review of Politics* 15 (January 1953), p. 78. See Note A appended to the English edition of Benjamin's "Theses on the Philosophy of History" (which Arendt edited in English): "Historicism contents itself with establishing a causal connection between various moments in history. But no fact that is cause is for that very reason historical. It became historical posthumously, as it were, through the events that may be separated from it by thousands of years. A historian who takes this as his point of departure stops telling the sequence of events like the beads of a rosary. Instead, he grasps the constellation which his own era has formed with a definite earlier one. Thus he establishes a conception of the present as the 'time of the now' which is shot through with chips of messianic time, W. Benjamin," *Illuminations,* ed., with an introduction by Hannah Arendt (New York: Schocken, 1969), p. 262.

9. Arendt, *The Origins of Totalitarianism,* p. 438.

10. Roland W. Schindler gives a very informative and balanced account of Hannah Arendt's theses concerning the nature of the National Socialist regime, and in particular of its policy on the extermination of the Jews, as seen within the context of contemporary historians' debates on these issues. Arendt's theory occupies a middle ground between "functionalist" patterns of explanation, which attribute some utilitarian means-ends rationality to the policy of the extermination of the Jews in the Third Reich, on the one hand, and "intentionalist" accounts, on the other, which see this policy as serving no utilitarian end but, instead, as following from the inexorable ideological logic of the National Socialist world-view. According to Arendt, the concept of an "objective enemy" did not serve an economic end but fortified the political purpose of total mastery and domination at which the Nazi regime aimed. Roland W. Schindler, "Hannah Arendt und die Historiker-Kontroverse um die 'Rationalität' der Judenvernichtung," in *Dialektik* (Frankfurt: Felix Meiner Verlag, 1994), pp. 146-160.

11. Arendt, *The Origins of Totalitarianism,* p. 443. See also Arendt's review called "The History of the Great Crime" of Leon Poliakov's *Breviary of Hate: The Third Reich and the Jews,* in *Commentary,* March 13, 1952, p. 304.

12. In Arendt's account of modern anti-Semitism, the historical-institutional role of the Jews in modern bourgeois society plays a major role. Nonetheless, it is important to recall

that the peculiarities of modern anti-Semitism cannot simply be explained by the identification of Jews with the sphere of circulation and exchange, with money, and with power in general. These equations are meaningful only because "enlightened" society has gotten rid of the figure of the Jew as the murderer of the Son of God and has replaced him or her with the image of the Jew as the potential carrier of an unreformable, unredeemable "vice," namely, the "fact" of Jewishness as such. Modern anti-Semitism focuses on Jewishness not as an act but as a condition, as a form of identity. For this reason, it is more insidious; it requires that this identity be changed or that the fact be eliminated. No doubt, the strange visibility of the Jews in modern European society made them the object of human resentments—from the bankers who financed the absolutist kings, to the assimilated bourgeoisie who used its connections established under the old regime to continue commercial relations in the new capitalist economy, to the Jews who, like money itself, seemed to be the one truly supra-European community—Jews remained members of the national state yet supranational in their historical ties, family relations, languages they spoke, and so on.

13. Ibid., p. 475.

14. See Manfred Funke, ed., *Totalitarismus: Ein Studien-Reader zur Herrschaftsanalyse moderner Diktaturen* (Düsseldorf: Proste, 1978).

15. See Hans Mommsen, "The Concept of Totalitarian Dictatorship Versus the Comparative Theory of Fascism," in *Totalitarianism Reconsidered*, ed. Ernest A. Menze (Port Washington, N.Y.: Kennikat, 1981), pp. 146-167.

16. See Karl Buchheim, "Totalitarismus: Zu Hannah Arendt's Buch 'Elemente und Ursprünge Totaler Herrschaft,' " in *Hannah Arendt: Materialien zu Ihrem Werk*, ed. Adalbert Reif (Vienna: Europaverlag, 1979), pp. 211 ff.

17. See Carl Friedrich and Zbigniew K. Brzezinski, *Totalitarian Dictatorship and Autocracy*, 2nd ed., revised by Carl J. Friedrich (Cambridge, Mass.: Harvard University Press, 1965). See in particular the preface to the first edition, pp. xi-xiii.

18. Of interest, in recent years, east European intellectuals and dissidents have been reviving this concept (Heller, Feher, Havel). See in particular F. Feher and A. Heller, *Eastern Left, Western Left: Totalitarianism, Freedom and Democracy* (Cambridge, UK: Polity, 1986).

19. See Robert C. Tucker, "Between Lenin and Stalin: A Cultural Analysis" in *Praxis International* 6, no. 4 (1987), pp. 470 ff.; and Alvin Gouldner, "Stalinism: A Study of Internal Colonialism," *Telos*, no. 34 (Winter 1977–1978), pp. 5-48. I would like to thank Paul Breines for his helpful discussion around this question.

20. These empirical and historical problems of Arendt's interpretation of totalitarianism still cannot distract from the work's greatness. Bernard Crick, for example, has argued that "if the book does seem unbalanced in the space it gives to Germany, perhaps this is a fault, to see it as a gross fault would be to misconceive the whole purpose and strategy of the book. It would be rather like, having been able to grasp that Tocqueville's *Democracy in America* is really meant to be about the whole of Western European civilizations, to then say that he should have given an equal and explicit space to France and England." Bernard Crick, "On Rereading *The Origins of Totalitarianism*," *Social Research* 44 (Spring 1977), pp. 113-114; reprinted in *Materialien zu Ihrem Werk*, ed. Reif, p. 224. I am personally less sanguine that this intelligent defense of Arendt's strategy can suffice to rectify the problems of her parallel treatments of National Socialism and Stalinism. What is more important in Bernard Crick's observation, and what might shed further light on the puzzles of Arendt's analysis of totalitarianism, is the affinity between Alexis de Tocqueville's *Democracy in America* and Arendt's *The Origins of Totalitarianism*.

21. Alexis de Tocqueville, *Democracy in America*, ed. J. P. Mayer; trans. George Lawrence (New York: Anchor, 1969), p. 12.

22. Arendt, *OT*, preface to the first edition (summer 1950), p. viii.

23. Tocqueville, *Democracy in America*, p. 192.

24. Ibid., p. 506.

25. Ibid., p. 508.

26. Ibid., p. 510.

27. Arendt, 1966 Preface to Part III, *The Origins of Totalitarianism*, pp. xxxi-xxxii.

28. See Hans Mommsen's introduction to the German edition of *Eichmann in Jerusalem: Ein Bericht von der Banalität des Bösen* (Munich: Piper Verlag, 1986), pp. i-xxxvii.

29. *OT*, pp. 310 ff.

30. See Andras Bozoki and Miklos Sukosd, "Civil Society and Populism in East European Democratic Transitions," *Praxis International* 13, no. 3 (1993), pp. 224-242; H. Gordon Skilling and Paul Wilson, eds., *Civic Freedom in Central Europe: Voices From Czechoslovakia* (New York: St. Martin's, 1991).

31. Agnes Heller, "An Imaginary Preface to the 1984 Edition of Hannah Arendt's 'The Origins of Totalitarianism,' " in *The Public Realm: Essays on Discursive Types in Political Philosophy*, ed. Reiner Schürmann (New York: SUNY Press, 1989), p. 254. See Arendt, Preface to Part III of *The Origins of Totalitarianism* (1966), p. xxxvi.

32. Heller, "An Imaginary Preface," p. 254.

33. Arendt, preface to Part III (1966), *OT*, pp. xxiii-xl.

34. I borrow the phrase from Nancy Fraser, who uses it to describe the formation of multiple public spheres under conditions of late-capitalist democratic societies. See Nancy Fraser, "Rethinking the Public Sphere: A Contribution to the Critique of Actually Existing Democracy" in *Habermas and the Public Sphere*, ed. Craig Calhoun (Cambridge: MIT Press, 1992), pp. 109-143.

35. Arendt, 1966 preface to Part III, *OT*, p. xxxvii.

36. See Andrew Arato, "Civil Society Against the State: Poland 1980–1981," *Telos* 47 (Spring 1981), pp. 23-47; "Empire vs. Civil Society: Poland 1981–1982," *Telos* 50 (Winter 1981–1982), pp. 19-48; and "Revolution, Civil Society and Democracy," *Praxis International* 10, nos. 1-2 (1990), pp. 24-38.

37. See in particular Jean Cohen and Andrew Arato, *Civil Society and Political Theory* (Cambridge: MIT Press, 1992).

38. An exception is George Kateb in *Hannah Arendt: Politics, Conscience, Evil* (Totowa, N.J.: Rowman and Allenheld, 1984), pp. 60 ff.; see also Anne Norton, "Heart of Darkness: Africa and African Americans in the Writings of Hannah Arendt," in *Feminist Interpretations of Hannah Arendt*, ed. Bonnie Honig (University Park: Pennsylvania State University Press, 1995), pp. 247-263; Norma Claire Moruzzi, "Re-placing the Margin: (Non)representations of Colonialism in Hannah Arendt's *The Origins of Totalitarianism*," *Tulsa Studies in Women's Literature* 10, no. 1 (1991), pp. 109-120.

39. Arendt cites the following figures: "Within less than two decades, British colonial possessions increased by 4 and ½ million square miles and 66 million inhabitants, the French nation gained 3 and ½ million square miles and 26 million people, the Germans won a new empire of a million square miles and 13 million natives." Arendt, *OT*, p. 124; quoting in turn Carlton J. H. Hayes, *A Generation of Materialism* (New York: Harper, 1941). See *OT*, pp. 127 ff., for the discussion of British empire building efforts in comparison with the French.

40. Arendt notes, "If race-thinking were a German invention, as it has been sometimes asserted, then 'German thinking' (whatever that may be) was victorious in many parts of the

spiritual world long before the Nazis started their ill-fated attempt at world conquest. . . . The historical truth of the matter is that race thinking, with its roots deep in the eighteenth century, emerged simultaneously in all Western countries during the nineteenth century. Racism has been the powerful ideology of imperialistic policies since the turn of our century." *OT,* p. 158.

41. The most vivid example of this connection is the statement attributed to Hitler, "Who remembers the Armenians today?" (in a speech delivered on August 22, 1939, to his military commanders). The massacre of Armenian peoples under the Ottoman regime is an example not only of the fragility of the "rights of man" but also an illustration of a case in which wars and massacres, seemingly at the periphery, sooner or later find their way to the center. See K. D. Bardakjian, *Hitler and the Armenian Genocide,* Special Report No. 3 (Cambridge, Mass.: Zoryan Institute, 1985).

42. Hannah Arendt, "Home to Roost," *New York Review of Books,* June 26, 1975, pp. 3-6.

43. Arendt refers to Lenin's text in *OT,* footnote 45, p. 148. See V. I. Lenin, *Imperialism: The Highest Stage of Capitalism,* 10th impression, vol. 22 of the *Works of Lenin* (Moscow: Foreign Language Publishing House, 1961).

44. Hannah Arendt's mother, Martha Arendt, was an ardent admirer of Rosa Luxemburg, and had taken her eleven-year-old daughter to demonstrations in Königsberg in support of the Spartacists League, which Rosa Luxemburg chaired with Karl Liebknecht. Hannah Arendt's husband, Heinrich Bluecher, had been a member of the Spartacists and later of the "KPD" (Kommunistische Partei Deutschlands), founded by Rosa Luxemburg and Karl Liebknecht. Debates between the Spartacists, on the one hand, the Russian Bolsheviks and German Social Democrats, on the other, were well known in the Arendt household. See Elisabeth Young-Bruehl, *For Love of the World* (New Haven: Yale University Press, 1982), pp. 124 ff.

45. Rosa Luxemburg, *The Accumulation of Capital,* trans. from the German by Agnes Schwarzschild, with an introduction by Joan Robinson (New York: Modern Reader Paperbacks, 1968), p. 368.

46. Hannah Arendt, "Rosa Luxemburg," in *Men in Dark Times* (New York: Harcourt Brace Jovanovich, 1968), p. 38.

47. See Young-Bruehl, *For Love of the World,* pp. 293 ff.

48. This is a dimension of Arendt's discussion that is totally ignored in Anne Norton's "Heart of Darkness." The only curious omission in Arendt's discussion is the colonization of the New World by the Spanish empire and the impact this confrontation with the "others" had on the development of early modern consciousness in Europe. See Tzvetan Todorov, *The Conquest of America: The Question of the Other,* trans. Richard Howard (New York: Harper & Row, 1982), for an exploration of this conquest.

49. See Edmund Burke, *Speeches on the Impeachment of Warren Hastings,* vols. 1 and 2, reprinted from the *Works of Edmund Burke,* vol. 8 (New Delhi: Discovery Publishing House, 1987); see also Connor Cruise O'Brien, *The Great Melody: A Thematic Biography and Commented Anthology of Edmund Burke* (Chicago: University of Chicago Press, 1992), pp. 255-385; see also Arendt, *OT,* p. 207.

50. Joseph Conrad, *Heart of Darkness,* ed. Robert Kimbrough (New York: Norton, 1988).

51. Anne Norton, "Heart of Darkness: Africa and African-Americans in the Writings of Hannah Arendt," p. 253.

52. Kwame Anthony Appiah, *In My Father's House: Africa in the Philosophy of Culture* (New York: Oxford University Press, 1992).

53. These dilemmas concerning the historiography of National Socialism, and the moral and political issues involved were repeated in the so-called historians' debate, which erupted

in German historiography in the 1980s. For documentation, see *Historikerstreit: Die Dokumentation der Kontroverse um die Einzigartigkeit der national-sozialistischen Judenvernichtung* (Munich: Serie Piper, 1987); Charles Maier, *The Unmasterable Past: History, Holocaust, and German National Identity* (Cambridge, Mass.: Harvard University Press, 1988).

54. Arendt, "A Reply," *Review of Politics*, p. 77.

55. Ibid., p. 79.

56. Ibid. See also Hannah Arendt, "The Crisis in Culture: Its Social and Its Political Significance," in *Between Past and Future: Six Exercises in Political Thought* (New York: Meridian, 1961), p. 221.

57. Arendt, "The Crisis in Culture," pp. 220-221; see also Seyla Benhabib, "Urteilskraft und die moralischen Grundlagen der Politik im Werk Hannah Arendts," in *Zeitschrift für Philosophische Forschung* 41, Heft 4 (October-December 1987): 521-547; revised English version, Benhabib, "Judgment and the Moral Foundations of Politics in Hannah Arendt's Thought," *Political Theory* 16, no. 1 (1988): 29-51.

58. When Arendt discusses Nietzsche extensively in *The Life of the Mind*, vol. 2, *Willing*, she treats him first and foremost as a philosopher of the will and not as an epistemologist (New York: Harcourt Brace Jovanovich, 1978), pp. 158-172. Nonetheless, Nietzsche's epistemic influence on Arendt is hard to miss. On Nietzsche's perspectivalism, see Alexander Nehamas, *Life as Literature* (Cambridge, Mass.: Harvard University Press, 1985).

59. I have dealt with some of the dilemmas of Arendt's moral theory in my article, "Judgment and the Moral Foundations of Politics." The obligation to take the standpoint of the other is part of a universalistic-egalitarian morality that needs a stronger justification in moral philosophy than Arendt was willing to offer. See Chapter 6 on these issues.

60. See Kateb, *Politics, Conscience, Evil*, pp. 61-63.

61. In light of post-Kuhnian developments in the social sciences in particular, some of Arendt's observations on the topic of generalization in these sciences have proved remarkably prescient; see, on the general topic, Richard J. Bernstein, *The Restructuring of Social and Political Theory* (Philadelphia: University of Pennsylvania Press, 1976).

62. "A Reply," *Review of Politics*, p. 83.

63. In Young-Bruehl, *For Love of the World*, p. 331, 367.

64. See the exchange with Karl Jaspers on this point in *Arendt-Jaspers Correspondence*, pp. 414 ff.

65. See Hans Mommsen, Vorwort to *Eichmann in Jerusalem: Ein Bericht von der Banalität des Bösen* (Munich: Serie Piper, 1986), pp. xiv-xviii.

66. See Voegelin, review of *The Origins of Totalitarianism, Review of Politics*, p. 71.

67. Arendt, "A Reply," *Review of Politics*, p. 79.

68. See Arendt, *Men in Dark Times*, p. 22; preface to *Between Past and Future*, p. 14. There is an excellent essay by David Luban, which is one of the few discussions in the literature dealing with Hannah Arendt's methodology of storytelling, see D. Luban, "Explaining Dark Times: Hannah Arendt's Theory of Theory," *Social Research* 50, no. 1, pp. 215-247; see also E. Young-Bruehl, "Hannah Arendt als Geschichtenerzählerin," in *Hannah Arendt: Materialien zu Ihrem Werk*, pp. 319-327.

69. Hannah Arendt, *The Life of the Mind*, vol. 1, *Thinking* (New York: Harcourt Brace Jovanovich, 1978), p. 212.

70. See her essays "What Is Authority?" and "What Is Freedom?" in *Between Past and Future*, pp. 91-143 and 143-173, respectively.

71. Arendt, *Thinking*, p. 210.

72. Arendt, *Thinking*, p. 212.

73. Arendt, "Walter Benjamin," in Arendt, *Men in Dark Times*, p. 193.

74. See M. P. d'Entrèves, *The Political Philosophy of Hannah Arendt* (London: Routledge, 1994), pp. 28-34, for one of the few discussions in the literature on this link between Arendt and Walter Benjamin.

75. Arendt, "Walter Benjamin," in Arendt, *Men in Dark Times*, p. 200.

76. In her essay on Brecht, Arendt quotes: "Of Poor B.B.".: "We have sat, an easy generation/In houses held to be indestructable./Thus we built those tall boxes on the/island of Manhattan/And those thin aerials that amuse the/Atlantic swell./Of those cities will remain what passed/through them, the wind!/The house makes glad the eater: he/clears it out./We know that we are only tenants, provisional ones/And after us will come: nothing worth talking/about." Arendt, "Bertolt Brecht," in *Men in Dark Times*, pp. 207-251; here, p. 219. See also B. Brecht, "Von Armen B.B.," in *Gedichte, 1918–1929* (Frankfurt: Suhrkamp, 1960), pp. 147-149.

77. Arendt, preface to *Between Past and Future*, p. 5.

4

The Dialogue With Martin Heidegger:
Arendt's Ontology of *The Human Condition*

The Meaning of Heidegger's Silence

In a letter to Karl Jaspers dated November 1, 1961, Hannah Arendt wrote,

> Heidegger—yes, it is a most irritating story . . . this open hostility, which
> he has never really displayed before. My explanation—putting aside for
> the moment the possibility of some kind of gossip—is that last winter I sent
> him one of my books, the *Vita Activa*, for the first time. I know that he finds
> it intolerable that my name appears in public, that I write books, etc. All
> my life, I've pulled the wool over his eyes, so to speak, acted as if none of
> that existed and as if I couldn't count to three, unless it was in the
> interpretation of his own works. Then he was always very pleased when it
> turned out I could count to three and sometimes even to four. Then I
> suddenly felt this deception was becoming just too boring, and so I got a
> rap on the nose. I was very angry for a moment, but I am not any longer. I
> feel instead that I somehow deserved what I got—that is, both for having
> deceived him and for suddenly having put an end to it.[1]

To the retrospective students of their thought, the personal drama contained in these few words is fascinating and irritating at the same time. The story of Martin Heidegger and Hannah Arendt fascinates, because the lives and personal relationship of these two powerful thinkers is like a parable of the twentieth century. We are fascinated by the story of a young German Jewess student of philosophy in Marburg during 1924–1925 who falls in love and has an affair with the brilliant young *dozent* of philosophy. We are fascinated that in 1933, as a refugee in Paris, she is working with a Zionist organization to settle children in Palestine, while he, for however brief a moment, becomes the rector of the University of Freiburg, in charge of bringing the university "in line" with the demands of the National Socialist Party. We are fascinated by the equanimity and magnanimity with which Arendt forgave Heidegger his "mistake," and by her continuing tortured attempts at a metaphysical justification of Heidegger's political error.[2]

The relationship of Martin Heidegger and Hannah Arendt also irritates. Despite her profound independence of mind and her unwavering pride, Hannah Arendt humbled herself in Heidegger's presence.[3] She even effaced herself as an intellectual in his eyes, feeding, in fact, a profoundly narcissistic male ego with her all-too-female erasure of her own intellectual power—until the day, that is, when she sent him a copy of the German translation of the *Human Condition,* which in German appeared as *Vita Activa.* "The active life" or "the life of action" is a better title for this work: as Arendt herself observed, she had meant to distinguish between the active life and the life of the mind; so the volume misleadingly called *The Human Condition* represents only one aspect of that condition, namely, the life of action as opposed to the life of the mind.[4]

How are we to interpret Heidegger's chilling silence in view of Arendt's philosophical work? Psychological explanations such as male narcissism, pettiness of character, envy, and jealousy may all be true, and unfortunately, they are borne out by historical accounts of Heidegger's personality.[5] But they do not explain the *philosophical significance* of Heidegger's silence. With her work *The Human Condition,* Arendt found her own philosophical voice.[6] As she expresses it in the letter to Jaspers cited above, she was no longer simply the *interpreter* of Heidegger's work, "count[ing] to three and sometimes even to four" in his arithmetic. Arendt now had her own equations to formulate and to solve. Heidegger, in my opinion, remained silent because he recognized how his former student had subverted the premises that were fundamental to his ontology; and she had done this within a framework that still bore the profound marks of his thought. This, I think, was unbearable to him and drove him to silence.

Plurality, the World, and the Solipsism of Heidegger's Ontology

I have discussed above (see the third section, "The Concept of the 'World' in Martin Heidegger's *Being and Time*," in Chapter 2) Arendt's claim that "it is almost impossible to render a clear account of Heidegger's political thoughts that may be of political relevance without an elaborate report on his concept and analysis of 'world.'"[7] Although Heidegger, through his analysis of *Dasein*'s being-in-the-world as a form of *Mitsein,* of "being-with," made human plurality constitutive of the human condition, the fundamental categories of his existential analytic, rather than illuminating human plurality, denigrated human togetherness to a form of being with the *das Man,* the "they." In her 1946 essay "What Is Existenz Philosophy?" Arendt suggests that the absence in Heidegger's philosophy of plurality, or being-with, as a constitutive dimension, is the reason that this philosophy can allow a "mechanical reconciliation" of "atomized selves" in an "Over-self" that carries them into action.[8] Certainly, the absence of a philosophical theorem of intersubjectivity, or of the co-constitution of subjects, is not enough to lead a thinker to espouse National Socialism. One can think of many counterexamples: most members of the Vienna school, including Rudolf Carnap, Alfred Tarski, and Maurice Schlick, were methodological individualists, as was Karl Popper. If anything, in the case of Popper, he established a deductive link—fallaciously, I believe—between thoughts of community and intersubjectivity and the espousal of National Socialism.[9] Indeed, what Arendt means is not that Heidegger's fundamental ontology led him to espouse National Socialism; rather, she suggests that Heidegger's inability to articulate the human condition of plurality led him to develop a conception of radically isolated selfhood from the standpoint of which an equally radical dissolution in a "whole," in a mass political movement, would appear plausible.[10] Applying one of the lessons of Arendt's theory of totalitarianism, we can say that the radical isolation of the individual makes this individual susceptible to being sucked in by collectivities that falsely promise solidarity and companionship. His inability to articulate the condition of plurality made Heidegger susceptible to promises of false solidarity in an authoritarian movement.

If, however, Heidegger had developed a concept of Dasein's being-in-the-world that revolutionized the modern epistemological tradition, why could he not have taken the step that led from "being-in-the-world-with" to human plurality? The answer lies with the absence of a concept of action as interaction in Heidegger's thought. The fundamental categories of the existential analytic in *Being and Time* deal with activities primarily referring to the manipulation of objects, to the bringing about of states of affairs in the world. Being-ready-to-hand *(Zuhandensein)* and being-ready-at-hand *(Vorhandensein)* each deal with modalities through which an individual brings about a state of affairs in the world, like building a house, planting a garden, or cooking a meal; or one makes something, for example, a pot or a table. Heidegger is concerned to analyze the way in which this world of things and objects, as well as the entire background of presuppositions and references that accompany them, make themselves present to Dasein. There are no categories in this framework for thinking of actions demonstrating generosity or cupidity, friendship or treachery, love or hostility.

Concerned being-with-others in the world—*Fürsorge*—is in its most authentic form a caring for others as they are unto-death, as they are finite creatures, caught in temporality. Guilt, resoluteness, being-unto-death are "Existentialia"—existential conditions—which remind Dasein of the fundamentals of its condition, namely, a temporality of finitude. Dasein is "thrown into" a world of facticity, of human circumstances, networks, and contexts that precede it and in which it is submerged. Only the step of pulling oneself back out of the facticity of everydayness to a condition of resolute coming-to-one's-senses *(Besinnung),* getting hold of one's existence, can enable Dasein to reach authenticity. This getting hold of one's senses does and must entail the possibility of being-unto-death, of choosing through an act of resoluteness one's own being-unto-death. "Does being-in-the-world have a higher instance for its potentiality-for-Being than its own death?" *(Hat das In-der-Welt-sein eine höhere Instanz seines Seinkönnens als seinen Tod?)*[11]

These passages on the ontology of death as the most authentic form of Dasein's being reveal the presence in Heidegger's work of sensibilities from different cultural and intellectual traditions. As Thomas Rentsch has written in his insightful introduction to the life and work of Heidegger, Heidegger develops "a godless theology."[12] The theological motifs of Christianity, the fallenness of men into an inauthentic world, the creature-like finitude of human existence destined to a life of "care"—*Sorge*—and finally the thought of one's fundamental finitude are vividly present. When we are confronted with death, we realize, in St. Augustine's sense, that we are not the ground of our being. Because Heidegger's theology is "godless," however, this realization does not lead to a further act of humbling. There is also in Heidegger's thought the existentialist ethos of transforming the knowledge of the groundlessness of one's being into an act of defiant courage by choosing one's own destiny, by giving oneself over to forces that call to one. The godless theology of Martin Heidegger now becomes the ideology of the male warrior. As Rentsch explains, at the time of the publication of *Being and Time* (1927),

> the World War . . . had just been over for a few years: don't phrases like "running into death" and "the most extreme possibility of self-sacrifice," remind one of the heroic picture of the soldier's existence. . . . Is this not the ideal of the front-fighter who is not afraid of death . . . the existential ideal of the masculine resolve of an officer . . . ?[13]

The philosophical categories of activity that dominate in *Being and Time* are either those of instrumental activity that concern forms of making or bringing about something in the world or the categories that reveal an existentialism of death, guilt, resoluteness, and fallenness. The most remarkable aspect of the latter is their complete methodological solipsism: they relate to none other than oneself. It is not those who mourn me and those whom I leave behind that matter, but that I, this single individual, must die. This is certainly and undeniably true; but even death is a social act and a social fact. My death concerns many more in addition to myself; it is mourned, remembered, lamented, or rejoiced over; met with sorrow or with glee—as the case may be. Think also of the social identities that may be affected: this death may mean the end of a dynasty or of a family; it may mean the death of one's only child and heir; it may mean the beginning of a new political era, as the death of a dictator usually signifies. One can multiply these descriptions of the pertinent human situations and relations that would characterize ad infinitum one's death as a social fact. For Heidegger, though, categories such as being-unto-death, guilt, resoluteness, as "existentials," are forms of "relating-oneself-to-oneself." Not only the existential but also the methodological solipsism of *Being and Time* prevents an intersubjective account of action as interaction, as acting-with, in Arendt's terms. From Heidegger's perspective, the human condition of plurality, of being-in-the-world-with-others in the manner of speech and action, is a condition of facticity into which one is thrown and in which one loses oneself.

In *The Human Condition,* Hannah Arendt resuscitates everyday-being-in-the-world with others as the basic condition of being human. Even a brief consideration of the fundamental categories of this work such as natality, plurality, and action reveal how profoundly they are opposed to those of Heidegger's *Being and Time.* Being-unto-death is displaced by natality; the isolated Dasein is replaced by a condition of plurality; and instead of instrumental action, a new category of human activity, action, understood as speech and doing, emerges. Everyday being-in-the-world, rather than being the condition of inauthenticity into which Dasein is thrown, now becomes that "space of appearance" into which we are inserted as acting and speaking beings and within which we reveal who we are and what we are capable of. Ironically, the full significance of Arendt's transformation of Heidegger's ontology requires a more detailed examination of Heidegger's reading of Aristotle in the period from 1923 to 1925. Arendt, as opposed to Heidegger, found in Aristotle's concept of *praxis* the key to a new revaluation of human action as interaction unfolding within a space of appearances.

Action, Narrative, and the Web of Stories

Without Heidegger's analysis of Dasein's condition as one of being-in-the-world-with-others, some of the fundamental categories of Hannah

Arendt's own political philosophy, such as natality, plurality, worldliness, and the public realm, could not have been formulated, because more often than not they were thought "in opposition" to Heidegger; yet it is also the case that Arendt undertook a fundamental transformation of Heidegger's ontology. Let us recall some of the key elements of her discussion in *The Human Condition*. Labor, work, and action each correspond "to one of the basic conditions under which life on earth has been given to man" (*HC*, p. 7). Labor is an activity necessitated by the biological rhythm of the human body itself: life must be renewed, sustained, nurtured; labor is activity geared to maintaining, under whichever social conditions, the constant care of the body and of the environment in which this body is situated. Procuring daily nourishment, cleaning and grooming the body and the space that humans inhabit, tending to the wear and tear of the everyday things around one, of the world of objects that humans need, all belong under the category of labor.

Work corresponds to the "unnaturalness of human existence" (*HC*, p. 7); work is the activity that creates a second nature of things—edifices, structures, buildings, monuments, cultural artifacts. Work is the activity that creates the *world* in the Heideggerian sense of the term. Through work, a world of more or less permanent objects emerges within which human life unfolds. This world of objects orients humans in their daily activities; at the same time, objects provide a certain durability and permanence that run across generations; they are, we may say, a material repository of memory. An example may clarify Arendt's meaning: when we visit ancient buildings, monuments, and cities, we try to immerse ourselves in the world of those who have lived in these buildings, who have carried out their activities in them. The presence of these things across time, their more or less contingent durability, allows us to establish a continuity with bygone generations.[14] To understand the world these past generations have inhabited means learning the referential contexts, the patterns of everyday use, the what and wherefor of their activities. Why did they build the spires of this castle so high? Why were the living chambers separated from the eating quarters in this way? Why were the ceilings so low? Is this object an instrument or a decorative piece? In what context of activity does it belong? By getting to know this world of things, artifacts, buildings, and, of course, cultural creations, we get to know each other across worlds.

> The objectivity of the world—its object- or thing-character—and the human condition supplement each other; because human existence is conditioned existence, it would be impossible without things, and things would be a heap of unrelated articles, a non-world, if they were not the conditioners of human existence. (*HC*, p. 9)

Action is the only activity that goes on directly between humans, and it corresponds to the human condition of plurality. Plurality entails both equality and distinction. If humans were not equal, they could not understand each other; if they were not distinct, they would need neither speech nor action to distinguish them from each other (*HC*, p. 175). Through speech and action, humans distinguish themselves from one another; they become the authors of "words and deeds." Through words and deeds, humans "appear" to one another, or reveal themselves to each other.

> This appearance, as distinguished from mere bodily existence, rests on initiative, but it is an initiative from which no human being can refrain and still be human. This is true of no other activity in the *vita activa*. Men can very well live without laboring, they can force others to labor for them, and they can very well decide to use and enjoy the world of things without themselves adding a single useful object to it. . . . A life without speech and action, on the other hand—and this is the only way of life that in earnest has renounced all appearance and all vanity in the biblical sense of the word—is literally dead to the world; it has ceased to be a human life because it is no longer lived among men. (*HC*, p. 176)

Action corresponds to the human condition of "natality"—that we are born or, in Heidegger's terms, "thrown" into a world that precedes our existence and within which alone we become who we are. Action is like a second birth (*HC*, p. 176); "its impulse springs from the beginning which came into the world when we were born and to which we respond by beginning something new on our own initiative" (*HC*, p. 177). The birth of the human infant has a biological as well as a psychic-social dimension. The human infant becomes a self by learning speech and action in the human community into which it is born. Through this process, the infant also becomes an individual, that is, the unique initiator of these words and deeds, the carrier of this life story. This condition is a social universal: no human community, as opposed to a merely accidental gathering of primates, can exist over time without teaching its young the language and actions characteristic of its way of life. The crucial point here is that in learning speech and action, every human child also becomes the initiator of new deeds and of new words. To learn a language is to master the capacity for formulating an infinite number of well-formed sentences in that language; to know how to act as a Hopi Indian, as an Ancient Greek, as a modern American is also to know—more or less—how to initiate both what is expected of one by the community and what is new, distinctive to this individual. Socialization and individuation are two sides of the same coin.

"In acting and speaking," writes Arendt,

> men show who they are, reveal actively their unique personal identities and thus make their appearance in the human world. . . . This disclosure of "who" in contradistinction to "what" somebody is—his qualities, gifts, talents, and shortcomings, which he may display or hide—is implicit in everything somebody says and does. (*HC*, p. 179)

Through speech and action, words and deeds, humans insert themselves "into a world of appearances." To be human is to appear in the world to others, to be present to them, to be perceived by them, to be in communication with them. For humans, being and appearance are one; there is no human essence hidden behind or beyond the appearances. Human life is life that unfolds within the human world of appearances. This means that all two-world metaphysics that seek to understand the human condition in the light of a principle that precedes, grounds, or antedates the world as appearance miss the essential human condition of action. To be alive as a human being, as opposed to being a mere body, is to act and speak with others in space and time. Being is being present, it is to appear; it is to manifest itself. As Sergio Belardinelli notes, Arendt's teaching of the space of appearances is unmistakably indebted to Heidegger's doctrine of *Erschlossenheit*, of being as disclosure. "With Heidegger's terminology we can say, that the existential-ontological structure of humans is such that, 'that Dasein is in the mode of being there.' "[15]

Yet precisely those passages in which Heidegger discusses Dasein's thrownness into the world, or fallenness within it, also reveal the fundamentally different accent that he and Arendt place on this phenomenon. Heidegger writes,

Dasein has, in the first instance, fallen away from itself as an authentic potentiality for Being its Self, and has fallen into the "world." "Fallenness" into the world means an absorption in Being-with-one-another, insofar as the latter is guided by idle talk, curiosity, and ambiguity. (*Being and Time,* p. 220/176)

This experience of absorbed being-in-the-world corresponds to "inauthenticity." Heidegger remarks that inauthenticity here does not signify a negation of Dasein's being, but it refers "to a quite distinctive kind of Being-in-the-world—the kind which is completely fascinated by the 'world' and by the Dasein-with of Others in the 'they' [*das Man*]" (*Being and Time,* p. 220).

The philosophical significance attributed to the world of appearances by Arendt and Heidegger could not be more different. Heidegger's language denigrates this realm. Despite all disclaimers, terms such as *fallenness, thrownness, inauthenticity, idle talk, the "they"* carry the unmistakable connotations of a Christian theology that views the world as the domain of fallen sinners who are condemned to live in finitude, contingency, accident, and death. We also recall Plato's allegory of the cave: those who are caught in the worldly appearance of objects and human affairs are like those who watch the shadows on the wall of the cave, without being able to ascend to the source of true light. The world, the space of appearance in which being discloses itself, is fundamentally ambivalent for Heidegger. The Platonic-Christian denigration and devaluation of this world is betrayed by his terminology, even if at times it contradicts his philosophical intentions.

Matters stand otherwise with Arendt. She clearly noted the profound affinity Heidegger shared with Plato in this respect; and her sensibilities on the worldliness of the world are more Homeric and Nietzschean than Christian. Arendt revalues what Heidegger devalues, because she has disclosed *the deep structure of human action as interaction.* The space of appearances is ontologically reevaluated by her, precisely because human beings can act and speak only with others, and insofar as they appear to others. One can live in solitude, one can think in solitude, but one cannot be generous or miserly, courageous or cowardly, kind or hurtful without the presence of others. Such actions can be identified as courageous, cowardly, miserly, and so on only insofar as we and others interpret them as "being-such-and-such," and not "so-and-so." The philosophical thesis here is that actions can only be identified through a narrative that is disclosed to others and to ourselves. The "whatness" of an action requires at the very least the identification of its doer, of his or her intentions, of the quality of the act, of the context within which it is engaged. These features of action, however, can only be identified narratively, by the stories we tell, by the narratives we construct of the who, the what, the why, the how, and the what for. Action is disclosure in speech.

One of Arendt's fundamental contributions to the history of twentieth-century philosophy is the thesis that the human space of appearances is constituted by "the web of relationships and the enacted stories." Action and speech go on between human beings, and "most action and speech is concerned with this in-between" (*HC*, p. 182). This in-betweenness, however, in addition to including the world of things, also includes an intangible dimension,

> since there are no tangible objects into which it could solidify; the process of acting and speaking can leave behind no such results and end products. But for all its intangibility, this in-between is no less real than the world of things we visibly have in common. We call this reality the "web" of human relationships, indicating by the metaphor its somewhat intangible quality. (*HC*, p. 183)

The metaphor of the "web" indicates the invisible, gossamerlike ties, networks, and contexts of human relationships that constitute the "horizon" of human affairs. The term *horizon* in phenomenology suggests the ever-present but never quite fully transparent presuppositions, contexts, and referential networks that we must always also take for granted when we are in the world. The horizon is ever present, and it recedes into infinity; at any point in time, it is only some aspect of it, some part of it on which we focus our attention, and this then becomes present to us and reveals itself to us.

For Hannah Arendt, the "web" of human relationships and enacted stories constitutes the horizon, in the phenomenological sense, of human affairs. Every speaking and acting human person finds such a horizon as the always already present background within which its life unfolds. An example may help here: think of how, even before a child is born, members of its family construct a "web" of stories and relationships into which it will be inserted. The mother may want a son who will become the great pianist she missed becoming because she started raising a family, or because she was not talented or disciplined enough. The father may want a daughter who will care for him in his old age; the sibling in the house may wish that a new child would never appear. We all begin life inserted into narratives, stories, and webs that were spun before us, and that will accompany us, and against which more often than not we will have to struggle.

This interminable and inexhaustibly intricate horizon of human affairs yields certain consequences: first, in acting there is always a necessary disjunction between intention and consequence. Not only are our actions always open to the reading and misreading of others, but also "because of this already existing web of human relationships, with its innumerable, conflicting wills and intentions . . . action almost never achieves its purpose" (*HC*, p. 184). Second, action is immersed in this medium through the stories it "produces," "as naturally as fabrication produces tangible things" (*HC*, p. 184). Actions are identified by their doers as well as by the spectators and those who suffer their consequences through various narrative tellings, and in this way they become part of the "web" of human affairs. "I thought I was being generous," I say, "whereas you thought I was being overbearing and protective." "This is treason," some say: "no, this is true patriotism," others respond. Such is the web of narratives within which human affairs unfold. Although we are all actors, none of us is the author or producer of his or her own life story. "In other words, the stories, the results of action and speech, reveal an agent, but this agent is not an author or producer. Somebody began it and is its subject in the twofold sense of the word, namely, its actor and sufferer, but nobody is its author" (*HC*, p. 184).

In the fragility, unpredictability, and complexity of human affairs Arendt saw the sources of the philosopher's contempt for this realm and ultimately the reason why the philosophical tradition repeatedly, from Plato to Marx, substituted "making" for "doing." In a passage that holds equally well for Heidegger, Arendt wrote,

> It is for this reason that Plato thought that human affairs (*ta ton anthropon pragmata*), the outcome of action (*praxis*) should not be treated with great seriousness; the actions of men appear like the gestures of puppets led by an invisible hand behind the scene, so that man seems to be a kind of plaything of a god. (*HC*, p. 185)

Aristotle, Arendt, and Heidegger

As opposed to Plato's contempt and ultimate turning away from the world of human affairs, Arendt saw in Aristotle's distinction between *poiesis* and *praxis,* between making and doing, the philosophical articulation of the concept of action as deeds and words. A principal manner in which Aristotle distinguishes between "making" and "acting" is through the analysis of the *telos* of each form of activity. "In the variable are included both things made and things done; making and acting are different . . .; so that the reasoned state of capacity to act is different from the reasoned state of capacity to make."[16] Whereas the end/purpose, telos, of making is in the thing produced, in the case of praxis, the doing itself, the quality of the deed, is the end of the activity. The doing cannot be separated from the doer in the way in which the thing made can be from the maker; for the doer and the deed are one; the doing is the revealing of who one is. The ultimate purpose of action is the doing of fine and noble deeds, as these come to constitute the unity of a lifetime. In Aristotle's words,

> Since every one who makes makes for an end, and that which is made is not an end in the unqualified sense (but only an end in a particular relation, and the end of a particular operation)—only that which is *done* is that; for good action is an end, and desire aims at this. (emphasis in the original)[17]

More important, though, than this teleological analysis is the view of praxis as a distinctive form of human actuality, of *energeia,* in fact, as the highest form of activity for humans qua human. Arendt cites Aristotle:

> To men the reality of the world is guaranteed by the presence of others, by its appearing to all; "for what appears to all, this we call being," and whatever lacks this appearance comes and passes away like a dream, intimately and exclusively our own but without reality. (*HC,* p. 199)

"For what appears to all, this we call being." Heidegger appropriated and interpreted Aristotle's concept of being through his own doctrine of truth as disclosure—*aletheia*—what is must manifest itself, must reveal itself. Being, he claimed, was a form of revealing presence, or of a specific kind of actuality, of motility, which he called *Bewegtheit.* A manuscript of Heidegger's from the year 1922, and first published in 1989, is titled *"Phänomenologische Interpretation zu Aristoteles (Anzeige der hermeneutischen Situation)"* (Phenomenological Interpretation of Aristotle: Definition of the Hermeneutical Situation). Named by Hans-Georg Gadamer "Heidegger's 'Theological' Early Writing,"[18] this text clarifies in a very compact space the reappropriation of Aristotle that Heidegger was undertaking at that time, and that left its indelible mark not only upon Hannah Arendt but upon Herbert Marcuse[19] as well as Leo Strauss and others.[20]

Heidegger is fully conscious in this manuscript of the novelty and radicalness of his approach to the history of philosophy:

> To understand in radical fashion what a past form of philosophical inquiry defined its own situation to be and how it identified its fundamental concern [*Grundbekuemmerung*]; understanding (*Verstehen*), this does not mean simply to ascertain certain things to be the case, rather it means repeating what has been understood in originary fashion and in the context of one's own situation.[21]

Heidegger follows these methodological insights with a series of propositions that clearly reveal him to be on the way to *Being and Time*. "The object of philosophical inquiry is human Dasein as it questions its own mode of Being" (p. 238). "Factical life has the character of being that bears its own self with difficulty" (Ibid.). "The fundamental meaning of the factical form of motility *(Bewegtheit)* characteristic of life is *Sorgen* (curare)" (p. 240, emphasis in the original). "The world is articulated according to the different directions of forms of care, and as the case may be, as the world around one *(Umwelt)*, the world with others *(Mitwelt)*, and the world of the self *(Selbstwelt)*." The doctrines of the fallenness of Dasein into ordinary life (p. 242), the leveling and obscuring quality of the ordinary concerns of everyday life (p. 243), the contempt for the "they" (das Man) (p. 243) are all present in this early manuscript.

It is hard to see how or why these fascinating phenomenological excursions require that "Aristotle be the theme of the inquiry" (p. 248). Heidegger himself answers the question that he poses with the following:

> At the same time, however, in his *Physics* Aristotle reaches a fundamentally new premise, out of which his ontology and logic will unfold. . . . The

central phenomenon, whose explication is the topic of the *Physics*, becomes being in the manner of its form of motility *(Bewegtseins)*. (p. 251)

Heidegger subsequently undertakes close readings of three passages from Aristotle's works: Book VI of the *Nicomachean Ethics*; *Metaphysics* alpha; and *Physics* alpha and beta.

An extremely detailed reading of Book VI of the *Ethics* is also at the center of Heidegger's lectures on Plato's dialogue the *Sophist*, which were given in the winter semester of 1924–1925 at the University of Marburg, and which Hannah Arendt attended.[22] In this section of the *Ethics*, Aristotle discusses the different modes of knowing as these correspond to different forms of being. He distinguishes scientific knowledge (episteme) from practical wisdom *(phronesis)*, from knowledge involved in making *(techne)*, from philosophical wisdom *(sophia)*, and from intuitive knowledge *(nous)*. There is little doubt that for Hannah Arendt the philosophical significance of the distinction between *praxis* (acting) and *poiesis* (making), between *phronesis* (practical wisdom) and *techne* (the knowledge involved in making), as the dionoetic virtues corresponding to these, became clear through Heidegger's lectures.

What is missing in these texts on Aristotle, however, which Gadamer notes as well,[23] is any special emphasis upon, or a detailed examination of, the Aristotelian practical philosophy, of the doctrine of virtue as the life of praxis that can be undertaken only in the political community of equals and friends. To as sharp a reader of Aristotle as Heidegger was, this intimate connection between the ethical doctrine of the good life and the political doctrine of the *politeia* as that form of regime that allowed humans the most ample opportunities for engaging in praxis, could not have gone unnoticed. Heidegger did not focus on the doctrine of the just city and the good life; instead, he focused on the *Sophist*, and on the characteristic Platonic distinction between the life of untruth, as lived by the sophists in the political community, and the search for truth by the philosopher, which leads away from the city. Heidegger ignored the fundamental doctrines of Aristotle's ethics and politics, as well as the centrality of praxis, as the doing of just and noble deeds, in human life.

We can speculate about what Heidegger was up to. No doubt in 1924–1925, Heidegger saw no signs of authentic political praxis anywhere; he insisted that philosophical truth lay beyond the life of human action in the city. Perhaps it was more fitting with his quasi-theological temperament to turn away from the chaos of the Weimar Republic toward Plato's *Sophist*, and to seek philosophical wisdom in those acts of withdrawal from the "fallen" world, in those moments of coming to one's senses about the contingency, futility, and frailty of human affairs. Had Heidegger exercised the turning away from the political that seemed to characterize his reading of Aristotle in this period several years later, in 1933 as well, the course of much of twentieth-century philosophy might have been different. Without a doubt, and however one interprets it, Heidegger's neglect of crucial features of Aristotle's teaching of ethics and politics was a meaningful omission, and one that did not escape the notice of his best students such as Hannah Arendt and Herbert Marcuse, who, each in his or her own way, went on to revive the missing concept of "praxis." Whereas Arendt reread Aristotle so as to reveal the ontological features of ethical and political action, thus gaining access to the notion of a "web" of human affairs, Marcuse read Aristotle's concept of praxis in Marxian terms as world-constitutive and historical laboring activity.[24] If one way to judge a philosophical doctrine or interpretation in retrospect is the depth of readings and creative misreadings it can give rise to, then there is little question that Heidegger's phenomenological appropriation of Aristotle remains one of the most significant chapters in the history of twentieth-century philosophy.

* * *

The preceding chapters of this work have been concerned to analyze the existential roots of Arendt's thought and to document the formative intellectual currents of her philosophy, namely, the search for a political homeland for the Jewish people as well as German "Existenz philosophy" of the 1920s, in particular the thought of Martin Heidegger. Heidegger's reading of Plato and Aristotle in his lectures of 1924 and 1925 left indelible marks upon Arendt's thinking, which she was all too ready to acknowledge. She wrote to Heidegger with reference to *The Human Condition*:

> You will see that the book has no dedication. If things had ever worked out properly between us . . . then I would have asked you if I could have dedicated the book to you. It grew right out of the first days in Marburg and so is in all respects indebted to you.[25]

The great tensions in Arendt's systematic reflections on politics and society, and the unresolved contradictions in some of her formulations, can be traced back to this twofold spiritual-intellectual legacy. Expressed in somewhat stylized form, while Hannah Arendt, the stateless and persecuted Jew is the philosophical and political modernist, Arendt, the student of Martin Heidegger, is the antimodernist Grecophile theorist of the polis and of an originary experience of praxis.

Corresponding to this duality of intellectual orientations are systematic ambiguities that run right through her key concepts such as action and the public sphere. Identifying such tensions and contradictions in a thinker's work can be both profoundly illuminating and deeply dissatisfying. Arendt herself no longer thought it either desirable or even possible to fit the world into a coherent "philosophical *Weltanschauung*." For her, political philosophy became a method of narration to "cull meaning from the past," an exercise in establishing distinctions that would enable us to think the meaning of our times and our actions, to "think what we are doing."[26] Certainly, for Arendt a thinking process that does not exhibit tensions and contradictions would be superficial as well as inadequate to grapple with the tasks at hand. Nonetheless, from the standpoint of the reader and the interpreter, identifying such dualisms is always accompanied by the urge to find principles such as to reconcile these dualisms via a yet more comprehensive interpretation or a fuller account of the corpus as a whole. At least, it is a guiding principle of any interpretive task to ask if such tensions and dualisms cannot be contained yet in a larger whole or reconciled via a different interpretive strategy than the one pursued hitherto.

My thesis is that the greatness of Hannah Arendt's political philosophy and its continuing contemporary import lie precisely in the controversial distinctions that she creates and the tensions that she identifies in the Western tradition of political thought. Some of the dualisms of her thought derive from the dualisms of the tradition within which she situates herself; the space of thinking is "between past and future"; it is located in the present. Some are her own creations. My goal in the remainder of this work will be to examine the dualisms and distinctions of Arendtian political thought, not to flatten them out by subsuming them under a more comprehensive interpretive umbrella, but to question, challenge, and contest them for the sake of illuminating the political phenomena at hand.

Notes

1. *Arendt-Jaspers Correspondence,* Letter 297, p. 457.

2. The relationship between Heidegger's philosophy and his politics, his involvement with the National Socialist Party and movement, his actions as rector of the University of Freiburg in 1933, the circumstances surrounding his resignation, the actions of the Denazification commission against him after the war, have been masterfully documented by Hugo Ott, in *Martin Heidegger: A Political Life,* translated from the German by Allan Blunden (New York: Basic Books, 1993). Ott's masterful study was preceded by Victor Farias's *Heidegger et le Nazisme: Morale et politique* (Paris: Lagrasse, 1987); English translation, *Heidegger and Nazism,* trans. Paul Burrell; ed. Joseph Margolis and Tom Rockmore (Philadelphia: Temple University Press, 1989). Thomas Sheehan's "Heidegger and the Nazis," *New York Review of Books* 15 (June 1988): 38-47, remains one of the best renditions of the complex issues involved. On the general relation between philosophy and politics in the thought of Heidegger, see also Richard Wolin, *The Politics of Being: The Political Thought of Martin Heidegger* (New York: Columbia University Press, 1990), and Tom Rockmore, *On Heidegger's Nazism and Philosophy* (Berkeley: University of California Press, 1992); see also Otto Pöggeler, *Der Denkweg Martin Heideggers* (Neske: Pfüllingen, 1963), reissue: trans. Daniel Mgurshah and Sigmund Barber (Atlantic Highlands, N.J.: Humanities Press, 1987), and Alexander Schwan, *Politische Philosophie im Denken Heideggers* (Opladen: Westdeutscher Verlag, 1965). Richard Wolin's *The Heidegger Controversy: A Critical Reader* (New York: Columbia University Press, 1991) includes some of the seminal texts and articles around the so-called Heidegger controversy.

For Heidegger's inability to acknowledge his "mistake," and to issue a public apology to his former Jewish students and colleagues, see Ott, *Martin Heidegger,* pp. 138 ff., 168 ff. See also Jürgen Habermas, "Work and *Weltanschauung:* The Heidegger Controversy From a German Perspective," *Critical Inquiry* 15 (Winter 1989): 431-456, and Habermas's comment: "With the help of an operation we might call 'abstraction via essentialization,' the history of Being is thus disconnected from political and historical events. . . . Heidegger dealt with the theme of humanism at a time when the images of the horror that the arriving Allies encountered in Auschwitz and elsewhere had made their way into the smallest German village. If his talk of an 'essential happening' had any meaning at all, the singular event of the attempted annihilation of the Jews would have drawn the philosopher's attention (if not already that of the concerned contemporary). But Heidegger dwells, as always, in the Universal. His concern is to show that man is the 'neighbor of Being'—not the neighbor of man" (p. 449).

3. It is widely reported that Martin Heidegger called Hannah Arendt "the passion of his life" (cited by Elisabeth Young-Bruehl, from a letter by Arendt to Hilde Fraenkel, February 10, 1950, and contained in Arendt's papers in the Library of Congress; Young-Bruehl, *For Love of the World,* New Haven, Conn.: Yale University Press, 1982, p. 247), and that their affair began in Marburg in February 1925. He was then 35 years old, she 19; she was a student of philosophy, and he was a married man with two children. After one year, their relationship appeared too risky to him, and perhaps desperate to her; she moved to Heidelberg to study philosophy with Karl Jaspers. But this was not the end of the story. After obtaining her address from a fellow student of hers, Heidegger wrote to her, and occasionally arranged meetings, the where and when of which he alone decided. In 1928, Heidegger obtained the professorship in Freiburg; in 1927, *Sein und Zeit* appeared. Hannah Arendt writes the follow-

ing letter to Martin Heidegger on August 22, 1928: "The way which you have shown for me is longer and harder than I had thought. It requires a whole life. . . . I would have lost my right to live, if I would have lost my love to you." The letter ends without a regular farewell; instead, Arendt writes, "And if there is a God, I will love you better after death." Arendt sought Heidegger out after the war, and they continued to see each other in her periodic trips to Europe. By then, Frau Heidegger as well as Arendt's husband, Heinrich Bluecher, were drawn into the picture. The terms of the relationship appeared to have been transformed into a friendship, and Arendt remained "true" to Heidegger until the very end, even upon those occasions, as when he received her copy of *The Human Condition,* when his behavior was less than friendly and magnanimous. See appendix, p. 221.

4. See Hannah Arendt, introduction to *The Life of the Mind,* vol. 1, *Thinking* (New York: Harcourt Brace Javanovich, 1977), p. 6.

5. The most compelling testimony into Heidegger's character is given by his comportment in his friendship with Husserl. Husserl took Heidegger under his wing from 1917 onward, promoted him in university circles, saw to it that Heidegger got the chair in Philosophy at the University of Freiburg. Heidegger in turn dedicated *Being and Time* to "Edmund Husserl in respect and friendship" on April 8, 1926. (See the English translation, Martin Heidegger, *Being and Time,* New York: Harper & Row, 1962.) Yet on April 7, 1933, the Reich law on the "reestablishment of a permanent civil service" came into effect, whereby all civil servants of non-Aryan origin, irrespective of religious denomination, were to be suspended from office—including those who, like Husserl, were living in retirement and who had converted to Protestantism. Heidegger joined the NSDAP on May 1, 1933, despite the fact that he knew of this law; the decree was rescinded in some form on April 28, 1933, but Husserl's son, Gerhart Husserl, lost his position at the Law Faculty of the University of Kiel and was not reinstated. Martin Heidegger's wife, Elfride Heidegger, wrote to Malvine Husserl on May 2, 1933, indicating how she had been shocked to read that their son had been suspended and expressing the hope that it was just a temporary measure, the work of some overzealous bureaucrat. "After all," Hugo Ott summarizes this letter, "the Husserl family had been staunch patriots during the First World War." As cited by Ott, *Martin Heidegger,* p. 175.

When the Reich citizenship law appeared in its fourth edition, after being approved at the Nuremberg Party Conference, on September 13, 1935, Husserl became a nonperson in the University of Freiburg; from 1936 onward, Husserl's name was not included among the university's faculty, and there was no commemoration of his death in April 1938. Heidegger, during these years, dissociated himself from Husserl; he did not write to Malvine Husserl after her husband's death, and in general exhibited great ingratitude and pettiness toward one who had helped him a great deal.

Right after the war, Hannah Arendt's knowledge of all these events was incomplete and inaccurate, as was that of many others. In her *Partisan Review* article of 1946, "What Is Existenz Philosophy?" she repeats the rumor that Heidegger had forbidden his friend and mentor to set foot in the Faculty in Freiburg because he was a Jew. See Hannah Arendt, "What Is Existenz Philosophy?" *Partisan Review* 8, no. 1 (1946), p. 46. Karl Jaspers corrected Arendt's claim after receiving the copy of the article she sent him, in his letter to her of June 9, 1946. "The facts in the note on Heidegger are not exactly correct. In regard to Husserl, I assume that you're referring to the letter that every rector had to write to those excluded by the government. . . . What you report is of course in substance true. However, the description of the actual process strikes me as not quite exact." *Arendt-Jaspers Correspondence,* p. 43. See also Ott's quite detailed presentation of the relation between Heidegger and Husserl in *Martin Heidegger,* pp. 172 ff.

6. The most extensive and philosophically most perspicacious analysis of Arendt and Heidegger to date has been provided by Jacques Taminiaux, in *La Fille de Thrace et le penseur professionnel: Arendt et Heidegger* (Paris: Éditions Payot, 1992). I am in agreement with Taminiaux about the transformation of Heideggerian ontology that Arendt undertook in *The Human Condition.* The only significant difference in our evaluations of this transformation is my emphasis on the "narrative structure of human action," as opposed to his more pronounced focus on the issue of plurality. See *La Fille de Thrace,* pp. 56 ff.

7. Arendt, "Concern With Politics in Recent European Philosophical Thought," in *Arendt: Essays in Understanding: 1930-1954,* ed. Jerome Kohn (New York: Harcourt Brace Jovanovich, 1994), p. 446.

8. Arendt, "What Is Existenz Philosophy?" p. 51.

9. See Karl Popper, *The Open Society and Its Enemies,* vol. 2, 5th ed., revised (Princeton, N.J.: Princeton University Press, 1971).

10. Karl Jaspers pondered the relation between philosophy and politics in Heidegger's thought as early as 1949. He writes, "Did Heidegger's passionate conversion to National Socialism have a philosophical meaning or not?

"Is it a mere mistake, a weakness, being seduced by the opportunities offered by power and influence? Or is it an indication of a symptom with deeper sources? an objective aspect of this philosophy? On this question: 1. The fundamental attitude of the dictatorial, the prophetic *(Verkuendenden)*—without demanding dogma yet requiring obedience—intolerance; 2. the blindness toward the real . . . 3. absolutistic formulations deriving from a philosophy of history . . . 4. the denial of the N.S. since 1934 (due to his failure in the eyes of the NS and being shoved to the side—still in 1937 demanding the Hitler greeting from students—first decidedly, and again towards the end of the War. . . . The continuing ambivalence—the lack of openness, the lack of straight answers *(Unaufrichtigkeit)*—does it lie in the whole philosophy?" Karl Jaspers, *Notizen zu Martin Heidegger,* ed. Hans Saner (Munich: Piper Verlag, 1989), pp. 53-54.

11. Heidegger, *Being and Time,* p. 361 (English ed.), sec. 63.

12. Thomas Rentsch, *Martin Heidegger: Das Sein und der Tod* (Frankfurt: Fischer Verlag, 1989), p. 149.

13. Rentsch, *Martin Heidegger,* p. 144.

14. The most beautiful illustration of this Arendtian point is P. B. Shelley's poem, "Ozymandias": "I met a traveller from an antique land/Who said: Two vast and trunkless legs of stone/Stand in the desert. . . . Near them, on the sand/Half sunk, a shattered visage lies, whose frown,/And wrinkled lip, and sneer of cold command,/Tell that its sculptor well those passions read/Which yet survive stamped on these lifeless things,/The hand that mocked them, and the heart that fed:/And on the pedestal these words appear:/'My name is Ozymandias, king of kings: Look on my works, ye Mighty, and despair!'/Nothing beside remains. Round the decay/Of that colossal wreck, boundless and bare/The lone and level sands stretch far away." *The Complete Poetical Works of Shelley,* ed., with textual notes by, Thomas Hutchinson (Oxford: Clarendon, 1904), p. 605.

15. See Sergio Belardinelli, "Martin Heidegger und Hannah Arendts Begriff von 'Welt' und 'Praxis,'" in *Zur philosophischen Aktualität Heideggers* (Frankfurt: Vittorio Klostermann, 1990), p. 132.

16. Aristotle, *Nicomachean Ethics,* Bk. 6, chap. 3, in *The Basic Works of Aristotle,* ed., with an introduction by, Richard McKeon (New York: Random House, 1966), 1140a 1-5, p. 1025.

17. Aristotle, *Nicomachean Ethics,* 1139b 1-4, p. 1024.

18. The Heidegger text and Hans-Georg Gadamer's introduction to it were published in *Dilthey-Jahrbuch*, ed. Frithjof Rodi, vol. 6 (Göttingen: Vandenhoeck and Ruprecht, 1989), pp. 228-269.

19. See my introduction to Herbert Marcuse's *Habilitationsschrift* called *Hegel's Ontology and the Theory of Historicity*, translated from the German by Seyla Benhabib (Cambridge: MIT Press, 1988), pp. ix-xlii.

20. "This interpretation has such momentum *(Schwung)*, that a listener of the Freiburg lectures, namely, Leo Strauss, was completely overwhelmed, and told everyone that not only Werner Jaeger, who certainly was a great Aristotle scholar, but even Max Weber, who no doubt displayed the strongest scientific temperament among German full professors of the period, would have to be considered a mere orphaned 'youth' *(Waisenknaben)* by comparison." Gadamer, "Heidegger's 'theologische' Jugendschrift," p. 232.

21. Martin Heidegger, "Phänomenologische Interpretation zu Aristoteles," p. 239. See also Ott's discussion of the academic expectations surrounding the Aristotle manuscript in the philosophical circles of Marburg and Freiburg in Ott, *Martin Heidegger*, pp. 123 ff.

22. These lectures are edited in Martin Heidegger, *Gesamtausgabe*, vol. 19, II, *Abteilung: Vorlesungen 1919-1944* (Frankfurt: Vittorio Klosterman, 1992), pp. 8 ff.

23. Gadamer writes, "What particularly called my attention in the whole interpretation was the predominance of the ontological interest, which is even apparent in the whole analysis of phronesis [practical wisdom]; the concept of 'ethos' is mentioned nowhere in this programmatic piece. Ethos is, however, precisely what is not disclosure or illumination *[Erhellung]*, but rather custom and usage *[Gewoehnung]*." Gadamer, "Heidegger's 'theologische Jugendschrift,'" p. 233.

24. The work that documents Marcuse's indebtedness to Heidegger is *Hegel's Ontology and the Theory of Historicity*, trans. Benhabib; see my introduction to this work, pp. ix-xlii, for further discussion of the Marcusean concept of praxis.

25. Ettinger, *Arendt-Heidegger: Eine Geschichte*, p. 114.

26. See Arendt, "Preface: The Gap Between Past and Future," in *Between Past and Future: Six Exercises in Political Thought* (New York: Meridian, 1961), p. 13.

5

The Art of Making and Subverting
Distinctions: With Arendt, Contra Arendt

The Ontological and Institutional Dimensions
of the Public Sphere

Although Hannah Arendt considered the art of making distinctions to be central to the vocation of the political theorist in this century, many subsequent commentators, even those most sympathetic to her work, such as Hanna Pitkin, Jürgen Habermas, and Richard Bernstein, have sought to show that her art of making distinctions often obscured rather than illuminated the phenomena at hand.[1] Consider some of Arendt's crucial distinctions, such as those between labor, work, and action; force, power, and violence; the social, the political, and the intimate. They have all been criticized, contested, and debated by other scholars.[2]

In this chapter, I would like to suggest that much of what has been irritating to commentators about the Arendtian art of making distinctions has its sources in a more basic dimension of her philosophical methodology, namely, her "phenomenological essentialism." This is Arendt's belief, particularly prominent in *The Human Condition,* that each type of human activity has a proper "place" in which it can be carried out. Labor, she claims, does not belong in the public realm, whereas work, although often carried out in solitude, must display its product in public. It is inherently ambiguous, however, whether in her view action can occur only in the public realm or whether the private spheres of love and friendship permit action as well. Arendt's phenomenological essentialism frequently leads her to conflate conceptual distinctions with social processes, ontological analyses with institutional and historical descriptions. This method has the virtue of throwing unprecedented light on social and political phenomena; at the same time, it often leaves us confused as to which level Arendt is operating on. This conflation of levels of analysis is most striking in the case of the two most crucial categories of the Arendtian corpus: action and the public realm. In criticizing Arendtian methodology and dichotomies in this chapter, her comment on Karl Marx's thought may serve us as a guide: "Inconsistencies, flagrant contradictions, if they do not occur, as they usually do not in second-rate writers, lead into the very center of most great thinkers where they belong to the most revealing clues of understanding."[3]

In his book, *The Political Philosophy of Hannah Arendt,* Maurizio Passerin d'Entrèves has produced an excellent analysis of the dualism in Arendt's concepts of action and the public sphere:

> Different assessments of Arendt's theory of action can be explained in terms of a fundamental tension in her theory between an *expressive* and a *communicative* model of action. . . . Communicative action is oriented to reaching understanding and it is characterized by the norms of symmetry and reciprocity between subjects who are recognized as equal. Expressive action, on the other hand, allows for the self-actualization or the self-realization of the person, and its norms are the recognition and confirmation of the uniqueness of the self and its capacities by others.

And d'Entrèves adds very accurately:

> Insofar as Arendt's theory of action rests upon an unstable combination of both expressive and communicative models (or action types), it is clear that her account of politics will vary in accordance with the emphasis given to one or the other. When the emphasis falls on the expressive model of action,

politics is viewed as the performance of noble deeds by outstanding individuals; conversely, when her stress is on the communicative model of action, politics is seen as the collective process of deliberation and decision-making that rests on equality and solidarity.[4]

Correlative with these two models of action are the two models of politics: the first being the agonal or the heroic model of politics as the activity of "performing great and memorable deeds" on the part of a civic republican elite, and the second being the kind of democratic or associative politics that can be engaged in by ordinary citizens who may or may not possess great moral prowess but who acquire the capacities of political judgment and initiative in the process of self-organization.[5]

In this analysis, d'Entrèves in turn draws upon the discussion of action types in Jürgen Habermas's *Theory of Communicative Action,* as outlined in my earlier book, *Critique, Norm, and Utopia.*[6] A more detailed examination of Habermas's indebtedness to Hannah Arendt, and his transformation of her philosophy of the public realm, will be undertaken in Chapter 6 of this volume. At this point, though, I would like to argue that the term *communicative action* does not quite capture the conceptual issues that Arendt, as opposed to Habermas, had in mind. Instead of *communicative action,* I shall use the terminology of the *narrative model of action.* Whereas *communicative action* is oriented to reaching understanding among conversation partners on the basis of validity claims raised in speech acts,[7] *narrative action,* in Arendt's theory, is action embedded in a "web of relationships and enacted stories." This "web of relationships and enacted stories" combines the constative as well as the expressive dimensions of speech acts; its rational core cannot be as clearly extricated as Habermas would like and as he attempts to do with his concept of validity claims. At this stage of the discussion, it is not necessary to arbitrate between the two models of action but, instead, to point to the way in which the ambiguities and dualism of the Arendtian concept of action are bound up with her phenomenological essentialism.

Instead of the terminology of *expressive* versus *communicative,* I shall refer to the pair as the *agonal* and the *narrative* models of action. Let me further explore some of the contrasts that seem typically associated with these models: whereas action in the agonal model is described through terms such as "revelation of who one is" and "the making manifest of what is interior," action in the narrative model is characterized through the "telling of a story" and "the weaving of a web of narratives." Whereas in the first model action appears to make manifest or to reveal an antecedent essence, the "who one is," action in the second model suggests that "the who one is" emerges in the process of doing the deed and telling the story. Whereas action in the first model is a process of discovery, action in the second model is a process of invention. In contemporary terms, we may say that the first model of action is essentialist while the second is constructivist.[8]

The following passages capture this contrast distinctively: "The *un-changeable identity of the person*," writes Arendt, "though disclosing itself intangibly in act and speech, becomes tangible only in the story of the actor's and speaker's life. . . . In other words, human essence . . . can come into being only when life departs, leaving behind nothing but a story" (*HC*, p. 193, emphasis added). Consider now the following passage that emphasizes the narrative and constructivist dimensions over and against the essentialist aspects of identity.

> The disclosure of the "who" through speech, and the setting of a new beginning through action, always fall into an already existing web where their immediate consequences can be felt. *Together they start a new process which eventually emerges as the unique life story of the newcomer. . . .* Although everybody started his life by inserting himself into the human world through action and speech, nobody is the author or producer of his own life story. In other words, the stories, the results of speech and action reveal an agent, but this agent is not an author or producer. *Somebody began it and is its subject in the twofold sense of the word, namely, its actor and sufferer, but nobody is its author.* (*HC*, p. 184, emphasis added)

The emphasis on the "unchangeable identity of the person" in the first passage stands in sharp contrast to the way in which, in the second passage, our actions and words, like waves in the water, are said to have beginnings and ends that we cannot identify. It is not only that we are the subject matter of the stories of others but also that we discover who we are and come to know ourselves for ourselves through the words and deeds we engage in, in the company of others.

These conceptual tensions and vacillations in Arendt's concept of action are duplicated in her concept of the public sphere as well. It has been rarely noticed that Arendt frequently runs together the pheno-menological concept of "the space of appearances" with the institutional concept of the "public space."[9] The two models of action discussed above correspond to this further dichotomy in that the agonal type of action presupposes a public space in which it can appear to others and be shared with others; narrative action, however, although it also needs a "space of appearance," does not need this to be a *public* space, accessible to all. Action, immersed in everyday web or narratives, can occur in the private-intimate realms as well; these are by their very nature restricted and cannot be shared by all. Private friendships and love, which Arendt says would be killed by the glare of the public light,[10] are action in this second sense, but they may or may not be action in the emphatic Greek sense of the "doing of great and fine deeds." Narrative action is ubiquitous, for it is the stuff out of which all human social life, all life together in the "mode of speech and action," is constituted. Agonal action is episodic and rare; only some human actions attain that quality of "shining forth" and "mani-festing a principle" that Arendt associated with agonal action. The "space of appearances" corresponds to the human condition of plurality, that is, that we are many and not one; it is only under certain very specific historical and institutional conditions that the human space of appearances assumes the form of a *public space.*

In the opening pages of *The Human Condition,* Arendt defines "the public realm" as follows: the term *public* signifies

> two closely interrelated but not altogether identical phenomena. . . . It means, first, that everything that appears in public can be seen and heard and has the widest possible publicity. For us, appearance—something that is being seen and heard by others as well as by ourselves—constitutes reality. (p. 50)

In its second meaning, the term *public*

> signifies the world in itself, in so far as it is common to all of us and distinguished from our privately owned place in it. . . . To live together in the world means essentially that a world of things is between those who have it in common, as a table is located between, relates and separates men at the same time. . . . The public realm, as the common world, gathers us together and yet prevents our falling over each other, so to speak. (*HC,* p. 52)

I have already investigated the origins of the concepts of world in Martin Heidegger's philosophy (Chapter 4) and documented Arendt's youthful attempts to construct Rahel Varnhagen's biography in terms of her search for a home in the world (Chapter 1). In Arendt's definition of the public, we see how the concept of the "world," which has been a leitmotif of her thinking from its early stages, is incorporated into her mature thought.

The two phenomenological dimensions of the public realm are (a) its quality as a *space of appearance* and (b) its quality of being *a common world*. These dimensions are phenomenological in that they are aspects of the human condition per se, under whatever sociohistorical conditions, in whatever epoch. Humans "appear" to each other in concentration camps, for being must appear—to speak with Aristotle and Heidegger (see above Chapter 4, the section "Aristotle, Arendt, and Heidegger"). But the aspect of the public realm as a common world is somewhat more fragile and more closely linked to certain sociohistorical conditions. Under conditions of extreme terror, isolation, domination, and violence, the public realm as a *common* world may be deeply damaged. Individuals may find it increasingly difficult to share a set of everyday references, background assumptions, and beliefs. Thus, totalitarian regimes aim to destroy the public realm as a common world of values, beliefs, and orientations, although they can never eliminate the public realm as a space of appearance without putting an end to human life itself.

Yet, in fact, societal conditions under totalitarianism also allow us to distinguish more clearly the ontological from the institutional dimensions of the public realm. Under totalitarian regimes, once they are past the movement, revolution, and war cycles, and have routinized the exercise of political authority, the public realm very often migrates into the private sphere, as paradoxical as this may sound. The public world is now relocated in churches and parish meetings, in people's drawing rooms, in semipublic meetings of artists and intellectuals, in political cabarets. Acts of friendship and everyday solidarity assume extraordinary meaning. A generation of distinguished antitotalitarian writers such as Václav Havel, Georg Konrad, and Milan Kundera[11] have documented a "phenomenology of life under totalitarianism," which serves as an interesting contrast to Arendtian concepts. The phenomenology of life under totalitarianism to be gleaned from the work of these authors documents how the institutional disappearance of the public realm can also affect the more fundamental structures of human life. Under totalitarianism, the public square is filled with the hollow signs of the regime's power, but a common world is re-created elsewhere. These regimes start toppling when the common world created elsewhere starts spilling over into the streets, the market-place, and into the city squares, thus constituting an alternative public sphere.

Arendt offers a clarification of the institutional and ontological dimensions of the public realm much later in *The Human Condition,* in section 28.

> The space of appearance comes into being wherever men are together in the manner of speech and action, and *therefore predates and precedes all formal constitution of the public realm and the various forms of government, that is, the various forms in which the public realm can be organized.* . . . Wherever people gather together, it is potentially there, but only potentially, not necessarily and not forever. (*HC,* p. 199, emphasis added)

Unfortunately, Arendt's writing about the public has not always been as clear as the above definition may suggest, with the consequence that the categories of space, appearance, common world, and public realm have frequently been run together. And precisely because these various dimensions have not been distinguished, the fundamental difference between the agonal and the narrative models of action has not been noted.

All action, including agonal action, is narratively constituted. The what of our actions and the who of the doer are always identified via a narrative, via the telling of what one does and who one is. As I stressed in the previous chapter, this is an ontological dimension of human action. The repertoire of bodily gestures and movements, the number and type of human grimaces, are all quite limited. The same smile can be an expression of love and irony, approbation as well as contempt; the nod of one's head sideways could be saying yes or no, expressing approval or disapproval. It is the narrative codes of action and interpretation available in the common sociocultural world that allow us to identify these gestures and movements as being "thus" and "not otherwise."

Seen from the vantage point opened by this phenomenological argument, the contrast between the agonal and the narrative models of action is overdrawn.[12] All action is narratively constituted, and some action may attain an agonal dimension. Action is agonal when it embodies or lets "shine forth" a principle or a virtue like justice, generosity, wisdom, and kindness, or when it expresses a passion, an emotion in its quintessential form, like Achilles' wrath, King Lear's despair, Hamlet's indecision, Billy Budd's mute rage, or the anonymous evil of the Holocaust.[13] Such action is rare; it transcends and in many ways transfigures everydayness and our understanding of ourselves. But the many small gestures and doings that constitute human everydayness do not usually attain such dimensions of brilliance of expression and intensity of passion. Action caught in the "web of relationships and enacted stories" is not recounted in either the epics of the poets or the annals of public-political history. Such actions, of which the story of our lives is composed, are usually remembered only by those closest to us, with whom we share the trivial and not so trivial intimacies and repetitions of everyday life. In everyday life, gossip is the quintessential narrative of action.

Having suggested the need to disentangle the phenomenological and institutional dimension of the concepts of action and public sphere, let me now delve deeper into the institutional issues. Under which sociohistorical conditions can one distinguish as sharply as Arendt does among work, labor, and action?

The Continuing Struggle With Karl Marx

The aspect of Arendt's theory of human activity that has been most criticized and discussed has not been the narrative constitution of action. Rather, it is the distinction between labor and work that has been hotly contested. Of course, behind this distinction lies Arendt's continuing struggle with Karl Marx's ideas.

The examination of Arendt's unpublished papers in the Library of Congress allows us to see the extent to which *The Human Condition* was conceived not only as a dialogue with Martin Heidegger but as a continuing argument with Karl Marx as well. A number of unpublished manuscripts, including one titled "Karl Marx and the Tradition of Western Political Thought,"[14] reveal Arendt working out crucial arguments that we subsequently encounter in *The Human Condition*. As Margaret Canovan has remarked, this encounter with Marx's work not only provides the background out of which *The Human Condition* emerged, but also is the missing link between *The Origins of Totalitarianism* of 1951 and *The Human Condition* of 1958.[15]

Attempts to distinguish among types of human activity, such as labor, work, and action in Arendt's case, labor and interaction in the case of the early Habermas, or communicative, instrumental, and expressive action in Habermas's later work,[16] are subject to a standard objection: it is pointed out that any complex human activity, from factory work, to writing a book, to making a meal, cannot simply be seen as an exemplar of a single action type. Industrial factory work, for example, is not just labor or instrumental activity; depending on the nature of the social relations of power on the shop floor, and between union and management, there are usually complex dimensions of social interaction involved. By building ten rather than fifteen chips per hour, workers may be engaging in a slowdown of production. Their activity in this case would not be merely instrumental labor; it would also be political activity. Equally, writing a poem may appear as a case of pure work in Arendtian terms, or as expressive activity in Habermasian terms; but if you are writing a poem as your weekly addition to a comic strip that you despise, far from being satisfying work, this activity may bear all the marks of drudgery of alienated, industrial wage labor. Finally, making a meal, the quintessential example of the repetitive, ephemeral labor that serves the needs of the body in Arendt's view, may be an expressive act for a gourmet chef, just as it may be an act of love among two or more individuals. When human activities are considered as complex social relations, and contextualized properly, what appears to be one type of activity may turn out to be another; or the same activity may instantiate more than one action type.

Nonetheless, I do not consider action typologies for this reason to be useless or unnecessary. Quite to the contrary. I agree with the tradition of interpretive social science, initiated by Max Weber, that understanding social action is the chief goal of all social inquiry, and that it is fundamental to construct "ideal types," or conceptual models, to guide us in such inquiry.[17] Of course, social reality and social processes are always more complex than our categories, but this is not an argument against making distinctions. At the most, we can question the perspicacity of the distinctions we make, while admitting that all thought means distinguishing and connecting at the same time. So the argument that social reality is more complex than Arendt's distinctions between labor, work, and action allow is not at first blush an argument against these categories. I believe that by distinguishing work from labor, and by linking some of the problems of Marx's philosophy of labor to the unresolved romanticism of his political thought at large, Hannah Arendt became one of the most useful and creative critics of Marxism in this century.

Arendt's basic critique of Marx is that Marx collapses the distinction between work and labor.[18] Work creates a durable permanent world of objects. Work shapes an enduring habitat and an environment through which human beings transform the earth into a home. All human life unfolds in such a habitat and an environment; without a world of more or less permanent objects, edifices, artifacts, and structures, which endure beyond the mere life span of a single mortal being, human life would be like the shadows in the cave in Plato's allegory. It would come and go without leaving a trace behind.

I think Arendt is right in claiming that Marx attributes to labor—*Arbeit*—the world-constitutive function that she thinks is more properly characteristic of work—*Werk*. Consider the following passage from the *Manuscripts of 1844* in which Marx is criticizing alienated labor:

> Labor, the *life activity, productive* life appears to individuals only as a *means* to the satisfaction of a need, namely, the maintenance of physical existence. But productive life is species life. It is life that generates life. The entire character of the species is contained in its kind of life-activity, and free conscious activity is the species character of humans. (emphasis added)[19]

Through laboring activity, the human species transforms nature into second nature; this is a dynamic process of self-transformation. Labor, for Marx, is an evolutionary engine through which the species changes itself in the course of changing its environment. Marx here translates into a philosophical-anthropological language Hegel's discovery in the *Phenomenology of Spirit* that Spirit *(Geist)* becomes and comes to know itself through its externalizations in history.[20] The model here is that of a subject facing an initially alien world of objectivity, which it successively "humanizes" or "makes its own," both by changing it actively and by comprehending it conceptually. Marx's definition of true communism is completely faithful to this Hegelian model of overcoming alienation through an act of reappropriation that brings reconciliation.

> True communism is the "positive" transcendence of *private property* as *human self-alienation,* and is therefore the *appropriation of human essence* through and for humans, thus it is the complete, conscious return of humans to themselves, within the limits of the entire wealth that has developed till today as social, that is humanized humans.[21]

By taking over the Hegelian language of subject-object, objectification *(Vergegenstaendlichung),* and externalization *(Entaüsserung),* Marx, in effect, analyzes the activities of labor as well as work at a more abstract-structural level than Hannah Arendt does. For Marx, as for Hegel, all human activity is a manifestation of the dynamic of initial unity, the breakdown of this unity through activity, and the restoration to the self via a movement of negation and reconciliation of what is opposed, strange, other, and alien.[22]

Put concisely, crucial to the Marxian critique of capitalism is the view that industrial wage labor robs human laboring activity of the world-constitutive characteristics that work possesses. Marx did not so much celebrate the advent of the *animal laborans,* of man as the laboring animal, as he searched for the dignity of *homo faber* in the activities of the animal laborans. The concepts of "alienation" and "alienated labor" are intelligible only against this background of the deification of world-constituting and world-transforming activity as manifested in work. Industrial capitalism thus robs humans of their capacity to express this activity through labor.

Yet, is the distinction between work and labor a transhistorical aspect of the human condition, as Arendt would lead us to believe? Arendt herself notes that with the beginning of industrial capitalism, more and more work assumes the character of labor: first, the activity of work as well as the objects of work lose their durable character and are swallowed up by anonymous processes of production and consumption. Think here of the work of an artisan who makes clay pots in a precapitalist economy; the identity of the individual, the skills and techniques of his or her craft, the few products of his or her labor have a place in the stable social hierarchy of production relations in such economies. With the advent of capitalism, the production process becomes anonymous, and the world speeds up: the potter is replaced by the factory workers in porcelain or ceramic factories; the skills and crafts are transformed increasingly into a know-how of the anonymous production process and are incorporated into the design of machinery and the technical organization of the production process; the number of pots and plates created per production time unit is now the most crucial concern. From the standpoint of the individual worker, there is indeed nothing personal, or self-affirming and self-confirming, in the innumerable commodities that amass with ever greater speed under capitalism. In criticizing this aspect of capitalism, Marx, like Arendt herself, hearkened back to the patterns and paradigms of production more characteristic of economic formations predating industrial capitalism.[23]

It is a tendency of the modernity initiated by industrial capitalism that increasingly more activities lose the quality of work and become like labor. What remains then as labor? Ironically, the only form of activity which, even under conditions of industrial and even postindustrial capitalism, approximates labor in the Arendtian sense is "housework." The daily sustenance and care of the human body and the tending to and mending of our daily habitat, are essential to housework. Indeed, as long as we are embodied, needy, fragile creatures, born of others like us, and on this earth for a limited period of time, the repetitive, cyclical, and incessant aspects of these activities will be dictated by the rhythms of nature to which our bodies are subject.

As Mary Dietz has remarked in an illuminating article, "Hannah Arendt and Feminist Politics," what astonishes the contemporary reader in Arendt's discussion of these categories is their gender subtext and the fact that it is left wholly "unplumbed" by Arendt herself. Dietz writes that

the laboring Arendt has captured so vividly is more readily recognizable for the feminist reader as that associated with women's traditional activities as childbearers, preservers, and caretakers within the household and the family. . . . The cyclical, endlessly repetitive processes of household labor—cleaning, washing, mending, cooking, sweeping, rocking, tending—have been time-honored female ministrations, and also conceived of and justified as appropriate to women. . . . It is indeed curious that Arendt never makes this central feature of the human condition an integral part of her political analysis.[24]

If we insert gender as a category of analysis into Arendt's discussion, several consequences follow: we see that household labor, as it has been traditionally identified with the women's domain, includes not only housework but child rearing as well. This activity, in turn, bears more the marks of "world-protection, world-preservation, and world-repair," which Arendt normally associated with work, than of the cyclical necessity characteristic of labor. For in raising a child, one is also transmitting to that child through every word and gesture, every sound and action, a world. Initially, one is concerned to make the world a home for the newborn and the infant; as a parent, one is concerned to nurture and develop the child's bodily as well as mental and emotional capacities to the point when the child can learn to be at home in the world for himself or herself. Parents preserve and transmit a world to their children through habit formation and moral-cognitive, cultural, and spiritual education. We teach the child what "the world is like"; we teach the child which aspects of the world around us we consider worthwhile to preserve and cultivate, which aspects make us feel at home in the world. And this work is not just work but action, in the emphatic Arendtian sense, "of the disclosure of the who through speech and action." Obviously, for Arendt, the philosopher of natality, this dimension of child raising and education of the young was not concealed. Arendt writes,

> The child, this in-between to which the lovers are now related and which they hold in common, is representative of the world in that it also separates them; it is an indication that they will insert a new world into the existing world. Through the child, it is as though the lovers return to the world from which love had expelled them. (*HC,* p. 242)

And, surely, it is no accident that the thinker who countered Western philosophy's love affair with death with her category of "natality"—that a child is born to us—was a woman. In fact, is not the household rather than the public sphere that space in which the "web of narratives and enacted stories" into which we are all thrust at birth unfold and initially envelop us? Are we all not children in the private realm before we become public beings? Is the action of educating and raising one's children well any less significant than the building of cities and the collective deliberation about the good and the just in a community?

In her essay "The Crisis in Education," Arendt is fully cognizant of this world-constituting dimension of rearing children and of education.

> Because the child must be protected against the world, his traditional place is in the family, whose adult members daily return back from the outside world and withdraw into the security of private life within four walls. These four walls, within which people's private family life is lived, constitute a shield against the world and specifically against the public aspect of the world.
>
> The responsibility for the development of the child turns in a certain sense against the world: the child requires special protection and care so that nothing destructive may happen to him from the world. But the world, too, needs protection to keep it from being overrun and destroyed by the onslaught of the new that bursts upon it with each new generation.[25]

If this is so, are not the walls that Arendt sought to erect between the public and the private more porous and more fragile than she would lead us to believe? If the adult members return to the family from the world outside, how well and how much can they leave behind the world of work and labor when crossing the threshold? The modern family, as Arendt well knew, is not independent of the marketplace. Furthermore, there are also instances in which not only the economy but also politics penetrate the realm of the family and of educational institutions. The demands of justice and equality require redressing relations of inequality, abuse, and oppression that may prevail, and often do prevail, in these realms. How can the fragile balance between the intimate and the public spheres be maintained? How can we both nurture the child and preserve the world, while seeing the inevitable and not always unsalutary interaction between work, labor, and action; between politics, the market, and the family?[26] It is clear that here too we must think with Arendt contra Arendt.

I began this section with Hannah Arendt's criticism of Marx's attributing to labor the characteristics of work; I am closing it with the observation that not only does most work become labor under industrial capitalism but also the one activity that retains the features of labor throughout centuries is household work. Yet here in the household, we confront two very different kinds of activities: the daily labor of cooking, cleaning, mending, tidying, and tending, and the bearing and raising of children. The raising and education of children, in turn, are less like labor, and more like work; furthermore, these activities are aspects of the human condition of natality, of the fact that we are born helpless to others like us on whose goodwill and nurturance our continued being depends. Action, immersed in a web of narratives and enacted stories, unfolds in this realm. This means that the private sphere, in the sense of the domestic-reproductive domain of the household, is just as essential to world-sustenance as the public realm is. Without the nurturance and protection of the child in this sphere, the public realm would not be inhabited by individuals but by shadows without selves.

It is not insignificant that this discussion of Arendt's critique of Marx led us into a consideration of gender and women's work. Let us recall a passage quoted in Chapter 1 of this book.

> The fact that the modern age emancipated the working classes and women at nearly the same historical moment must certainly be counted among the characteristics of an age which no longer believes that bodily functions and material concerns should be hidden. It is all the more symptomatic of the nature of these phenomena that the few remnants of strict privacy even in our own civilization relate to the "necessities" in the original sense of being necessitated by having a body. (*HC*, p. 73)

It is as if in this passage Arendt is lamenting the transformations brought about by the modern age: the emancipation of laborers and women go hand in hand with the belief that bodily conditions and material concerns should no longer be hidden. Yet the body and its necessities still remain in a domain of privacy. What is the distinction between the social and the political that Arendt is invoking in this passage? Furthermore, where does the line between the public and the private run, as she draws it? We now have reached the systematic kernel of Arendt's political thought and of its contemporary import. Any case we may be able to make for Arendt's continuing relevance must include some defensible reconstruction of her hotly contested distinctions between the social and the political, the public and the private.

The Social and the Political:
An Untenable Divide

Commenting on the passage cited from *The Human Condition* above in which Arendt discusses the emancipation in the modern age of workers and of women, Hanna Pitkin has written,

> Can it be that Arendt held so contemptible a doctrine—one that denies the possibility of freedom, a truly human life, and even reality, to all but a handful of males who dominate all others and exclude them by violence from privilege? And when the excluded and miserable do enter history, can it be that Arendt condemns them for their rage, their failure to respect the "impartiality of justice and laws"? Impartiality! Justice! Where were these principles when that immense majority was relegated to shame and misery?[27]

Following this devastating commentary, Pitkin voices the second most common reaction experienced in the face of Arendt's works by contemporary feminist theorists, namely, puzzlement. "But there is more wrong here than injustice. On this account, I suggest, one cannot even make sense of politics itself. . . . Yet, can this really be what Arendt means?" she writes, "Why should she so undermine her own efforts to save public, political life?"[28]

There is no simple answer to this question. My goal in the preceding chapters of this work has been to show that Hannah Arendt's understanding of modern society, and of the cultural, economic, and political changes initiated by modernity, are much more complex, rich, and nuanced than the simple *Verfallsgeschichte* model, the history of the decline of the public space from the Greek polis to conditions of modern mass society, which dominates *The Human Condition*. The author of *The Origins of Totalitarianism,* of the section on imperialism and the rights of man, of the historical ironies of Zionism and of the search for a Jewish homeland in the twentieth century, was no philosopher of antimodernity. Hannah Arendt was a reluctant modernist, but a modernist nonetheless, who celebrated the universal declaration of the rights of man and citizen; who took it for granted that women were entitled to the same political and civic rights as men; who denounced imperialist ventures in Egypt, India,

South Africa, and Palestine; who did not mince her words in her critique of the bourgeoisie and of capitalism, or in her condemnation of modern nationalist movements. Furthermore, Arendt celebrated the revolutionary tradition, which she likened to a fata morgana that appears and disappears at unexpected moments in history. How then to reconcile these complex historical-cultural analyses with the categorical oversimplifications that stare at us from the pages of *The Human Condition*? Let us return to the distinction between the social and the political.

In Chapter 1, I observed that by the term *social,* Arendt referred to three distinct, but nevertheless interrelated, social processes. First, the term *social* in Arendt's usage meant "the rise of commodity exchange relations in a capitalist economy." Second, it referred to mass society, and to the models of behavior, action, and mentality characteristic of individuals in a mass society. In the third and least explored sense, I suggested that the term *social* referred to those social and cultural processes of association, interaction, and sociability emerging in Western modernization processes in the transition from the ancien régime to modern civil society. The senses of the social that dominate in *The Human Condition* are the first and the second. Now when Arendt criticizes the eclipse of public-political life, and laments the "rise of the social," she is criticizing the transformation of political life brought about both by a capitalist market economy and by the eventual rise of mass society. But is her critique merely an exercise in nostalgia? Are there any hopes for reconstructing the public sphere under these conditions? Or is politics in the contemporary world to be settled beyond the social and economic realms? And what kind of politics could this be?

I would like to suggest that in thinking through the distinctions between the "social" and the "political," we should ferret out three levels of analysis. First, the social and the political can be taken to refer to different *contents* of *object domains.* For example, at a very crude level, whereas issues of economic distribution would be termed *social,* in the Arendtian sense of the term, which includes the economic as well as the more properly social domains, constitutional debates about the meaning, scope, and purpose of the First Amendment would be named *political.* Second, these domains can also be distinguished along *attitudinal* lines. The social is "the form in which the fact of mutual dependence for the sake of life and nothing else assumes public significance and where the activities concerned with sheer survival are permitted to appear in public" (*HC*, p. 46). This attitude would involve a concern for economic survival, a preoccupation with amassing and keeping wealth and objects of consumption; also, the treatment of others as means to one's own ends. For Arendt, the most vivid illustration of this mentality is the bourgeoisie's imperialistic ventures and the ambition of this class to transform the state into a joint-stock company solely protecting its interests. Third, the social and the political can also be understood as an *institutional* distinction: the *social* would refer to the economy as well as the civil society; whereas the *political* would refer to the public sphere, the state and its institutions.

Each of these ways of redrawing the line between the social and the political has its problems: if we assume that what distinguishes the social-cum-economic from the political are content- or object-domain specific distinctions, are we not then obscuring power relations that underlie the economic domain? For economics not only includes the distribution of commodities but also involves complex relations that distribute access to resources and decision-making processes. The struggle over the length of the working day is not simply a struggle over wages; it is a fundamental struggle about the quality of life together as political beings in a commonwealth; it is about the value a collectivity should place upon the world of work as opposed to that of civic sociability or family life. These issues can easily become political, in the emphatic Arendtian sense of raising fundamental questions about our life together as a collectivity of citizens.

It would seem then that economic and social and cultural issues are by themselves neither simply of one kind or of another: perhaps then the social and the political refer to *attitudinal* rather than to *content-specific* orientations. Indeed, I think that at the end of the day, this will be the most defensible way to salvage the Arendtian distinction. However, how realistic is this quasi-aristocratic separation of bread and politics? How far beyond well-being and self-interest can any understanding of politics in the modern world settle itself? Is Arendt not committing the same error as Engels[29] by presupposing a society of abundance in which political struggles over scarce resources will one day cease to exist and become administrative problems alone?

Finally, if the political in the institutional sense is identical with the public realm for Arendt, what does this public realm include over and beyond citizens acting together in concert for the common good? What about the state, the bureaucracy, the legal system, the media? Is the Arendtian concept of public space sophisticated and rich enough to do justice to the sociological complexity and variety of modern institutions? I would like to argue that the only tenable and productive way of distinguishing the social from the political is in the light of *attitudinal* orientations: neither content-bound distinctions nor Arendt's sociology of the social and political are rich enough to carry the burden of this distinction. Three episodes in Arendt's writings may help us think through these issues: (a) Arendt's discussion of the labor movement in *The Human Condition*; (b) her controversial article on school desegregation in Little Rock, Arkansas; and (c) her critique of the French Revolution in *On Revolution*.

The Legacy of the European Labor Movement

Arendt's discussion of "The Labor Movement" in *The Human Condition* is pivotal for understanding much that she is claiming concerning the social, the political, and economic realms. Arendt begins by observing that laboring activity, although performed together with others and never in isolation, does not generate a political community and a sense of collectivity if such forms of togetherness are merely limited to the production process. "The sociability arising out of those activities which spring from the human body's metabolism with nature rest not on equality but on sameness" (*HC*, p. 213).The equality attending the public realm is an equality of unequals, and hence cannot be based upon the experience of the *animal laborans*. Arendt observes that when the European working classes entered history, they did so not in their capacity as *animal laborans* but as representatives of the masses of the people excluded from social power.

Arendt's attempt to exclude the formation of community or a collective spirit around interactions occurring in the laboring process is fairly unsubstantiated anthropologically as well as historically. Her references concern Greek slavery (*HC*, pp. 215 ff.). But contemporary working-class historiography, particularly in the wake of E. P. Thompson's monumental work *The Making of the English Working Class,* shows that there is much more to working-class culture, associations, and sociability than Arendt thought or may have been familiar with. E. P. Thompson discusses, for example, how silk weavers' societies were organizations in which not only trade secrets and skills were transmitted but political bonds were formed and sociability established.[30] Sociability and community are much more closely linked to production processes than Arendt envisaged.

Fortunately, though, what is of interest in Arendt's discussion of the labor movement does not depend exclusively on her phenomenological essentialism, namely, her belief that each human activity has its proper place and can only reveal its essence properly in that place. In her observations on the European labor movement, Arendt is after a much more important distinction, a distinction between the working class as an *economic client and/or interest group,* on the one hand, and the working class as a *political actor,* on the other. She is full of sympathy and solidarity with the latter's struggles, while the former, as inevitable as it is, she thinks is not of political consequence as such. She writes,

> From the revolutions of 1848 to the Hungarian revolution of 1956, the European working class, by virtue of being the only organized and hence the leading section of the people, has written one of the most glorious and probably the most promising chapter of recent history. However, although the line between political and economic demands, between political organizations and trade unions, was blurred enough, the two should not be confused. The trade unions, defending and fighting for the interests of the working class, are responsible for its eventual incorporation into modern society, especially for an extraordinary increase in economic security, social prestige and political power. The trade unions were never revolutionary in the sense that they desired a transformation of society together with a transformation of the political institutions in which this society was represented, and the political parties of the working class have been interest parties most of the time. . . . A distinction appeared only in those rare and yet decisive moments when during the process of a revolution it suddenly turned out that these people, if not led by official party programs and ideologies, had their own ideas about the possibilities of democratic government under modern conditions. (*HC,* pp. 215-216)

The form of government to which Arendt is referring is the "Council" form, or the "Soviets," the *"Räterepubliken,"* established again and again by the European working classes. Originating during the Paris Commune of 1871, then in the aftermath of the defeat of the German Kaiserreich at the end of World War I in Munich and Berlin, and during the Kronstadt Sailors' Rebellion in 1917 in the Russian Revolution, this spontaneous government of the working masses displayed the formation of acting and deliberating bodies without differentiation of legislative and executive functions. "The councils say: We want to participate, we want to debate, we want to make our voices heard in public, and we want to have a possibility to determine the political course of our country."[31]

Arendt is not the first theorist to distinguish so sharply between the economic interests of the working classes and their political missions. In his well-known propaganda piece, *What Is to Be Done?* V. I. Lenin berated the trade unionism of the working classes and argued for the necessity of bringing to them a revolutionary consciousness from the outside, via a vanguard elite. Through this importation of consciousness from the outside, the working class would abandon its narrow focus on economic interests alone, and grasp its revolutionary mission.[32]

Georg Lukacs, in *History and Class Consciousness,* appropriated Lenin's teaching and changed it into the infamous distinction between the "class in-itself" and the "class for-itself."[33] The working class, argued Lukacs, following Marx and Weber, suffered in its everyday activities from a profound form of alienation, namely, a "reification of its consciousness and activities," a rendering thinglike of one's activities and one's relation to fellow human beings. Interestingly, at the phenomenological level, Lukacs is pointing to the same phenomena of worldlessness and lack of genuine human companionship that Arendt also finds to be the condition of the *animal laborans.* In Lukacs's scenario, by a process of revolutionary praxis and transformation, this class-in-itself would become a class-for-itself by understanding the social causes of its misery and by transforming the totality of social relations that have put it in this position. The class-for-itself, in Lukacs's philosophy, is not distinguished by a specific vision of the economic but by a cultural-social-philosophical goal to put an end to cultural alienation and socioeconomic reification.

The distinction between the economic and the political missions of the working class was commonplace in debates of twentieth-century Marxism. Of course, Arendt has little sympathy for the political authoritarianism that would inevitably follow from the vanguardist theories of Lenin and Lukacs. Taking Rosa Luxemburg's side in her dispute with Lenin,[34]

Arendt emphasized rather the transformative and politically educative aspects of the economic struggle: it was the process of struggle that transformed the *animal laborans* into a citizen of a potentially new public sphere. In 1957 Arendt could write,

> For this political and revolutionary role of the labor movement, which in all probability is nearing its end, it is decisive that the economic activity of its members was incidental and that its force of attraction was never restricted to the ranks of the working class. If for a time it almost looked as if the movement would succeed in founding, at least within its own ranks, a new public space with new public standards, the spring of these activities was not labor—neither the laboring activity itself nor always the utopian rebellion against life's necessity—but those injustices and hypocrisies which have disappeared with the transformation of a class society into a mass society and with the substitution of a guaranteed annual wage for daily or weekly pay. (*HC*, p. 219)

It is hard to know exactly which society Arendt was referring to as having substituted an "annual wage" for daily or weekly pay. In no capitalist society, or even in statist, mixed economies, has the practice of a guaranteed annual wage taken hold. Arendt herself was either technocratic or utopian when it came to matters of economic distribution. What is interesting, though, is that she saw the revolutionary mission of the working class in its establishing a "new public space with new public standards." "The workers," she observes, which at one time "could represent the people as a whole," today "are no longer outside of society; they are its members, and they are jobholders like everybody else" (*HC*, p. 219).

Despite her curious optimism about the formation of a future mass society that will guarantee an annual minimum wage, Arendt is neither wrong nor particularly original in predicting the transformation of the European working classes into tame players of the postwar social-democratic game in the Keynesian and post-Keynesian capitalist welfare state. It is rather her distinction between the economic and political struggles of the working class that is important. Arendt does not deny that in their struggle to unmask the hypocrisy of class society, the working classes give voice to economic demands and to questions of social justice. But they do so from a standpoint that can constitute a "new public space with new political standards."

This is the crucial point. The constitution of a public space always involves a claim to the generalizability of the demands, needs, and interests for which one is fighting. In struggling for the eight-hour working day, or against child labor, or for universal health insurance, one is also struggling for justice, for interests that we as a political community have in common. We feel that it is not just that a society potentially capable of so much abundance should still distribute wealth on the basis of wages per labor hour spent; we argue that it is unjust as well as exploitative to permit child labor; we maintain that universal health insurance should be the right of all members of a political community rather than a privilege only of the few. Whichever class or social group enters the public realm, and no matter how class or group specific its demands may be in their genesis, the process of public-political struggle transforms the *attitude of narrow self-interest into a more broadly shared public or common interest.* This, I think, is the fundamental distinction between the "social-cum-economic" and "political" realms for Hannah Arendt. Engaging in politics does not mean abandoning economic or social issues; it means fighting for them in the name of principles, interests, values that have a generalizable basis, and that concern us as members of a collectivity. The political for Arendt involves the transformation of the partial and limited perspective of each class, group, or individual into a broader vision of the "enlarged mentality." As Hanna Pitkin has noted,

> The first outlook, the mentality of *homo faber,* characterizes us when we come to politics with our private interests firmly in hand, seeking by any means necessary to get as much as we can out of the system. . . . Drawn into public life by personal need, fear, ambition or interest, we are there forced to acknowledge the power of others and appeal to their standards, even as we try to get them to acknowledge our power and standards. . . . In the process, we learn to think about the standards themselves, about our stake in the existence of standards, of justice, of our community, even of our opponents and enemies in the community; so that afterwards we are changed. Economic man becomes a citizen.[35]

"Only in public life can we jointly, as a community, exercise the human capacity 'to think what we are doing,' and take charge of the history in which we are all constantly engaged by drift and inadvertence."[36]

Drawing out the implications of Pitkin's perspicacious observations, we can conclude that the "political" for Arendt need not define a given and predetermined set of issues, nor refer only to certain specific institutions. Rather, what constitutes the political is a certain quality of the life of speech and action, of talking and acting in common with others who are one's equals. This quality is characterized by the willingness to give reasons in public, to entertain others' points of view and interests, even when they contradict one's own, and by the attempt to transform the dictates of self-interest into a common public goal. Hannah Arendt was to work out the epistemological bases of this concept of public life and the political much later, in her posthumously published *Lectures on Kant's Political Philosophy.*[37] On one occasion, though, Hannah Arendt's ability to draw distinctions, and in particular her insistence upon a razor-edge separation between the "social" and the "political," seriously misled her. Unlike her observations on the European labor movement, which initiate a halfway workable and defensible differentiation among the economic and political agendas and goals of the working classes, Arendt's reflections on court-ordered school desegregation in Little Rock, Arkansas applied the distinction between the social and the political to radically different conditions and failed.

"Reflections on Little Rock"

This essay was written in 1957 at the request of the editors of *Commentary,* but did not appear until 1959 when it was published by *Dissent.* The editorial disclaimer that announces that the article was published not because the editors agreed with it but, to the contrary, because "they believe in freedom of expression even for views that seem to us entirely mistaken,"[38] already anticipates the tone of shock and acrimony with which liberal white and black intellectuals were to meet it. In this essay, Arendt discusses the civil rights program of the Eisenhower administration, and in particular enforced school desegregation. The essay is not only a provocative meditation upon black-white race relations in the United States but also the most extensive application of her controversial distinction between the social and the political to contemporary conditions.

What disturbed friends and critics alike were statements such as the following:

> However, the most startling part of the whole business was the Federal decision to start integration in, of all places, public schools. It certainly did not require too much imagination to see that this was to burden children, black and white, with the working out of a problem which adults for generations have confessed themselves unable to solve. (p. 50)

Furthermore:

> To force parents to send their children to an integrated school against their will means to deprive them of rights which clearly belong to them in all free societies—the private right over their children and the social right to free association. As for the children, forced integration means a very serious conflict between home and school, between their private and their social life, and while such conflicts are common in adult life, children cannot be expected to handle them and therefore should not be exposed to them. (p. 55)

Finally Arendt states, "Segregation is discrimination enforced by law, and desegregation can do no more than abolish laws enforcing discrimination; *it cannot abolish discrimination and force equality upon society, but it can, and indeed, must enforce equality within the body politic*" (p. 50, emphasis added).

Arendt's concern for the rights of the parents to decide about the education of their children, and her fears that social wrongs are being righted by adults on the backs of children, follow directly from her desire to preserve some domain of private autonomy and nurturance intact under conditions of a growing mass society. The question is, though, whether these fears are the appropriate ones in the face of black-white relations that dominated at the time, and in particular with respect to integration in the schools. Certainly, for Hannah Arendt the persecuted Jew, discrimination in the schools was not unknown. Her mother, Martha Arendt, had instructed her that whenever one of her teachers made anti-Semitic remarks in the classroom, she was to report this at home, whereupon Ms. Arendt would send one of her endless notes to the school authorities.[39] Indeed, at the beginning of her article, Arendt appeals to her position as an "outsider" writing on these issues. "I have never lived in the South," she says,

> and have even avoided occasional trips to Southern states because they would have brought me into a situation that I personally find unbearable. Like most people of European origin, I have difficulty understanding, let alone sharing, the common prejudices of Americans in this area. Since what I wrote may shock good people and be misused by bad ones, I should like to make it clear that as a Jew I take my sympathy for the cause of the Negroes as for all oppressed or underprivileged peoples for granted and should appreciate it if the reader did likewise. (p. 46)

This is one of the rare occasions in the Arendtian corpus when she appeals to one's identity rather than to one's arguments, beliefs, and positions in public as supporting evidence for one's views. Arendt knew very well, through her reflections on Palestine and Zionism, that being a member of a persecuted minority was not a guarantee of the validity of one's views. Her attempt to distance herself from American racism, on the grounds that like "most people of European origin" she had difficulty understanding it, is also painfully self-contradictory. The author of the sections on "race-thinking before racism" in *The Origins of Totalitarianism* surely knew that racism was no exclusively American phenomenon; and Europeans were not untainted by it! In a rare moment of blatant self-contradiction, she exculpates North Americans for the evil of slavery, putting the blame instead on the Europeans.

> The color question was created by the one great crime in America's history and is soluble only within the political and historical framework of the Republic . . . for the color problem in world politics grew out of the colonialism and imperialism of European nations—that is, the one great crime in which America was never involved. (p. 46)

This remark that now implicates European imperialism and colonialism in "the one great crime in America's history" is historically just as inadequate as her previous observation that somehow Europeans did not share racial prejudices against black people. Arendt seems bent on putting the blame on either one or the other pole, without paying heed to the fact that European colonialism was part and parcel of the legacy of the white settlers of North and South America in their encounters with Native American populations of the Americas. Equally, patterns of consciousness and behavior characteristic of the European "scramble for Africa" would be reproduced in the southern plantations of the United States and in the treatment of the black American slave population. What is at stake in these personal disclaimers and historically untenable generalizations?

I would like to explicate the uneasy oscillations of judgment and observation in this essay through the use of a metaphor. Arendt looked at the experience of black-white race relations in the United States through glasses whose lenses were crafted in another context. This is the context of European anti-Semitism and discrimination against Jews. She drew an erroneous analogy between the desire of the emancipated Jews in Europe to be integrated into a society that excluded and rejected them from its social and cultural elites and centers, and the wish of the black American population to end discrimination as well as segregation. When she writes that "segregation is discrimination enforced by law," and that desegregation can abolish laws enforcing segregation but that it cannot abolish discrimination (p. 50), she appears to be saying that for the self-conscious pariah, what matters is that segregation be abolished because it is against human rights and dignity; but discrimination is the coin of the realm in the social domain, and it is only the social parvenu who cares about social acceptance and conformism. The distinction between the pariah and the parvenu, which was so illuminating in her analysis of patterns of European anti-Semitism and Jewish responses to them, now fails her.

It is in this context that Arendt launches into an extensive discussion of the "social," which otherwise would appear curiously out of place in an article on school desegregation and race relations in the South. "Society," she writes,

> is that curious, somewhat hybrid realm between the political and the private in which, since the beginning of the modern age, most men have spent the greater part of their lives. . . . In American society, people group together, and therefore discriminate against each other, along lines of profession, income, and ethnic origin, while in Europe the lines run across class origin, education, and manners. . . . In any event discrimination is as indispensable a social right as equality is a political right. The question is not how to abolish discrimination, but how to keep it confined within the social sphere,

where it is legitimate, and even prevent its trespassing on the political and the personal sphere where it is destructive. (p. 51)

What does Arendt mean by "social discrimination"? She means the right and freedom of like-minded individuals to associate, to communicate, and to create a space in common without making this accessible to all. Social discrimination appears as the obverse side of the right to freedom of association. Her examples are hotels, recreation areas, and places of amusement, some of which are designated exclusively for Jews, for example (p. 52). But surely there is no unlimited right of free association in any polity, and Arendt is fully cognizant of this. In fact, she establishes a hierarchy of rights, the inalienable human rights of "life, liberty and the pursuit of happiness," where the latter includes the right to marry whomever one wishes. She believes in this context that laws against miscegenation are a far more fundamental violation of human rights than discriminatory laws concerning the use of public facilities, buses, and so on (p. 49). Universal rights to vote and eligibility for office follow human rights in order of importance insofar as they are fundamental political rights in a democracy; civil rights to "attend an integrated school, the right to sit where one pleases on a bus, the right to go into any hotel or recreation area or place of amusement, regardless of one's skin or color or race" are tertiary in her view. These universal human and political rights limit discriminatory practices in the social realm as well as drawing boundaries around the right to freedom of association. Arendt's query is how the concept of equal civil rights would lead to a redefinition of the boundaries between the social and the political.

Arendt insists that there is a distinction between hotels, resorts, and other amusement and entertainment-oriented associations, on the one hand, and buses, railroad cars, and public facilities, on the other, because

we are dealing with services which, whether privately or publicly owned, are in fact *public services that everyone needs in order to pursue his business and lead his life. Though not strictly in the political realm, such services are clearly in the public domain where all men are equal.* (p. 52, emphasis added)

This right of access to public services, which are needed because they are "necessary to pursue one's business and lead one's life," is a curiously hybrid argument on her part if one takes the strict separation between the social and the political. Arendt appears to be suggesting a right of access to public services to secure a decent human life—a curious echo in her formulations of welfare state considerations.[40]

But how does this distinction between social associations and public services, which must be accessible to all, redefine the extent of civil rights? In the light of Arendt's conception of a public service in the public domain, it is quite hard to see why she would think that schools would be more like vacation resorts in their public-political status than like buses, railroad stations, and movie houses. Schools are major public institutions in any society, whether they are funded publicly or privately, in that they are settings through which the future generations of a polity are formed. Schools are not "services"; they are crucibles of identity formation. In Arendtian language, a world is passed on to future generations not only in the family but also, and equally significantly, in the schools. How can schools segregate and discriminate against certain groups in a political community while the polity upholds principles of political equality? As a Jewish child growing up after Jewish emancipation and assimilation, Arendt was not prevented from attending public schools in Germany. Why could she not see that the desegregation of publicly funded schools was essential to respecting the equality of black American children as citizens of this republic, equally entitled to public resources and services as white children were? Schools, like many other associations that exist in the social realm—civic and political organizations, parties, religious associations, and the like—have a hybrid status because as formal organizations with a charter, they become institutions in the public domain, which must comply with the constitutional essentials of the liberal-democratic state.

Viewed in this light, Arendt's attempt to build a *cordon sanitaire* around resorts and vacation places is also untenable. Why should the liberal-democratic constitutional state accept the incorporation of an institution, and hence its emergence as a quasi-public entity, even if it provides private services, when the charter and rules of associations of such organizations violate fundamental rights of nondiscrimination? If the state endorses such institutions, it also endorses the legitimacy of practices of discrimination. Arendt's example of vacation resorts reserved for Jews only is not different in its discriminatory logic than country clubs, corporations, or men's clubs that do not allow blacks, Jews, Asian Americans, or women among their members. A distinction between *informal social practices* of association and affiliation, on the one hand, and *formal institutions* in the public sphere, on the other, would have helped Arendt here. Discrimination at the level of informal practices, of modes and habits of thought, feeling, and association will no doubt continue to exist in society among all forms of social groups, classes, and races; but whether formal institutions in a liberal-democratic state can establish themselves via a public charter, which would have to be approved by procedures of the due process of law, if they are based on a denial of civic as well as political equality, is a contestable issue. The rights of freedom of association and of free speech may be contested through other principles, as, for example, in contemporary debates about the use of hate speech in schools and universities, or the legality or illegality of neo-Nazi groups. Arendt cannot have it both ways: political equality and social discrimination cannot simply coexist. Social discrimination is always essentially contestable through the principle of political equality. Her formula, "discrimination is as indispensable a social right as equality is a political right," is an inherently unstable one. Not only are certain amounts of social and economic equality—access to the basic services in order to lead a decent human existence, as formulated above—indispensable to the exercise of political equality, but certain forms of social discrimination, insofar as they formalize the public exclusion of certain groups of human beings on the basis of their identities, are incompatible with political equality. Indeed, precisely because equality is a value created by the political process, it requires constant vigilance, redefinition, redeployment, and extension into the social sphere. It is one question whom I invite to dinner or spend my vacations with, but another to have the major institutions of a society, like the schools, be segregated along racial, ethnic, or religious lines. Again, the distinction between the social and the political, as Arendt draws it in this context as well, does not serve her well and collapses under closer scrutiny.

Before concluding this discussion, I would like to address briefly the issue of black-white race relations in the U.S. context as they surface through Hannah Arendt's article. There is little question that the civil rights movement, Martin Luther King, Jr.'s social leadership, the subsequent radicalization of black America, the eruption of urban violence in the ghettoes, and the formation of the Black Panther Party were all events that deeply concerned and agitated Hannah Arendt.[41] She "trembled" many times for the "republic" of the United States of America, and stated explicitly that the "one great crime in America's history"—that is, the chattel slavery of black people—needed to be addressed at the constitutional level through drawing up a new social contract with black Americans that would explicitly make them members of the republic.[42] As early as January 29, 1946, she wrote to Karl Jaspers:

> The fundamental contradiction in this country is the coexistence of political freedom and social oppression. The latter is, as I've already indicated, not total; but it is dangerous because the society organizes and orients itself along "racial lines." . . . *The racial issue has to do with a person's country of origin, but it is greatly aggravated by the Negro question; that is America has a real "race" problem and not just a racial ideology.* (emphasis added)[43]

But Arendt's comments a few lines later about a Jewish woman friend of hers who met non-Jewish Americans for the first time in her home[44] may signal the problem in her perception of these issues. Arendt did not think of the "race question" exclusively in terms of black-white relations; for her, relations between Jews and Gentiles were also race issues. The problem of American blacks seemed to her to be one among many other "racial divisions" that existed in this country.

In resisting casting the category of race in terms of "white/black" alone, and in enriching our understanding of racism through her treatment of "race thinking before racism," Arendt was not wrong. Where she was wrong, in my view, was in not taking public cognizance of the fact that it is not racism as such but a *racially based condition of social slavery* that marks relations between white and black peoples in North America as well as in other countries in the American hemisphere—Brazil and Cuba, for example—where chattel slavery has existed.[45] Racially based chattel slavery is not to be compared with conditions of Greek slavery either, for some Greek slaves had been free men at one time. Some, though not all of them, were ethnic Greeks, coming from neighboring city-states that had lost in war. Arendt was not sufficiently sensitive to distinctions between Greek slavery and the slavery of the black people, who were considered members of an inferior race, at times judged to be barely human.[46]

It was Ralph Ellison who pointed to the gravest error of perception in Arendt's "Reflections on Little Rock." He berated her tone for its "Olympian authority,"[47] ironically drawing attention through this phrase not only to Arendt's more than mortal distance from the events but also casting a jibe at her "Grecophilia." In his interview with Robert Penn Warren, in *Who Speaks for the Negro?* Ellison stated,

> At any rate, this too has been part of the American Negro experience, and I believe that one of the most important clues to the meaning of that experience lies in the idea, the *ideal* of sacrifice. Hannah Arendt's failure to grasp the importance of this ideal among Southern Negroes caused her to fly way off into left field in her "Reflections on Little Rock," in which she charged Negro parents with exploiting their children during the struggle to integrate the schools. But she has absolutely no conception of what goes on in the minds of Negro parents when they send their kids through those lines of hostile people. . . . And in the outlook of many of these parents (who wish that the problem didn't exist), the child is expected to face the terror and contain his fear and anger *precisely* because he is Negro American. Thus he's required to master the inner tensions created by his racial situation, and if he gets hurt—then this is one more sacrifice. It is a harsh requirement, but if he fails this basic test, his life will be even harsher.[48]

In a personal letter to Ralph Ellison, Arendt acknowledged that she had not understood this "ideal of sacrifice" or the "element of stark violence, bodily fear in the situation."[49] It would have been desirable for Arendt to have made her communication to Ellison public; it would have been important for her friends and opponents to know what she herself had learned through this exchange and what had gone wrong in her judging black parents to be like the Jewish parvenus of a different era and a different culture. In not doing so, Arendt failed to articulate in appropriate public terms her views of black-white relations around the school desegregation issue. No doubt, Arendt, the immigrant Jew who escaped persecution and extermination in Europe, was and remained grateful to the new republic whose citizen she had become. She was protective of her new country and homeland, although never becoming an apologist for it. Perhaps precisely for this reason, she could not really empathize with the standpoint of those who were brought to this country forcibly, under conditions of inhuman violence, whose cultures, villages, histories, and identities in Africa were decimated by slave catchers and their helpers. Arendt tried to exercise the art of "enlarged mentality" in thinking about the issue of school desegregation. Instead, however, of truly presenting to herself the standpoint of the others involved, she projected her own history and identity onto those of others. The "Reflections on Little Rock" essay shows not only the failure of the distinction between the social and the political but also the failure of the art of practicing "enlarged mentality" in the public realm. Oddly enough, Arendt was to be accused of the same failure one more time in her life: during the Eichmann controversy and vis-à-vis her own people.

On Revolution and the "Social Question"

Arendt was confronted with harsh criticisms of her distinction between the social and political realms already during her lifetime, and, in fact, increasingly so in the final years of her life. During a conference at the University of Toronto dedicated to her work, it was none other than her longtime friend, Mary McCarthy, who confronted her with some of the questions I have been discussing in this chapter. McCarthy asks,

> I would like to ask a question that I have had in my mind a long, long time. It is about the very sharp distinction that Hannah Arendt makes between the political and the social. It is particularly noticeable in her book *On Revolution,* where she demonstrates, or seeks to demonstrate, that the failure of the Russian and French Revolutions was based on the fact that these revolutions were concerned with the social, and concerned with suffering—in which the sentiment of compassion played a role. Whereas, the American Revolution was political and ended in the foundation of something. Now I have asked myself: "What is somebody supposed to do on the public stage, in the public space, if he does not concern himself with the social? That is, what's left?" . . . On the other hand, if all questions of economics, human welfare, busing, anything that touches the social sphere, are to be excluded from the political scene, then I am mystified. I am left with war and speeches. But the speeches can't be just speeches. They have to be speeches about something.[50]

In her answer to Mary McCarthy, Hannah Arendt concedes that she has asked herself this question, and that topics of public conversation and public interest at every given period change constantly, but that there will

always be affairs that are "worthy to be talked about in public."[51] Pressed
by other participants to this conversation, such as Richard J. Bernstein,
Albrecht Wellmer, and C. B. MacPherson, as to how one decides what is
"worthy to be talked about in public," Arendt retorts,

> There are things where the right measure can be figured out. These things
> can really be administered and are not then subject to public debate. Public
> debate can only deal with things which—if we want to put it negatively—
> we cannot figure out with certainty. . . . On the other hand, everything
> which can really be figured out, in the sphere Engels called the adminis-
> tration of things—these are social things in general. That they should then
> be subject to debate seems to me phony and a plague.[52]

The example that Arendt then discusses is the housing problem. "The
social problem," she says, is "adequate housing. But the question of
whether this adequate housing means integration or not is *certainly* a
political question."[53] But what constitutes "adequate housing"? Just consider the conceptions of urban and civic space, of the domestic sphere, of
the neighborhood, of the city, let alone issues of entitlement and merit,
which would be involved in such a debate. The question of adequate
housing and, indeed, as Albrecht Wellmer notes, any major social problem, such as education, transportation, and health care, are "unavoidably
political problems."[54] Arendt admits that "with every one of these questions there is a double face. And one of these should not be subject to
debate."[55] Yet the decision about what should not be subject to debate,
what should be left to the experts and the administrators, is itself a political
decision. As Richard Bernstein observes about this same conversation,
"Indeed, the question whether a problem is itself properly social (and
therefore not worthy of public debate) or political is itself frequently the
central *political* issue."[56]

I said above that the only defensible way to draw the distinction
between the social and the political was an attitudinal one. Engaging in
the public-political sphere involves the transformation of the partial and
limited perspective of each class and group into a broader vision of the
enlarged mentality. What is public-political must be defensible by giving
reasons in public, by entertaining others' points of view, and must attempt
to transform the dictates of self-interest into a common public goal.
Arendt, by contrast, insists on wanting to make a content- or issue-based

distinction, suggesting that although issues that are "worthy of public debate" change throughout history, some issues permit "administrative" solutions and hence can be removed from the public-political arena.

As Mary McCarthy had observed, the distinction between the social and the political was particularly salient in Arendt's work *On Revolution,* in which the dominance of the "social question" in the French and Russian Revolutions was blamed for their political failure to usher in a new order. I think Arendt's text is more complex than this reading suggests; and although it will not alter the principal difficulties concerning the distinction between the social and the political that I have discussed in this chapter, a brief consideration of her argument can help develop her concept of the political more fully.

At first blush, the argument of *On Revolution* appears to be a paean to the American Revolution and revolutionaries who exemplified the genius to found a new political order—a *novus ordo saeclorum.* The French Revolution, by contrast, was doomed to end in a cycle of terror and revolutionary wars because of the entry of the masses of the *sans-culottes,* of the disenfranchised, the poor, downtrodden, and despised into the scene of history. The "social question," which in this context Arendt identifies with the "problem of poverty" (*OR,* pp. 54 ff.), appeared on the scene. In her rather dramatic words:

> When they appeared on the scene of politics, necessity appeared with them, and the result was that the power of the old regime became impotent and the new republic was stillborn; freedom had to be surrendered to necessity, to the urgency of the life process itself. (*OR,* p. 54)

Read in this fashion, Arendt's "reflections on the Revolution in France" can be placed alongside a notable tradition of European political thought, beginning with Edmund Burke and ending with Francois Furet's farewell to the "revolutionary ideal."[57]

Indeed, *On Revolution* continues Arendt's "phenomenological essentialism," in that Arendt's account reads as if what condemned the one revolution and saved the other was that the entry of *"les enragés"* (the enraged) into the scene of history in the French Revolution violated the proper place of each condition and activity. Poverty, hitherto considered a private and individual condition, became a generally visible public predicament; shame, misery, and deprivation, associated with bodily humiliation and want, thus appeared in public. The necessity associated with the urgency of bodily need satisfaction entered the scene of history—nature overwhelmed culture.

> In this stream of the poor, the element of irresistibility, which was found so intimately connected with the original meaning of the word "revolution," was embodied. . . . All rulership has its original and most legitimate source in man's wish to emancipate himself from life's necessity, and men achieved such liberation by means of violence, by forcing others to bear the burden of life for them. This was the core of slavery, and it is only the rise of technology, and not the rise of modern political ideas as such, which has refuted the old and terrible truth that only violence and rule over others could make some men free. Nothing we might say could be more obsolete than the attempt to liberate mankind from poverty by political means; nothing could be more futile and more dangerous. . . . The result was that necessity invaded the political realm, the only realm where men can be truly free. (OR, p. 110)

Arendt's attempt to separate the political from the economic via an ontological divide between freedom and necessity is, as I have argued, futile and implausible. The realm of necessity is permeated through and through by power relations: power over the distribution of labor, of resources, over authority, and so on. There is no neutral and nonpolitical organization of the economic; all economy is political economy. Even household labor is permeated by gender-based power relations and the sexual division of labor in the family.

To this hapless ontological divide Arendt now adds the technocratic argument. Economic issues, and, in particular, questions about the distribution of scarce resources, are now viewed as matters to be solved by technology. She insists that technology, not politics, would put an end to the question of poverty. Although Arendt is not wrong in calling our attention to the increase in human productivity and the tremendous accumulation of commodities made possible by the rise of mechanized and by-now automated production processes, it is astonishing how neglectful she is of forms of misery and deprivation that have accompanied and will continue to accompany this mode of production on a global scale. If anything, in a world civilization in which nations and peoples exist at increasingly unjustifiable levels of disparity and enjoy incomprehensibly unequal levels of scientific, technological, and productive know-how, poverty becomes all the more a political issue. I am inclined to turn Arendt's sentence around: "Nothing, we might say today, could be more urgent than to attempt to liberate mankind from poverty by political means."

Yet Arendt's ontological technocratism in distinguishing the economic from the political is only one aspect, and fortunately not the deeper aspect, of her theses concerning the American and French Revolutions. Rather, Arendt's account builds around a series of distinctions between liberation and freedom, between socioeconomic transformation and the establishment of a new political order of freedom. Liberation, at its most basic level, is human emancipation from conditions of necessity, which have their origin in the realm of necessity: the needs of the body and the urgency to satisfy them. Liberation also signifies the capacity to choose and to act according to one's personal wishes and desires. "The notion of liberty implied in liberation can only be negative," writes Arendt; therefore, "even the intention of liberating is not identical with the desire for freedom" (*OR*, p. 22). Freedom, by contrast, is the consensual generation and exercise of power among equals; freedom can only be actualized through the consensual acts of deliberation and decision of a group of humans who consider each other equals. "Freedom itself needed therefore a place where people could come together—the agora, the market-place, or the polis, the political space proper" (*OR*, p. 24).

Modern revolutions aimed both at attaining liberation and at guaranteeing freedom. And Arendt herself admits that these conditions are indeed interdependent and not separable by an ontological wall:

> And since liberation, whose fruits are absence of restraint and possession of "the power of locomotion," is indeed a condition of freedom . . . it is frequently very difficult to say where the mere desire for liberation, to be free from oppression, ends, and the desire for freedom as the political way of life begins. (*OR*, p. 25)

This insight into the interdependence of liberation and freedom, or rather the interdependence of socioeconomic conditions and of political freedom, considerably complicates the Arendtian narrative of the two revolutions.

The "social question" was not absent from the American Revolution; "we are tempted to ask ourselves," writes Arendt,

> if the goodness of the poor white man's country did not depend to a considerable degree upon black labor and black misery—there lived roughly 400,000 Negroes along with approximately 1,850,000 white men in America in the middle of the eighteenth century, and even in the absence of reliable statistical data we may be sure that the percentage of complete destitution and misery was considerably lower in the countries of the Old World. From this, we can only conclude that the institution of slavery carries an obscurity even blacker than the obscurity of poverty; the slave, not the poor man, was "wholly overlooked." (OR, p. 66)

Arendt did not neglect black slavery in the New World, but this forceful insight does not become a main theme in her narrative of the American Revolution. Instead, it is the clash between liberalism and republicanism, between the pursuit of happiness, understood as the search for private-interest satisfaction, and the pursuit of public happiness, understood as the life of political freedom and participation, that come to dominate her narrative of the American Revolution. Had Arendt made the problem of slavery central to her account, she would have to see that the American Revolution also had its share of violence and terror, when a century later, from 1861 to 1865, the Civil War exploded. From this perspective, the contrast between the civility of the American Revolution and the carnage and violence of the French appears moot, because we can argue that the violence of the American Revolution erupted a century later, in the Civil War. Neither the absence of the social question alone nor the absence of violence are convincing grounds upon which to draw the contrast in the story of the two revolutions. Is there then a contrast to be drawn at all?

No doubt, Arendt's historiographic account has been greatly surpassed by scholars of the American Revolution such as Gordon Wood, and scholars of the French Revolution such as François Furet and Simon Shama. Recent historians such as Patrice Higonnet and Joyce Appleby have also thrown light on the interdependence of the two revolutions.[58] Nonetheless, there are elements of Arendt's account that will stand the test of these later historiographies as well. Arendt's central concern is with the *institutionalization of public freedom* in revolutions.

The entry of the *sans-culottes* into the scene of the Revolution, with their demands for bread and justice, is a complex social process. Arendt overemphasizes one side of this process. She is concerned to stress how an alliance formed between revolutionaries of virtue, such as Robespierre, and *le peuple,* who are identified with *les misérables.* With this alliance, equality departed as a political principle and gave way to pity and compassion; the search for public freedom was sacrificed to enabling the happiness of the masses. Like those of G. W. F. Hegel, Alexis de Tocqueville, and Edmund Burke before her, Arendt's narrative is also concerned with the loss of freedom in the French Revolution, the transformation of the search for virtue into a "reign of terror," and the establishment of revolutionary dictatorship.

In different ways, all these accounts address the same central problem: what led the Revolution to eat its children? In Hegel's famous words, how did Robespierre's "republic of virtue" become a "republic of terror"? Hegel saw the seeds of this transformation in the revolutionaries' abstract and faulty concept of freedom, understood as the radical self-determination of the will under laws that it legislates to itself.[59] Hegel argues that this formula of freedom is as vacuous as it is dangerous, because what is to prevent the will from legislating injustice and irrationality? And who can say what exactly this self-legislation is to consist of?

In *The Old Regime and the French Revolution,* Tocqueville also addresses the problem of freedom.[60] For him, the revolution only carries to its logic the centralizing trends of the ancien régime under which the nobility had lost its traditional liberties and its taste for political self-governance. The excesses of the revolution were programmed by a greedy absolutist monarchy that had robbed the nobility of its local liberties and had thus already depoliticized the elites of the country, while leaving the peasants dependent upon a corrupt and weak social class of *seigneurs.*

Burke, whose *Reflections on the Revolution in France* (1790) preceded Hegel's as well as Tocqueville's works, combined a philosophical critique of the revolutionaries' concept of freedom with an institutional critique. For Burke, the French Revolution showed the triumph of an abstract philosophy of natural law and natural rights.[61] Based upon the false view that "Man, and not men" inhabited the commonwealth, the French revolutionaries saw in traditional liberties and the political order of the ancien régime nothing but a system of corrupt and illogical privileges. In their contempt for tradition, for the local, and the particular, they set out to create a tabula rasa; to erect a commonwealth anew. Given that the exercise of liberty always depends upon a fragile balancing of rights and responsibilities, privileges and obligations, argued Burke, the French revolutionaries could not but destroy the essence of liberty.

Arendt's account, like these classics, focuses upon the fate and institutionalization of political freedoms. She shares Hegel's and Burke's criticism of "natural right dogmatisms," without participating in their antidemocratic disenfranchisement of the people. After all, genuine revolutions allow "public happiness"; the actual content of public freedom "is participation in public affairs, or admission to the public realm" (OR, p. 25). Arendt, like Tocqueville, also emphasizes social class dynamics; her story is about the manipulation by the Jacobins of the sans-culottes for their political ends. At times, she suggests that this alliance was not so much a manipulation as an ideological necessity: the natural right philosophy of Robespierre and his search for the republic of virtue would have to create the people in the image of the "noble savage." In an illuminating passage, Arendt writes,

> Historically speaking, compassion became the driving force of the revolutionaries only after the Girondins had failed to produce a constitution and to establish a republican government. The Revolution had come to its turning point when the Jacobins, under the leadership of Robespierre, seized power, not because they were more radical but because they did not share the Girondins' concern with forms of government, because they believed in the people rather than in the republic, and "pinned their faith on the natural goodness of a class" rather than on institutions and constitutions. (OR, p. 70)

This alliance between the people and the Jacobins led to the replacement of political diversity by national unity, led to an ideology of homogenization whereby the people, the object of compassion and manipulation, became a mythical instance to which ultimate appeal was made. The sovereign people was raised to a criterion of legitimacy; thereby unity dominated over diversity and plurality, which are the chief virtues of the political realm; consent, "with its overtones of deliberate choice and considered opinion, was replaced by the word 'will,' which essentially excludes all processes of exchange of opinions and an eventual agreement between them" (*OR*, p. 71). The equality of equal citizens now became the equality of all who were good and pure in the heart. Pity and compassion replaced respect as the political sentiments among the revolutionaries. In short, the "republic of virtue" could be erected only by destroying the true revolutionary spirit of the deliberative exercise of power among equals.

What remains questionable in Arendt's account are the dynamics of these transformations, whether, indeed, the unitary logic of popular sovereignty, for which she takes Rousseau and the Jacobins to task, is in any historical way related to the entry of the people onto the political scene. Here as well, Arendt minimizes the new political spaces created by the people and for the people—the revolutionary societies, the clubs, the municipal councils and militia, women's associations.[62] Robespierre also turned against the people and crushed these spaces. The people were not the hapless objects of manipulation, as Arendt's account often makes them out to be: even if they entered the revolutionary scene to "demand bread," and were promised "cake instead," in the process there was a politicization, the formation of political organizations and associations, a "nascent public sphere." Women's historians have impressively documented this process with respect to women's bread riots in revolutionary times.[63]

Was the American Revolution, though, wholly exempt from such dynamics? After all, the teachings of natural right theories were not any less significant for them than they were for the French revolutionaries. They also believed in natural law and natural rights, and in the unity of the sovereign people (*OR*, pp. 179 ff.).[64] The American revolutionaries no less than their French counterparts faced the "paradoxes of revolutionary beginnings."[65] The "need for an absolute" manifests itself in the political sphere in two ways. On the one hand, there is the need to ground law in a source of authority beyond law. The source of authority of all human laws is thought to reside in an instance outside them, thus bestowing legitimacy upon them. A completely self-grounding law would be the equivalent of the divine will in the human realm: it would contain both will and legitimacy, power and might, reason and action in one. In the most extreme forms of democratic theory, the will of the sovereign people becomes the source of a new divine will, a source of despotism.

The second need reflected in the search for absolutes in the political realm concerns the circularity of the foundational act, the act of new beginning. If the will of the united people is the source of all legitimacy, then whence does this people derive its authority? If it is the constitution that a united people gives to itself that forms and declares it as a body politic, whence does the constitution derive its authority? The act of foundation seems to send us around in a circle: the revolutionary will of the people is said to be the foundational act that lends legitimacy to the constitution; on the other hand, the will of the people is declared the highest law of the land because the constitution legitimizes it to bear this authority. Abbé Sièyes's distinction between *pouvoir constituant* and *pouvoir constitué* was an attempt to solve this paradox of republicanism; the *pouvoir constitué* (constituted power) would have to derive its authority from the constituent power, the *pouvoir constituant*, but this could be no other than the will of the nation, "which itself remained outside and above all government and all laws" (*OR*, p. 162). The French solution to the paradox of revolutionary beginnings was thus not a solution, and left the door open for a perpetual series of crises of legitimacy.

Yet the solution cannot be, solely or even primarily, a conceptual one. The thinking of the American revolutionaries was just as equivocal as that of the French. The famous lines from the preamble to the Declaration of Independence—which state: "We hold these truths to be self-evident, that all men are created equal, that they are endowed by their Creator with certain unalienable Rights, that among these are Life, Liberty, and the pursuit of Happiness"[66]—are equivocal. On the one hand, there is the mutual agreement of those who have embarked upon a course of revolution to respect each other as equals—"we hold these truths to be self-evident"; that is, we, the people. On the other hand, the appeal to self-evidence and to God's law is an appeal to an absolute that needs no agreement. Such truths compel without argumentative demonstration and political persuasion. For the Age of Enlightenment, which believed in the compelling power of natural truths to thrust themselves upon reason, there is no contradiction here. As the issues of slavery and of the exclusion of women and Native Americans from the status of rights-bearing person-hood demonstrated, the appeal to "self-evident truths" is never self-evident in politics. The light of reason does not shine equally on all, except insofar as they can be persuaded by argument and speech.

It was not the political philosophy of natural law and natural reason that enabled the American revolutionaries to develop a workable solution to the problem of revolutionary beginnings. "The great and fateful misfortune of the French Revolution" (*OR*, p. 164) was avoided in the American case only because, as a matter of historical and social arrangements,

> the delegates to the provincial congresses or popular conventions which drafted the constitutions for state governments had derived their authority from a number of subordinate, duly authorized bodies—districts, counties, townships; to preserve these bodies unimpaired in their power was to preserve the source of their own authority intact. (*OR*, p. 164)

Arendt also sees in the historical circumstances surrounding the experience of the thirteen colonies the rearticulation of the essence of power. This new concept of power was mistakenly expressed through the terminology of the social contract, which referred both to the contract among individual persons that gave birth to society, and the contract between the ruler and ruled that thereby established a legitimate political authority (*OR*, p. 169). For Arendt, the conundrums of social contract theory are less important than the principle of power, which she sees as underlying the first contractual model.

> The mutual contract by which people bind themselves together in order to form a community is based on reciprocity and presupposes equality; its actual content is a promise, and its result is indeed a "society" or "cosociation" in the old Roman sense of *societas*, which means alliance. (*OR*, p. 169).

The American revolutionaries conceived of society as such an association of associations and, in doing so, they avoided the paradoxes of revolutionary beginnings by leaving unarticulated the ultimate source of authority of the constitution, and by creatively interpreting and appropriating the royal and company charters that had originally legalized their establishment. Arendt concludes,

> Hence, binding and promising, combining and covenanting are the means by which power is kept in existence; where and when men [*sic*] succeed in keeping intact the power which sprang up between them during the course

of any particular act or deed, they are already in the process of foundation, of constituting a stable worldly structure to house, as it were, their combined power of action. There is an element of the world-building capacity of man in the human faculty of making and keeping promises. Just as promises and agreements deal with the future and provide stability in the ocean of future uncertainty where the unpredictable may break in from all sides, so the constituting, founding, and world-building capacities of man concern always not so much ourselves and our own time on earth as our "successor," and "posterities." The grammar of action: that action is the only human faculty that demands a plurality of men; and the syntax of power: that power is the only human attribute which applies solely to the worldly in-between space by which men are mutually related, combine in the act of foundation by virtue of the making and keeping of promises, which, in the realm of politics, may well be the highest faculty. (*OR*, p. 175).

This beautiful passage, lyrical in its tone, powerfully articulates the *normative core of the Arendtian conception of the political*: the creation of a common world through the capacity to make and keep promises among a plurality of humans who mutually respect one another. Only when humans give the space of appearance in which all action and speech unfold a visible and stable form, and create institutions, do they create a public space. For readers of Arendt, like myself, who believe in this normative core of her conception of the political, the annoyance and the puzzles remain: is it obvious that this normative vision can be retained only if one defends, as Arendt attempted to do, the political against the floods of the economic, the social, and even the intimate? Suppose we turned the arrow of influence around and asked ourselves: what if we were to extend this form of human relations, based upon the mutual promise-giving and keeping of equals, to the economic, the social, and the intimate realms? What would Arendtian politics look like then? As Jean Cohen and Andrew Arato ask in their compelling critique of the sociological short-comings of Arendt's vision: "Could it be that the despised terrain of the social could after all become the scene of repoliticization in the context of movements that constitute a new public sphere and thereby mediate between the private and the public?"[67]

Notes

1. Jürgen Habermas, "Hannah Arendt's Communications Concept of Power," in *Social Research* 44, no. 1 (1977), pp. 3-25; Hanna Fenichel Pitkin, "Justice: On Relating Private and Public," *Political Theory* 9, no. 3 (1981), pp. 327-352; Richard J. Bernstein, "Rethinking the Social and the Political," in R. J. Bernstein, *Philosophical Profiles* (Philadelphia: University of Pennsylvania Press, 1986), pp. 238-260.

2. For a good illustration of the urge to "stir and mix" Arendtian distinctions until they become totally fluid, see the collection of essays edited by Bonnie Honig, *Feminist Interpretations of Hannah Arendt* (University Park: Pennsylvania State University Press, 1995).

3. Hannah Arendt, "Karl Marx and the Tradition of Western Political Thought" (1953), Hannah Arendt Papers in the Library of Congress, originally in container 64, now in container 71, p. 4. Note that Arendt's syntax in this unpublished manuscript is clumsy; a similar thought is expressed at the beginning of her discussion of Karl Marx in *The Human Condition*, pp. 79 ff.

4. Maurizio Passerin d'Entrèves, *The Political Philosophy of Hannah Arendt* (London: Routledge, 1994), pp. 84-85.

5. These dualisms have been noted in the literature by Peter Fuss and Bikhu Parekh. See Peter Fuss, "Hannah Arendt's Conception of Political Community," *Idealistic Studies* 3, no. 3 (1973), reprinted in *Hannah Arendt: The Recovery of the Public World*, ed. Melvyn A. Hill (New York: St. Martin's, 1979), pp. 157-177; Bhikhu Parekh, *Hannah Arendt and the Search for a New Political Philosophy* (London: Macmillan, 1981); Seyla Benhabib, "Models of Public Space: Hannah Arendt, the Liberal Tradition, and Jürgen Habermas," in *Habermas and the Public Sphere*, ed. Craig Calhoun (Cambridge: MIT Press, 1992), pp. 73-99.

6. See Seyla Benhabib, *Critique, Norm, and Utopia: A Study of the Foundations of Critical Theory* (New York: Columbia University Press, 1986), pp. 137-139.

7. Jürgen Habermas, *The Theory of Communicative Action: Reason and the Rationalization of Society*, vol. 1, trans. T. A. McCarthy (Boston: Beacon, 1984), pp. 286-337.

8. For a good theoretical statement of the "essentialism/constructivism" divide, in particular as it applies to issues of gender, see Joan W. Scott, "Gender: A Useful Category of Historical Analysis," in *Gender and the Politics of History* (New York: Columbia University Press, 1988), pp. 28-53.

9. Margaret Canovan notes the significance of the concepts of "world and "public" in tracing out the philosophical relationship between Hannah Arendt and Martin Heidegger; see Margaret Canovan, *Hannah Arendt: A Reinterpretation of Her Political Thought* (London: Cambridge University Press, 1992), pp. 110 ff. Yet she does not distinguish "the space of appearances" from the "public realm," as in the following passage: "Although Arendt does not entirely identify the 'public' with the political, she does tend to assume that the link between publicity and the disclosure of reality in its fullness must also be a link between reality and free politics" (p. 113). What Canovan names "public" in the first half of her statement is the public sphere as a space of appearance and a common world in the phenomenological sense of the term; that is why a link can even be considered to exist between "reality" and "free politics." I regard this as a conflation of levels of analysis on Arendt's part, which is then perpetrated by one of her most skillful interpreters.

10. Hannah Arendt, "The Crisis in Education," in *Between Past and Future: Six Exercises in Political Thought* (New York: Meridian, 1961), p. 186.

11. See Václav Havel, "The Power of the Powerless" and "Politics and Conscience" in *Living in Truth* (London: Faber and Faber, 1987); Georg Konrad, *Antipolitics* (New York: Harcourt Brace, 1984); and Milan Kundera, *The Incredible Lightness of Being*, trans. Michael Henry Heim (New York: Harper & Row, 1984).

12. In recent years, there has been renewed attention to the "agonal" elements of Arendt's views of action; see in particular, Bonnie Honig, "Arendt, Identity, and Difference," in *Political Theory* 16, no. 1 (1988), pp. 77-99; and Dana Villa, "Beyond Good and Evil: Arendt, Nietzsche, and the Aestheticization of Political Action," *Political Theory* 20, no. 2 (1992), pp. 274-309.

13. Arendt discusses this concept of a principle of action in her essay, "What Is Freedom?" in *Between Past and Future*, pp. 152 ff.

14. Hannah Arendt, "Karl Marx and the Tradition of Western Political Thought," first and second drafts (1953), container 71 in the Hannah Arendt Papers in the Library of Congress. Arendt had applied for a Guggenheim fellowship grant with the title, "Totalitarian Elements of Marxism," which she was awarded in 1952. See also the essay, "Von Hegel zu Marx," container 79, Library of Congress holdings.

15. Canovan, *A Reinterpretation*, pp. 63 ff.

16. See Jürgen Habermas, "Labor and Interaction: Remarks on Hegel's *Jena Philosophy of Mind*," in *Theory and Practice*, trans. John Viertel (Boston: Beacon, 1973), pp. 142-170; Habermas, *The Theory of Communicative Action*, vol. 1.

17. See Max Weber, "The Meaning of Ethical Neutrality in the Social Sciences," in Weber, *The Methodology of the Social Sciences*, ed. and trans. E. A. Shils and Henry A. Finch (New York: Free Press, 1949), pp. 40 ff.

18. In *The Human Condition*, Arendt writes that the "Unutopian ideal" that guides Marx's theories is that "the distinction between labor and work would have completely disappeared; all work would have become labor because all things would be understood, not in their worldly, objective quality, but as results of living labor power and functions of the life process" (*HC*, p. 89). But Marx not only reduced work to labor; in his early writings at least, he sought to elevate labor to the status of work. For Arendt's comments on Marx's deification of labor, see also "Karl Marx and the Tradition of Western Political Thought," Hannah Arendt Papers, Library of Congress, container 71, p. 4. This argument is incorporated into the essay "Tradition and the Modern Age," in *Between Past and Future*, pp. 17-41.

19. Karl Marx, *The Economic and Philosophical Manuscripts of 1844*, trans. Dirk J. Struik (New York: International Publishers, 1964), p. 57.

20. I have dealt extensively with this Hegelian model of expressive activity, and Marx's indebtedness to it, in *Critique, Norm, and Utopia*, pp. 43-69.

21. Karl Marx, *Manuscripts of 1844*, p. 75, emphasis in the original.

22. In *Critique, Norm, and Utopia*, I have argued that there is a more radical strain in Marx's thinking, which stresses human plurality, intersubjectivity, and the essential dependence of human beings on others as well as on the objects around them. I have called this position "sensuous finitude." If these aspects of Marx's thought had dominated over his Hegelianisms, the condition of human plurality and the narrative structuration of action could easily have been made compatible with Marx's philosophical anthropology. Already in *Critique, Norm, and Utopia*, I attempted a synthesis of Arendt's thought and the insights of the critical Marxian tradition; see pp. 58 ff., 346 ff.

23. For a brilliant analysis of this dimension of Marxian thinking, see Andre Gorz, *Farewell to the Working Class* (Boston: South End Press, 1982).

24. Mary G. Dietz, "Hannah Arendt and Feminist Politics," in *Feminist Interpretations and Political Theory,* ed. Molly Shanley and Carole Pateman (Oxford: Polity, 1991), pp. 239-240.

25. Arendt, "The Crisis in Education," in *Between Past and Future,* p. 186.

26. For a contemporary exploration of these issues, see Susan Moller Okin, *Justice, Gender, and the Family* (New York: Free Press, 1989).

27. Pitkin, "Justice," p. 336.

28. Ibid., pp. 338-339.

29. See Arendt's statement: "After all, the world in which we live has to be kept. We cannot permit it to go to pieces. And this means that 'administration of things,' which Engels thought such a marvelous idea, and which actually is an awful idea, but which is still a necessity. And this can be done in a more or less central manner." In *The Recovery of the Public World,* ed. Hill, pp. 327-328.

30. E. P. Thompson, *The Making of the English Working Class* (New York: Vintage, 1966).

31. Hannah Arendt, *Crises of the Republic* (New York: Harcourt Brace Jovanovich, 1969), p. 23.

32. V. I. Lenin, *What Is to Be Done?,* trans. Joe Fineberg and George Hanna (London: Penguin, 1962); rev., trans. Robert Service (London: Penguin Classics, 1988).

33. Georg Lukacs, "Class Consciousness," in *History and Class Consciousness,* trans. Rodney Livingstone (Cambridge: MIT Press, 1971), pp. 46-83.

34. See Rosa Luxemburg's writings "Social Reform or Revolution?" and "Organizational Questions of Russian Social Democracy," in *Selected Political Writings of Rosa Luxemburg,* ed. Dick Howard (New York: Monthly Review Press, 1971).

35. Pitkin, "Justice," p. 347.

36. Ibid., p. 344.

37. Hannah Arendt, *Lectures on Kant's Political Philosophy,* ed., with an interpretive essay by, Ronald Beiner (Chicago: University of Chicago Press, 1982).

38. Hannah Arendt, "Reflections on Little Rock," *Dissent* 6, no. 1 (1959), pp. 45-56. Included in the same issue were criticisms by David Spitz and Melvin Tumin. In *Dissent* 6, no. 2 (1959), Arendt replied to these criticisms, pp. 179-181. The editorial note cited here precedes the article on p. 45. All references in the text are to this edition.

39. Elisabeth Young-Bruehl, *Hannah Arendt: For Love of the World* (New Haven, Conn.: Yale University Press, 1982), p. 11.

40. For a criticism of Arendt's rather offhanded remarks about matters of distributive justice, see Richard J. Bernstein, "Rethinking the Social and the Political," pp. 251 ff.

41. See Arendt's essay *On Violence* (New York: Harcourt, Brace, 1969), pp. 18 ff., 65 ff., 95-96. Arendt was particularly concerned with the outbreak of violence among the student movements of 1968, and addressed what she saw as the political faults of the Black Power movement in this context.

42. See her remarks in the essay "Civil Disobedience": "We know that this original crime could not be remedied by the Fourteenth and Fifteenth Amendments; on the contrary, the *tacit* exclusion from the *tacit* consensus was made more conspicuous by the inability or unwillingness of the federal government to enforce its own laws. . . . An explicit constitutional amendment, addressed specifically to the Negro people of America, might have underlined the great change more dramatically for these people who had never been welcome." *Crises of the Republic,* pp. 90-91.

43. Hannah Arendt to Karl Jaspers on January 29, 1946, *Arendt-Jaspers Correspondence*, p. 31.

44. Ibid.

45. Orlando Patterson, *Slavery and Social Death* (Cambridge, Mass.: Harvard University Press, 1982).

46. A belated recognition of some dimensions of these issues came in 1969, when Arendt wrote, "Racism, white or black, is fraught with violence by definition because it objects to natural organic facts—a white or black skin—which no persuasion or power could change; all one can do, when the chips are down, is to exterminate their bearers. Racism, as distinguished from race, is not a fact of life, but an ideology, and the deeds it leads to are not reflex actions, but deliberate acts based on pseudo-scientific theories." Arendt, *On Violence*, p. 76.

47. Ralph Ellison, "The World and the Jug," in *Shadow and Act* (New York: Random House, 1964), p. 108.

48. Ralph Ellison, "Leadership From the Periphery," in *Who Speaks for the Negro?* ed. Robert Penn Warren (New York: Random House, 1965), pp. 343-344.

49. Quoted in Young-Bruehl, *For Love of the World*, p. 316.

50. In "On Hannah Arendt," in *The Recovery of the Public World*, p. 315.

51. In *The Recovery of the Public World*, p. 316.

52. Ibid., p. 317

53. Ibid., p. 318.

54. Albrecht Wellmer, in "On Hannah Arendt," in *The Recovery of the Public World*, p. 318.

55. Arendt, *The Recovery of the Public World*, p. 318.

56. R. J. Bernstein, "Rethinking the Social and the Political," p. 252.

57. See Edmund Burke, *Reflections on the Revolution in France*, ed. Connor Cruise O'Brien (Middlesex, England: Penguin, 1969), and Francois Furet, *Interpreting the French Revolution*, trans. Elborg Forster (Cambridge: Cambridge University Press, 1981).

58. See Gordon Wood, *The Creation of the American Republic: 1776–1787* (New York: Norton, 1969); Furet, *Interpreting the French Revolution*; Simon Shama, *Citizens: A Chronicle of the French* Revolution (New York: Knopf, 1989); Patrice Higonnet, *Sister Republics: The Origins of French and American Republicanism* (Cambridge, Mass.: Harvard University Press, 1988); Joyce Appleby, *Liberalism and Republicanism in the Historical Imagination* (Cambridge, Mass.: Harvard University Press, 1992).

59. G. W. F. Hegel, "Absolute Freedom and Terror," in *Phenomenology of Spirit*, trans. A. V. Miller (Oxford: Clarendon, 1977), pp. 355-364.

60. Alexis de Tocqueville, *The Old Regime and the French Revolution*, trans. Stuart Gilbert (New York: Doubleday and Anchor, 1955).

61. See Burke, *Reflections on the Revolution in France*, pp. 149 ff.

62. See Joan Landes's excellent discussion of these issues in "Novus Ordo Saeclorum: Gender and Public Space in Arendt's Revolutionary France," in *Feminist Interpretations of Hannah Arendt*, ed. Bonnie Honig (University Park: Pennsylvania State University Press, 1995), pp. 195-221.

63. See Olwen Hufton, *Women and the Limits of Citizenship in the French Revolution*, Donald G. Creighton Lectures (Toronto: Buffalo University Press, 1992); Joan Landes, *Women and the Public Sphere in the Age of the French Revolution* (Ithaca, N.Y.: Cornell University Press, 1988); Lynn Hunt, *Politics, Culture, and Class in the French Revolution* (Berkeley: University of California Press, 1984); Joan Wallach Scott, *Gender and the Politics of History* (New York: Columbia University Press, 1988), Pt. III.

64. See Samuel H. Beer's masterful discussion on these issues in *To Make a Nation: The Rediscovery of American Federalism* (Cambridge, Mass.: Harvard University Press, 1993), especially Pts. II and III; also Appleby, "The American Model for the French Revolutionaries," in *Liberalism and Republicanism*, pp. 232-253. Judith Shklar has argued that Hannah Arendt has neglected the political significance of one's identity as a wage earner in the American republic; see Judith N. Shklar, *American Citizenship: The Quest for Inclusion* (Cambridge, Mass.: Harvard University Press, 1991).

65. For a provocative analysis of the paradoxes of foundation, see Bonnie Honig, "Declarations of Independence: Arendt and Derrida on the Problem of Founding a Republic," *American Political Science Review* 85 (1991): 97-113; and my "Democracy and Difference: Reflections on the Metapolitics of Lyotard and Derrida," *Journal of Political Philosophy* 2, no. 1 (1994): 1-23. Bruce Ackerman has analyzed the constitutional and theoretical issues involved in the concept of "foundations" for democratic politics in his important work *We the People: Foundations* (Cambridge, Mass.: Harvard University Press, 1991).

66. The Declaration of Independence, July 4, 1776, as printed in Edmund S. Morgan, *The Birth of the Republic: 1763-1789* (Chicago: University of Chicago Press, 1977), p. 159.

67. Jean Cohen and Andrew Arato, *Civil Society and Political Theory* (Cambridge: MIT Press, 1992), p. 199.

6

From the Problem of
Judgment to the Public Sphere:
Rethinking Hannah Arendt's Political Theory

The preceding chapter reached a largely negative conclusion: I argued that Hannah Arendt's distinction between the social and the political realms, so central to her critique of modern society, is untenable; furthermore, the phenomenological essentialism that each human activity has its proper place in the world is also to be rejected, because it conflates categories of her action theory with questionable institutional analyses. What remains then of the characteristically Arendtian doctrines concerning the political? Can one think through issues and problems facing contemporary polities through Arendtian categories? Or is the attempt to recoup Arendtian political thought itself an "exercise in nostalgia" in much the same way that Arendt's own analysis of the *polis,* on one reading at least, could be accused of being?

Let us recall that in treating tradition and the past, Arendt herself exercised two methodologies: the phenomenological methodology of Heidegger and Husserl, which sought to recover the "originary" meaning of terms and conditions of phenomena; and a fragmentary methodology, inspired by Walter Benjamin, according to which one treats the past by acting either as a collector or as a pearl diver, digging down for those treasures that lie now disjointed and disconnected.[1] In appropriating Arendt's political thought, it is the latter methodology that we must follow.

This chapter will exercise such a method of fragmentary historical appropriation by focusing on several aspects of Arendt's thought: beginning with the Eichmann controversy, I will move to discuss the problem of judgment as it arises through Arendt's *Lectures on Kant's Political Philosophy*;[2] exploring some implications of her reading of Kant, I will then analyze the lack of normative foundations of politics in her thought. My considerations will finally turn to the concept of "public space," as it is transformed by Jürgen Habermas into that of the "public sphere." What is the role of this concept in contemporary democratic theory? What remains of the Arendtian divide between the private and the public realms in the light of contemporary feminist criticisms?

Thinking and Judging:
Rereading *Eichmann in Jerusalem*

Hannah Arendt's incomplete reflections on judgment, intended to be the third volume of her last work, *The Life of the Mind*, are puzzling.[3] The perplexing quality of these reflections does not derive primarily from the burden on contemporary students of her thought to seek to understand and imaginatively complete what an author might have intended to but was unable to say in her lifetime. Rather, this hermeneutic puzzle arises from three sets of claims that Arendt makes about judgment and that stand in tension with each other.

First, in the introduction to the first volume of *The Life of the Mind*, Arendt clarifies that her preoccupation with the mental activities of thinking, willing, and judging had two different origins.[4] The immediate impulse came from her attending the Eichmann trial in Jerusalem; the secondary, but equally important, prompting was provided by her desire to explore the counterpart of the *vita activa* (the active life, which in

English translation misleadingly appeared as *The Human Condition*), which is the *vita contemplativa* (the contemplative life). In coining the phrase "the banality of evil" and in explaining the moral quality of Eichmann's deeds not in terms of the monstrous or demonic nature of the doer, Arendt became aware of going counter to the tradition of Western thought, which saw evil in metaphysical terms as ultimate depravity, corruption, or sinfulness. The most striking quality of Eichmann, she claimed, was not stupidity, wickedness, or depravity but what she described as "thoughtlessness." This in turn led her to this question:

> Might the problem of good and evil, our faculty for telling right from wrong, be connected with our faculty of thought? . . . Could the activity of thinking as such, the habit of examining whatever happens to come to pass or attract attention, regardless of results and specific contents, could this activity be among the conditions that make men abstain from evil-doing or even actually "condition" them against it?[5]

Arendt pursued this question in a lecture, "Thinking and Moral Considerations," written in 1971, around the same time that she was composing the volume *Thinking*. Again she asked, "Is our ability to judge, to tell right from wrong, beautiful from ugly, dependent upon our faculty of thought? Does the inability to think and a disastrous failure of what we commonly call conscience coincide?"[6]

As these passages indicate, in approaching the problem of judgment Arendt was primarily interested in the interrelationships of thinking and judging as moral faculties. She was concerned with judgment as the faculty of "telling right from wrong."

In the second place, and in contrast to her interest in judgment as a moral faculty, Arendt also focused on judgment as the retrospective faculty of culling meaning from the past, as a faculty essential to the art of storytelling. In the "Postscriptum" to the volume *Thinking,* she briefly outlines how she proposes to handle the problem of judgment in Volume 3. She still intends to discuss judgment as it is related to "the problem of theory and practice and to all attempts to arrive at a halfway plausible theory of ethics."[7] But her last paragraph to the "Postscriptum" turns from ethics to the problems of historiography. She intends to deny history's right of being the ultimate judge—"Die Weltgeschichte ist das Weltgericht" (Hegel)—without denying history's importance. As Richard Bernstein and Ronald Beiner have observed, in these subsequent reflections Arendt's interest appears to have shifted from the standpoint of the actor, judging so as to act, to that of the spectator, judging so as to cull meaning from the past.[8]

Lastly, Arendt's reflections on judgment not only vacillate between judgment as a moral faculty, guiding action versus judgment as a retrospective faculty, guiding the spectator or the storyteller; there is an even deeper philosophical perplexity about the status of judgment in her work. This concerns her attempt to bring together the Aristotelian conception of judgment as an aspect of *phronesis* with the Kantian understanding of judgment as the faculty of "enlarged thought" or "representative thinking." As Christopher Lasch has observed,

> On the one hand, Arendt's defense of judgment as the quintessential political virtue seems to lead to an Aristotelian conception of politics as a branch of practical reason. On the other hand, her appeal to Kant as the source of her ideas about judgment appeals to a very different conception of politics, in which political action has to be grounded not in the practical arts but in universal moral principles. . . . Arendt's discussion of judgment, instead of clarifying the difference between ancient and modern conceptions of morality and politics, seems to confuse the two.[9]

In the following, I will attempt to disentangle some of the very complex issues that are suggested by Arendt's inconclusive and, as we shall see, paradoxical reflections on the question of judgment. Of these, the hardest still remains Arendt's meaning and intentions in writing *Eichmann in Jerusalem*.[10]

Eichmann in Jerusalem: A "Cura Posterior"?[11]

Among all of Hannah Arendt's writings, the controversy generated by *Eichmann in Jerusalem* remains the most acrimonious, the most tangled, and the one hardest to put to rest. In fact, it is likely that with the publication of the Hannah Arendt-Martin Heidegger and the Hannah Arendt-Mary McCarthy correspondences,[12] the debate around this book will be rekindled. Perhaps what makes this work and the controversy surrounding it still so unwieldy is the weaving together of sociohistorical narratives and philosophical reflections. There are at least three sociohistorical narratives in this work: in the first place, there is Arendt's reporting of the circumstances of Eichmann's arrest, detention, and trial by the Israeli authorities, including the behavior of Chief Prosecutor Gideon Hausner during the proceedings. Second, there is Arendt's attempt to come to grips with the behavior of so-called ordinary German citizens during the Nazi regime, and the Holocaust in particular. Eichmann becomes for her a paradigm case for analyzing how neither particularly evil nor particularly smart people could get caught in the machinery of evil and commit the deeds that they did. Third, there is Arendt's account of the role of the Jewish councils—the *Judenraete*—the special committees appointed by the Nazis, with a decree of September 21, 1939, in the administration of the Jewish populations of Poland, the Baltic countries (Lithuania, Latvia, and Estonia), and the occupied areas of the former Soviet Union (Byelorussia and Ukraine); and of their role in cooperating with the Nazis in the carrying out of the final solution.[13] It is the convergence of these narratives with her philosophical thesis concerning the "banality of evil" that baffled her readers. At one level, it seemed as if Arendt was accusing her own people and their leaders of being complicitous in the Holocaust, whereas she was exculpating Eichmann and other Germans through naming their deeds "banal."[14] Could these have been Hannah Arendt's intentions? Could she have been so mistaken in her judgments?

No doubt, the phraseology of "the banality of evil" and of "thoughtlessness" to describe Eichmann's deeds did not help. Arendt forced the English language into a procrustean bed to get across her own complex, and perhaps even ultimately confused, reflections on the issues of "personal responsibility under dictatorships." Arendt did not mean that Eichmann's cooperation in the extermination of the Jews, and of other peoples, by the Nazis was banal. She referred rather to a specific quality of mind and character of the doer himself.[15] The Mary McCarthy–Hannah Arendt correspondence throws some light on these terminological infelicities.[16] On August 10, 1945, McCarthy wrote to Hannah Arendt with a philosophical query: She had been pondering Raskolnikov's old problem in Dostoyevsky's *Crime and Punishment,* "Why shouldn't I murder my grandmother if I want to? Give me one good reason."[17] Arendt responded with a professorial gesture that acknowledged the depth as well as the difficulty of McCarthy's question: "The philosophic answer would be the answer of Socrates: Since I have got to live with myself, am in fact the only person from whom I never shall be able to part, whose company I shall have to bear forever, I don't want to become a murderer; I don't want to spend my life in the company of a murderer."[18] Mary McCarthy is unconvinced: "The modern person I posit would say to Socrates, with a shrug, 'Why not? What's wrong with a murderer? And Socrates would be back where he started.' "[19]

Nearly twenty years later, they return to the same question. Arendt had sent her manuscript for "Thinking and Moral Considerations" to Mary McCarthy to be edited. McCarthy complains, not for the first time, about Arendt's tendency to force the English language to mean what it does not mean.[20] McCarthy observes that *thoughtlessness* in English would mean "heedlessness, neglect, forgetfulness," and that Arendt should come up with a synonym like "inability to think." Even with this terminological correction, Mary McCarthy remains unconvinced that what Eichmann suffered from was not extraordinary moral wickedness or depravity but "thoughtlessness." She writes that "Eichmann was profoundly, egregiously stupid. . . . Here I rather agree with Kant . . . that stupidity is caused . . . by a wicked heart."[21]

The questions posed for moral philosophy by Arendt's attempts to link thoughtlessness, lack of judgment, and evildoing will be taken up below. It is the link between the sociohistorical narrative and the moral questions that is still the hardest to establish properly. Recent historical research has shown that on a number of issues, Arendt's judgments were either insufficiently documented, ill-founded, or both. In his excellent introduction to the 1986 reedition of *Eichmann in Jerusalem,* the German historian Hans Mommsen writes,

> A number of statements were not sufficiently critically examined. A number of conclusions show that she was insufficiently familiar with the material that was available by the beginning of the 1960s. The presentation of historical developments relies on two studies: in addition to the older study of Gerald Reitlinger, in particular that of Raul Hilberg's on the extermination of European Jewry which appeared in 1961. She was extremely critical of his general interpretation, although this matched her own views of the matter on important issues. At the same time, in her role as a journalist, she

occasionally uses *[verwertet]* information, whose truth content could only be established through painstaking historical analysis, and which, for the most part, could only be clarified after access to the proper documentation."[22]

Hans Mommsen lists several such historical issues: Hannah Arendt had minimized the resistance against Hitler, and in the original edition had mentioned the anti-Hitler conspiracy of July 20, 1944, only incidentally;[23] she still held on to the questionable view that German communists had entered the NSDAP *(National Sozialistische Deutsche Arbeiter Partei)* in massive numbers; she underestimated the communist resistance to Hitler.[24] Mommsen observes,

> She was unable to analyze the deeper causes for the lack of the willingness to resist *[Widerstandswillen]*. Just as in the case of the cooperation of many Jewish functionaries, in this instance too, she took as the measure *[Maßstab]* of her judgment, the individual's lack of readiness to sacrifice his/her life.[25]

Indeed, of all the difficult historical and moral issues touched upon by Hannah Arendt, her evaluation of the behavior of the Jewish councils remains the most difficult. It was also her passing judgment on these events and the individuals involved in them that earned her the wrath, rejection, condemnation, and contempt of the established Jewish community.[26] Historians agree that Arendt should have distinguished more carefully among the various stages of the "silent" cooperation between the Nazi regime and Jewish organizations and committees. Hans Mommsen observes that before 1936, there was some collaboration between the Gestapo and Zionist organizations that shared "a negative identity of goals,"[27] in that each wanted, in one way or another, for the Jewish population to leave Germany and other European territories. Until 1938, the Central Committee of German citizens of Jewish faith retained the hope of being able to find some modus vivendi with the regime. Hannah Arendt used the term *der jüdische Führer* (the Jewish führer) to describe the activities of Leo Baeck, the former Chief Rabbi of Berlin, a terminology that she dropped in later editions of the book.[28]

Arendt was concerned about the role of the Jewish councils from the very beginning of the Eichmann controversy. She wrote to Karl Jaspers on December 23, 1960, before the beginning of the trial:

> I'm afraid that Eichmann will be able to prove, first of all, that no country wanted the Jews (just the kind of Zionist propaganda which Ben Gurion wants and that I consider a disaster) and will demonstrate, second, to what a huge degree the Jews helped organize their own destruction. That is, of course, the naked truth, but this truth, if it is not really explained, could stir up more anti-Semitism than ten kidnappings.[29]

A few years later, Arendt was still convinced that the reason the Jewish "establishment" (her term) was taking such extraordinary interest and going to such massive expense in attacking her was that

> the Jewish leadership [Jewish agency before the state of Israel was founded] has much more dirty laundry to hide than anyone had ever guessed—at any rate, I don't know very much about it. As far as I can see, ties between the Jewish leadership and the Jewish Councils may be involved.[30]

Establishing the extent, nature, and motives of the cooperation between the Nazis and various Jewish organizations, which were faced with extremely diverse territorial and demographic conditions, extending from the Jewish organizations of Berlin to the Jewish councils of the ghettos of Lodz, Vilna, and Bialystok, will be the task of future historians of the Holocaust. Hannah Arendt's position on the role of the Jewish councils remains ambiguous: on the one hand, one can read her as if her sole concern was the lack of Jewish resistance and uprising, of the kind that took place in the Warsaw ghetto. Given her left Zionist sympathies, which went back to her student days, this reaction was, of course, understandable. On the other hand, she was extremely critical of Chief Prosecutor Gideon Hausner in the Eichmann trial, who would ask the witnesses precisely why they did not resist. Arendt herself considered this line of questioning "cruel and silly."[31]

What then were her own motives in raising these questions? Was it so difficult to understand that Jewish communities and their leaders could not grasp the magnitude, as well as the unprecedentedness, of the crime that was being perpetrated against them? Was it so hard to grasp that they would interpret Nazi extermination policy as a more massive form of the traditional anti-Semitism to which they had been subjected since time immemorial?[32] Was it so impossible to see that the Jewish councils tried to keep a semblance of order and everydayness in running the lives of their communities, and somehow still entertained the hope that they could influence and maybe even postpone the worst from happening to them?[33] If it was "cruel and silly" to ask the Jews to have resisted under such circumstances, as Hannah Arendt accused Gideon Hausner's line of questioning of being, than what was she after herself? I do not have the answers to these questions.

I am inclined to think that Hannah Arendt played the role of Cassandra here: she had decided that the time had come to ask these questions, if only because Eichmann himself was going to raise them in his own self-defense, and it would be more appropriate, she thought, for the Jewish community worldwide to examine itself and its own conscience about the Holocaust. Her letter to Karl Jaspers of December 23, 1960, clearly supports this reading.[34] Perhaps this is also what she had in mind when she wrote to Mary McCarthy in October 1963 that

> you were the only reader to understand what otherwise I have never admitted—namely, that I wrote this book in a curious state of euphoria. And that ever since I did it, I feel—after twenty years [since the war]—light-hearted about the whole matter. Don't tell anybody; is it not proof positive that I have no "soul"?[35]

The use of the term "light-hearted" in this context may be another terminological infelicity on Arendt's part; she means rather that her heart was lightened by having gotten rid of a burden. By voicing in public the shame, rage, and sadness she had carried in private for thirty years, she was finally unloading some of the burden history had imposed upon her. Certainly, Hannah Arendt had written about totalitarianism, anti-Semitism, the extermination camps, the Nazi death machinery before. What was unprecedented in the Eichmann affair was that for the first time a struggle broke out among the Jewish community and the survivors of the Holocaust as to how and in what terms one should appropriate the memory of the Holocaust and its victims. Hannah Arendt, despite the contentiousness of many of her judgments, is to be credited for being among the first to encourage this line of questioning.[36] Arendt was confronted with the question: who spoke for the memory of the victims, if anyone at all? In what terms could one do so?[37] Her attempt to retain a position outside the established organizations of the state of Israel and world Jewry got her into trouble. Who was she anyway? Where was she speaking from?

Oddly enough, the Eichmann book is Hannah Arendt's most intensely Jewish work, in which she identifies herself morally and epistemologically with the Jewish people, and this despite the fact that others, such as Gershom Scholem, would accuse her of lacking *Ahabath Israel* (love of the Jewish people).[38] It is as if some of the deepest paradoxes of retaining a Jewish identity under conditions of modernity come to the fore in Arendt's own attempts to find the moral, political, and jurisprudential bases upon which the trial and sentencing of Adolf Eichmann took place. Hannah Arendt struggled to bring together the universal and the particular, her modernist cosmopolitanism with her belief in some form of collective Jewish self-determination. Her reflections here return us to some of the central preoccupations of her political philosophy. Again, the correspondence with Karl Jaspers offers many insights.

After Eichmann's kidnapping in Argentina by the Israeli Secret Service on May 11, 1960, both Karl Jaspers and Hannah Arendt are anguished about the illegality of this act, and about the moral and legal issues involved in his being tried by an Israeli court.[39] Arendt is convinced to the very end that the state of Israel had committed a "clear violation of international law in order to bring him to justice."[40] She also noted that what enabled Israel to get away with this in the international community was in fact Eichmann's de facto statelessness. Neither postwar Germany nor Argentina, where he had settled under false pretenses, were to claim him as their citizen.

Inasmuch as she questioned the justifiability of the circumstances surrounding Eichmann's capture, Hannah Arendt did not differ from Karl Jaspers. Yet, although the latter wanted Israel to hand over the jurisdiction of the trial to an international court or body, she defended Israel's right to bring Eichmann to trial and to pass judgment on him.[41] There were three kinds of objections raised to the Eichmann trial. First, there was the objection raised in the case of the Nuremberg trials as well, that Eichmann was tried under a retroactive law and appeared in the court of the victors. To this objection, Hannah Arendt thought that the Israeli court's reply was justifiable: the Nuremberg trials were cited in the Jerusalem Court as precedent, and the Nazi Collaboration (Punishment) Law of 1950 in Israel was based on this.[42] Arendt's observations on the principle *"nullum crimen, nulla poena sine lege"* (no crime, no wrongdoing without the law) are interesting. She observes that the principle of retroactivity, that no one can be condemned for an act that was not against the law at the time it was committed, only "meaningfully applies to acts known to the legislator."[43] If a crime that was unknown before makes its appearance in human history, such as the crime of genocide perpetrated by the Holocaust, justice in this instance demands a new and unprecedented law. The Eichmann trial did not violate the principle of retroactivity, for prior to the Nuremberg trials there was no law established by a human legislator under which he could have been tried.[44] The Nuremberg trials established such a law through the Charter (the London agreement of 1945), and Israel invoked its own law against genocide in 1950, which was based on the 1945 Nuremberg Charter. Hannah Arendt was not, therefore, particularly concerned with the argument that the justice meted out at the Nuremberg trials as well as in the case of Eichmann was "the justice of the victor" *(Siegerjustiz),* because she held to the view that the crimes of the Nazi regime were of such an unprecedented nature that one needed new categories, new criteria for judging actions and events around one. The Eichmann trial posed the dilemmas of judging "without bannisters" for everyone involved, from the jurors to the journalists and to world public opinion.

To the objection that the court in Jerusalem was not competent to stand trial over Eichmann, Arendt gave a more equivocal answer, for this issue concerned the state of Israel's right to represent and speak in the name of all the victims of Adolf Eichmann. Arendt is firm that insofar as Eichmann had participated in the killing of Jews *because* they were Jews, and not because they were Poles, Lithuanians, Rumanians, and so on, a Jewish political entity could represent his victims. The basis on which Israel could do so, she maintained, could be made consistent with the Genocide Convention, adopted by the United Nations General Assembly on December 9, 1948. This convention provided that "persons charged with genocide . . . shall be tried by a competent tribunal of the States in the territory of which the act was committed or by such an international penal tribunal as may have jurisdiction."[45]

Arendt's gloss on this rather technical question of defining territorial jurisdiction leads to some rather surprising conclusions. "Israel," she writes,

> could easily have claimed territorial jurisdiction if she had only explained that "territory," as the law understands it, is a political and legal concept, and not merely a geographical term. It relates not so much, and not primarily, to a piece of land as to the space between individuals in a group whose members are bound to, and at the same time separated and protected from, each other by all kinds of relationships, based on a common language, religion, a common history, customs, and laws. Such relationships became spatially manifest insofar as they themselves constitute the space wherein the different members of a group relate to and have intercourse with each other. No State of Israel would have ever come into being if the Jewish people had not created and maintained its own specific in-between space throughout the long centuries of dispersion, that is, prior to the seizure of its old [sic] territory.[46]

This is indeed a curious claim. If a citizen of a particular country or the consular space of a certain country is attacked in foreign territory, the government of the country of the victim would have the territorial competence to judge the perpetrators and ask for their extradition, and so on. But is Hannah Arendt suggesting that the state of Israel has a claim to represent all Jews in the world, even those who are not Israeli citizens, on the grounds that this state itself could never have come into being "if the Jewish people had not created and maintained its own specific in-between"? The main objection to this formulation would be that it does not derive membership in a state from an act of consent, choice, or other indication of positive will, but makes it dependent on a resultant of one's ethnic identity. This analysis collapses the categories of citizenship and ethnicity by almost suggesting that all ethnic Jews are potential Israeli citizens. This is a principle accepted by Israel's Law of Return; the obverse side of this law is, of course, the denial of full citizenship rights to those whose ethnic identity or nationality is not Jewish but who nonetheless live in the territories under the jurisdiction of the state of Israel. Arendt's reflections on the matter of Israel's territorial jurisdiction to judge Eichmann run contrary to her otherwise careful distinctions between citizenship rights and ethnic identity.

This unresolved tension between the universal and the particular is nowhere more evident than in her articulation of the central category under which she thinks Eichmann should have been condemned, namely, "crimes against humanity." Arendt criticized the sentence of the Israeli court for its juridical confusions. In particular, she was critical that the Israeli court had used the category of "crimes against humanity"

> to include genocide if practiced against non-Jewish peoples (such as the Gypsies or the Poles) and all other crimes, including murder, committed against either Jews or non-Jews, provided that these crimes were not committed with intent to destroy the people as a whole.[47]

For Arendt, this way of stating the question was utterly wrongheaded and was based on a fundamental misunderstanding of the category itself. The unprecedented category of "crimes against humanity" was invented, she insisted, precisely to name a new kind of act: namely, the act of genocide that was perpetrated upon a people simply because they existed on the face of this earth as *this specific kind* of people, as exemplifying one way of being among the many possible modes of "human diversity." Jews were killed not because they were enemies of the regime, class traitors, spies against the *Führer,* or the like but because qua Jews they were said to be certain kinds of beings that had no right to be on this earth. Genocide requires some form of race thinking as its basis because it aims at the elimination of a people in virtue of the collective characteristics that it is constructed as possessing. All genocide is a form of "ethnic cleansing," as the war in Yugoslavia has taught us. Arendt observes,

> Had the court in Jerusalem understood that there were distinctions between discrimination, expulsion and genocide, it would immediately have become clear that the supreme crime it was confronted with, the physical extermination of the Jewish people, was a crime against humanity, perpetrated upon the body of the Jewish people, and that only the choice of victims, not the nature of the crime could be derived from the long history of Jew-hatred and anti-Semitism. Insofar as the victims were Jews, it was right and proper that a Jewish court should sit in judgment; but insofar as the crime was a crime against humanity, it needed an international tribunal to do justice to it.[48]

Arendt wanted finally to reconcile the universal and the particular, the ideal of humanity and the fact of human particularity and diversity. The concept of "crimes against humanity" immediately invokes the concept of the "right to have rights," discussed in *The Origins of Totalitarianism* (pp. 290 ff.). In both cases, an anthropological normative universal is being invoked. In virtue of our humanity alone, Arendt is arguing, we are beings entitled to be treated in certain ways, and when such treatment is not accorded to us, then both wrongs and crimes are committed against us. Of course, Arendt was thinking along Kantian lines that we are "moral persons," and that our humanity and our moral personality coexist. Yet these are not the terms that she will use; nor will she, like Kant, seek to ground the mutual obligation we owe one another in our capacity for acting in accordance with the principles of reason. Even her formula the "right to have rights" is frustratingly ambiguous: if we have a right to have rights, who could have removed it from us? If we do not already all have such a right, how can we acquire it? Furthermore, what is meant by "a right" in this formula: a legally recognized and guaranteed claim by the lawgiver? Or a moral claim that we, qua members of a human group, address to our fellow human beings, to be recognized as their equals? Clearly, it is the second, moral, meaning of the term *rights* that Arendt has in mind. But she is not concerned to offer a justification here.[49] She was not a foundationalist thinker and she stayed away from strategies of normative justification. Her belated reflections on Kant's doctrine of judgment reveal, however, the extent to which she was and remained a moral universalist and modernist. The Eichmann trial was a watershed of sorts because it brought to the fore the contradictions with which Hannah Arendt had struggled existentially and conceptually all her life.

Judgment in Kant's Moral Philosophy and Arendt's Reappropriation

The Eichmann affair showed the centrality of judgment for human affairs in many and varied ways: there was the retrospective judgment that every historian and narrator of past events exercised; there was the moral judgment of the contemporaries who conducted the trial against

Eichmann, his actions and doings; and there was also the lack of a faculty of judgment on Eichmann's own part. Rereading *Eichmann in Jerusalem,* one almost feels Hannah Arendt's bafflement at Eichmann's persona and conduct before and during the trial. Writing in the "Postscript" that she would have welcomed a general discussion of the concept of the "banality of evil," she continues,

> Eichmann was not Iago and not Macbeth, and nothing would have been farther from his mind than to determine with Richard III "to prove a villain." . . . He *merely,* to put the matter colloquially, *never realized what he was doing.* It was precisely this lack of imagination which enabled him to sit for months on end facing a German jew who was conducting the police interrogation. . . . It was sheer thoughtlessness—something by no means identical with stupidity—that predisposed him to become one of the greatest criminals of that period. . . . That such remoteness from reality and such thoughtlessness can wreak more havoc than all the evil instincts taken together which, perhaps, are inherent in man—that was, in fact, the lesson one could learn in Jerusalem. (emphasis in the original)[50]

To solve or, more correctly, to think through the philosophical problem of judgment, which this trial had raised for her in all its urgency, Hannah Arendt turned to Kant's moral and political philosophy.

As Richard Bernstein has noted, one of the most perplexing aspects of Arendt's discussion of judgment in Kant's philosophy consists of the following:

> Arendt well knew that, even though she invokes the name of Kant, she was radically departing from Kant. There is no question in Kant that the "ability to tell right from wrong" is a matter of practical reason and not the faculty of reflective judgment which ascends from particulars to generals or universals.[51]

Kant, in fact, did not completely ignore the role of judgment in practical philosophy. Judgment, "as the faculty of thinking the particular under the universal," is determinant when the universal is given and the particular is merely to be subsumed under it.[52] It is reflective, if only the particular is given and the universal has to be found for it. Given that, according to Kant, the moral law, as the universal guiding moral action, is in all circumstances given, moral judgment is determinant rather than reflective. But this conclusion is too hasty, for even according to Kant's own reasoning, moral judgments cannot be merely determinant; they do not merely entail the subsumption of the particular under the universal law.

In the section "Of the Topic of Pure Practical Reason" in the *Critique of Practical Reason,* Kant wrote, "To decide whether an action which is possible for us in the sensuous world is or is not a case under the rule requires practical judgment, which applies what is asserted universally in the rule *(in abstracto)* to an action *in concreto.*"[53] This problem presents special difficulties. Because an action determined by the law of practical reason must contain no other ground for its performance than the conception of the moral law, and because "all instances of possible action," according to Kant, "are only empirical and can belong only to experience and nature," it is absurd to wish to find an instance in the world of sense that allows the application of the law of freedom to it.[54] Kant sums up the difficulty as follows:

> The morally good, on the contrary, is something, which, by its object, is supersensuous; nothing corresponding to it can be found in sensuous intuition; consequently, judgment under laws of pure practical reason seems to be subject to special difficulties, which result from the fact that a law of freedom is to be applied to actions which are events occurring in the world of sense and thus, to this extent, belonging to nature.[55]

In this discussion, Kant assumes that every human action is an event in the world falling under natural laws. Yet, for freedom to be possible, he also has to admit that although all actions, once performed, become events in the world, some actions must be caused by the idea of the moral law alone. What distinguishes a moral from a nonmoral action is the ground of its determination, that is, the nature of the principles governing one's maxims alone. Furthermore, only such actions can be morally good.

As is often the case, in his considerations on this matter Kant conflates two issues. First is a question we may name the epistemology of human actions. How can they be identified and individuated?[56] Kant's metaphysics of two worlds, the noumenal and the phenomenal, leads him to the view that all actions, once they become deeds in the world, are events. The problem, however, is not whether actions are not also events, but whether the language of natural events is epistemologically adequate to describe human actions. Even as events in the world, human actions can be understood only with reference to reasons, that is, with reference to the meaningful grounds or principles that act as their causes. Reasons are of such a kind that they require to be understood; they can be described only from the participants' or actors' own perspectives.[57] Under the spell of the exaggerated promises of Newtonian science, Kant dissolves all distinctions between the natural, human, and social sciences, and simply takes it for granted that a natural, Newtonian science of human action is possible.

The second question that guides Kant is the distinction between the morally right and the morally good. Actions that are morally right are *in conformity* with the moral law; but only those done with *the duty to conform* to the moral law as their sole ground, or motivational purpose, are morally good. The distinction between the morally right and the morally good is not counterintuitive, for it is possible to do the right thing for the wrong reasons. The intentions of the doer are obviously an essential, though by no means the sole, component of the moral quality or virtue of an action. Where Kant seems to go wrong, though, is in his insistence that we can never know if an action was morally virtuous in this sense at all, because the morally good defies embodiment in the phenomenal world. Thus, although Kant does not ignore the role of judgment in practical philosophy, his reflections on this matter get mired in the problem of his two-world metaphysics and preclude a closer examination of what may be involved in the exercise of moral judgment.

Are we now in a position to explain why Hannah Arendt, who repeatedly emphasized that judgment was a faculty of "telling right from wrong,"[58] and not just the beautiful from the ugly, continued to appeal to Kant's doctrine of reflective judgment as a model for judgment in general? Clearly, Arendt had no use for Kant's two-world metaphysics and for the denigration of human action that resulted from it. In this respect, Kant only shared the contempt for the *vita activa* characteristic of the philosophical tradition as a whole. Arendt's entire theory of action, as it unfolds in the space of appearances, presents us with a powerful alternative to the Kantian two-world theory of metaphysics. What Arendt saw in Kant's doctrine of aesthetic judgment was something else: in Kant's conception of reflective judgment, restricted by Kant himself—erroneously in Arendt's eyes—to the aesthetic realm alone, Arendt discovered a procedure for ascertaining intersubjective agreement in the public realm. This kind of intersubjective agreement clearly transcended the expression of simple preference, while falling short of the a priori and certain validity demanded by Kantian reason. Let us recall Kant's description of "reflective judgment":

> By the name *sensus communis* is to be understood the idea of a public sense, i.e. a critical faculty which in its reflective act takes account (a priori) of the mode of representation of everyone else, in order, as it were, to weigh its judgment with the collective reason of mankind, and thereby avoid the illusion arising from subjective and personal conditions which could readily be taken for objective. . . . This is accomplished by weighing the judgment, not so much with actual, as rather with the merely possible, judgments of others, and by putting ourselves in the position of everyone else.[59]

In her early essay "The Crisis in Culture," Arendt provides an illuminating gloss on this passage. She writes,

> The power of judgment rests on a potential agreement with others, and the thinking process which is active in judging something is not, like the thought process of pure reasoning, a dialogue between me and myself, but finds itself always and primarily, even if I am quite alone in making up my mind, in an anticipated communication with others with whom I know I must finally come to some agreement. From this potential agreement judgment derives its specific validity. This means, on the one hand, that such judgment must liberate itself from the "subjective private conditions," that is from the idiosyncracies which naturally determine the outlook of each individual in his privacy and are legitimate as long as they are only privately held opinions but which are not fit to enter the market place, and lack all validity in the public realm. And this enlarged way of thinking, which as judgment knows how to transcend its individual limitations, cannot function in strict isolation or solitude; it needs the presence of others "in whose place" it must think, whose perspective it must take into consideration, and without whom it never has the opportunity to operate at all.[60]

The answer to the question as to why Arendt did not explore her departure from Kant in these matters is primarily that in Kant's discovery of the "enlarged mentality," Arendt saw the model for the kind of inter-subjective agreement we could hope to attain in the public realm. Such capacity for judgment is not empathy, as Arendt also observes, for it does not mean assuming, accepting the point of view of the other. It means merely making present to oneself what the perspectives of others involved are or could be, and whether I could "woo their consent" in acting the way I do. Recovering one of the early themes of Hannah Arendt's biography of Rahel Varnhagen, we can say that "enlarged thought" displays the qualities of judgment that are essential to grasp the perspectivality of the public world.

Is there any reason to assume that this model of enlarged thought, which enjoins us actually to engage in or simulate in thought a moral dialogue with all concerned, helps us recover that thread among thinking, judg-ment, and moral considerations that Hannah Arendt had sought? It is again one of the perplexities of Arendtian thinking on these matters that al-though she readily acknowledged the relevance of "enlarged thought" as a principle in the public-political realm, in her considerations on morality, she reverted to the Platonic model of the unity of the soul with itself. In her 1971 essay "Thinking and Moral Considerations," following Socrates in the *Gorgias,* she described conscience as the harmony or oneness of the soul with itself.[61] Although I would not want to deny the relevance of this experience for moral considerations, as Mary McCarthy also ob-served, Arendt was too quick in assuming that out of the self's desire for unity and consistency a principled moral standpoint could emerge. Let me simply remind you of Walt Whitman's famous lines: "Do I contradict myself? Very well then I contradict myself, I am large, I contain multi-tudes."[62]

Although Arendt emphasized *harmony* as the morally relevant experi-ence, she regarded *plurality* as the political principle par excellence. But through this emphasis on unity or harmony, she presented a quasi-intuitionist conception of moral, as opposed to political, judgment. For if the basis of the validity of our moral judgments is that they allow us "to be at home with ourselves," or to be at one with ourselves, are we not in fact making validity a matter of the idiosyncrasies of the individual psyche? Was it not one of the most perplexing characteristics of Eichmann in Arendt's eyes precisely that he seemed "at home" with himself? Arendt fails to convince that an attitude of moral reflection and probing, such as enjoined by the procedure of enlarged thought, and the Platonic emphasis on unity or harmony of the soul with itself can be reconciled. In fact, the capacity for enlarged thought may well lead to moral conflict and alienation, but in a world in disarray an attitude of moral alienation may be more at home in the world than an attitude of simple harmony with oneself.

In her inconclusive considerations on thinking and judging, Hannah Arendt used two different models for understanding the relationship of these faculties. On the one hand, the faculty of thinking, as the capacity to examine "whatever happens to come to pass or attract attention, regardless of results and specific contents,"[63] is closely associated with moral qualities such as autonomy, consistency, tenacity, independence, and steadfastness of judgment. On the other hand is the model of judging, and in particular judging when the general rule, or in Kantian language, the "universal" under which we should subsume the particular, is missing. Under such circumstances, judging becomes an activity of "enlarged mentality," a capacity for presenting to oneself the perspectivality of the world, of taking cognizance of the many points of view through which a matter must be seen and evaluated. This capacity is not empathy, in that it does not mean "feeling with others," but signifies instead a cognitive ability to "think with others." Judgment requires the moral-cognitive capacities for worldliness, that is, an interest in the world and in the human beings who constitute the world, and a firm grasp of where one's own boundaries lie and where those of others begin. Rahel Varnhagen's circle of friends were caught in "romantic inwardness" precisely because at one point they lost the capacity to distinguish between what the world was like and what they would have liked or wished the world to be like; in mood, the boundaries between the "inner" and the "outer" are washed away, as Arendt herself had noted. Whereas thinking requires autonomy, consistency, tenacity, independence, and steadfastness, judging requires worldliness, an interest in one's fellow human beings, and the capacity to appreciate the standpoint of others without projection, idealization, and distortion.

These two models are related insofar as consistency is a virtue of all cognitive processes, and not just of judging. Furthermore, there is also a relationship between the steadfastness of one's thinking process and one's capacity to appreciate the boundaries between oneself and others. Nonetheless, thinking and judging are also distinct in that independence of mind and appreciation of perspectivality may contradict one another; consistency may lead one to want to smooth out contradictions, ambiguities, and ambivalencies; it may lead one to want to develop a *Weltanschauung,* a form of thinking that Arendt herself derided for believing that it had "the key" to every political issue. Tenacity of thought may lead one to ignore others' claims upon one and to deny the presence of their different perspectives. Thus, thinking and judging stand in tension with each other, and the link that Arendt sought to establish between them remains tenuous at best.

There is a profound irony in these reflections—one that no doubt Arendt herself was aware of. The irony is that Martin Heidegger, the greatest thinker of this century in Arendt's eyes, who restored to the word *thinking* its original Greek meaning of "wonder at the phenomena," was also the one who lacked the capacity for judgment.[64] Arendt herself saw a certain kind of "worldlessness," a certain loss of interest in the world and a certain distancing of oneself from it, to be the true mark of the philosopher as opposed to those who, like herself, engaged in the world of human affairs and were moved by "a love of the world." Yet all this suggests is that the one who could think like no other, namely, Martin Heidegger, and the one who could not think at all, namely, Adolf Eichmann, ended up being tempted by the same political ideology and political movement. What then is the relationship between thinking, judging, and acting?

To explore the relationships between thinking, judging, and acting would have required a treatise in moral philosophy. Hannah Arendt leaves unexplored the motivational question of how perspicacious thinking and good judgment could be translated into action. Cognition and action, though, are distinct; not only must one know what to do, under which circumstances, in what fashion, and the like, but one must also have the proper motivation to translate judgment into action. Maybe what Heidegger and Eichmann lacked were not so much, or even primarily, the cognitive skills of thinking in the one case and judging in the other, but the motivational habits of civic courage and civic virtue, capacities for independent political action, and the ability to exercise the "enlarged mentality."

The Missing Normative Foundations of Arendtian Politics

There is an irony in these reflections. The kinds of historical situations that led Arendt to her ruminations on thinking and moral considerations, most notably National Socialism and totalitarianism in our century, were precisely instances when the intersubjectivity constitutive of the social world was so disrupted and damaged that the motivation as well as the capacity of individuals to engage in enlarged thought disappeared. The moral attitude of enlarged thought seems to be missing when we most need it, that is, in those situations of moral and political upheaval when the fabric of moral interactions that constitute everyday life are so destroyed that the obligation to think of the other as one whose perspective I must weigh equally alongside my own disappears from the conscience of individuals.

This realization creates a melancholia in Hannah Arendt's work. Her inconclusive reflections and ruminations on the fragility of human rights, her belief that we are not born equal but we become equals through being recognized as members of a moral and political community, and her ironic acknowledgment that Eichmann, the former Nazi, was a "stateless" person like herself, the persecuted Jew, and that neither would be protected by an international legal and normative order—these episodes are some of the more salient instances when her melancholia about this century comes to the fore.

Arendt's skepticism that moral beliefs and principles would ever be able to restrain or control politics in the twentieth century, and give it a direction compatible with human rights and dignity, leads to a normative lacuna in her thought. There is a resistance on her part to justificatory political discourse, to the attempt to establish the rationality and validity of our beliefs in universal human rights, human equality, the obligation to treat others with respect. Although Hannah Arendt's conception of politics and of the political is quite inconceivable, unintelligible even, without a strongly grounded normative position in universalistic human rights, equality, and respect, one does not find her engaging in any such exercises of normative justification in her writings.

This issue has not gone unnoticed in the secondary literature. George Kateb, for example, has written,

> Arendt in her Greek thinking suggests that political action does not exist to do justice or fulfill other moral purposes. The supreme achievement of political action is existential, and the stakes are seemingly higher than moral ones. This is the gist of Arendt's radicalism. But we must persist with at least one question: Does Arendt's Greek theory provide moral *limitations* on political action, even though it rejects moral *motivation*? (emphasis in the original)[65]

Although with this question, Kateb focuses on elements of Arendt's theory of action that derive from the agonistic appropriation of the Aristotelian conception of praxis, his criticism can be generalized: it is not only Arendt's theory of action that leaves the relationship between action and moral limitations unanswered, but also her view of *political institutions* at large that leaves questions of justice, equality, and mutual recognition unexplored. Not only are Arendt's reflections on morality cursory and unconvincing, but the absence of a justification of the normative dimension of the political, that is, of the question of social and political justice in her work, is deeply disturbing.

Margaret Canovan and Martin Jay approach this issue through the category of "political existentialism" (Jay) or "existentialism politicized" (Canovan).[66] Canovan's observations are instructive:

> Totalitarianism had left human beings without moral certainties, in need of "a new foundation for human community." But Arendt's contention, . . . was that although no absolute moral rules exist which could provide such a foundation, and although even the most authentic of personal moral experiences cannot supply it, nevertheless a foundation for sound human coexistence and a guard against totalitarianism *can* be found in the funda-

mental human condition of plurality itself, in acceptance of the fact that we share the earth with others who are both like and unlike ourselves.[67]

I am not convinced, as Margaret Canovan seems to be, that these observations put Hannah Arendt in the camp of "anti-foundationalist politics," or whether this is such a desirable position for Arendt to be in. I have presented my objections to anti-foundationalisms in ethics and politics in other contexts; they bear no repetition here.[68] Canovan's observations on Arendt's concept of "plurality" suggest to me a reading of the question of the normative foundations of the political in Arendt's work different from anti-foundationalism, and it is this possibility that I would like to explore.

Hannah Arendt's thinking is deeply grounded in a position that I shall call "anthropological universalism." *The Human Condition* treats human beings as members of the same natural species, to whom life on earth is given under certain conditions, namely, those of natality, plurality, labor, work, and action. This philosophical anthropology proceeds from a level of abstraction that treats all forms of cultural, social, and historical differentiation among humans as irrelevant when measured up against the "fundamentals" of their condition. There is an implicit ethical gesture in approaching the human condition from this level of abstraction, one that proceeds from our fundamental equality and commonality as members of the same species. This philosophical anthropology can be viewed as a form of coming to one's senses morally, that is, as a form of *Besinnung,* a form of taking hold of one's senses by grasping what it is to be human. What are some of the elements of such coming to one's senses? In the first place, an awareness of our natality as well as mortality, a cure against the sin, in St. Augustine's terms, of thinking that we are the ground of our being. We are not, however: we are fundamentally dependent creatures, born promiscuously to others like us, and radically dependent upon the goodwill and solidarity of others to become who we are. Furthermore, we are embodied creatures whose material needs must be satisfied by a constant engagement and metabolism with nature. This process of material engagement with the world is also one of world constitution and world creation. Like the anthropology of the young Marx in the *Manuscripts of 1844,* Hannah Arendt also stresses the world- and object-creating qualities of human activities through her distinction between labor and work. We are creatures immersed in a condition of plurality: we are sufficiently like other members of our species so that we can always in some sense or other communicate with them; yet, through speech and action, we individuate ourselves, we reveal how distinctive we are. Plurality is a condition of equality and difference, or a condition of equality-in-difference.

This anthropological universalism contains an ethics of radical inter-subjectivity, which is based on the fundamental insight that all social life and moral relations to others begin with the decentering of primary narcissism. Whereas *mortality* is the condition that leads the self to withdraw from the world into a fundamental concern with a fate that can only be its own, *natality* is the condition through which we immerse ourselves into a world at first through the goodwill and solidarity of those who nurture us, and subsequently through our own deeds and words. Insight into the condition of natality, although it enables the decentration of the subject, is not adequate to lead to an attitude of moral respect among equals. The condition of natality involves inequality and hierarchies of dependence. By contrast, Arendt describes mutual *respect* as "a kind of 'friendship' without intimacy and without closeness; it is a regard for the person from the distance which the space of the world puts between us" (*HC*, p. 243). It is the step leading from the constituents of a philosophical anthropology (natality, worldliness, plurality, and forms of human activity) to this attitude of respect for the other that is missing in Arendt's thought. Her anthropological universalism does not so much justify this attitude of respect as presuppose it. For, in treating one another as members of the same species, we are in some sense already granting each other recognition as moral equals. Arendt does not examine the philosophical step that would lead from a description of the *equality of the human condition* to the *equality that comes from moral and political recognition*. In Kantian terms, to the question of *quaestio juris*, by what reason or on what ground should I respect the other as my equal? Arendt answers with a *quaestio facti*, a factual-seeming description of the human condition. The path leading from the anthropological plurality of the human condition to the moral and political equality of human beings in a community of reciprocal recognition remains philosophically unthematized, precisely because it seems so historically contingent. It is only in her reflections on Kant's theory of reflective judgment, as they extend into the ethical domain, that we see Arendt developing the elements of a procedure of intersubjective validation and justification in ethics. This is contained in her ingenious reading of Kant's theory of the "enlarged mentality."

Yet, aren't those existentialist and anti-foundationalist impulses in her political philosophy precisely what make Hannah Arendt so attractive to many today? Was she not a postmodernist *avant la lettre*? A number of provocative recent interpretations have attempted to push Hannah Arendt's thought toward a more Nietzschean and less Kantian bent. Emphasizing in particular her conception of action and freedom contained in essays such as "What Is Freedom?,"[69] Dana Villa has explored the relation between Arendt's views of action as "agonistic performance" and certain Nietzschean themes. In *Arendt and Heidegger: The Fate of the Political,* he writes,

> The force of Arendt's reading of Aristotle should now be clear. If the idea of *praxis* is to be effectively deployed in the fight against an undemocratic instrumentalization of action, then the first order of business is the thorough deconstruction of the teleological context from which this concept emerged. . . . This is the radical shift of ground that Arendt affects in order to "recover" praxis. The project is revolutionary, the formulations it yields paradoxical and often disturbing. . . . Motives, goals, conditions, consequences: all become largely secondary to grasping action's peculiar significance and reality.[70]

According to Villa's reading, Arendt becomes a "high modernist" who insists "on politics for the sake of politics."[71] I have indicated my disagreements with any analysis of Arendt's theory of action that ignores the dimension of its narrative constitution (see pp. 125 ff., this volume). This selective emphasis on Arendtian agonistics, which subsumes Arendt under Nietzsche's shadow, also underestimates her major contribution to twentieth-century philosophies of action, which is the radical discovery of the link between action, narration, and interpretation. Although action is a central category in Arendt's thought, without being placed in its proper context alongside natality and plurality, emphasis on it alone yields a truncated access to her thought. Hannah Arendt was not just a thinker of political action; she was also a thinker of human culture and institutions, political parties and movements, individual and collective identities, historical trends and future possibilities. It is only when we place her more philosophical reflections on action, identity, and plurality in the context of the development of her political thought as a whole that we note the persistence of the central tension in her work: between her moral and political universalism in thinking through the issues of this century from Zionism through imperialism to the fate of stateless peoples and the Eichmann trial, and her continuing allegiance to the philosophical ethos of Greek thought as transmitted via Martin Heidegger's 1924–1925 lectures. It is this tension that makes Hannah Arendt a reluctant modernist.

To be sure, it is well-known that every interpretation is necessarily selective. Reading is a dialogue between the author, the reader, and the community of past and present interpreters with whom one is in dialogue. All reading is polyphonic; it is perhaps less like an ordered conversation than a symphony of voices. What makes Arendt's voice so present for us is that she offers the possibility of a desirable politics in the post-totalitarian moment. Whether we name this a form of "republican existentialism," as Margaret Canovan proposes, or whether we call it "radical democracy," with Maurizio Passerin d'Entrèves, we must face a central paradox:[72] Hannah Arendt's sociology of modern institutions and her distinction between the social and the political are so problematic that it is hard to see where or how her normative vision of the political could be anchored in contemporary institutions. What we need is not only a reinterpretation of Hannah Arendt's thought but a *revision* of it as well; for if we are to think "with Arendt against Arendt," we must leave behind the pieties of textual analyses and ask ourselves Arendtian questions and be ready to provide non-Arendtian answers.

It is impossible to come to grips with Hannah Arendt's political thought without raising the question of the recovery of the public sphere. It remains one of her central contributions to political philosophy that she made us aware of the centrality of the concept of the public sphere for any egalitarian and participatory democratic project. Yet her neglect, particularly in *The Human Condition*, of the alternative genealogy of modernity that was suggested in her work as early as her biography of Rahel Varnhagen leaves her concept of public space institutionally unanchored, floating as if it were a nostalgic chimera on the horizon of politics.

From Public Space to Public Sphere:
Hannah Arendt and Jürgen Habermas

In 1962, Jürgen Habermas published *The Structural Transformation of the Public Sphere*.[73] Although the very first pages of this work reveal the centrality of Habermas's dialogue with Arendt,[74] the complexity of their interchange and the magnitude of his intellectual debt to her have not been given their due. Jürgen Habermas is indebted to Hannah Arendt not only through the latter's rediscovery of the concept of the public space—*der öffentliche Raum*. Habermas's crucial distinction between "labor" and "interaction," which is at the origin of his concept of "communicative action," is deeply indebted to Arendt's critique of Karl Marx in *The Human Condition* and to her own differentiation between work, labor, and action.[75] At times, Habermas has referred to Arendt's work summarily as being part of a "neo-Aristotelian" revival of the category of *praxis*.[76] The label of "neo-Aristotelianism," however, hides the differences between thinkers like Hans-Georg Gadamer and Hannah Arendt. Certainly, they were both deeply indebted to a certain Heideggerian reading of Aristotle, the elements of which I have examined in Chapter 4. Gadamer revives the Aristotelian category of *praxis* within the context of a philosophy of *phronesis,* of a philosophy of practical reason and judging, and of concern with the particulars of ethical and political situations. He juxtaposes this form of *phronesis* to modern philosophy's Cartesian emphasis on methodical and abstract forms of knowing.[77] Hannah Arendt takes a different route[78] and explores the "linguistic structure of human action." Her claim that "most deeds are in the form of words" (*HC,* pp. 178 ff.) is crucial. Arendt is not arguing that speech itself is a form of action, as J. L. Austin and John Searle have done with their "speech act theories"; she is claiming that human action is linguistically structured, in that it can be identified, described, and recognized for what it is only through a narrative account. Both the doer of deeds and the teller of stories must be able to say in speech what it is that they are doing. Arendt's discovery of the linguistic structure of human action, in my opinion, gave one of the principal impetuses to Habermas's subsequent theory of communicative action. Arendt's concept of public space is the second and equally important conceptual legacy that she imparted to Habermas.

After *The Human Condition,* Jürgen Habermas's *The Structural Transformation of the Public Sphere* was the first work to call to our attention the centrality of this concept for modern, as opposed to just ancient, politics. In the move from the Arendtian concept of the "public space" to the Habermasian concept of the "public sphere," certain crucial transformations took place: first, whereas Arendt sees a decline of the public sphere under conditions of modernity, Habermas notes the emergence of a new form of publicity in the Enlightenment, that is, the public of private individuals reasoning together about public matters.[79] The bourgeois reading public of the early Enlightenment, which constitutes *in nuce* the critical-political public of the late eighteenth and early nineteenth centuries, exercises its reason about public matters by discussing a third voice, the voice of the absent author. There is a shift from the model of an *occular* to an *auditory* public; the public is no longer thought of as a group of humans seeing each other, as in the case of the united *demos.* Rather, the public is increasingly formed through impersonal means of communication such as the printing press, newsletters, novels, and literary and scientific journals.

Second, whereas the Arendtian conception of the public is bound to topographical and spatial metaphors such as "space of appearance," "the city and its walls," Habermas focuses on the transformations brought about in the identity of the public with the rise of the printed media. The public becomes a virtual community of readers, writers, and interpreters.[80] For Habermas, the public sphere is not just, or even principally, an arena of action but an impersonal medium of communication, information, and opinion formation. The terminological shift in German allows us to capture this point more readily: whereas Arendt writes of *der öffentliche Raum,* Habermas uses the term *die Öffentlichkeit,* translated into English variously as the *public sphere, publicity,* and *public opinion.* The public becomes increasingly desubstantialized in this process.

In Hannah Arendt's theory, the concept of the public sphere is so intimately related to her understanding of action in the space of appearances in general that the crucial place of this concept in a *theory of democratic legitimacy* is obscured. Through Habermas's systematic transformations of this Arendtian concept, it becomes possible for us to reestablish the link between the public sphere and democratic legitimacy.[81] To appreciate this transformation, let me introduce two terms to delineate the *functions* of public space in the Arendtian view of the political.

When Arendt links the public space with the space of appearances, as she often does, she primarily has in mind a model of face-to-face human interactions. Not only does this view privilege direct human interaction, it also presupposes a fair degree of homogeneity and convergence around a certain shared ethos. For how otherwise would action be "manifest" to others in its meaning? How, without a fair degree of cohesion around interpretation, would a group of humans recognize the "whatness" of an action, and the "whoness" of the doer? Cohesion does not signify unanimity but a certain amount of convergence in interpretation. I would like to name this the *holistic* function of public space. Public space, according to this view, is a space in which a collectivity becomes present to itself and recognizes itself through a shared interpretive repertoire.

Public space also has an *epistemic* function. This dimension is particularly salient in Arendt's attempt to distinguish sharply between the social and the political realms. In doing so, she emphasizes that the process of public-political struggle must transform narrow self-interest into a more broadly shared public or common interest. What constitutes the authentic political attitude is the capacity and the willingness to engage in "the enlarged mentality"; to give reasons in public, to entertain others' point of view, to transform the dictates of self-interest into a common public goal. As Arendt put it beautifully in her commentary on Kant's theory of judgment,

> The power of judgment rests on a potential agreement with others, and the thinking process which is active in judging something is not, like the thought process of pure reasoning, a dialogue between me and myself, but finds itself always and primarily, even if I am quite alone in making up my mind, in an anticipated communication with others with whom I know I must finally come to some agreement.[82]

This is the epistemic function of public space, and such "anticipated communication with others" transcends the boundaries of the face-to-face society.

The holistic and epistemic models of public space are both central to any theory of democratic legitimacy, whether ancient or modern, that holds that government is essentially for the people, through the people, and by the people. Nonetheless, there are interesting differences of emphases between the more radical-democratic participatory traditions and the liberal-representative ones. If we take Jean-Jacques Rousseau, Thomas Jefferson, or the young Karl Marx as theorists of radical participatory democracy, the emphasis is on the presence of the united will of the people gathered together as a deliberative or decisional community.

If we stress, by contrast, the liberal tradition's claim that all legitimate government derives from the consent of the governed, the public sphere can be viewed as a mechanism through which such consent is expressed. As opposed to participatory democrats' emphases on the actual embodied presence of the people, the liberal tradition is more willing to accept that the consent of the people may be expressed in more mediated fashion and through more complex institutions in civil society as well as the state. At some level, the ingenuity of Habermas's discussion in *The Structural Transformation of the Public Sphere* was that he subjected the liberal principle of political legitimation, the use by citizens of their private reason to test public matters, to a radical-democratic critique.[83]

Habermas establishes the connection between the concept of the public sphere and modernist forms of political legitimacy that regard the voluntary union of equal citizens as the basis of such legitimacy. In Kantian language, the "public exercise of one's reason"[84] is essential because it is through submitting one's point of view on public matters to the judgment of others, in confronting it with theirs, that a generalizable point of view can emerge. If the reasonable and voluntary consent of citizens, or their mutual promises in Arendtian language, are the basis of legitimacy in the political realm, then a public sphere of the exchange of opinion, of the sifting through of arguments, and of mutual deliberation is fundamental to modern political institutions. Habermas clearly shows the link between modernist understandings of political legitimacy and the public sphere through this analysis. Elements of such a perspective were already implicit in some of Arendt's later essays, such as "Civil Disobedience,"[85] but a systematic argument connecting political legitimacy, in its democratic or liberal forms, and the public sphere could not be culled from the Arendtian theory. Instead, her thoughts on the public realm often were left mired in a romantic invocation of the power that emerges whenever and wherever the people are united together through mutual promises. Such recoveries of the "lost treasures of the revolutionary tradition" seldom found institutional anchorings in the modern world.

Even if the history of political thought teaches us how crucial a certain understanding of the public is, for democratic as well as for liberal theory, all normative theories of the public sphere have been suspect for quite some time of being profoundly irrelevant to contemporary political life. This is the point at which Arendtian questions elicit non-Arendtian responses.

The Contested Public Sphere:
Arendt, Habermas, and Beyond

In 1927, Walter Lippmann published *The Phantom Public*.[86] Written against the background of growing despair and disillusionment about the viability of representative democracies in Europe and North America, in this work Lippmann decried the "ideal of sovereign and omnicompetent citizens" to be a fiction at best and a phantom at worst.[87] Lippmann's elitist and pessimistic assessment concerning the fictional quality of collective deliberation processes by ordinary citizens elicited a spirited response from John Dewey in *The Public and Its Problems*. Granting that the experience of industrial and urban modern societies undermined "the genuine community life" out of which American democracy had developed, Dewey admitted that "the public seems to be lost. . . . If a public exists, it is surely as uncertain about its whereabouts as philosophers since Hume have been about the residence and make-up of the self."[88] Nonetheless, Dewey tried to articulate a vision of radical democracy according to which individuals could be reconstituted as democratic citizens by revitalizing those ties of community out of which the American experience with democracy in New England towns was born.

Indeed, theories of the public sphere, from Walter Lippmann to Hannah Arendt, from John Dewey to Jürgen Habermas, appear to be afflicted by a nostalgic trope: where once there was a public sphere of action and deliberation, participation and collective decision making, today there no longer is one; or, if a public sphere still exists, it is so distorted, weakened, and corrupted as to be a pale recollection of what once was. Whether one chooses the Athenian polis as a paradigm, or looks at the experience of republican city-states in the Italian Renaissance; whether one locates the authentic public in the coming together of private persons of the Enlightenment to use their "private reason to discuss public matters" (Habermas), or whether one idealizes the New England town meetings, there is always a curious "what was then and what no longer is" quality to these theories. The public is a phantom that will not go away: even after the many funeral rites and orations it has ben subjected to, it comes back to haunt conscience and memory.

In the concluding pages of *The Structural Transformation of the Public Sphere,* Habermas quoted C. Wright Mills precisely on the distinction concerning *public* and *mass.* A public, according to Mills, refers to a form of communication in which as many people express opinions as receive them, where there is a channel of immediate and effective answer-back, and in which opinion can find an effective outlet in action. In a human "mass," by contrast, far fewer people express opinions than receive them; it is either difficult or impossible to answer back; and the realization of opinion in action is controlled by authorities who organize and control the channels of such action. The mass has no autonomy from institutions of control.[89]

With the spread of industrialization and new technologies, the dominance of the printed media gives way first to the wireless and the radio, then to the electronic media, and in our day to information technologies. As the means of communication unite ever larger numbers of people and enable their access to ever more impersonal channels of information and communication, the "public" loses its metaphorical anchoring in some form of body and becomes desubstantialized or decorporealized. In new media of communication such as e-mail, those communicating neither see one another nor hear each other's voices. They are present only as senders and receivers of electronic messages. The new public increasingly has no body or location in space. It is constituted by an anonymous *public conversation* taking place in multiple spaces in society and in which potentially infinite voices can participate. Lippmann's and Dewey's public citizen today has become the faceless speaker and listener in an anonymous *public conversation.*

Can such an anonymous public conversation be the medium through which democratic deliberations take place? Neither Lippmann nor Dewey thought that under these social and technological circumstances a "conversation" could take place, let alone a process of public deliberation. In fact, all around us we are confronted today with the apparent contradiction that as access to public means of communication has increased, the *quality* of public debate and reasoning has decreased. Radio talk shows have not encouraged public deliberation; rather, the public sphere is filled with the voices of resentment, prejudice, and unanalyzed opinions that are exposed to others, more often than not, in acts of exhibitionist defiance. The more impersonal the public conversation has become, the more the temptation is increasing to "let it all hang out"; the line between intimacy and publicity has been corroded.

The idea of the sovereign people deliberating collectively about matters of common concern to all is a *regulative ideal* of the democratic form of government, and disquiet about the public sphere is at bottom anxiety about democracy in modern, complex, multicultural, and increasingly globalized polities. The regulative principle of democracy requires the idea of an autonomous public sphere as the process through which self-governance through the deliberation of a collectivity can take place. Between this constitutive ideal of democracy and the increasingly desubstantialized carriers of the anonymous public conversation of mass societies, a hiatus exists; it is this hiatus that transforms the regulative ideal of democracy into a *constitutive fiction,* and it is this fiction that causes continuous anxiety.

Let us be clear, though, that this regulative ideal itself is and has always been highly problematic. Despite its normative force, it is misleading in a number of crucial ways for understanding the project of democracy. A reconsideration of the ideal of the public sphere and the democratic project should begin with a fresh analysis of this constitutive fiction of democracy itself. I would like to list four ways in which the principle of the sovereign deliberative body of citizens is problematic: (a) identity of the body politic, (b) social complexity, (c) rationality of procedures, (d) myth of democratic sovereignty and constitutionalism.

Identity of the body politic. All hitherto known "publics" have rested on the exclusion of certain groups of individuals from participation or deliberation on the bases that these individuals lacked the cognitive, emotional, economic, political, or cultural virtues and abilities that were considered essential to take part in the public. Throughout history, and in different cultures and societies, women, laborers who used their bodies, those who did not own property, as well as members of certain racial, religious, ethnic, and linguistic groups have been excluded from participation in the public sphere. The *public* is a term of inclusion as well as exclusion: it is based upon defining the "we" and the "they," that which is properly public and that which is private. As Hannah Arendt has noted, it is one of the ironies of complex democracies of the twentieth century that the so-called decline or transformation of the public sphere has coincided with the unprecedented opening of the public to hitherto excluded groups. Could it be then that the regulative ideal of democracy, that of the sovereign people, can never be adequately realized, precisely because as an ideal it must always be questioned and challenged for the exclusions it creates, the boundaries it delineates? The "sovereign people" in a democracy can never be a fixed quantity; it is of the essence of democracy that the boundaries between the "we" who decide and the "they" about whom decisions are made will always be subject to questioning and contestation.

Social complexity. As *The Human Condition* has demonstrated, the sociological configuration of modernity radically alters the meanings of private and public. The *private* now refers to the *domestic-intimate* sphere; the *economic* sphere of private property and contractual transactions; and the *civil sphere* of multiple associations that increasingly include an autonomous domain of science, literature, and other cultural and religious pursuits. From Rousseau to the young Hegel, from Hannah Arendt to the young Marx, modern social theorists see an incompatibility between the project of democracy and the social complexity of modern capitalist civil societies.

Theorists sympathetic to the project of modernity, by contrast, like the old Hegel of the 1821 *Philosophy of Right,* Benjamin Constant, Alexis de Tocqueville, and John Stuart Mill, argue that the project of democratic self-governance and individual liberty are not incompatible but may even be complementary. The claim here is that democracy in the polis could be attained only at the cost of stifling individuality, creativity, and self-development. The liberties of the ancients, as lofty as they were, crushed individual liberty when the two were in conflict. The challenge is to reenvisage the democratic project under conditions of social, cultural, and moral heterogeneity.

It is the legacy of the more thoughtful liberal observers of modern civil society to have introduced two principles into democratic theory: the necessity of representative and mediating institutions in civil society, which articulate at the level of the state the interests and views of an increasingly diverse group of citizenry that constitute modern civil societies; in addition, an independent sphere of public opinion that is formed within, rather than outside, the boundaries of civil society.

From a conceptual point of view, the more challenging attack against the regulative ideal of democratic theory came from observers of the changing nature of legislative and parliamentary bodies, such as Carl Schmitt, who published his critique of liberal democracies, *The Crisis of Parliamentary Democracy,*[90] in 1928, a year after Lippmann's *The Phantom Public* (1927). Schmitt delineated a phenomenon that is still very much with us, although the consequences he drew from this analysis pointed in a rather different direction than the project of revitalizing democracy. Schmitt theorized that parliamentary bodies in liberal democracies were being transformed from bodies that deliberated about the public good into organizations in which powerful private-corporatistic bodies negotiated and bargained over interests. Increasingly, public legislation was delegated to powerful committees, working in back rooms, while the arena of public deliberation and debate was emptied out. For Carl Schmitt, this changing nature of legislative bodies in liberal democracies was an unmasking of the illusion of government by debate on which these systems rested. The more government by debate was replaced by negotiations among powerful groups, the more one would recognize the ultimate and nondebatable moment of decision upon which all political power rested. The sovereign is not the united body of citizens but the one who has the power to decide in an emergency situation. Carl Schmitt's authoritarian, and ultimately fascist, theory of sovereignty dispensed with the public sphere altogether.

The transformation of legislative and representative bodies in democracies from deliberative organs into bargaining ones; the increasing distance between the decision-making processes of democratic representatives, social and technological elites, on the one hand, and the ordinary public, on the other; and the epistemic complexity of the issues facing both the public and its representatives are all aspects of social complexity that challenge the ideal and practice of democracy.

Rationality and collective deliberation. Even among democratic theorists, the notion of collective processes of deliberation has always aroused suspicion. Rousseau thought that the united people could not deliberate, because this would only produce factions.[91] Rather, the "people" should be present to itself through rituals, ceremonies, and public symbolic observances. Madison supported the principle of democratic cultivation of the public through the wise, just, and noble decisions of a public elite, while Jefferson saw the town ward system as the only size compatible with public deliberative processes. But more than size is at stake here. Deliberative processes require rules, procedures, as well as limitations of time and closure to attain a modicum of rationality. Hannah Arendt was unduly neglectful of this procedural dimension. Publicity and rationality are not always compatible; public debate and deliberation must respect procedures to ensure some form of rationality. The principle of democratic legitimacy requires that all those whose interests are affected by collectively agreed upon rules of action have the possibility of participating in deliberative processes concerning the justifiability of such decisions. Democratic legitimacy requires maximum publicity, but it is the task of just institutions and wise procedures to ensure that the outcomes of democratic processes of debate, deliberation, and decision making are also at least minimally rational. The irrationality of majoritarian decisions has been the thorn in the side of democracy since the condemnation of Socrates to death in the city of Athens. The "people" is sovereign in a democracy, but it is neither always just nor always wise.

Sovereignty and constitutionalism. A fundamental conceptual and institutional innovation of liberal democracies that enables a mediation between rationality and legitimacy, democratic sovereignty and justice, consists in the establishment of constitutional courts and the procedure of judicial review. In fact, in most contemporary democracies, an increasingly complex tug-of-war between the principle of democratic sovereignty and of constitutional review is under way. From a theoretical standpoint, procedures of constitutional review are innovative answers to the paradoxes of democratic legitimacy: what if the sovereign people is unjust in violating the rights of certain groups within its boundaries? What if the resolutions of the sovereign people violate the principles of its own constitution? Contemporary democracies are evolving into increasingly complex conversations between legislative, judicial, and electoral bodies and outcomes. No doubt, the results of such conversations can be anti-democratic and against the express wishes of the majority; but they can also be more progressive than majoritarian opinions as well as more just in protecting minority rights.

In conclusion: while the ideal of the sovereign public collectively deliberating about the common good is a regulative ideal as well as a constitutive fiction of democracy, historical, social, and institutional developments show the need to qualify this ideal. The boundaries of the body politic are never set but always essentially contestable. The social complexity of contemporary societies mandates institutions of repre-sentation as well as self-organization at the level of a free civil society. The principle of democracy can be carried out in a modern civil society along many different axes, dealing with many different issues. Delibera-tive rationality requires procedures as well as institutions that guarantee equality, freedom, and participation rights to all those who are affected by the outcome of certain decisions. In a democracy, the seat of the sovereign people must remain empty, for majoritarian decisions can themselves be subject to scrutiny, contestation, and criticism by constitutional courts and other organs of judicial review. In a democracy, the sovereign people has the final but not the ultimate say. In fact, it is best to define complex democracies as self-regulating and self-criticizing institutions of delib-eration as well as decision making.

* * *

What about the public and its problems? We know now that the phantom will not go away, and that in fact it should not. As Hannah Arendt's work has poignantly reminded us, as a regulative ideal of the democratic form of self-government, the public is not only a sociological quantity but a norm and a principle in the name of which we can criticize the fairness of outcomes, the judiciousness of decisions, and the wisdom of deliberations.

To breathe new life into this phantom under contemporary conditions will require a transgression and a remapping of all the boundaries that Arendt drew between the political and the social, the administrative and the legal. Precisely because of the daunting complexity of most issues facing representatives and citizens alike in democratic polities, the democratic mandate requires new and more innovative means of translating complex legislative deliberations and decisions into publicly intelligible information. Furthermore, the challenges to democratic polities under conditions of social complexity require *innovative institutional designs*. There is indeed all around us an exhaustion of utopian energies (Habermas),[92] and our social imagination appears to be abandoning us at the point when we most need it. This exhaustion of utopian energies is accompanied by a dizzying sense of contingency about history, society, and culture. It seems that everything can be or could have been otherwise, yet our political cultures are increasingly too dull to generate innovative solutions. Revitalizing the public sphere is necessary under these conditions for polities to put forth their social imaginary, their utopian hopes for the future. Reflexive processes of self-innovation and examination must be encouraged across the broad spectrum of our institutions.

In today's global world, the public sphere has a crucial role in molding the elective identities of anonymous citizens in increasingly complex nation-states. The public sphere has always acted as the mirror in which a polity has seen its identity reflected, magnified, distorted, or clouded. The cultural construction of the public in diverse human societies at different points in history offers the most direct access to understanding the self-definition of a collectivity. To recognize its own diversity, and to come to grips with the implications this diversity may have for its own self-understanding, a democratic people needs to reenact its identity in the public sphere. As with both individuals and collectivities, threats of being different that are not diffused turn into resentment toward others who are not like oneself. The free public sphere in a democratic polity must allow equal access to all groups within civil society to re-present themselves in public. In entering the public, every new social, cultural, political group presents its point of view to others, or it re-presents itself to others, in the sense of refashioning itself as a presence in the public. This process of self-representation and articulation in public is still the only means through which the civic imagination can be cultivated. The process of articulating good reasons in public forces one to think from the standpoint of all others to whom one is trying to make one's point of view plausible and cogent, and to whom one is trying to tell one's own story. The ability of individuals and groups to take the standpoint of others into account, to reverse perspectives and see the world from their point of view, is a crucial virtue in a civic polity, certainly one that becomes most necessary and most fragile under conditions of cultural diversity and social opacity. The public sphere is like the pupil in the eye of the body politic; when its vision is murky, cloudy, or hindered, the sense of direction of the polity is also impaired.

Rethinking Privacy

We not only owe to Hannah Arendt's political philosophy the recovery of the public as a central category for all democratic-liberal politics; we also are indebted to her for the insight that the public and the private are interdependent.[93] These are terms of a binary opposition: the public is inconceivable without the private, and vice versa. Let me reiterate the multiple meanings that are associated with the term *private:* with the emergence of a commodity exchange economy and the development of modern state institutions, the term *private* refers to a wide range of institutional phenomena: the domestic/reproductive realm of the household; the economic order of production, exchange, distribution, and consumption in a free marketplace, and, finally, the sphere of civil, cultural, religious, scientific, literary, and artistic associations within civil society.[94]

What is distinctive in Hannah Arendt's approach to the concepts of the public and the private is not the institutional framework, the sociological weaknesses of which I have challenged at various points in this book, but rather her phenomenological account. Consider the following passage from *The Human Condition*:

> Although the distinction between private and public coincides with the opposition of necessity and freedom, of futility and permanence, and, finally, of shame and honor, it is by no means true that only the necessary, the futile, and the shameful have their proper place in the private realm. The most elementary meaning of the two realms indicates that there are things that need to be hidden and others that need to be displayed publicly if they are to exist at all. (p. 73)

Arendt here is proposing some conception of human balance and psychic integrity that could be maintained only if the private and the public realms stood in a certain relation to one another. In this context, by *privacy* Arendt does not mean the freedom of religion and conscience that historically has been understood as the fundamental privacy right in the liberal polity; nor does Arendt think that there is a privacy right to economic wealth.[95] By *privacy* in the above quote—"there are things that need to be hidden and others that need to be displayed publicly"—Arendt means primarily the necessity that some aspect of the "domestic-intimate" sphere be hidden from the glare of the public eye. What aspect then of this "domestic-intimate" sphere must remain hidden from the public eye and sheltered from political action? An answer to this question can be interpolated by considering the distinction in her thought between *privacy* and *intimacy*. And here a surprising meeting between contemporary feminist concerns and Arendt's political theory will become visible.

Hannah Arendt distinguished between *intimacy* and *privacy*. In the emergence of modernity in the West in the course of the sixteenth and seventeenth centuries, Arendt saw not only the transformation of the political-public into the social-public but also the transformation of the private into the "intimate." For her, the preoccupations with intimacy and with individual subjectivity were aspects of the same process. Isolating individuals and forcing them into the confines of anonymous public activities such as the commodity exchange market, the modern age also brought forth the cult of individuality, the preoccupation and concern with the uniqueness, authenticity, and psychic harmony of the self. For Arendt, the mark of the turn to individuality and to intimacy is the accompanying "worldlessness" of these human relations.

Arendt stresses that there is a sense of privacy distinct from intimacy and its form of worldlessness. She writes,

> The second outstanding non-privative characteristic of privacy is that the four walls of one's private property offer the only reliable hiding place from the common public world, not only from everything that goes on in it but also from its very publicity, from being seen and being heard. A life spent entirely in public, in the presence of others, becomes, as we would say, shallow. While it retains its visibility, it loses the quality of rising into sight from some darker ground which must remain hidden if it is not to lose its depth in a very real non-subjective sense.
>
> The only efficient way to guarantee the darkness of what needs to be hidden against the light of publicity is private property, a privately owned place to hide in. (*HC*, p. 71)

Certainly, Arendt's call in this passage for "a privately owned place to hide in" is not a call to own a condominium or a private house—as far as I know, she rented an apartment in New York City and never owned anything. A privately owned place means one that provides the self with a center, with a shelter, with a place in which to unfold capacities, dreams, and memories, to nurture the wounds of the ego, and to lend to it that depth of feeling that, as Arendt puts it, allows it to "[rise] into sight from some darker ground." This passage is an affirmation of "the home." Viewed against the background of massive homelessness in our societies, the perspicacity of Arendt's insight is clear: the home not only lends the self the depth without which it is nothing but a shadow in the streets, but the home also provides the space that protects, nurtures, and makes the individual fit to appear in the public realm. The homeless self is the individual ready to be ravaged by the forces of the social against which it must fight daily to protect itself.

With Arendt's concept of the "home"—not her terminology but mine—we reach the most significant sense of *privacy* in her theory, which contemporary feminist theory must cultivate. Let me distinguish, though, between a specific domestic structure, the monogamous nuclear male-headed family, and the "home." This is a distinction that Hannah Arendt herself did not make, and that is the central reason her affirmation of the private realm so often reads like an ahistorical justification of a specific gender division of labor that historically confined modern bourgeois women to the home. While feminists have shown that the patriarchal family was no "home" for most women, the Gay Liberation movement in the last two decades has also made public that there are many ways to be a family and to share a home.

The concept of the home invokes several moral and political goods as well as principles. They may be named intimacy, domesticity, and the space of individuality. What form of sexual relations best expresses intimacy can no longer be dictated in terms of categories of biologically grounded gender identity; homosexual as well as heterosexual human relations may succeed or fail in creating intimacy for the individuals involved. Domestic arrangements are those designed to sustain the human body and meet its daily needs; to raise, nurture, and educate children; and to provide the self with a space into which it can withdraw. These tasks can be carried out, and historically have been carried out, by many different forms of kinship and familylike arrangements other than the male-headed nuclear family.

Together, intimacy and domesticity contribute to the nourishment and unfolding of individuality. In this sense, the primary moral and cultural purpose of the household under conditions of modernity is the development and flourishing of autonomous individualities. One very important consequence of this reformulated concept of privacy is not only the redefinition of the family unit but also the encouragement of legislation protecting children and their care providers on the basis of the right to a home, understood as the moral and political entitlement of the child to the physical, material, and spiritual preconditions that would enhance the development of his or her personality.

Although this explication expands Hannah Arendt's categories considerably and takes them in directions that she herself could not have anticipated, they are compatible with her deep reflections on the meaning of the private sphere. After two decades of criticizing the private/public split, and the way in which this dichotomy has served to camouflage domestic violence, child molestation, and marital rape in the private realm, contemporary feminist theory is entering a new phase of thinking about these issues. The binarity of the public and the private spheres must be reconstructed, and not merely rejected. From abortion rights to debates about pornography, from the struggles of gay and lesbian couples to become foster parents and to be recognized as "domestic partnerships," a renewed affirmation of the value of the private sphere is afoot.[96] For, as Hannah Arendt has so well shown, without a robust private sphere, which fulfills our needs for intimacy, domesticity, and individuality, we would exist only in the glare of the light of the public that is all-consuming. The recovery of the public world is impossible and unlikely without a parallel reconstruction of the private sphere. In this task as well, Hannah Arendt's political thought is an indispensable guide. From her reflections on the paradoxes of the nation-state and the rights of man to her cultural sociology of the pariah and the parvenu, and to her firm faith in the capacity of ordinary citizens to reignite the embers of civic and democratic activism, Hannah Arendt's legacy continues to inspire.

Notes

1. Hannah Arendt, "Walter Benjamin," in Arendt, *Men in Dark Times* (New York: Harcourt Brace Jovanovich, 1968), pp. 200 ff.

2. Hannah Arendt, *Lectures on Kant's Political Philosophy,* ed., with an interpretive essay by, Ronald Beiner (Chicago: University of Chicago Press, 1982).

3. A version of the following section has appeared previously as S. Benhabib, "Judgment and the Moral Foundations of Politics in Hannah Arendt's Thought," *Political Theory* 16, no. 1 (1988): 29-51; also included in *Situating the Self: Gender, Community and Postmodernism in Contemporary Ethics* (New York: Harcourt Brace Jovanovich, 1992), pp. 121-148.

4. Hannah Arendt, *Thinking,* vol. 1, *The Life of the Mind* (New York: Harcourt Brace Jovanovich, 1977), p. 3.

5. Arendt, *Thinking,* p. 5.

6. Hannah Arendt, "Thinking and Moral Considerations: A Lecture," (1971, reprinted in *Social Research,* 50th Anniversary issue, Spring/Summer 1984), p. 8.

7. Arendt, *Thinking,* p. 216.

8. Ronald Beiner, "Hannah Arendt on Judging," in *Lectures on Kant's Political Philosophy,* pp. 117 ff.; R. J. Bernstein, "Judging—The Actor and the Spectator," in *Philosophical Profiles* (Philadelphia: University of Pennsylvania Press, 1986), pp. 221-238. See also Arendt's distinction between the standpoint of the actor and that of the spectator in *Lectures on Kant's Political Philosophy,* pp. 44 ff., 54 ff.

9. Christopher Lasch, introduction to *Salmagundi,* special Hannah Arendt issue, ed. Christopher Lasch, no. 60 (1983): xi. I have outlined a possible way of reconciling the Aristotelian and the Kantian perspectives in moral philosophy in my article "Judgment and the Moral Foundations of Politics," pp. 29-51.

10. Hannah Arendt, *Eichmann in Jerusalem: A Report on the Banality of Evil.* I am using the 1992 edition (New York: Penguin), which is based on the revised and enlarged 1965 edition. The original 1963 edition was published by Viking, New York. All references in the text are to the Penguin edition.

11. In the last pages of the *Origins of Totalitarianism,* Hannah Arendt had written of the Holocaust and in particular of the extermination camps as the appearance of "radical evil" on earth (p. 443). This term, which originates in Immanuel Kant's *Religion Within the Limits*

of Reason Alone (trans., with an introduction and notes by, Theodore M. Greene and Hoyt H. Hudson [New York: Harper & Row, 1960], p. 32), was subsequently dropped by Hannah Arendt. Writing the Eichmann book was a "cura posterior" (a subsequent cure) for her; see Elisabeth Young-Bruehl, *For Love of the World* (New Haven, Conn.: Yale University Press, 1982), pp. 367 ff. Exactly why this was so is harder to explain, for Hannah Arendt did not give up her claim that with the concentration and death camps "some radical evil, previously unknown to us" had occurred (*OT*, p. 443). What occurred defied all moral standards and confronted us with the realization that "something seems to be involved in modern politics that actually should never be involved in politics as we used to understand it." Arendt repeats at the end of *Eichmann in Jerusalem* "that every act that has once made its appearance and has been recorded in the history of mankind stays with mankind as a potentiality long after its actuality has become a thing of the past . . . that the unprecedented, once it has appeared, may become a precedent for the future, that all trials touching upon 'crimes against humanity' must be judged according to a standard that is today still an 'ideal' " (*Eichmann in Jerusalem*, p. 273).

12. See Elzbieta Ettinger, *Hannah Arendt-Martin Heidegger* (New Haven, Conn.: Yale University Press, 1995); and *Between Friends: The Correspondence of Hannah Arendt and Mary McCarthy*, ed., with an introduction by, Carol Brightman (New York: Harcourt Brace Jovanovich, 1995).

13. See the authoritative volume by Isaiah Trunk, *Judenrat: The Jewish Councils in Eastern Europe Under Nazi Occupation*, introduction by Jacob Robinson (New York: Macmillan, 1972); Raul Hilberg, *Perpetrators, Victims, Bystanders: The Jewish Catastrophe 1933-1945* (New York: Harper Collins, 1992).

14. In his letter to Hannah Arendt of December 13, 1963, Karl Jaspers provides the following interesting bit of information on this much-disputed phrase: "Alcopley told me that Heinrich [Bluecher—Hannah Arendt's husband] suggested the phrase 'the banality of evil' and is cursing himself for it now because you've had to take the heat for what he thought of. Perhaps the report isn't true, or my recollection of it is garbled. I think it's a wonderful inspiration and right on the mark as the book's subtitle. The point is that *this* evil, not evil per se, is banal." *Arendt-Jaspers Correspondence*, p. 542.

15. See Jacob Robinson, *And the Crooked Shall Be Made Straight: The Eichmann Trial, the Jewish Catastrophe, and Hannah Arendt's Narrative* (New York: Macmillan, 1965). Robinson makes clear in his preface that his task is to "correct" Hannah Arendt: "Miss Arendt does not convey reliable information. She has misread many of the documents and books referred to in her text and bibliography. She has not equipped herself with the necessary background for an understanding and analysis of the trial" (p. viii). See also the acrimonious exchanges between Arendt and Gershom Scholem, and Arendt and Walter Laqueur, collected in Hannah Arendt, *The Jew as Pariah: Jewish Identity and Politics in the Modern Age*, ed., with introduction by, Ron H. Feldman (New York: Grove, 1978), pp. 240 ff.

16. See Arendt's description of Eichmann's last words on the gallows, and her statement: " 'After a short while, gentlemen, *we shall all meet again*. Such is the fate of all men. Long live Germany, long live Argentina, long live Austria. *I shall not forget them.*' . . . It was as though in those last minutes he was summing up the lesson that his long course in human wickedness had taught us—the lesson of the fearsome, word-and-thought-defying *banality of evil*" (*Eichmann in Jerusalem*, p. 252, emphasis in the original).

17. See my review of their correspondence that appeared in the *Nation*, March 27, 1995, pp. 423-425.

18. *Between Friends*, ed. Brightman, p. 19.

19. Ibid., p. 22.

20. Ibid., p. 27.

21. Ibid., p. 296.

22. Hans Mommsen, "Hannah Arendt und der Prozess gegen Adolf Eichmann," in Hannah Arendt, *Eichmann in Jerusalem: Ein Bericht von der Banalität des Bösen*, translated from the English by Brigitte Ganzow (Munich: Piper Verlag, 1986), p. ii (my translation).

23. See her own comments on this issue in the "Note to the Reader" of the 1964 edition; reprinted in the 1992 Penguin edition used here.

24. Mommsen, "Hannah Arendt und der Prozess," p. xxii.

25. Ibid., p. xxii.

26. Hannah Arendt was accused of every possible posture, extending from Jewish self-hatred to anti-Zionism, from insensitivity to tastelessness and, of course, arrogance. The reaction of the American Jewish community has been documented by Alan D. Krinsky's senior thesis (Boston University, 1990), called "The Controversy" (on file with the author). I would like to thank Professor Hillel Levine of Boston University for making this thesis available to me. For documentation of the German controversy, see *Die Kontroverse: Hannah Arendt, Eichmann und die Juden*, ed. F. A. Krummacher (Munich: Nymphenburger Verlag, 1964). See also the references in note 15 above.

27. Mommsen, "Hannah Arendt und der Prozess," p. xix.

28. On the circumstances surrounding this question, see Young-Bruehl, *For Love of the World*, pp. 363 ff. The reference is missing in the revised edition; see Arendt, *Eichmann in Jerusalem*, p. 119.

29. Hannah Arendt, Letter to Karl Jaspers, December 23, 1960, in *Arendt-Jaspers Correspondence*, p. 417.

30. Hannah Arendt, Letter to Karl Jaspers, October 29, 1963, in *Arendt-Jaspers Correspondence*, p. 524.

31. Hannah Arendt, *Eichmann in Jerusalem*, p. 12.

32. Hannah Arendt herself suggests this question in the epilogue to *Eichmann in Jerusalem*, p. 267.

33. For a masterful analysis of the "rationality" that may have guided the behavior of the Jewish councils, in particular in those situations where there was a Jewish workforce employed in various German factories, see Dan Diner, "Historical Understanding and Counterrationality: The *Judenrat* as Epistemological Vantage," in *Probing the Limits of Representation: Nazism and the "Final Solution,"* ed. by Saul Friedlaender (Cambridge, Mass.: Harvard University Press, 1992), pp. 128-143.

34. *Arendt-Jaspers Correspondence*, pp. 414 ff.

35. *Between Friends*, ed. Brightman, p. 168.

36. See Michael R. Marrus's statement: "Up to the time of the Eichmann trial in Jerusalem, in 1961, there was relatively little discussion of the massacre of European Jewry. . . . Since then scholarship has proceeded apace. . . . Hannah Arendt's *Eichmann in Jerusalem*, originally an assessment of the trial for the *New Yorker*, prompted a debate in the historical literature that echoes to our own time." Michael R. Marrus, *The Holocaust in History*, the Tauber Institute for the Study of European Jewry Series (Toronto: Lester and Orpen Dennys, 1987), pp. 4-5.

37. The volume edited by Saul Friedlaender contains many interesting perspectives on these issues; see his introduction, as well as Yael S. Feldman's "Whose Story Is It, Anyway? Ideology and Psychology in the Representation of the Shoah in Israeli Literature," in *Probing the Limits of Representation*, ed. Friedlaender, pp. 223-240.

38. Gershom Scholem, " 'Eichmann in Jerusalem': An Exchange of Letters Between Gershom Scholem and Hannah Arendt," *Encounter* 22 (January 1964): 51-56; reprinted in Feldman, ed., *The Jew as Pariah,* pp. 240 ff; here p. 241.

39. See *Arendt-Jaspers Correspondence,* pp. 413 ff.

40. Arendt, epilogue, *Eichmann in Jerusalem,* p. 263.

41. Arendt, *Arendt-Jaspers Correspondence,* p. 414.

42. Arendt, epilogue, *Eichmann in Jerusalem,* p. 254.

43. Ibid., p. 254.

44. For a masterful analysis of the Nuremberg trials, see Judith N. Shklar, *Legalism: An Essay on Law, Morals and Politics* (Cambridge, Mass.: Harvard University Press, 1964).

45. Arendt, quoted in *Eichmann in Jerusalem,* p. 262.

46. Arendt, *Eichmann in Jerusalem,* p. 263.

47. Ibid., pp. 244-245.

48. Ibid., p. 269.

49. See Frank Michelman, "Parsing 'A Right to Have Rights.'" In *Constellations: An International Journal of Critical and Democratic Theory* 3, no. 2:200-209.

50. Arendt, *Eichmann in Jerusalem,* pp. 287-288.

51. Bernstein, "Judging—The Actor and the Spectator," pp. 232-233.

52. Immanuel Kant, *Critique of Judgment,* trans., with an analytical index by, J. C. Meredith (Oxford: Clarendon, 1964), p. 10. I have also consulted "Kritik der Urteilskraft," in *Kants Werke: Akademie-Textausgabe,* vol. 5 (Berlin: Walter d'Gruyter, 1968).

53. Immanuel Kant, "Critique of Practical Reason," in *Critique of Practical Reason and Other Writings in Moral Philosophy,* trans., with an introduction by, L. W. Beck (New York: Garland, 1976), p. 176.

54. Ibid., p. 176.

55. Ibid., p. 177.

56. There is a fundamental connection between the tradition's ignoring of the question of judgment in moral life and the neglect of the specificity of action as speech and action or communicative interaction. Once we see moral action as interaction, performed toward others and in the company of others, the role of judgment becomes particularly salient. I have explored these themes in Benhabib, "Judgment and the Moral Foundations of Politics," pp. 34-36.

57. There is an extensive literature on this topic. Some of the seminal contributions to this debate have been Charles Taylor, "Interpretation and the Sciences of Man," *Review of Metaphysics* 25 (1971): 3-51; R. J. Bernstein, *The Restructuring of Social and Political Theory* (Philadelphia: University of Pennsylvania Press, 1978); A. Giddens, *Studies in Social and Political Theory* (London: Hutchinson, 1977).

58. See Arendt, introduction to *The Life of the Mind,* vol. 1, *Thinking,* p. 5; Arendt, "Thinking and Moral Considerations: A Lecture," p. 8. We also know from the notes of her students who attended her course on Kant's *Critique of Judgment* at the University of Chicago in 1971 that "although Kant had withheld questions of right and wrong from the sphere of reflective (aesthetic) judgment . . . Arendt herself was convinced that in doing so he had made a major mistake." Michael Denneny, "The Privilege of Ourselves: Hannah Arendt on Judgment," in *Hannah Arendt: The Recovery of the Public World,* ed. Melvyn A. Hill (New York: St. Martin's, 1979), p. 266.

59. Immanuel Kant, "Critique of Judgment," p. 151; see Hannah Arendt's discussion of this passage in her *Lectures on Kant's Political Philosophy,* pp. 71 ff.

60. Hannah Arendt, "Crisis in Culture," in Arendt, *Between Past and Future: Six Exercises in Political Thought* (New York: Meridian, 1961), pp. 220-221.

61. Plato, *Gorgias*, in *The Collected Dialogues of Plato*, ed. Edith Hamilton and Huntington Cairns, Bollingen Series 71 (Princeton, N.J.: Princeton University Press, 1973), p. 265.

62. Walt Whitman, "Song of Myself," in *Leaves of Grass and Selected Prose*, ed., with an introduction by, John Kouwenhoven (New York: Modern Library, 1950), p. 74, stanza 51.

63. Arendt, *The Life of the Mind*, vol. 1, *Thinking*, p. 5.

64. See Arendt's essay, "Martin Heidegger at Eighty," reprinted in Michael Murray, ed., *Heidegger and Modern Philosophy* (New Haven, Conn.: Yale University Press, 1978), p. 295.

65. George Kateb, *Hannah Arendt: Politics, Conscience, Evil* (Totowa, N.J.: Rowman and Allanheld, 1984), p. 31.

66. See Martin Jay and Leon Botstein, "Hannah Arendt: Opposing Views," *Partisan Review* 45, no. 3 (1978), p. 351; reprinted in Martin Jay, *Permanent Exiles* (New York: Columbia University Press, 1986); Margaret Canovan, *Hannah Arendt: A Reinterpretation of Her Political Thought* (Cambridge: Cambridge University Press, 1992), p. 190. Canovan is referring to L. P. and S. K. Hinchman, "Existentialism Politicized: Arendt's Debt to Jaspers," *Review of Politics* 53, no. 3 (1991), pp. 447-449. There is an excellent reply to Jay's position in Maurizio Passerin d'Entrèves's *The Political Philosophy of Hannah Arendt* (London: Routledge, 1994), pp. 85-90.

67. Canovan, *A Reinterpretation*, p. 191.

68. Ibid., p. 191, fn. 137; also see my *Situating the Self*, pp. 89-148.

69. Hannah Arendt, "What Is Freedom?" in *Between Past and Future*, pp. 143-173.

70. Dana Villa, *Arendt and Heidegger: The Fate of the Political* (Princeton, N.J.: Princeton University Press, 1996), pp. 52-53.

71. Ibid., p. 55.

72. Canovan, *A Reinterpretation*, pp. 201 ff; d'Entrèves, *The Political Philosophy of Hannah Arendt*, pp. 139 ff.

73. Jürgen Habermas, *Strukturwandel der Öffentlichkeit* (Darmstadt: Hermann Luchterhand, 1962), translated into English by Thomas Burger, with the assistance of Frederick Lawrence, as *The Structural Transformation of the Public Sphere: An Inquiry Into a Category of Bourgeois Society* (Cambridge: MIT Press, 1991).

74. See Habermas, *The Structural Transformation*, pp. 4 ff.

75. Habermas acknowledged this debt in "On the German-Jewish Heritage," *Telos* (Summer 1980): 182. See also Margaret Canovan, "A Case of Distorted Communication: A Note on Habermas and Arendt," *Political Theory* 11, no. 1 (1983): 105-116.

76. See Habermas, *The Structural Transformation*, p. 4; see also Herbert Schnädelbach, "What Is Neo-Aristotelianism?" in *Praxis International* 7, nos. 3-4 (1987-1988): 225-238, and the reply by Maurizio Passerin d'Entrèves, "Aristotle or Burke? Some Comments on H. Schnädelbach's 'What Is Neo-Aristotelianism?' " in the same issue, pp. 238-246.

77. See Hans-Georg Gadamer, "What Is Practice? The Conditions of Social Reason," and "Hermeneutics as Practical Philosophy," and "Hermeneutics as a Theoretical and Practical Task," all in *Reason in the Age of Science*, trans. Frederick G. Lawrence (Cambridge: MIT Press, 1983), and Hans-Georg Gadamer, *Philosophical Hermeneutics*, trans. and ed. David E. Linge (Berkeley: University of California Press, 1976).

78. Albrecht Wellmer has argued that the category of judgment is significant not only in the realm of politics but in theoretical philosophy as well; see Albrecht Wellmer, "Hannah Arendt on Judgment: The Unwritten Doctrine of Reason," in *Hannah Arendt: Twenty Years Later*, ed. Larry May and Jerome Kohn (Cambridge: MIT Press, 1996).

79. Habermas, *The Structural Transformation*, pp. 28 ff.

80. Ibid., pp. 36 ff.

81. See Habermas's statement: "Public debate was supposed to transform *voluntas into a ratio* that in the public competition of private arguments came into being as the consensus about what was necessary in the interest of all" in *The Structural Transformation*, p. 83.

82. Arendt, "Crisis in Culture," in *Between Past and Future*, pp. 220-221.

83. See his statement, "The public sphere of civil society stood or fell with the principle of universal access. A public sphere from which specific groups would be *eo ipso* excluded was less than merely incomplete; it was not a public sphere at all." Habermas, *The Structural Transformation*, p. 85.

84. Immanuel Kant, "An Answer to the Question: 'What Is Enlightenment?' " in *Kant: Political Writings*, ed., and introduction and notes by, Hans Reiss; trans. H. B. Nisbet (Cambridge: Cambridge University Press, 1994), pp. 54-61.

85. Hannah Arendt, "Civil Disobedience," in *Crises of the Republic* (New York: Harcourt Brace Jovanovich, 1972), pp. 49-103.

86. Walter Lippmann, *The Phantom Public*, with a new introduction by W. M. McClay (New Brunswick, N.J.: Transaction, 1993 [1927]).

87. Ibid, pp. 4 ff.

88. John Dewey, *The Public and Its Problems* (Chicago: Swallow, 1954 [1927]), p. 117.

89. Mills introduces into his reflections on the distinction between *public* and *mass* elements of his social control theory. It is doubtful that in the days of radio talk shows, cable TV, ham radio stations, and other innumerable forms of access to means of communication by diverse groups, Mills's social control theory of the masses would hold water. In the contemporary situation, the carriers of this anonymous public conversation have become so diffuse, inchoate, and varied that even the contrast between the "public" and "mass" is too flat to capture the changing nature of the public in the age of the information revolution. See C. Wright Mills, *The Power Elite* (New York: Oxford University Press, 1956).

90. Carl Schmitt, *The Crisis of Parliamentary Democracy*, trans. Ellen Kennedy (Cambridge: MIT Press, 1985).

91. See Jean-Jacques Rousseau, *The Social Contract*, trans., with an introduction by, Maurice Cranston (Middlesex, England: Penguin, 1968 [1762]), Bk. II, chap. 3.

92. J. Habermas, "The New Obscurity," in *The New Conservatism: Cultural Criticism and the Historian's Debate*, ed. and trans. by S. W. Nicholsen (Cambridge: MIT Press, 1988), pp. 48-70.

93. Portions of this concluding discussion have appeared in S. Benhabib, "Feminist Theory and Hannah Arendt's Concept of Public Space," in *History of the Human Sciences* 6, no. 2 (1993): 97-114. Used with permission.

94. I discussed some of the political puzzles surrounding the status of these "private" associations in the liberal-democratic state when considering Hannah Arendt's "Reflections on Little Rock," above.

95. For Arendt, property and wealth are distinct. Although property, in the sense of a place of my own and that part of the world that sustains my daily well-being, is private, wealth is public, and its appropriation always subject to political action and public policy (Arendt, *HC*, pp. 109 ff.)

96. Some of the reasons for rethinking privacy rights within feminist theory debates have been well outlined by two recent articles: see Jean Cohen, "Redescribing Privacy: Identity, Difference, and the Abortion Controversy," *Columbia Journal of Gender and Law* 3, no. 1 (1992): 43-117; and Nicola Lacey, "Theory Into Practice? Pornography and the Public/ Private Dichotomy," *Journal of Law and Society* 20, no. 1 (1993): 9313.

Appendix:
The Personal is not the Political*

Hannah Arendt's life is a parable of the twentieth century. Born in 1906 in Hannover to an assimilated Jewish family, she was forced to leave Germany in 1933, after being arrested for researching documentation on the exclusion of Jews from major professional organizations. Crossing the border to Czechoslovakia, and then to Paris, she proceeded to work with Jewish organizations helping to settle children in Palestine. In 1940 she came to the United States with her second husband, Heinrich Bluecher, and both became American citizens. She thus experienced persecution, statelessness, exile, a brief internment in a detention camp, immigration, success, and public recognition.

The posthumous publication of her extensive correspondences with Karl Jaspers, her mentor and teacher; with Henrich Bluecher, her husband; with Kurt Blumenfeld, her friend the Zionist leader; and with Mary McCarthy,

---

*This Appendix is a revised and abridged version of a review essay that originally appeared by Seyla Benhabib as "The Personal is not the Political," *Boston Review* (October–November 1999), pp. 45-48.

her "best girlfriend," add to the current fascination with Arendt's life and work. But the wealth of biographical detail also presents scholars with a dilemma. How should we understand the relationship between the personal and political, intimate and public, aspects of Arendt's own life? Three possibilities suggest themselves. One is to use personal, in particular psychoanalytic, categories as a prism for understanding Arendt's political thought. A second would be to see Arendt's personal life as an expression of the categories of her political thought. The third is to treat the public and private sides of her life separately, as distinct spheres which are to be understood and assessed on their own terms. Here we would follow Arendt herself, who embraced a crisp distinction between public and private, and expressed concern about our contemporary "eagerness to see recorded, displayed and discussed in public what were once strictly private affairs and nobody's business."

Difficult though it may be to find the right angle of approach, the task has become all the more pressing. In 1999, the Frankfurt publisher Klostermann printed the latest book of Arendt correspondence—her letters to and from the German philosopher Martin Heidegger. The two met in 1924 when Arendt, then eighteen years old, was a student of Heidegger's seminars at the University of Marburg. The brief but passionate love affair that ensued will always remain touched by the ironies, perplexities, and horrors of this century. For in 1933, the same year Arendt fled Germany and became a stateless Jewish refugee in Paris, professors sympathetic to the Nazis elected Heidegger Rector of Freiburg University. If we are going to think through the personal and the political, the intimate and the public, in all their fraught interconnections, we might start with this relationship.

II

Ursula Ludz, the German editor of the Arendt–Heidegger correspondence, titles its earliest phase "Der Blick," which in English could be rendered either as "the sighting" or "the gaze." The first letter, dated February 10, 1925, shortly after Arendt's arrival in Marburg, is from Heidegger. It addresses Arendt as "Liebe Fräulein Arendt," and announces that "he must come to her tonight and speak to her heart." Subsequent letters are addressed to "Liebe Hannah," or simply to "Hannah!" The growing intensity of emotional and erotic involvement is evident, and Heidegger, in the stilted and stylized prose so familiar to us from his other writings, confesses: "*Das Daemonische hat mich getroffen. Nie noch ist mir so etwas geschehen.*" ("I have been touched by the demonic. Nothing like this has ever happened to me before.") After a year and a half of a clandestine love affair with the married professor seventeen years her elder, Arendt flees to Heidelberg to study with Karl Jaspers. In 1929, she writes to Heidegger to let him know that she is engaged to marry Guenter [Stern] Anders, a fellow Heidegger student.

The second chapter begins in the winter of 1950, when Arendt first returns to Europe after the war. By then she is working for the Committee for Jewish Reconstruction, traveling through various European cities collecting the remains of Jewish cultural artifacts. She resumes contact with Heidegger. On February 7, he invites her to his home, to meet with him and his wife Elfride. What follows is an astonishing confirmation of a continuing bond—I am not sure whether to call it "love," since this word can say so much and so little at once. Arendt writes to Heidegger a few days after their first meeting: "This evening and this morning are a confirmation [*Bestaetigung*] of a whole life time. As the waiter called out your name (I did not expect you actually, since I had not received your letter), it was as if time stood still."

It may have seemed so to the two of them, but in the meantime Heidegger had confessed his affair to his wife. Frau Elfride's reaction, though dignified and controlled, is understandably far from embracing. It is clear from other sources that Arendt could not stand her. Arendt thought Frau Elfride was openly anti-Semitic and behind much of Heidegger's political misfortune. This second phase, in which Arendt visits Heidegger whenever she is in Europe, even once attending his seminar, is interrupted when Frau Elfride throws a fit after one of Arendt's visits. On June 5, 1952, Heidegger asks her not to write any more and not to visit him. There is still occasional contact, but after 1959 the letters become sparser, and there is no correspondence at all from 1960 to 1966.

The third phase, poetically titled "The Fall" by Ludz, begins with Heidegger wishing Arendt a "Happy 60th Birthday" in 1966. The ensuing exchange of letters, which ends with Arendt's death in 1975, reveals a growing tenderness and concern among Heidegger, his wife, Arendt, and

Heinrich Bluecher, who meets the Heideggers during one of his visits to Germany. With the *Sturm* and *Drang* of youth finally behind them, Arendt and Heidegger for the first time engage each other philosophically. Unfortunately, the fleeting references to Kant, language, Merleau-Ponty, Nietzsche, and metaphysics merely whet the reader's appetite. Their exchange is not a philosophical correspondence; it is a deeply personal one, revealing an attachment that is astonishing, touching, and bewildering.

The last document in the collection is a letter from Heidegger to Hans Jonas, dated December 27, 1975. Jonas, who met Arendt at Heidegger's seminars at Marburg in 1924–1925, was her lifelong friend and colleague at the New School for Social Research. He had written to Heidegger, informing him of Arendt's death. Heidegger's response bears the title "Bound to the Circle of Friends in Deep Sorrow." It is brief, elegant, and to the point. Recalling that Arendt had visited him and Elfride in August that year, and that they only knew that she had been preparing to give her lectures in Scotland later that fall, Heidegger writes: "A higher fate has ruled and contrary to human designs. For us remain only the sorrow and the recollection [*das Andenken*]."

Though the newly published correspondence fills in many previous blanks in our understanding, the basic outlines of the relationship between Arendt and Heidegger have been known since the 1982 publication of Elisabeth Young-Bruehl's biography, *Hannah Arendt: For Love of the World*. Since then, commentators have cited it as evidence of Arendt's foolish female side (Elzbieta Ettinger)[1] or her deeply troubled relation to her Judaism (Richard Wolin).[2] To such critics, Arendt herself appears to have issued a warning. She concludes her famous essay, "Martin Heidegger is Eighty," originally delivered as a birthday laudatorio to Heidegger, with the lines: "May those who come after us, when they are commemorating our century and its individuals in the attempt to remain true to them, not forget the sand storms which have turned our lives into deserts and which have dispersed each of us [like specks of sand] and each in their own way, here and there; they should remember nonetheless that in this century this man and his work have been possible." Arendt's prayer has not been answered. Posterity has not looked upon Heidegger's involvement with the Nazis in the spirit of forgiving compassion and meditative recollection which she enjoins in these lines. To the contrary, Arendt's own loyalty to Heidegger has cast aspersions upon her own controversial, but nonetheless illustrious, public career. In the United States in particular, the disclosure of the Arendt–Heidegger relationship caused consternation. The editors of the *New Republic* even called it a "scandal."

III

In 1995, Ettinger published *Hannah Arendt: Martin Heidegger.* Ettinger, who used previously inaccessible excerpts from Arendt's papers, created a great deal of pre-publicity for her work by giving an interview on the subject to the *Frankfurter Allgemeine Zeitung.*[3] Later, in his meticulous *Martin Heidegger: The Master-Thinker from Germany,*[4] Ruediger Safranski relied on material from this interview and other excerpts from the letters. Ettinger proceeded to sue Safranski and his publisher, Hanser Verlag. After this incident, Lotte Koehler, the director of the Arendt Literary Trust, closed access to this material to other scholars. Under the weight of circumstances generated by these events, Heidegger's son, Hermann, agreed to the publication of his father's papers. So we owe the publication of this correspondence to a combination of voyeuristic curiosity, intellectual opportunism, and cultural scandal. Of the 168 documents in this volume, only a quarter are Arendt's. We do not know what happened to the rest of her letters. Did Heidegger destroy them in his efforts to conceal the affair? Did Arendt get rid of her own correspondence? Whatever the circumstances, Heidegger's voice and presence dominate the volume.

As one of the scholars who was denied access to these letters in 1995 and 1996, when I was completing my book, *The Reluctant Modernism of Hannah Arendt,* I approached this correspondence with one question in mind: What did Arendt know about Heidegger's involvement with the Nazis, and when? The answer might explain a series of related issues. Why did she seek him out after the war? How could she justify to herself, as a persecuted Jewish émigré and public intellectual who reflected deeply and brilliantly about Jews, Germans, and the Holocaust, her continuing friendship, affection, and loyalty to this man? Was Arendt simply "a woman in love"—as if love should blind us to ethical principle and public responsibility?

The correspondence does not shed much light on the first question, except to indicate that Arendt had been hearing rumors about Heidegger's anti-Semitism as early as 1932. In answer to a letter inquiring about these rumors, an angry Heidegger writes back an *apologia sua*, listing all the doctoral students and undergraduates of his who are Jewish. He enumerates his personal friendships with Edmund Husserl and Ernst Cassirer, among others, concluding: "This really can hardly affect my relationship to you." Of course, this answer does not preclude that Heidegger could have personal friendships with members of a hated group but continue to disdain them collectively.

This exchange remains one of the few instances in which Heidegger shows a temper and some anger. Otherwise, he is an unmoved colossus. As Germany collapses around him, he retains his doggedly steadfast sense of abstraction and dedication to his work. Except, of course, for that brief period, in the spring of 1933, one month after being elected rector of the university, when he joined the Nazi Party. Arendt did not know, neither immediately after the war nor in the 1950s, the full extent of Heidegger's activities in this period, as they have since been meticulously reconstructed by historian Hugo Ott.

Heidegger wrote in "Facts and Thoughts," a text prepared for the Denazification Committee:

> In April 1933, I was elected rector by unanimous vote of the University's plenary council. On the morning of the election I was still not sure about it and wanted to withdraw my candidacy. I had no connections with the relevant government or Party officials; I was not a Party member myself, nor had I ever been politically active in any way.

Ott shows, however, that in the first few days of April 1933 the "new Nazi secretary for higher education at the ministry of Home Affairs in Karlsruhe, Eugen Fehrle, came to Freiburg on a fact-finding visit," talked with officials in the university, and met with a small group of Nazi professors. According to the report prepared by one of the professors present in these discussions, "concerning the alliance of National Socialist university teachers, we have ascertained that Professor Heidegger has already entered into negotiations with the Prussian Ministry of Education. He enjoys our full confidence, and we would therefore ask you to regard him for the present as our spokesman here at the University of Freiburg."[5] Arendt did not know all this, and continued to insist on her own interpretation that Heidegger was an "unpolitical" person who lacked worldly wisdom and judgment. Heidegger, in fact, was a conniving opportunist; only occasionally did Arendt see this about him. More often than not, she chose to neglect what her close friend and mentor, Karl Jaspers, would occasionally reveal to her about the nature and extent of Heidegger's political involvement.

One rumor about Heidegger's short-lived tenure as rector deeply disturbed Arendt: he supposedly forbade his old teacher, Edmund Husserl, to enter the university and use its facilities because he was a Jew. Arendt mentions this in a footnote to her essay, "What is Existenz Philosophy?," which she published in *Partisan Review* in 1946. Jaspers corrected Arendt after receiving a copy of the article. "The facts on the note on Heidegger are not exactly correct," Jaspers wrote. "In regard to Husserl, I assume that you're referring to the letter that every rector had to write to those excluded by the government. What you report is of course in substance true. However the description of the actual process strikes me as not quite exact." Jaspers, as it turns out, also had it partially wrong. As rector and department head, Heidegger did not issue a ban against Edmund Husserl's use of the university or department library, perhaps because a Nazi law made his doing so superfluous.[6] But Heidegger did officially join the Nazi Party in 1933 and according to eyewitness accounts continued to wear the party badge on his lapel as late as 1938.

In the early 1960s, psychiatrist Leslie H. Farber, who was interested in Heidegger's influence upon postwar Swiss psychiatry, wrote a letter to Arendt inquiring about Heidegger's responsibility in Husserl's removal from the university. Arendt answered, confirming information that Dr. Farber had obtained from other sources—namely, that there was no basis to the Husserl story. Arendt's letter, which is contained in her papers in the Library of Congress in Washington, D.C., and has not been published, continues:

> As to the initial lecture [the so-called "Rektoratsrede," the inaugural lecture Heidegger had to give upon assuming the position] I must confess I have not read it since that time and am not overeager to read it now. I remember, however, quite clearly, that the speech, though in spots unpleasantly nationalistic, was by no means an expression of Nazism. I doubt that Heidegger at that time had any clear notion of what Nazism was all about. But he learned comparatively quickly, and after about 8 to 10 months, his whole "political

past" was over. . . . Do these things after nearly 30 years really need to be apologized for? And do we, living in the Republic of Letters, really have to ask questions such as: Were you ever a member of this or that party? Which, properly or improperly are included in the questionnaires of the police?

To be sure, one can understand Arendt's reluctance to go into an exegesis of the "Rektoratsrede" after thirty years. The speech, which addresses German youth in the most authoritarian tone and orders them to undertake a commitment to theoretical and scientific work in the spirit of patriotic duty, is full of contorted formulations of "world historical duty" to Germany's fate. But Arendt's elegant dismissal of Dr. Farber's question about Heidegger's political activities, with the assertion that the mores of a "Republic of Letters" should be distinguished from intellectual McCarthyism, is disingenuous. Thinking has consequences; intellectuals have responsibilities; words can be actions. Arendt could not deny this. The truth of the matter is that she was never consistent on this score. In her long struggles with the question of the political consequences of Heidegger's philosophy, she followed two tracks of interpretation and eventually settled for the second.

In "What is Existenz Philosophy?" Arendt argued that Heidegger's radically individualist vision of the self as *Dasein* (literally "being-there"), easily lent itself to an equally facile collectivism in which the self would disappear. Such a collectivity could promise individuals some more authentic form of being-with-others in the world than the banalities of bourgeois, everyday existence. Heidegger's sympathy for the Nazis could thus be seen, she maintained, as the flip side of his contempt for the liberal-bourgeois, individualist world of political institutions and dealings.

By the time she wrote Heidegger's birthday lauditorio, however, Arendt had shifted her perspective. In this piece, her early and biting critique of the irresponsible political consequences of Heidegger's ontology disappears. This time she honors Heidegger by likening his involvement with the Nazis to Plato's involvement with tyrants of Sicily. Philosophers, she argues, lack political judgment and worldly wisdom. It is a "deformation professionelle" which leads to their political errors! This latter interpretation allowed Arendt to codify her reflections on the Heidegger mystery through a series of dualisms she developed in her own philosophy: thinking versus acting, philosophy versus politics, withdrawal from the world versus engagement with it. These categories, she maintained, always stood in tension with one another and could hardly be reconciled. Thus, one could be the greatest philosopher of the century and not be more advanced in one's political judgment than the proverbial fellow on the street. In fact, Arendt at times suggested that the fellow on the street may possess more healthy common sense on political matters than those great philosophers, who could only make sense of the world by departing from it.

The dualisms of philosophy and politics, great thought and good judgment, permitted Arendt to make sense of Heidegger and his doings and to retain her conviction that she alone had, in some ways, understood this man and his passion. Arendt built a myth around "Heidegger, the unworldly genius." Even her correspondence with her husband, Heinrich Bluecher, contains passages expressing her concern, in the wake of several trips, that Heidegger is not working properly, and that he is not writing the way he can. Bluecher goes along with this myth of "Heidegger, the genius of the century."

IV

In one episode of their correspondence, Arendt's readiness to indulge Heidegger's cultivated sense of his own political naïveté takes a toll on her forthrightness. In an astonishing passage in a letter of April 12, 1950, Heidegger, a lifelong anti-communist, rejects attitudes of pessimism and despair in response to the beginning of the Cold War, and enjoins Arendt to comprehend "being" without reducing it to mere historical occurrence. The "fate [*Schicksal*] of Jews and Germans has its own truth that cannot be reached by our historical reckoning," he writes. "When evil has happened and happens, then Being ascends from this point on for human thought and action into mystery; for the fact that something is does not mean that it is good and just." He ends: "I am neither experienced nor talented in the domain of the political."

What is Heidegger saying here? What mystery of Being does the fate of the Jews and the Germans reveal? Isn't this passage an abdication of individual responsibility in the face of history? Isn't the appeal to higher forces simply a fancy excuse? What gave Arendt the patience to listen to such second-rate mystifications of political processes which she, as a political theorist, fought so hard to make accessible to human intelligence—so that, in Tocqueville's words, which she quoted in her preface to *The Origins of Totalitarianism,* "the mind of man may not aimlessly wander" for lack of comprehension? At the time, Arendt was struggling with the question of "radical evil" in *The Origins of Totalitarianism.* She used this category to describe how human beings could act to render, through genocide and massacre, other human beings "superfluous" on this earth by denying them the right to be. Why did she not engage Heidegger on this point? In fact, when she finally does send him a copy of *The Origins of Totalitarianism,* Heidegger, in a sublime put-down, tells her that he cannot read English but that perhaps his wife, Elfride, could take a look!

Finally, in 1961, Arendt reaches a moment of truth. In a letter to Jaspers, she writes: "I know that he finds it intolerable that I appear in public, that I write books, etc. All my life, I've pulled the wool over his eyes, so to speak, acted as if none of that existed and as if I could not count to three and sometimes even to four. Then I suddenly felt this deception was becoming just too boring, and so I got a rap on the nose." A year before Arendt had sent Heidegger a copy of *The Human Condition,* translated into German, with the following note: "Dear Martin, I asked the publisher to send you one of my books. I want to say something about this. You will see that there is no dedication in the book. If things had ever worked out between us—I mean 'between,' neither just me nor you—I would have then asked you if I could dedicate the book to you. It has its origins in those first days in Freiburg and is indebted to you in all respects. As things are now, this seemed impossible; but somehow I wanted to inform you of the bare facts." There is no response from Heidegger. The next letter in the correspondence is dated April 13, 1965. Heidegger, as was so often the case with him, is simply silent. And Arendt? How do we explain her contradictions?

Clearly, this was a difficult relationship, full of half-uttered feelings and unsettled accounts, a relationship in which neither party could relax with the other. But it is also a very partial window on Arendt's life. We can only begin to understand the complexities of Arendt's life and personality when we put together all the many voices that are revealed in her correspondences with Bluecher, Jaspers, McCarthy, Blumenfeld, and others. The affectionate bantering, the open expression of sexual passion and warmth, and the sheer joy of togetherness that her correspondence with her husband reveals stand in sharp contrast to the controlled, stilted, and anxious voice that dominates the Heidegger correspondence.

Throughout the 1950s, as she is traveling through Europe, Arendt writes to Bluecher. If his letters arrive more than a week late, she feels lost. "I cannot wander around in the world, if you do not write," she writes in 1950. He answers:

> Certainly I am the man who is not capable *to make a living* [in English in the original]. Be calm, nothing can come between us, neither the spoken nor the written word. I love you and am very close to you. I have experienced homelessness, and this distinguishes me from Jaspers, and I could always say 'Wherever I am, there I am not at home.' But nonetheless right here in the middle of this world, and not in some superwordly Zion, I have managed to build a home [*ein Zuhause*] through you and my friends, so that I can also say: Where one or more of you are with me there is my homeland [*Heimat*], and where you are with me, there is my home.

It was Bluecher, the working-class kid from Berlin, the former member of the Spartacist League who broke with his comrades when they turned Stalinist, the autodidact who taught art history at Bard College, who mesmerized the intelligentsia of Greenwich Village of the 1940s and 1950s through his lectures on modern art though he could not also surmount his writer's block to publish—it was he, not Heidegger, who provided Arendt with a "home," and without whom she felt "like a lost wheel," spinning around the world. Arendt and Bluecher also shared a passion for politics. Not only did she learn a great deal from him about Soviet-style Marxism and totalitarian communism, but he, more than anyone else, understood her involvement in Jewish politics and her left-Zionist sympathies.

The beginning of their love affair in 1936 coincides with Arendt's activities on behalf of the World Zionist Congress and her clandestine work to help Jewish children escape from Europe into Palestine. Bluecher follows these efforts with approval; he is in Paris organizing among various left groups, and through his exposure to the milieu of many Zionist Socialists—in particular the Jewish Bundists, who wanted to build a Jewish state within the post-revolutionary Soviet Union—he has knowledge, sympathy, and affection for Jewish politics. His Berliner dialect, which he often puts on in his letters to cheer Arendt up, is full of Yiddish expressions. With

Bluecher, Arendt was at home, for she could combine the passion for politics, her life as a public intellectual, her commitment to Jewish causes, and her femininity. With Heidegger this mixture was not possible; at the most she remained the adoring and intelligent, attractive but quiescent female, pretending to count, as she put it, "to three and sometimes even to four" only in his arithmetic—until that time when she dared to send Heidegger a copy of one of her books. Heidegger remained for her a messenger from another realm—the realm of metaphysics and philosophy, and the symbiosis of Greek and German thought.

V

As the details of Hannah Arendt's life and friendships become increasingly public through the posthumous publication of her correspondence, as well as the numerous recent studies of her work and person, a question presses itself upon us: How should we integrate all this historical–contextual detail into our understanding of Arendt as a political philosopher? Is there a mode of analysis that can successfully synthesize life and thought, and the work and the person, without falling into voyeurism on the one hand and mere historical recounting of facts on the other?

Hannah Arendt did not leave us a "doctrine" of politics or the state, or a "theory of justice." Her work demonstrates how one can "think" about politics while resisting the temptation to system building. She is one of the few witnesses of this century whose insights still throw light on the perplexities of our times. We read her today precisely because of the problematic distinctions and juxtapositions she creates, and not despite them; we read her because she helps us think politically, not because she answers our political questions. Above all, Arendt teaches us that without a measure of personal intimacy, nurturing, and privacy, "shielded from the public eye," there can be no vibrant, fulfilling public life. And that without distinguishing economic questions about the just distribution of scarce resources from political questions about how we, as a collectivity, will form the institutions that will govern us, we cannot be free citizens.

"The personal is not the political": That is the message of Arendt's life and work. Politics is the space we create in common by virtue of what we can share with each other in the public sphere. The personal becomes the political when one's identity as a Jew, as a woman, as a refugee, etc.—an identity one shares with others—is attacked by the larger society. But to translate an identity under attack into a political project, one needs to transcend the vicissitudes of individual life and find what is common and what can be shared by all in the public sphere. The term "interest," as Arendt points out, originally had nothing to do with the highly individualist meaning we attribute to it today. *Inter-est* means, literally, what is between us, what binds us together and draws us apart. Arendt maintained that good politics was about the public interest and about the commitment to create a vibrant public life. Good politics should not invade the fragile domain of human attachments and friendships, nor should it force individuals to make public the shadowy and obscure recesses of the human heart. Arendt's poignant loyalty to Martin Heidegger, but also her deep attachments to her many friends, are a testimony to her own practice of this subtle "art of separation."

Notes

1. See Elzbieta Ettinger, *Hannah Arendt-Martin Heidegger* (New Haven, Conn.: Yale University Press, 1995).

2. See Richard Wolin, "An Affair to Remember: Hannah and the Magician," *New Republic* (October 9, 1995), pp. 27-37.

3. *Frankfurter Allgemeine Zeitung*, February 6, 1993.

4. Ruediger Safranski, "Ein Meister aus Deutschland: Heidegger und Seine Zeit." Munich: Carl Hanser Verlag, 1994.

5. Hugo Ott, *Martin Heidegger: A Political Life*, trans. Allan Blunden (New York: Basic Books, 1993), pp. 143-44.

6. On April 6, 1933, the provincial Nazi governor, or *Reichskommissar*, Roberg Wagner issued a decree suspending from office all civil-servants of "non-Aryan" origin. As a professor emeritus of Freiburg University, which stood under the jurisdiction of the government of Baden, Husserl was formally notified of his "enforced leave of absence." On April 28, 1933, this provincial decree was rescinded and superseded by the national Reich law on making the German civil service *judenfrei*. Heidegger knew of this new decree and did not need to take further personal action against Husserl.

Bibliography

Works by Hannah Arendt

Arendt, Hannah. 1929. *Der Liebesbegriff bei Augustin: Versuch einer philosophischen Interpretation*. Berlin: Julius Springer Verlag. Translated into English by E. B. Ashton, "Love and St. Augustine: An Essay in Philosophical Interpretation," Hannah Arendt Papers, Library of Congress, containers 66 and 67. Translation as *Love and Saint Augustine*, with an interpretive essay by, Joanna V. Scott and Judith C. Stark. Chicago: University of Chicago Press, 1996. (All references in the text are to the E. B. Ashton translation.)

———. 1941. "Die jüdische Armee—der Beginn einer jüdischen Politik." *Aufbau*, November 14, 1-2.

———. 1942. "Die 'sogenannte Jüdische Armee.' " *Aufbau*, May 2, 20.

———. 1944. "Von der Armee zur Brigade." *Aufbau*, October 6, 15-16.

———. 1946. "What Is Existenz Philosophy?" *Partisan Review* 18, no. 1: 35-46. In German, "Was ist Existenz-Philosophie?" In *Hannah Arendt: Sechs Essays*. Heidelberg: Schneider. Reprinted as "What Is Existential Philosophy?" In *Arendt: Essays in Understanding: 1930-1954*. Ed. Jerome Kohn, pp. 163-187. New York: Harcourt Brace & Company, 1994.

———. 1952. "The History of the Great Crime." Review of Leon Poliakov, *Breviary of Hate: The Third Reich and the Jews*. *Commentary*, March 13, pp. 300-304.

235

——. 1953. A reply. Exchange with Eric Vögelin about his review of *The Origins of Totalitarianism*. *Review of Politics* 15 (January).

——. 1953. "Karl Marx and the Western Political Tradition." Hannah Arendt Papers, Library of Congress, originally in container 64, now in container 71.

——. 1959. "Reflections on Little Rock." *Dissent* 6, no. 1: 45-56. With criticisms by David Spitz and Melvin Tumin.

——. 1959. Reply to critics. *Dissent* 6, no. 2: 179-181.

——. 1961. *Between Past and Future: Six Exercises in Political Thought*. New York: Meridian.

——. 1963. *On Revolution*. New York: Viking.

——. 1968. *Men in Dark Times*. New York: Harcourt, Brace.

——. 1969. *On Violence*. New York: Harcourt, Brace.

——. 1972 [1969]. *Crises of the Republic*. New York: Harcourt Brace Jovanovich.

——. 1973 [1958]. *The Human Condition*. 8th ed. Chicago: University of Chicago Press. (All page references in the text are to this edition.)

——. 1974 [1957]. *Rahel Varnhagen: The Life of a Jewish Woman*. Rev. ed. Translated into English by Richard and Clara Winston. New York: Harcourt Brace Jovanovich. (All page references in the text are to this edition.)

——. 1975. "Home to Roost." *New York Review of Books*, June 26, 3-6.

——. 1978. "Heidegger at Eighty." In *Heidegger and Modern Philosophy*. Ed. Michael Murray. New Haven, Conn.: Yale University Press. Originally published in German in *Merkur* 10 (1969): 893-902. Translated into English by Albert Hofstadter for *New York Review of Books* 17, no. 6 (October 21, 1971): 50-54.

——. 1978. *The Jew as Pariah: Jewish Identity and Politics in the Modern Age*. Ed., with an introduction by, Ron H. Feldman. New York: Grove.

——. 1978 [1977]. *The Life of the Mind*. New York: Harcourt Brace Jovanovich.

——. 1979. "On Hannah Arendt." In *Hannah Arendt: The Recovery of the Public World*. Ed. Melvyn A. Hill. New York: St. Martin's.

——. 1979 [1951]. *The Origins of Totalitarianism*. New York: Harcourt Brace Jovanovich. Originally published in Britain as *The Burden of Our Time*. London: Secker and Warburg, 1951.

——. 1982. *Lectures on Kant's Political Philosophy*. Ed., and with an interpretive essay by, Ronald Beiner. Chicago: University of Chicago Press.

——. 1971. "Thinking and Moral Considerations: A Lecture." *Social Research*, Reprinted in 50th Anniversary issue (Spring/Summer 1984).

——. 1986. "Wir Flüchtlinge." In *Hannah Arendt zur Zeit: Politische Essays*. Berlin: Rotbuch Verlag. Originally published as "We Refugees." *Menorah Journal*. Reprinted in *The Jew as Pariah: Jewish Identity and Politics in the Modern Age*. Ed., with an introduction by, Ron H. Feldman, pp. 55-67. New York: Grove.

——. 1992 [1965]. *Eichmann in Jerusalem: A Report on the Banality of Evil*. Rev., enlarged ed. New York: Penguin. Originally published in 1963 by Viking, New York. Published in German as *Eichmann in Jerusalem: Ein Bericht von der Banalität der Bösen*. Trans. Brigite Ganzow. Introduction by Hans Mommsen. Munich: Piper Verlag, 1986.

——. 1994. *Arendt: Essays in Understanding: 1930-1954*. Ed. Jerome Kohn. New York: Harcourt Brace Jovanovich.

——. 1994. "Concern With Politics in Recent European Philosophical Thought." In *Hannah Arendt: Essays in Understanding: 1930-1954*. Ed. Jerome Kohn. New York: Harcourt Brace Jovanovich.

————. 1994 [1932]. "On the Emancipation of Women." Review of *Das Frauenproblem der Gegenwart*, by Alice Ruehle-Gerstel. In *Arendt: Essays in Understanding: 1930-1954*. Ed. Jerome Kohn. New York: Harcourt Brace Jovanovich. Originally published in *Die Gesellschaft* 10 (1932): 177-179.

————. 2000. *Within Four Walls: The Correspondence Between Hannah Arendt and Heinrich Bluecher, 1936-1968*. Ed. and Intro. Lotte Kohler. Trans. Peter Constantine. New York: Harcourt, Inc.

————. n.d. *Von Hegel zu Marx*. Hannah Arendt Papers, Library of Congress, container 79.

Arendt, Hannah, and Karl Jaspers. 1992. *Hannah Arendt-Karl Jaspers Correspondence 1926-1969*. Ed. Lotte Köhler and Hans Saner. Trans. Robert and Rita Kimber. New York: Harcourt Brace Jovanovich. Originally printed in German as *Hannah Arendt-Karl Jaspers Briefwechsel*. Ed. Lotte Köhler and Hans Saner. Munich: Piper Verlag, 1985. (All page references are to the English translation.)

Arendt, Hannah, and Mary McCarthy. 1995. *Between Friends: The Correspondence of Hannah Arendt and Mary McCarthy, 1949-1975*. Ed., with an introduction by, Carol Brightman. New York: Harcourt Brace Jovanovich.

Other Works

Ackerman, Bruce. 1991. *We the People: Foundations*. Cambridge, Mass.: Harvard University Press.

Anders, Günther (Stern). 1979. "Wenn ich verzweifelt bin, was geht's mich an?" In *Die Zerstörung einer Zukunft: Gespräche mit emigrierten Sozialwissenschaftlern*. Ed. Matthias Greffrath. Hamburg: Rowohlt.

Appiah, Anthony. 1992. *In My Father's House: Africa in the Philosophy of Culture*. New York: Oxford University Press.

Appleby, Joyce. 1992. "The American Model for the French Revolutionaries." In *Liberalism and Republicanism in the Historical Imagination*, pp. 232-253. Cambridge, Mass: Harvard University Press.

————. 1992. *Liberalism and Republicanism in the Historical Imagination*. Cambridge, Mass: Harvard University Press.

Arato, Andrew. 1981. "Civil Society Against the State: Poland 1980-1981." *Telos* 47 (Spring): 23-47.

————. 1981-1982. "Empire vs. Civil Society: Poland 1981-1982." *Telos* 50 (Winter): 19-48.

————. 1990. "Revolution, Civil Society and Democracy." *Praxis International* 10, nos. 1-2: 24-38.

Aristotle. 1966. *Nicomachean Ethics*. In *The Basic Works of Aristotle*. Ed., with an introduction by, Richard McKeon. New York: Random House.

Ash, Timothy Garton. 1990. *The Magic Lantern*. New York: Random House.

Barnouw, Dagmar. 1990. *Visible Spaces: Hannah Arendt and the German-Jewish Experience*. Baltimore: Johns Hopkins University Press.

Bedford, Sybille. 1958. "Emancipation and Destiny." Review of *Rahel Varnhagen: The Life of a Jewish Woman* by Hannah Arendt. *Reconstructionist*, December 12, 22-36.

Beer, Samuel H. 1993. *To Make a Nation: The Rediscovery of American Federalism*. Cambridge, Mass.: Harvard University Press.

Beiner, Ronald. 1982. "Hannah Arendt on Judging." Introduction to Hannah Arendt's *Lectures on Kant's political Philosophy*. Ed. Ronald Beiner. Chicago: University of Chicago Press.

———. 1997. "Love and Worldliness in Hannah Arendt's Reading of St. Augustine." In *Hannah Arendt: Twenty Years Later*. Ed. Larry May and Jerome Kohn, pp. 269-284. Cambridge: MIT Press.

Belardinelli, Sergio. 1990. "Martin Heidegger und Hannah Arendts Begriff von 'Welt' und 'Praxis.' " *Zur philosophischen Aktualität Heideggers*. Frankfurt: Vittorio Klostermann.

Benhabib, Seyla. 1986. *Critique, Norm, and Utopia: A Study of the Foundations of Critical Theory*. New York: Columbia University Press.

———. 1987. "Urteilskraft und die moralischen Grundlagen der Politik im Werk Hannah Arendts." *Zeitschrift für Philosophische Forschung* 41, Heft 4: 521-547. Revised English version: "Judgment and the Moral Foundations of Politics in Hannah Arendt's Thought." *Political Theory* 16, no. 1 (1988): 29-51; also included in *Situating the Self: Gender, Community and Postmodernism in Contemporary Ethics*. New York: Routledge, 1992.

———. 1988. "Hannah Arendt und die erlösende Kraft des Erzählens." *Zivilisationsbruch: Denken nach Auschwitz*. Ed. Dan Diner, pp. 150-175. Frankfurt: Fischer. This article has appeared in altered form as "Hannah Arendt and the Redemptive Power of Narrative." *Social Research* 57, no. 1 (1990): 167-196.

———. 1989. Introduction to Herbert Marcuse's *Hegel's Ontology and the Theory of Historicity*. Trans. Seyla Benhabib. Cambridge: MIT Press.

———. 1992. "Models of Public Space: Hannah Arendt, the Liberal Tradition, and Jürgen Habermas." In *Habermas and the Public Sphere*. Ed. Craig Calhoun, pp. 73-99. Cambridge: MIT Press.

———. 1992. *Situating the Self: Gender, Community and Postmodernism in Contemporary Ethics*. New York: Routledge.

———. 1993. "Feminist Theory and Hannah Arendt's Concept of Public Space." *History of the Human Sciences* 6, no. 2: 97-114.

———. 1994. "Democracy and Difference: Reflections on the Metapolitics of Lyotard and Derrida." *Journal of Political Philosophy* 2, no. 1: 1-23.

———. 1995. "The Pariah and Her Shadow." In *Feminist Interpretations of Hannah Arendt*. Ed. Bonnie Honig. University Park: Pennsylvania State University Press. Originally published in *Political Theory* 23, no. 1 (February 1995): 5-24.

———. 1995. Review of *Between Friends: The Correspondence of Hannah Arendt and Mary McCarthy*. *Nation*, March 27, 423-425.

Benjamin, Walter. 1969. *Illuminations*. Ed., with an introduction by, Hannah Arendt. New York: Schocken.

———. 1977. *The Origin of German Tragic Drama*. Trans. by John Osborne. London: New Left Books.

Bernstein, Richard J. 1976. *The Restructuring of Social and Political Theory*. Philadelphia: University of Pennsylvania Press.

———. 1986. "Judging—The Actor and the Spectator." In *Philosophical Profiles*, pp. 221-238. Philadelphia: University of Pennsylvania Press.

———. 1986. "Rethinking the Social and the Political." In *Philosophical Profiles*, pp. 238-260. Philadelphia: University of Pennsylvania Press.

Bozoki, Andras, and Miklos Sukosd. 1993. "Civil Society and Populism in East European Democratic Transitions." *Praxis International* 13, no. 3, 224-242.

Bradshaw, Leah. 1989. *Acting and Thinking: The Political Thought of Hannah Arendt.* Toronto: University of Toronto Press.

Brecht, Bertolt. 1960. "Von Armen B.B." In *Gedichte, 1918-1929.* Frankfurt: Suhrkamp.

Broszat, Martin, Elke Frölich, and Falk Wiesemann, eds. 1977. *Bayern in der NS-Zeit: Soziale Lage und politisches Verhalten der Bevölkerung im Speigel vertraulicher Berichte.* Munich: R. Oldenburg Verlag.

Buber, Martin. 1983 [1921]. "Nationalism." In *A Land of Two Peoples: Martin Buber on Jews and Arabs.* Ed., with commentary by, Paul R. Mendes-Flohr. New York: Oxford University Press.

Buchheim, Karl. 1979. "Totalitarismus: Zu Hannah Arendt's Buch 'Elemente und Ursprünge totaler Herrschaft." In *Hannah Arendt: Materialen zu ihrem Werk.* Ed. Adalbert Reif. Vienna: Europaverlag.

Burke, Edmund. 1969. *Reflections on the Revolution in France.* Ed. Connor Cruise O'Brien. Middlesex, England: Penguin.

———. 1987. *Speeches on the Impeachment of Warren Hastings.* Vols. 1 and 2. Reprinted from the *Works of Edmund Burke.* Vol. 8. New Delhi: Discovery.

Calhoun, Craig, ed. 1992. *Habermas and the Public Sphere.* Cambridge: MIT Press.

Canovan, Margaret. 1974. *The Political Thought of Hannah Arendt.* London: J. M. Dent.

———. 1983. "A Case of Distorted Communication: A Note on Habermas and Arendt." *Political Theory* 11, no. 1: 105-116.

———. 1992. *Hannah Arendt: A Reinterpretation of Her Political Thought.* London: Cambridge University Press.

Cohen, Jean. 1992. "Redescribing Privacy." *Columbia Journal of Gender and Law* 3, no. 1: 43-117.

Cohen, Jean, and Andrew Arato. 1992. *Civil Society and Political Theory.* Cambridge: MIT Press.

Conrad, Joseph. 1988. *Heart of Darkness.* Ed. Robert Kimbrough. New York: Norton.

Crick, Bernard. 1977. "On Rereading the Origins of Totalitarianism." *Social Research* 44 (Spring 1977). Reprinted in *Hannah Arendt: Materialen zu ihrem Werk.* Ed. Adalbert Reif. Vienna: Europaverlag.

Denneny, Michael. 1979. "The Privilege of Ourselves: Hannah Arendt on Judgment." In *Hannah Arendt: The Recovery of the Public World.* Ed. Melvyn A. Hill. New York: St. Martin's.

D'Entrèves, Maurizio Passerin. (1987). "Aristotle or Burke? Some Comments on H. Schnädelbach's 'What Is Neo-Aristotelianism?' " *Praxis International* 7, nos. 3-4: 238-246.

———. 1994. *The Political Philosophy of Hannah Arendt.* London: Routledge.

Dietz, Mary G. 1991. "Hannah Arendt and Feminist Politics." In *Feminist Interpretations and Political Theory.* Ed. Molly Shanley and Carole Pateman. Oxford: Polity.

Diner, Dan, ed. 1988. *Zivilisationsbruch: Denken nach Auschwitz.* Frankfurt: Fischer.

———. 1992. "Historical Understanding and Counterfactuality: The Judenrat as Epistemological Vantage." In *Probing the Limits of Representation: Nazism and the "Final Solution."* Ed., with an introduction by, Saul Friedlaender, pp. 128-143. Cambridge, Mass.: Harvard University Press.

Dossa, Shiraz. 1989. *The Public Realm and the Public Self: The Political Theory of Hannah Arendt.* Waterloo, Ontario: W. Laurier University Press.

Elias, Norbert. 1994. *The Civilizing Process.* Trans. E. Jephcott. Oxford, UK: Blackwell.

Ellison, Ralph. 1964. "The World and the Jug." In *Shadow and Act*. New York: Random House.

———. 1965. "Leadership From the Periphery." In *Who Speaks for the Negro?* Ed. Robert Penn Warren. New York: Random House.

Elon, Amos. 1971. *The Israelis: Founders and Sons*. New York: Holt, Rinehart & Winston.

Ettinger, Elzbieta. 1995. *Hannah Arendt-Martin Heidegger.* New Haven, Conn.: Yale University Press.

Farias, Victor. 1987. *Heidegger et le Nazisme: Morale et politique*. Paris: Lagrasse. Translated into English by Paul Burrell, *Heidegger and Nazism*. Ed. Joseph Margolis and Tom Rockmore. Philadelphia: Temple University Press.

Feher, F., and A. Heller. 1986. *Eastern Left, Western Left: Totalitarianism, Freedom and Democracy*. Cambridge: Polity.

Feilchenfeldt, Konrad. 1987. "Die Berliner Salons der Romantik." In *Rahel Levin Varnhagen: Die Wiederentdeckung einer Schriftstellerin*. Ed. Barbara Hahn and Ursula Isselstein, pp. 152-163. Göttingen: Vandenhoeck & Ruprecht.

———. 1987. "Rahel Philologie im Zeichen der antisemitischen Gefahr (Margarete Sussman, Hannah Arendt, Käte Hamburger)." In *Rahel Levin Varnhagen: Die Wiederentdeckung einer Schriftstellerin*. Ed. Barbara Hahn and Ursula Isselstein, pp. 187-195. Göttingen: Vandenhoeck & Ruprecht.

Feldman, Yael S. 1992. "Whose Story Is It, Anyway? Ideology and Psychology in the Representation of the Shoah in Israeli Literature." In *Probing the Limits of Representation: Nazism and the "Final Solution."* Ed., with an introduction by, Saul Friedlaender, pp. 223-240. Cambridge: Harvard University Press.

Foucault, Michel. 1977. *Discipline and Punish: The Birth of the Prison*. Trans. Alan Sheridan. New York: Pantheon.

Fraser, Nancy. 1992. "Rethinking the Public Sphere: A Contribution to the Critique of Actually Existing Democracy." In *Habermas and the Public Sphere*. Ed. Craig Calhoun, pp. 109-143. Cambridge, Mass.: MIT Press.

Friedlaender, Saul, ed. 1992. *Probing the Limits of Representation: Nazism and the "Final Solution."* Cambridge, Mass.: Harvard University Press.

Friedrich, Carl, and Zbigniew K. Brzezinski. 1965. *Totalitarian Dictatorship and Autocracy*. 2d ed., revised by Carl Friedrich. Cambridge, Mass.: Harvard University Press.

Funke, Manfred, ed. 1978. *Totalitarismus: Ein Studien-Reader zur Herrschaftsanalyse moderner Diktaturen*. Düsseldorf: Proste.

Furet, Francois. 1981. *Interpreting the French Revolution*. Trans. Elborg Forster. Cambridge, UK: Cambridge University Press.

Fuss, Peter. 1973. "Hannah Arendt's Conception of Political Community." *Idealistic Studies* 3, no. 3. Reprinted in *Hannah Arendt: The Recovery of the Public World*. Melvyn Hill, ed., pp. 157-177. New York: St. Martin's, 1979.

Gadamer, Hans-Georg. 1975. *Truth and Method*. Ed. Garrett Barden and John Cumming. New York: Seabury.

———. 1976. *Philosophical Hermeneutics*. Trans. and ed. David E. Linge. Berkeley: University of California Press.

———. 1983. "Hermeneutics as a Theoretical and Practical Task." In *Reason in the Age of Science*. Trans. Frederick G. Lawrence. Cambridge: MIT Press.

———. 1983. "Hermeneutics as Practical Philosophy." In *Reason in the Age of Science*. Trans. Frederick G. Lawrence. Cambridge: MIT Press.

———. 1983. *Reason in the Age of Science*. Trans. Frederick G. Lawrence. Cambridge: MIT Press.

———. 1983. "What Is Practice? The Conditions of Social Reason." In *Reason in the Age of Science*. Trans. Frederick G. Lawrence. Cambridge: MIT Press.

———. 1989. "Heidegger's Theologische Jugendschrift." In *Dilthey-Jahrbuch*, vol. 6. Ed. Frithjof Rodi. Göttingen: Vandenhoeck and Ruprecht.

Gerhardt, Marlis. 1983. "Einleitung: Rahel Levin, Friedériké Robert, Madame Varnhagen." In *Rahel Varnhagen: Jeder Wunsch und Frivolität genannt. Briefe und Tagebucher.* Darmstadt: Luchterhand.

Giddens, A. 1977. *Studies in Social and Political Theory.* London: Hutchinson.

Godelier, Maurice. 1977. *Perspectives in Marxist Anthropology*. Trans. Robert Brain. London: Cambridge University Press.

Gordon, Daniel. 1994. *Citizens Without Sovereignty: Equality and Sociability in French Thought, 1670-1789.* Princeton, N.J.: Princeton University Press.

Gorz, Andre. 1982. *Farewell to the Working Class.* Boston: South End Press.

Gottsegen, Michael S. 1993. *The Political Thought of Hannah Arendt.* Albany: SUNY University Press.

Gouldner, Alvin. "1977-1978: Stalinism: A Study of Internal Colonialism." *Telos* 34 (Winter): 5-48.

Habermas, Jürgen. 1962. *Strukturwandel der Öffentlichkeit.* Darmstadt: Hermann Luchterhand. Translation in hard cover, 1989; in paperback, 1991.

———. 1970. "Technology and Science as 'Ideology.' " In *Toward a Rational Society.* Trans. Jeremy J. Shapiro. Boston: Beacon.

———. 1973. "Labor and Interaction: Remarks on Hegel's *Jena Philosophy of Mind.*" In *Theory and Practice.* Trans. John Viertel, pp. 142-170. Boston: Beacon.

———. 1977. "Hannah Arendt's Communications Concept of Power." *Social Research* 44, no. 1: 3-25.

———. 1980. "On the German-Jewish Heritage." *Telos* 44 (Summer 1980): 127-130.

———. 1984. *The Theory of Communicative Action: Reason and the Rationalization of Society.* Vol. 1. Trans. T. A. McCarthy. Boston: Beacon.

———. 1989. "The New Obscurity." In *The New Conservatism: Cultural Criticism and the Historian's Debate.* Ed. and trans. Shierry Weber Nicholsen, pp. 48-70. Cambridge: MIT Press.

———. 1989. *The Structural Transformation of the Public Sphere.* Trans. T. Burger and F. Lawrence. Cambridge: MIT Press.

———. 1989. "Work and Weltanschauung: The Heidegger Controversy From a German Perspective." *Critical Inquiry* 15 (Winter): 431-456.

Havel, Václav. 1987. "Politics and Conscience." In *Living in Truth.* London: Faber and Faber.

———. 1987. "The Power of the Powerless." In *Living in Truth.* London: Faber and Faber.

Hayes, Carlton J. H. 1941. *A Generation of Materialism.* New York: Harper.

Hegel, G. W. F. 1973 [1821]. *Hegel's Philosophy of Right.* Trans., with notes by, T. M. Knox. Oxford: Oxford University Press.

———. 1975 [1802-1803]. *Natural Law.* Trans. T. M. Knox. Introduction by H. B. Acton. Philadelphia: University of Pennsylvania Press.

———. 1977. "Absolute Freedom and Terror." In *Phenomenology of Spirit.* Trans. A. V. Miller, pp. 355-364. Oxford: Clarendon.

Heidegger, Martin. 1962. *Being and Time.* Trans. John Macquarrie and Edward Robinson. New York: Harper & Row.

———. 1963 [1927]. *Sein und Zeit.* 10th ed. Tübingen: Max Niemeyer Verlag.

———. 1989. "Phänomenologische Interpretation zu Aristoteles." In *Dilthey-Jahrbuch,* vol. 6. Ed. Frithjof Rodi. Göttingen: Vandenhoeck and Ruprecht.

———. 1992. *Gesamtausgabe.* Vol. 19, II. *Abteilung: Vorlesungen 1919-1944.* Frankfurt.

Heller, Agnes. 1989. "An Imaginary Preface to the 1984 Edition of Hannah Arendt's 'The Origins of Totalitarianism.' " In *The Public Realm: Essays on Discursive Types in Political Philosophy.* Ed. Reiner Schürmann. New York: SUNY Press.

Hertz, Deborah. 1988. *Jewish High Society in Old Regime Berlin.* New Haven, Conn.: Yale University Press.

Herzberg, Arthur, ed. 1959. *The Zionist Reader: A Historical Analysis and Reader.* New York: Athäneum.

Higonnet, Patrice. 1988. *Sister Republics: The Origins of French and American Republicanism.* Cambridge, Mass.: Harvard University Press.

Hilberg, Raul. 1992. *Perpetrators, Victims, Bystanders: The Jewish Catastrophe 1933-1945.* New York: Harper Collins.

Hill, Melvyn A., ed. 1979. *Hannah Arendt: The Recovery of the Public World.* New York: St. Martin's.

Hinchman, Lewis P., and Sandra K. Hinchman. 1991. "Existentialism Politicized: Arendt's Debt to Jaspers." *Review of Politics* 53, no. 3: 447-449.

———. 1993. *Hannah Arendt: Critical Essays.* Albany: SUNY Press.

Honig, Bonnie. 1988. "Arendt, Identity, and Difference." *Political Theory* 16, no. 1: 77-99.

———. 1991. "Declarations of Independence: Arendt and Derrida on the Problem of Founding a Republic." *American Political Science Review* 85: 97-113.

Honig, Bonnie, ed. 1995. *Feminist Interpretations of Hannah Arendt.* University Park: Pennsylvania State University Press.

hooks, bell. 1984. *Feminist Theory From Margin to Center.* Cambridge, Mass.; South End Press.

Hufton, Olwen. 1992. *Women and the Limits of Citizenship in the French Revolution.* Donald G. Creighton Lectures. Toronto: Buffalo University Press.

Hunt, Lynn. 1984. *Politics, Culture, and Class in the French Revolution.* Berkeley: University of California Press.

Isaac, Jeffrey C. 1992. *Arendt, Camus, and Modern Rebellion.* New Haven, Conn.: Yale University Press.

Jaspers, Karl. 1989. *Notizen zu Martin Heidegger.* Ed. Hans Saner. Munich: Piper Verlag.

Jay, Martin, and Leon Botstein. 1978. "Hannah Arendt: Opposing Views." *Partisan Review* 45, no. 3. Reprinted in Martin Jay, *Permanent Exiles.* New York: Columbia University Press, 1986.

Johanbegloo, Ramin. 1992. *Conversations With Isaiah Berlin.* London: Peter Halban.

Judt, Tony. 1995. "At Home in This Century." *New York Review of Books* 42, no. 6 (April 6): 9-15.

Kant, Immanuel. 1960. *Religion Within the Limits of Reason Alone.* Trans., with an introduction and notes by, Theodore M. Greene and Hoyt H. Hudson. New York: Harper & Row.

———. 1964. *Critique of Judgment.* Trans., with an analytical index by, J. C. Meredith. Oxford: Clarendon.

———. 1968. "Kritik der Urteilskraft." In *Kants Werke: Akademie-Textausgabe.* Vol. 5. Berlin: Walter de Gruyter.

———. 1976. "Critique of Practical Reason." In *Critique of Practical Reason and Other Writings in Moral Philosophy.* Trans., with an introduction by, L. W. Beck. New York: Garland.

———. 1994. "An Answer to the Question: 'What is Enlightenment?' " In *Kant: Political Writings.* Ed., with an introduction and notes by, Hans Reiss. Trans. H. B. Nisbet, pp. 54-61. Cambridge: Cambridge University Press.

Kateb, George. 1984. *Hannah Arendt: Politics, Conscience, Evil.* Totowa, N.J.: Rowman and Allanheld.

Konrad, Georg. 1984. *Antipolitics.* New York: Harcourt Brace Jovanovich.

Krinsky, Alan D. 1990. "The Controversy." Senior thesis, Boston University. On file with the author.

Kundera, Milan. 1984. *The Incredible Lightness of Being.* Trans. Michael Henry Heim. New York: Harper & Row.

Lacey, Nicola. 1993. "Theory Into Practice? Pornography and the Public/Private Dichotomy." *Journal of Law and Society* 20, no. 1: 93-113.

Landes, Joan B. 1988. *Women and the Public Sphere in the Age of the French Revolution.* Ithaca, N.Y.: Cornell University Press.

———. 1995. "Novus Ordo Saeclorum: Gender and Public Space in Arendt's Revolutionary France." In *Feminist Interpretations of Hannah Arendt.* Ed. Bonnie Honig, pp. 195-221. University Park: Pennsylvania State University Press.

Laqueur, Walter. 1972. *A History of Zionism.* New York: Holt, Rinehart & Winston.

Lasch, Christopher. 1983. "Introduction." *Salmagundi* 60, special Hannah Arendt issue, ed. Christopher Lasch.

Lazare, Bernard. 1948. *Job's Dungheap: Essays on Jewish Nationalism and Social Revolution.* Trans. Harry Lorin Binsse. Preface by Hannah Arendt. New York: Schocken.

Lenin, Vladimir Ilyich. 1961. *Imperialism: The Highest Stage of Capitalism.* 10th impression. Vol. 22, *Works of Lenin.* Moscow: Foreign Language Publishing House.

———. 1962. *What Is to Be Done?* Trans. Joe Fineberg and George Hanna. London: Penguin. Rev. translation by Robert Service. London: Penguin Classics, 1988.

Löwith, Karl. *Martin Heidegger and European Nihilism.* Trans. Gary Steiner. New York: Columbia University Press.

Luban, David. 1983. "Explaining Dark Times: Hannah Arendt's Theory of Theory." *Social Research* 50, no. 1: 215-247.

Lukacs, Georg. 1971. "Class Consciousness." In *History and Class Consciousness.* Trans. Rodney Livingston, pp. 46-83. Cambridge, Mass.: MIT Press.

Luxemburg, Rosa. 1968. *The Accumulation of Capital.* Trans. Agnes Schwarzschild. Introduction by Joan Robinson. New York: Modern Reader Paperbacks.

———. 1971. "Organizational Questions of Russian Social Democracy." In *Selected Political Writings of Rosa Luxemburg.* Ed. Dick Howard. New York: Monthly Review Press.

———. 1971. "Social Reform or Revolution?" In *Selected Political Writings of Rosa Luxemburg.* Ed. Dick Howard. New York: Monthly Review Press.

MacIntyre, Alasdair. 1981. *After Virtue.* Notre Dame, Ind.: Notre Dame University Press.

Maier, Charles. 1988. *The Unmasterable Past: History, Holocaust, and German National Identity.* Cambridge, Mass.: Harvard University Press.

Marcuse, Herbert. 1988. *Hegel's Ontology and the Theory of Historicity.* Trans., with an introduction by, Seyla Benhabib. Cambridge, Mass.: MIT Press.

Marcuse, Herbert, and Frederick Olafson. 1977. "Heidegger's Politics: An Interview." *Graduate Faculty Philosophy Journal* 6, no. 1 (1977): 28-40.

Marrus, Michael R. 1987. *The Holocaust in History.* Tauber Institute for the Study of European Jewry Series. Toronto: Lester & Orpen Dennys.

Marx, Karl. 1964. *The Economic and Philosophical Manuscripts of 1844.* Trans. Dirk J. Struik. New York: International.

———. 1972 [1843]. "On the Jewish Question." In *The Marx-Engels Reader.* Ed. Robert C. Tucker, pp. 26-53. New York: Norton.

———. 1973. *Grundrisse: An Introduction to the Critique of Political Economy.* Trans. Martin Nicolaus. Middlesex, England: Penguin.

———. 1983 [1848]. "Manifesto of the Communist Party." In *The Portable Karl Marx.* Ed. Eugene Kamenka. New York: Penguin.

Merleau-Ponty, Maurice. 1955. *Les aventures de la dialectique.* Paris: Gallimard.

Michelman, Frank. 1996. "Parsing 'A Right to Have Rights.'" In *Constellations: An International Journal of Critical and Democratic Theory* 3, no. 2: 200-209.

Mills, C. Wright. 1956. *The Power Elite.* New York: Oxford University Press.

Mitrovic, Petra. 1982. "Zum Problem der Konstitution von Ich-Identität in den Briefen der Rahel Varnhagen." Master's thesis, University of Frankfurt, Institut für Deutsche Sprache und Literatur.

Mommsen, Hans. 1981. "The Concept of Totalitarian Dictatorship Versus the Comparative Theory of Fascism." In *Totalitarianism Reconsidered.* Ed. Ernest A. Menze, pp. 146-167. Port Washington, N.Y.: Kennikat.

———. 1986. "Hannah Arendt und der Prozess gegen Adolf Eichmann." Introduction to Hannah Arendt, *Eichmann in Jerusalem: Ein Bericht von der Banalität des Bösen.* Trans. Brigitte Ganzow. Munich: Piper Verlag.

Morgan, Edmund S. 1977. *The Birth of the Republic: 1763-1789.* Chicago: University of Chicago Press.

Morss, Susan Buck. 1977. *The Origin of Negative Dialectics: Theodor W. Adorno, Walter Benjamin and the Frankfurt Institute.* New York: Free Press.

Moruzzi, Norma Claire. 1995. "Re-placing the Margin: (Non)representations of Colonialism in Hannah Arendt's *The Origins of Totalitarianism.*" *Tulsa Studies in Women's Literature* 10, no. 1: 109-120.

Nehemas, Alexander. 1985. *Life as Literature.* Cambridge: Harvard University Press.

Nordmann, Ingeborg. 1987. "Fremdsein ist gut: Hannah Arendt über Rahel Varnhagen." In *Rahel Levin Varnhagen: Die Wiederentdeckung einer Schriftstellerin.* Ed. Barbara Hahn and Ursula Isselstein, pp. 196-207. Göttingen: Vandenhoeck & Ruprecht.

Norton, Anne. 1995. "Heart of Darkness: Africa and African Americans in the Writings of Hannah Arendt." In *Feminist Interpretations of Hannah Arendt.* Ed. Bonnie Honig, pp. 247-263. University Park: Pennsylvania State University Press.

O'Brien, Connor Cruise. 1992. *The Great Melody: A Thematic Biography and Commented Anthology of Edmund Burke.* Chicago: University of Chicago Press.

Okin, Susan Moller. 1989. *Justice, Gender, and the Family.* New York: Free Press.

Ott, Hugo. 1993. *Martin Heidegger: A Political Life.* Trans. Allan Blunden. New York: Basic Books.

Parekh, Bikhu. 1981. *Hannah Arendt and the Search for a New Political Philosophy.* London: Macmillan.

Patterson, Orlando. 1982. *Slavery and Social Death.* Cambridge, Mass.: Harvard University Press.

Pitkin, Hanna. 1981. "Justice: On Relating Private and Public." *Political Theory* 9, no. 3: 327-352.

———. 1995. "Conformism, Housekeeping and the Attack of the Blob: The Origins of Hannah Arendt's Concept of the Social." In *Feminist Interpretations of Hannah Arendt.* Ed. Bonnie Honig, pp. 51-83. University Park: Pennsylvania State University Press.

Pöggeler, Otto. 1987 [1963]. *Der Denkweg Martin Heideggers.* Neske: Pfüllingen. Reissue: Trans. Daniel Mgurshah and Sigmund Barber (Atlantic Highlands, N.J.: Humanities Press, 1987).

Polanyi, Karl. 1871. "Aristotle Discovers the Economy." In *Trade and Market in the Early Empires: Economics in History and Theory.* Ed. Karl Polanyi, C. M. Arensberg, and Harry W. Peasner. Chicago: Regnery.

Popper, Karl. 1971. *The Open Society and Its Enemies.* 5th ed., rev. Princeton, N.J.: Princeton University Press.

Rentsch, Thomas. 1989. *Martin Heidegger: Das Sein und der Tod.* Frankfurt: Fischer Verlag.

Rich, Adrienne. 1979. "Conditions for Work: The Common World of Women." In *On Lies, Secrets, and Silence.* New York: Norton.

Robinson, Jacob. 1965. *And the Crooked Shall Be Made Straight: The Eichmann Trial, the Jewish Catastrophe, and Hannah Arendt's Narrative.* New York: Macmillan.

Rockmore, Tom. 1992. *On Heidegger's Nazism and Philosophy.* Berkeley: University of California Press.

Safranski, Rüdiger. 1994. *Ein Meister aus Deutschland: Heidegger und seine Zeit.* Munich: Carl Hanser Verlag.

Schindler, Roland W. 1994. "Hannah Arendt und die Historiker-Kontroverse um die 'Rationalitat' der Judenvernichtung." In *Dialektik,* pp. 146-160. Frankfurt: Felix Meiner Verlag.

Schmitt, Carl. 1985. *The Crisis of Parliamentary Democracy.* Trans. Ellen Kennedy. Cambridge: MIT Press.

Schnädelbach, Herbert. 1987. What Is Neo-Aristotelianism? *Praxis International* 7, nos. 3-4: 225-238.

Scholem, Gershom. 1946. *Major Trends in Jewish Mysticism.* New York: Schocken.

———. 1964. " 'Eichmann in Jerusalem': An Exchange of Letters Between Gershom Scholem and Hannah Arendt." *Encounter* 22 (January): 51-56. Reprinted in Hannah Arendt, *The Jew as Pariah: Jewish Identity and Politics in the Modern Age.* Ed., with an introduction by, Ron H. Feldman. New York: Grove, 1978.

Schwan, Alexander. 1987 [1965]. *Politische Philosophie im Denken Heideggers.* Opladen: Westdeutscher Verlag.

Scott, Joan W. 1988. "Gender: A Useful Category of Historical Analysis." In *Gender and the Politics of History,* pp. 28-53. New York: Columbia University Press.

———. 1988. *Gender and the Politics of History.* New York: Columbia University Press.

Seebacher-Brandt, Brigitte. 1993. "Der aufgehobene Zweifel: Hannah Arendt und Martin Heidegger." *Frankfurter Allgemeine Zeitung,* "Bilder und Zeiten" section, no. 31, February 6 (1993).

Seibert, Peter. 1987. "Der Salon als Formation im Literaturbetrieb zur Zeit Rahel Levin Varnhagens." In *Rahel Levin Varnhagen: Die Wiederentdeckung einer Schriftstellerin.* Ed. Barbara Hahn and Ursula Isselstein, pp. 164-172. Göttingen: Vandenhoeck & Ruprecht.

Shama, Simon. 1989. *Citizens: A Chronicle of the French Revolution.* New York: Knopf.

Sheehan, Thomas. 1988. "Heidegger and the Nazis." *New York Review of Books* 15 (June): 38-47.

Shelley, P. B. 1904. *The Complete Poetical Works of Shelley.* Ed., with textual notes by, Thomas Hutchinson. Oxford: Clarendon.

Shklar, Judith. 1964. *Legalism: An Essay on Law, Morals and Politics.* Cambridge, Mass.: Harvard University Press.

———. 1991. *American Citizenship: The Quest for Inclusion.* Cambridge, Mass.: Harvard University Press.

Skilling, H. Gordon, and Paul Wilson, eds. 1991. *Civic Freedom in Central Europe: Voices From Czechoslovakia.* New York: St. Martin's.

Smith, Charles. 1988. *Palestine and the Arab-Israeli Conflict.* New York: St. Martin's.

Taminiaux, Jacques. 1992. *La fille de Thrace et le penseur professionel: Arendt et Heidegger.* Paris: Éditions Payot.

Taylor, Charles. 1971. "Interpretation and the Sciences of Man." *Review of Metaphysics* 25: 3-51.

Thompson, E. P. 1966. *The Making of the English Working Class.* New York: Vintage.

Tocqueville, Alexis de. 1955. *The Old Regime and the French Revolution.* Trans. Stuart Gilbert. New York: Doubleday and Anchor.

———. 1969. *Democracy in America.* Ed. J. P. Mayer. Trans. George Lawrence. New York: Anchor.

Todorov, Tzvetan. 1982. *The Conquest of America: The Question of the Other.* Trans. Richard Howard. New York: Harper & Row.

Trunk, Isaiah. 1972. *Judenrat: The Jewish Councils in Eastern Europe Under Nazi Occupation.* Introduction by Jacob Robinson. New York: Macmillan.

Tucker, Robert C. 1987. "Between Lenin and Stalin: A Cultural Analysis." *Praxis International* 6, no. 4 (1987): iv-xvi.

Varnhagen, Rahel. 1983. *Gesammelte Werke,* 10 vols. Ed. Konrad Feilchenfeldt, Uwe Schweikert, and Rahel E. Steiner. Munich: Matthes and Seitz Verlag.

Villa, Dana. 1992. "Beyond Good and Evil: Arendt, Nietzsche, and the Aestheticization of Political Action." *Political Theory* 20, no. 2: 274-309.

———. 1996. *Arendt and Heidegger: The Fate of the Political.* Princeton, N.J.: Princeton University Press.

Weber, Max. 1946. "The Meaning of Ethical Neutrality in the Social Sciences." In *The Methodology of the Social Sciences.* Ed. and trans. E. A. Shils and Henry A. Finch. New York: Free Press.

———. 1964. *The Theory of Social and Economic Organization.* Ed., with an introduction by, Talcott Parsons. New York: Free Press.

Wellmer, Albrecht. 1996. "Hannah Arendt on Judgment: The Unwritten Doctrine of Reason." In *Hannah Arendt: Twenty Years Later.* Ed. Larry May and Jerome Kohn. Cambridge, Mass.: MIT Press.

Wirsing, Sybille. 1984. "Urworte, nicht orphisch, sondern weiblich." Review of the *Gesammelte Werke* of Rahel Varnhagen. *Frankfurter Allgemeine Zeitung,* no. 18 (January 21).

Wolin, Richard. 1990. *The Politics of Being: The Political Thought of Martin Heidegger.* New York: Columbia University Press.

———. 1991. *The Heidegger Controversy: A Critical Reader.* New York: Columbia University Press.

————. 1995. "An Affair to Remember: Hannah and the Magician." *New Republic*, October 9, 27-37.

————. 1995. "Karl Löwith and Martin Heidegger—Contexts and Controversies: An Introduction." In *Martin Heidegger and European Nihilism*. Ed. Karl Löwith. Trans. Gary Steiner. New York: Columbia University Press.

Wood, Gordon. 1969. *The Creation of the American Republic: 1776-1787*. New York: Norton.

Young-Bruehl, Elisabeth. 1979. "Hannah Arendt als Geschichtenerzählerin." In *Hannah Arendt: Materialen zu ihrem Werk*. Ed. Adalbert Reif, pp. 319-327. Vienna: Europaverlag.

————. 1982. *Hannah Arendt: For Love of the World*. New Haven, Conn.: Yale University Press.

Zangwill, Israel. 1937 [1903]. "Zion, Whence Cometh My Help?" In *Speeches, Articles, and Letters of Israel Zangwill*. Ed. Maurice Simon. Foreword by Edith Aryton Zangwill. London: Soncino.

Index

Action:
agonal model of, 125-126, 127, 129-130
as interaction, 105, 109, 111-113
communicative, 124-125, 199
distinction from behavior, 25-26
dualism in concept of, 124-125
expressive, 124-125
freedom and, 197-198
Heidegger on, 105
in Arendt's political philosophy, 197-198
intentions of, 188
interpreted by others, 113
Kant's view of, 187-188
linguistic structure of, 199
morality of, 188
narrative model of, 92, 125-126, 129-130, 199
purpose, 114
relationship with thinking and judging, 192-193
speech and, 109, 112-113
See also Labor; Work

Africa:
European colonies, 82-86
Europeans in, 84-86
political distinctions within, 85

African Americans. *See* Race relations; Racism

Agonal model of action, 125-126, 127, 129-130

Alienation, 132-133, 143

American Zionist Congress, 39

Analogical thinking, 89-90

Anders, Günther, 52

Anthropological universalism, 195-197

Anti-Semitism:
compared to racism, 149
German, in 19th century, 7, 13, 18
in Arendt's schools, 147
modern, 27, 30, 66, 68
Russian, 68

About the Author

Seyla Benhabib is the Eugene Meyer Professor of Political Science and Philosophy at Yale University, and Director of the Program in Ethics, Politics, and Economics. She was born in Istanbul, Turkey, in 1950 and studied philosophy and political theory at Brandeis University, Yale University, and Johann-Wolfgang Goethe Universitaet in Frankfurt, Germany.

She is the author of *Critique, Norm and Utopia* (1986); *Situating the Self: Gender, Community and Postmodernism in Contemporary Ethics* (1992); coauthor with Judith Butler, Drucilla Cornell, and Nancy Fraser of *Feminist Contentions: A Philosophical Exchange* (1994). She has edited with Drucilla Cornell, *Feminism as Critique* (1987); with Fred Dallmayr, *The Communicative Ethics Controversy* (1990); and with Wolfgang Bonss and John McCole, *On Max Horkheimer: New Perspectives* (1994). She is also editor of *Democracy and Difference: Contesting the Boundaries of the Political* (1996).

Her most recent publications include *Transformations of Citizenship: Dilemmas of the Nation-State in the Era of Globalization* (2001) and *The Claims of Culture: Equality and Diversity in the Global Era* (2002).

7946339R00174

Printed in Great Britain
by Amazon.co.uk, Ltd.,
Marston Gate.